Cannon County Tennessee

Deed Books "A-L"

- 1836-1857 -

By:
Thomas E. Partlow

Southern Historical Press, Inc.
Greenville, South Carolina

Please Direct All Correspondence and Book Orders to:

Souther Historical Press, Inc.
PO Box 1267
375 West Broad Street
Greenville, S.C. 29602

ISBN # 0-89308-714-9

Printed in the United States of America

This Book

Is

Respectfully Dedicated

To

A Very Special Cousin

JANE BASS JONES

PREFACE

Cannon County was established in 1836. It was named in honor of Newton Cannon, Governor of Tennessee from 1835-39. It is surrounded by Wilson, Rutherford, Warren, Coffee, and De-Kalb Counties.

This book contains the early deeds and wills of Cannon County. It should be of interest to people not only to people with ancestors in Cannon County, but the surrounding counties as well.

These abstracts contain all pertinent genealogical information. If the place of residence is not given for the individual, then that person resided in Cannon County.

Thomas E. Partlow
Lebanon, Tennessee

Whereas by an Act of the General Assembly of the State of
Tennessee passed on the 31st day of Jan 1836 entitled an Act to
establish a new county of the name of Cannon to be composed of
parts of the counties of Warren, Rutherford, and Smith and
whereas by the said Act refferance being thereto had for greater
certainty Johnathan Webster of Coffee County, John S. Ru   )
of Williamson County, and George Elliot of Sumner County were
appointed commissioners to locate and fix the seat of Justice
for the said County of Cannon, crated and established by the said
Act of Assembly at some point within or not exceeding five miles
from the town of Danville and to purchase a tract of land not less
than fifty acres whereon to build and establish a seat of Justice
or county town for said county and whereas after due examination
of all the scites suitable for towns within the boundaries named,
the said committee, that is to say, the said Johnathan Webster
and John S. Ru   ) being a majority of said commissioners with
lawful authority to act in the absence of the said George Elliot
have on this day selected the place and location on which the
town of Danville (on the upper part of the east fork of Stone's
River) now stands with the addition of adjoining lands purchased
by them for and as the scite of said county town or seat of
justice for the said County of Cannon and have bestowed and giving
the name of Woodberry in honor of the honorable Levie Woodberry
of New Hampshire to the town to be established on said scite so
selected as by law. It was their duty to do and whereas the said
land was purchased from various persons as is herein after recited
and partley by the donation of certain of individuals in land and
town lots in said town of Danville as is herein after recited.
This Indenture further witnesseth that on this 15th day of Apr
1836 Joseph Pinkerton, Abel McBroom, Henry D. McBroom, William Y.
Henderson, Robert Vinson, W. M. Young, Patsey Gannon, Nathan
(Neeley), Adam Elrod, Henry Trott, Jr., Mary Gannon, and Martha
Gannon for and in concideration of the establishment of the seat
of Justice for the said county of Cannon at Danville and so as
to include Danville and in consideration of a price stipulated
to be paid for twenty-nine acres of land included in this deed on
east end of the town of Danville by Abel McBroom and Henry D.
McBroom and to Martha Gannon for two acres on the south side of
said town have this day bargained, sold, and convey and by these
persons do bargain, sell, and convey to Johnathan Webster and
John S. Ru   ), the commissioners aforesaid, and to thare suc-
cessors in office and to thair heirs and assignees forever a
certain tract of land beginning at the southwest corner of Lot
number one as described in the original plan of the town of Danville. . . 15 Apr 1836. (Pp. 1-3)

James Taylor to John S. Ru) and Johnathan Webster for
location a seat of justice for the County of Cannon 20 acres and
31 poles. One acre now in the possession of Widow Gannon is ex-
cepted. 15 Apr 1836. (Pp. 3-4)

Benjamin Pendleton to Benjamin C. Stephens 79½ acres in the
County of Warren. 1 Jun 1835. (Pp. 4-5)

Washington Kennedy of Warren County to Benjamin C. Stephens
ten acres on Hill's Creek in Warren County. 4 Oct 1835. (P. 5)

1

John Wright and Pumphrey Bynuns of Rutherford County to Charles Espey of the same place 72 acres on the east fork of Stone's River. 8 May 1835. (P. 6)

James M. Brown of Cannon County was appointed by the County Court of Warren County as the guardian of Frances Ann and Henry Wiley, minor heirs of Henry Wiley deceased and entered into bond with David Young, John Brown, William Henderson, and Benjamin Pendleton. 11 May 1836. (Pp. 7-8)

Thomas W. Duncan of Smith County to Wills Anderson his interest as one of the heirs of Josiah Duncan deceased and to the one tenth part of a tract of land in Smith County on Smith's Fork. 4 Nov 1835. (P. 9)

Henry Frith to Wills Adamson a one tenth part of a tract of land in Smith County on which Josiah Duncan lived and died. The one tenth part is the distributive share of W. F. Cochran and wife Jane for which I have taken their quit claim. 4 Nov 1835. (Pp. 9-10)

Charles Jenkins and wife Mary; Basdel Garrison and wife Sally; David Allen; and Ana Hathaway to John Allen their interest in the estate of John Allen deceased, it being the land on Smith's Fork on which John Allen lived and died. It being the same land whereon his widow lately lived and died. 24 May 1836. (Pp. 10-11)

Thomas Whaley of Smith County to Leonard Lamberson of the same place one half of two tracts of land called the Mill Tract and joining the town of Liberty. 23 Jan 1835. (Pp. 11-12)

David Fite of Smith County to Leonard Lamberson 27 acres on Smith's Fork. 5 Dec 1833. (Pp. 12-13)

Thomas Whaley of Smith County to David Fite 14 acres adjoining the town of Liberty. 19 Jan 1835. (Pp. 13-14)

Moses Fite of Smith County to Edward Robinson of Wilson County 277 acres in Smith County on the west side of Smith's Fork. 2 Oct 1835. (Pp. 14-15)

Brent Spence and John M. Bass of Davidson County to Hugh Reed of Rutherford County 416 acres in Rutherford County on Carson's Fork of Stone's River. 27 Oct 1835. (Pp. 15-16)

James M. Brown to David Young and Joseph D. Morgan of Warren County, John Brown, William Henderson, and Benjamin Pendleton a deed of trust. 11 May 1836. (Pp. 16-18)

Thomas Hopkins to James Dillard two bonds for deeds. 22 Aug 1835. (Pp. 18-19)

Articles of agreement between Jessa Sapp and G. B. Sapp in which personal property is given to the said G. B. Sapp in exchange for supporting the said Jessa Sapp in her days of affliction and distress. 8 Apr 1836. (P. 19)

Michael Bickle of Warren County to B. L. McFerrin of Rutherford County 90 acres in Rutherford County on Brally's Fork. 15

May 1832. (P. 20)

Hugh Reed of Rutherford County to John Cooper of the same place 58 acres on Carson's Fork of Stone's River. Witness: John H. Reed. 3 Nov 1836. (Pp. 20-21)

Alexander McKnight to Drury Matthews of the same place 28 acres on the head waters of McKnight's Creek, a part of the tract of land on which the said McKnight now lives. 4 Apr 1836. (Pp. 21-22)

William Craft to Joel Cherry 100 acres. 2 May 1836. (P. 22)

Thomas Hopkins, attorney for the heirs of G. B. Ross of Warren County, to Martha Gooding of Rutherford County 100 acres in Rutherford County. 16 Dec 1836. (Pp. 22-23)

Robert Carson to Jonathan Jones an acre on the east fork of Stone's River. Also one hundred acres on which the said Carson now lives. 2 Jun 1836. (P. 24)

Commissioners to locate the county seat of Cannon County to to the Commissioners of Cannon County 62 acres. Bounded: south west corner of Lot #1 in the original plan of the town of Danville. 5 May 1836. (Pp. 24-25)

W. S. Cummins of Rutherford County to Robert L. Fagan 50 acres on Brally's fork of Stone's River. 3 Jun 1836. (Pp. 25-27)

Commissioners relinquish to the Commissionera appointed by the Legislature one acre for one dollar. 13 May 1836. (P. 27)

Abel McBroom and Henry D. McBroom to Joseph Clark and the other commissioners appointed by the County Court to lay off the town of Woodbury one half acre on the south side of the Stage Road east of the stone wall. 18 May 1836. (P. 28)

James M. Brown to Henry Trott, Jr. a deed of trust on 72 acres. 6 Jun 1836. (Pp. 28-30)

Elisha Bullard to Henry Bullard 100 acres on the north side of Sink Creek. 15 Mar 1836. (Pp. 30-31)

James H. Alexander to B. L. McFerrin four and one half acres on Brally's Fork of Stone's River. 13 Mar 1833. (P. 31)

Arthur Warren of Warren County to Joseph Fowler of Rutherford County a tract of land in Warren County on the waters of Stone's River. 13 Mar 1828. (P. 32)

Joseph Fowler of Rutherford County to James Taylor of Warren County 260 acres on the south side of the east fork of Stone's River. 20 Sep 1834. (Pp. 32-33)

Micajah Hollis of Rutherford County to John Hollis 75½ acres on the waters of Stone's River, it being part of a grant granted to Captain John Welch in the 13th year of independency of the United States. 29 Jan 1820. (Pp. 33-34)

Thomas P. Nichols and wife Delinda of Fayette County, Illinois to Jessa B. Robinson of Rutherford County their quit claim to a tract of land in Rutherford County, it being Entry #928, dated 18 Dec 1826. 15 Apr 1836. (Pp. 34-35)

Lydia Moody of Warren County to Henry Dosier of the same place 50 acres in Warren County on the dry fork of the east fork of Stone's River. 19 Oct 1833. (Pp. 35-36)

James Simmons of Warren County to James Sisson of Rutherford County 75 acres on the head waters of Carson's Fork of Stone's River. 30 Dec 1834. (P. 36)

Aaron Byford of Rutherford County to James Sisson one acre in Rutherford County. 2 Sep 1835. (Pp. 36-37)

James Mitchell to B. L. McFerrin, both of Rutherford County, 20 acres on Brally's Fork of Stone River. 11 Sep 1834. (Pp. 37-38)

James Taylor to the commissioners appointed by the County Court a tract of land on   south side of Stone's River adjoining the town of Woodbury. 12 May 1836. (P. 38)

Abel McBroom and Henry D. McBroom to the commissioners appointed by the County Court to sell the lots in the town of Woodbury and to superintend the publick buildings a tract of land on the south side of the east fork of Stone's River and adjoining the town of Woodbury so as to include the town spring. The land is donated. 12 May 1836. (P. 39)

Acalus Alexander to James Taylor 45 acres on Halacre's Creek. 10 Jan 1835. (Pp. 39-40)

David W. Anglin to James Taylor town lots #2 and 7 in the town of Danville. 9 Sep 1829. (P. 40)

John Reed of Maury County to Robert George of Warren County a tract of land in Rutherford County on the north side of Stone's River. 4 Feb 1828. (P. 41)

Robert George of Warren County to George Gannon of Rutherford County 100 acres on the north side of the east fork of Stone's River. 20 Nov 1830. (P. 42)

Daniel Dasher of Warren County to Richard P. Dasher of the same place 30 acres in Warren County on the dry fork of the east fork of Stone's River. 2 Sep 1831. (P. 43)

Daniel Dasher to Richard P. Dasher 44 acres in Warren County. 16 Oct 1830. (P. 44)

Elizabeth Brown and D. Q. Brown of Rutherford County a negro girl named Rody, about 10, for $300. 3 Mar 1834. (P. 45)

Ancil Milton to Stephen Cantrell, both of Warren County, 30 acres in Warren County on the east fork of Stone's River. 15 Aug 1834. (Pp. 45-46)

James Milton of Warren County to Stephen Cantrell 12 acres. 12 Aug 1834. (Pp. 46-47)

John Milton to Stephen Cantrell 15 acres in Warren County. 15 Aug 1834. (Pp. 47-48)

James Wood to Josiah Youngblood 90½ acres in Warren County on the east fork of Stone's River. 19 Dec 1834. (Pp. 48-49)

Commissioners appointed by the County Court to James Taylor a town lot in the town of Woodbury known as Lot #54. 13 Jun 1836. (P. 49)

Commissioners to Joseph Pinkerton a town lot in the town of Woodbury know as lot #2. 13 Jun 1836. (P. 50)

Commissioners to Richard Vinson town lot #43 in the town of Woodbury. 13 Jun 1836. (P. 51)

John Wood, Sr. to Archibald Stone, his son in law, for love and affection 50 acres on the waters of Locke's Creek. 25 Apr 1836. (P. 52)

Arthur Smith of Fulton County, Illinois to Sterling Alman and William Alman of Cannon County the exclusive right of making and using a moulding machine called Fake's Brick Moulder. 6 Jul 1836. (P. 53)

Commissioners to Charles Ready Lot #28 in the town of Woodbury. 13 Jun 1836. (Pp. 54-55)

Commissioners to Charles Ready Lot #28 in the town of Woodbury. 13 Jun 1836. (Pp. 56-57)

Arthur Smith of Fulton County, Illinois to Benjamin Sapp a machine for moulding brick to be used within the State of Alabama and the Territory of Florida and no place else. 9 Jul 1836. (P. 56)

Thomas L. Todd to Nathan Neely a negro boy named Sampson, about 5, for $200. 1 Nov 1835. (P. 57)

John Jones; Hayman and Polly Barrett; George and Sally King, being three of the heirs of Joseph Jones deceased of Warren County, state that they know that Betsy Haas, now Betsy Brownfield, formerly Betsy Jones, daughter of the said deceased, did purchase and pay for 30 acres of land on which the said Betsy now lives. They relinquish their claims to the said land. 28 Feb 1829. (P. 57)

Robert Stephens of Warren County to Jobe Stephens 68½ acres in Warren County on the head of Mountain Creek. 26 Nov 1831. (Pp. 58-59)

State of Tennessee Grant #126 to Haymon Barrett for 90 acres. 8 Mar 1828. (P. 59)

James Miles to H. D. and Abel McBroom 30½ acres in Warren County on the east fork of Stone's River. 28 Mar 1832. (P. 60)

Samuel Moore to Micajah Petty his one eighth interest in two negro boys that descended to him by virtue of relationship to Elizabeth Moore deceased (said boys known by the name of) being the same that my father left her. 1836. (Pp. 60-61)

William Bates to William Cunningham 160 acres in Phillips County, Arkansas. 19 Jul 1836. (P. 61)

John B. Meadleton of Marian County, Illinois to Jessa L. Perry of Warren County 200 acres in Warren County on the head waters of the east fork of Stone's River. 6 Apr 1836. (P. 62)

Thomas Oliver of Rutherford County to Robert Vinson of Warren County Lot #9 in the town of Danville. 4 Dec 1832. (Pp. 62-63)

Sheriff John Graves of Warren County to John Graham Lot #15 in the town of Danville. 8 Jul 1836. (Pp. 63-64)

John Graham to P. W. Campbell and R. H. Wallace Lot #15 in the town of Danville. 25 Jul 1836. (Pp. 64-65)

Edmund Tennison of Rutherford County to Brinkley Lasiter 100 acres. 18 Jul 1836. (Pp. 65-66)

Brinkley Lasiter to Larner Watson 100 acres on the west of the east fork of Stone's River. 18 Jul 1836. (Pp. 66-67)

John Brown of Warren County to Thomas Barrett ten acres in Warren County on Hill's Creek. 13 Oct 1836. (P. 67)

William Parton to John Pendleton 52 acres in Warren County on the head of Stone's River. 15 Mar 1836. (P. 68)

Edmund Jones to Harmon Barrett 50 acres, it being the land where the said Barrett now lives. 29 Jul 1836. (P. 69)

John Tucker to John Pendleton 120 acres on the head waters of Stone's River. 21 Jun 1836. (P. 70)

Arthur Warren of Warren County to Henry Warren of Rutherford County 89¼ acres in Rutherford County on the south side of the east fork of Stone's River. 20 Dec 1825. (P. 71)

Archebal Edwards to David O. Spicer 84 acres on Dry Creek. 30 Jul 1836. (P. 72)

James Pistole of Cannon County, formerly Smith, to Pleasant Pistole two tracts of land on the waters of the clear fork of Smith's Fork. 7 Mar 1836. (P. 73)

Marcus D. L. Bruce and wife Jane of Jefferson County, Illinois to M. S. West their one undivided share in a tract of land on Smith Fork. Bounded: the heirs of John Allen, Thomas West, and the heirs of John M. Bennett. 20 Jul 1836. (Pp. 74-75)

Leonard Fite and wife Elizabeth of Wilson County; Leonard Lamberson and wife Mary D., Pascal W. Brien and wife Narcissy B., all of Cannon County, to Wills Adamson their interest the tract of land on the south side of Smith's Fork, it being the land that Looney deeded to Josiah Duncan deceased. 14 May 1836. (Pp. 75-76)

Commissioners to John Brown 53½ poles in the town of Woodbury known as Lot #17. 13 Jun 1836. (Pp. 76-77)

Commissioners to John Brown Lot #51 in the town of Woodbury.

13 Jun 1836. (Pp. 77-78)

Commissioners to James Ferrell Lot #65 in the town of Wood-bury. 13 Jun 1836. (P. 79)

Commissioners to John Brown Lot #58 in the town of Woodbury. 13 Jun 1836. (P. 80)

Commissioners to William Bates Lot #19 in the town of Wood-bury. 13 Jun 1836. (P. 81)

Commissioners to William Bates Lot #6 in the town of Wood-bury. 13 Jun 1836. (P. 82)

Commissioners to Smart & McBroom Lot #27 in the town of Woodbury. 13 Jun 1836. (P. 83)

Commissioners to Elijah Stephens Lot #22 in the town of Woodbury. 13 Jun 1836. (P. 84)

Commissioners to Edmund Taylor Lot #55 in the town of Wood-bury. 13 Jun 1836. (P. 85)

Commissioners to Abel McBroom Lot #1 in the town of Woodbury. 13 Jun 1836. (P. 86)

Commissioners to Adam Elrod Lot #50 in the town of Woodbury. 13 Jun 1836. (P. 87)

Commissioners to Joseph Ramsey Lot #18 in the town of Woodbury. 13 Jun 1836. (P. 88)

John Moore to Henry Warren of Rutherford County 268 acres in Rutherford County on the waters of the east fork of Stone's River. 18 Aug 1832. (P. 89)

Commissioners to Abel McBroom 80 poles in the town of Wood-bury. 20 Aug 1836. (P. 90)

Samuel Moore to Henry Warren 77 acres, it being a tract of land that fell to the said Samuel Moore by heirship from Jesse G. Moore. 1 Aug 1836. (P. 91)

Commissioners to Henry Trott, Jr. Lot #52 in the town of Woodbury. 13 Jun 1836. (P. 92)

Commissioners to Henry Trott, Jr. Lot #13 in the town of Woodbury. 20 Jul 1836. (P. 93)

Commissioners to Henry Trott, Jr. Lot #30 in the town of Woodbury. 13 Jun 1836. (P. 94)

Commissioners to Henry Trott, Jr. Lot #49 in the town of Woodbury. 13 Jun 1836. (P. 95)

Commissioners to Henry Trott, Jr. Lot #61 in the town of Woodbury. 13 Jun 1836. (P. 96)

State of Tennessee Grant #4675. 30 acres in Smith County to Lemuel Turney. 25 Nov 1826. (P. 97)

Lemuel Turney to Jasper Rugle 30 acres on the waters of Clear Fork in Cannon County. 7 Aug 1836. (P. 98)

Articles of agreement between James M. Brown, Administrator for the heirs of Henry Wiley deceased, and Gabriel (Hume). 27 Aug 1836. (Pp. 98-99)

William McCormack to Richard Butcher a deed of trust on some livestock. 3 Aug 1836. (P. 100)

Commissioners to William Alman Lot #32 in the town of Woodbury. 13 Jun 1836. (P. 101)

John E. Sullivan of Warren County to Richard Lemay of the same place 150 acres in Warren County on the waters of Stone's River. 29 Nov 1834. (P. 102)

Commissioners to William Alman Lot #21 in the town of Woodbury. 13 Jun 1836. (P. 103)

Elijah Stephens to B. C. Stephens Lot #22 in the town of Woodbury. 27 Aug 1836. (P. 104)

Henry Bullard to Elisha Bullard, his nephew, a certain sorrel mare. 1 Jun 1836. (P. 105)

Samuel Laswell of Rutherford County to Henry Warren nine acres in Rutherford County on the east fork of Stone's River. 27 Mar 1833. (Pp. 105-106)

Commissioners to John A. Dunn Lot #38 in the town of Woodbury. 13 Jun 1836. (Pp. 106-107)

James Phillips to John Jarrell a gray mare. 21 Aug 1836. (P. 107)

Elizabeth Baker to James Henson a deed of gift for love and affection a certain black cow. 5 Sep 1836. (Pp. 107-108)

Thomas Cavat to G. W. Rose a deed of trust. 9 Sep 1836. (Pp. 108-109)

Joseph H. Haas to James Scott ten acres on the east fork of Stone's River. 17 Sep 1836. (Pp. 109-110)

Joseph H. Haas to James Scott 125 acres on the east fork of Stone's River. 17 Sep 1836. (Pp. 110-111)

James H. Alexander to Peter Simpson four and a fourth acres in Rutherford County on Stone's River. 11 Sep 1833. (Pp. 111-112)

Hiram Rawson of Rutherford County to John Rodgers of the same place 50 acres in Rutherford County on Carson's Fork of Stone's River. 5 Oct 1835. (P. 112)

Hugh Reed to James Sisson 100 acres on Carson's Fork of Stone's River. 15 Aug 1836. (P. 113)

Commissioners to Robert Vinson Lot #34 in the town of Woodbury. 13 Jun 1836. (Pp. 113-114)

Hugh Reed to Henry Pendergrass 56 acres, it being the place where the said Pendergrass now lives. 5 Sep 1836. (Pp. 114-115)

David Tackett to Peter Simpson, both of Rutherford County, 50 acres. 2 Mar 1829. (Pp. 115-116)

James H. Alexander of Rutherford County to Peter Simpson 87½ acres in Rutherford County on the waters of the middle fork of the east of Stone's River. 11 Sep 1833. (Pp. 116-117)

John Cooper to James Gipson 58 acres in Rutherford County on Carson's Fork of Stone's River. 14 Mar 1836. (P. 117)

James M. Brown to the firm of Barton & Ramsey a parcel of ground on the Public Square in the town of Woodbury. 30 Sep 1836. (P. 118)

. Nathaniel Linder of Warren County to Watson Cantrell his power of attorney to sell 100 acres, it being on the south side of Sink Creek. 2 Feb 1828. (P. 119)

John T. Lowe of Rutherford County to Walter Lowe of Cannon County a negro man named Jack, about 40, for $1000. 8 Aug 1836. (Pp. 119-120)

Jordan H. Ford and Abram W. Ford to John Reynolds a certain mule colt of a brown color. 3 Oct 1836. (Pp. 120-121)

Thomas Hopkins to Peterson Gilly 26 acres on the east fork of Stone's River. 8 Mar 1836. (Pp. 121-122)

Zavener Martin to Edward W. Edge of Wilson County 20 acres in Cannon County in the 1st District on the waters of Eagle Creek. 26 Sep 1836. (P. 122)

Zavener Martin to Edward W. Edge 180 acres in the 1st District of Cannon County. 26 Sep 1836. (P. 123)

Josias Hendrickson to Cinthia Kemp and John Goodner 50 acres on Helton's Creek of Smith County. 7 Jun 1834. (Pp. 123-124)

Solomon Redman to John Davis of Warren County 269 acres on both sides of Pine Creek of Caney Fork. 29 Aug 1836. (P. 125)

Isaac Brownston, Daniel Brownston, and Frederic Jones of Smith County to Josias Hendrickson a tract of land on Helton's Creek of Smith's Fork. 1 Oct 1828. (Pp. 125-126)

Isham Keaton to John Lawrence 50 acres in Smith County on the south side of Smith's Fork. 14 Mar 1829. (P. 127)

James Dillard to Thomas Hopkins a note. 11 Mar 1836. (Pp. 127-128)

Cantrell Bethel of Smith County to Thomas W. Duncan of the same place 15 acres on the north side of Smith's Fork in Smith County. 2 Mar 1831. (P. 128)

Gabriel Elkins to Thomas Elkins 173 acres in Warren County on Prater's Branch of the east fork of Stone's River. 22 Dec 1834. (Pp. 128-129)

Samuel Pogue to Thomas Parker 20 acres on Stone's River. 3 Feb 1827. (P. 129)

Sterling Whitlock to James Hendrickson 70 acres on Helton's Creek of Smith's Fork. 24 Sep 1836. (P. 130)

William Moore to Joseph Ramsey two negro or mulatto servants, namely two boys Isaac and Westley which interest descended to me by virture of relationship to Elizabeth Jane Moore. Also, two other boys, Lewis and Peter, and Levina and Lucinda and her child Mary which descended to me by virtue of Jesse G. Moore's will. It is stipulated that the said William Moore must not surrender his interest to the slaves until the time appointed in the Will of Jesse G. Moore. 26 Oct 1836. (P. 131)

Thomas James (one of the heirs of Daniel James) to Daniel Shackelford his one fifteenth part of two tracts of land on the east fork of Stone's River. 28 Oct 1836. (Pp. 131-132)

William L. Sullivan to James M. Brown two tracts of land on the east fork of Stone's River. 29 Oct 1836. (Pp. 132-133)

Allen Jaragin to Henderson Yoakum of Rutherford County 55 acres on Brawley's Fork of the east fork of Stone's River. 23 Nov 1836. (Pp. 133-134)

Samuel Lawing of Warren County to John Brown of the same place ten acres on Hill's Creek. 14 Mar 1835. (Pp. 134-135)

Matthew Edwards to John J. McElroy ten acres on Stone's River. 7 Nov 1836. (P. 135)

James Barkley to Thomas Cavatt 115 acres on the north side of the east fork of Stone's River. 11 Jun 1836. (P. 136)

Henry R. Perry, Administrator of Jesse L. Perry, to John Brown 100 acres on Stone's River. 7 Nov 1836. (Pp. 136-137)

Jesse L. Perry of Warren County bound to James M. Brown in the sum of one thousand dollars. 27 Jan 1836. (P. 137)

Thomas Clymer to John Daniels 50 acres on Mountain Creek in the 1st District. 10 Nov 1817. (P. 138)

Abram C. Pallet of Layfaett County, Missouri to Matthew Edwards 25 acres. Bounded: Abram Pallet. 1 Mar 1836. (Pp. 138-139)

Edwin Hickman of Shelby County to John P. Hickman his power of attorney to sell 228 acres on Helton's Creek. 25 Jan 1836. (P. 139)

Edwin Hickman to Samuel Vannatta 228 acres on Helton's Creek. 7 Jan 1836. (P. 140)

Hezekiah Bowers to John Vantrease 108 acres on Helton's Creek, a branch of Smith's Fork. 18 Nov 1836. (P. 141)

Catharine A. Spicer to her daughter and two sons, to wit, Lucy W. Spicer, Robert G. Spicer, and David O. Spicer to take effect at her death the following property a negro man named Kitt, about 25; a negro woman named Lydia, about 27; a negro girl named America, about 14; and three negro children named Judia, Ellin, and Peter. 1 Dec 1836. (Pp. 141-142)

Archebald Edwards to Richard P. Mosier 13¼ acres on the dry fork of the east fork of Stone's River. 3 Aug 1833. (Pp. 142-143)

Isham Adams to Henry Trott, Jr. a deed of trust. 15 Dec 1836. (Pp. 143-144)

Elizabeth Lyon to Nathan Neeley the following negroes, to wit, Nancy, about 38; Stephen, about 20; David, about 18; Louisa, about 16; Ema, about 10; Franky, about 8. 14 Apr 1836. (Pp. 144-145)

Blake Sageley to Jesse Jarnagin 50 acres on the east fork of Stone's River. 25 Jun 1836. (P. 145)

Thomas Glover of Smith County to Phillip Haas of the same place 15 acres on Helton's Creek of Smith's Fork. 16 Aug 1833. (P. 146)

Winphrey Weatherspoon to John Johnson 45 acres. 24 Nov 1836. (Pp. 146-147)

William W. Milligan to Daniel Shackleford 112 acres. 8 Nov 1836. (Pp. 147-148)

Tabitha Trewitt, Wingate Trewitt, Edward Robinson and wife Peggy, heirs of William Trewitt, of Smith County to Elijah Trewitt 132 acres in Smith County. 26 Oct 1835. (Pp. 148-149)

Nancy Trewitt, heir of William Trewitt, of Cannon County to Elijah Trewitt 44 acres which is the same that the said William Trewitt bought of John Donaldson and died seized and possessed of. 1 Dec 1836. (P. 149)

Lewis Hicks to James Yeargan 25 acres on Dismal Creek. 4 Aug 1836. (P. 150)

John Fite, Sr. of Smith County to Henry Fite of the same place 200 acres that the said Fite bought of Sampson Williams. 19 Nov 1835. (Pp. 150-151)

Elijah Trewitt to Henry Fite 20 acres on Smith Fork. 13 Dec 1836. (Pp. 151-152)

Moses Fite of Smith County to Elijah Trewitt of the same place ten acres on Smith Fork. 15 Apr 1835. (Pp. 152-153)

Polly Turney appoints Lemuel Turney her power of attorney to collect that which is due her from the estate of her father, John Gilliam, who deceased in Franklin County in the latter part of the year 1836. 5 Dec 1836. (P. 153)

Thomas Merit to Richard Eddings 25 acres on the east fork of Stone's River of Hollis' Creek. 8 Nov 1836. (Pp. 153-154)

William Young and Alexander Young, Executors of Henry Young, to Richard Eddings 25 acres on the east fork of Stone's River of Hollis' Creek, adjoining the lands of John Eddings, Sr. 8 Nov 1836. (Pp. 154-155)

11

Mrs. Elizabeth Good of Rutherford County binds her son, Christopher Good, to William E. McLin to learn the art and trade of saddling. 15 Nov 1836. (Pp. 155-156)

Elijah Stephens to Gabriel Williams and McKisack Williams Lot #22 in the town of Woodbury. 12 Nov 1836. (P. 156)

Richard A. Lemay to Archebald Stone a negro woman of black color named Mary Ann, about 17. 15 Dec 1836. (Pp. 156-157)

Daniel Parkhurst of Johnson County, Indiana appoints Job B. Stephens his power of attorney to convey a tract of land. 30 Nov 1836. (Pp. 157-158)

Joel Cherry of Warren County to Mitchell Daniels of the same place 100 acres on the head waters of the barren fork of Collins River. 1 Jan 1835. (P. 158)

State of Tennessee Grant No. 4574. 61 acres in Warren County to Augustus S. Oliver. 6 Oct 1835. (Pp. 158-159)

Augustine S. Oliver to Isham Adams 61 acres on Spring Fork and Berges Creek. 6 Oct 1835. (Pp. 159-160)

Paul Rigsby of Warren County to William Cummings 44 acres on the east fork of Stone's River. 3 Oct 1829. (Pp. 160-161)

James Scott to Edward E. Hooper 130 acres on the Caney Fork. 23 Dec 1836. (Pp. 161-162)

William Parton to Churchill B. Ransdell 414½ acres on the head waters of Stone's River. 8 Sep 1836. (Pp. 162-163)

Stanford Smith to Henry Hayes a trust of deed. 24 Dec 1830. (P. 163)

George T. Ford to Josiah Youngblood a tract of land on the fork of Stone's River. 2 Jan 1837. (P. 164)

William Parton to Washington Kennedy 500 acres on the head waters of the Barren Fork of Collins' River. 8 Apr 1835. (Pp. 164-165)

Robert Stephens to Jesse Johnson five acres on Mountain Creek. 30 Jun 1835. (Pp. 165-166)

Thomas Cavett to William Wood several tracts of land. 11 Jun 1836. (Pp. 166-167)

William Wood, Joseph Wood, Thomas Wood, and James Wood of Philadelphia, Pennsylvania to George T. Ford 260 acres in Warren County. 15 Jan 1836. (Pp. 167-168)

Archebald Edwards to Samuel Burke 43 acres in Warren County on Dry Creek. 3 Aug 1833. (P. 168)

Arthur Youngblood to Henry Trott, Jr. a trust deed. 9 Jan 1837. (P. 169)

Moses McKnight to David Wendell 100 acres on the east fork of Stone's River. 10 Jan 1837. (Pp. 169-170)

George T. Ford to Isaiah Neeley 25 acres on Cavender's Branch and joining the lands of Joshua Neeley. 16 Jan 1837. (Pp. 170-171)

John R. Sullivan to Charles P. Alexander a trust deed on a town lot in Woodbury. 16 Jan 1837. (Pp. 171-172)

Edwin A. Keeble, Administrator, and Harriet R. Brady, Administratrix of William Brady, both of Rutherford County to Robert Locke and Charles R. Abbott a deed of trust. 16 Jan 1837. (Pp. 172-173)

John Yeargin to John C. Cannady 185 acres in Warren County. 23 Dec 1834. (Pp. 173-174)

William Cooper to Allen Johnson, both of Warren County, 100 acres on Eagle Creek. 31 Jan 1833. (Pp. 174-175)

Thomas L. Turner and others to Henry Trott, Jr. a deed of trust. 27 Jan 1837. (Pp. 175-176)

John Morgan of Warren County to Judge C. Campbell 250 acres on Barren Fork of Collins River. 16 Aug 1836. (Pp. 176-177)

John B. Stone to Henry Trott, Jr. a trust deed. 4 Feb 1837. (Pp. 177-178)

Thomas Nokes, Jr. of Warren County to G. W. Rose of the same place ten acres. 7 Nov 1834. (Pp. 178-179)

Thomas Nokes, Jr. to G. W. Rose ten acres on the head waters of dry fork of Smith's Fork. 7 Nov 1834. (P. 179)

James Melton of Warren County to G. W. Rose a tract of land on dry fork of Smith's Fork. 5 Dec 1833. (Pp. 179-180)

Samuel F. McKnight to Alexander McKnight 73 acres on McKnight's Creek where the said Samuel now lives. 4 Apr 1836. (Pp. 180-181)

Henry Saul to Andrew Bogle 25 acres on Sanders' Fork near the dividing ridge. 28 Oct 1836. (Pp. 181-182)

Lemuel Turney to Abraham Adams 41 acres on the south draught of Smith's Fork. 28 Jan 1837. (P. 182)

Benjamin Pendleton of Warren County to William West 60 acres. 3 Sep 1830. (P. 183)

John Wright and Pumphrey Bynun to Daniel Hoover and Martha S. Hoover 153 acres on Brawley's Fork of the east fork of Stone's River. 11 Mar 1836. (Pp. 183-184)

Henry Medford to William Elkins some personal property. 7 Feb 1837. (Pp. 184-185)

John Wright and Pumphrey Bynun to Winphrey Witherspoon 161 acres. 11 Mar 1836. (Pp. 185-186)

Joseph Ramsey is bound to Robert G. Spicer in the sum of fifty dollars. Mentions his slaves America, Judia, Ellen, and Peter. 8 Feb 1837. (P. 186)

Robert G. Spicer to Joseph Ramsey his one third part in

six negroes now in the possession of George St. Johns and are
named Lida, about 25; Kit, about 24; America, about 4; India,
about 10; Ellen, about 8; and Peter, about 6. 8 Feb 1837.
(Pp. 186-187)

William West to Elisha Reynolds Lot #36 in the town of
Woodbury. 1836. (Pp. 187-188)

Samuel Bryson to George Bogle 71 acres in the 13th District.
25 Feb 1837. (P. 188)

Frances Northcutt to George W. Mears 45 acres in the 6th
District. 10 Feb 1837. (Pp. 188-189)

Samuel Vance to Thomas Vance a trust deed. 16 Feb 1837.
(P. 189)

Robert Orr of Rutherford County to Amos Saffel 95 acres in
Rutherford County. 29 Feb 1832. (P. 190)

Margaret Work to James Clark, both of Rutherford County,
her interest in the following negroes, to wit, a man named Bob;
a woman named Mist with her five children, Anderson, Elis, Burton, Thornton, and Zack. 10 Feb 1837. (Pp. 190-191)

John Gossett of Wayne County to Richard Dodd of Wilson County
100 acres in Wilson County on the waters of the sycamore fork of
the clear fork. 4 Jan 1833. (P. 191)

Richard Dodd to Richard Hancock 100 acres in Cannon County
on the waters of the sycamore fork of clear fork. 25 Feb 1837.
(P. 192)

William James to Eli Bailey 55 acres on the east fork of
Stone's River. 11 Jan 1830. (Pp. 192-193)

Johnathan Bateman to Blake Sagely a trust deed. 6 Mar 1837.
(Pp. 193-194)

Rachel Palmer, Hannah M. Davis, and John D. Jones to Pleasant A. Thomason a trust deed. 4 Feb 1837. (Pp. 194-195)

Daniel Parkhurst of Warren County to Jesse Johnson of the
same place 20 acres in Warren County on Mountain Creek. 30 Jun
1835. (Pp. 195-196)

Peter Crips to Henry Hart his interest in a tract of land
lying in the Smoke House Hollow on the waters of Dry Creek. 16
Aug 1836. (P. 196)

Robert Vinson to George Bishop a trust deed. 8 Feb 1837.
(P. 197)

Joseph Evans and wife Sarah to Thomas W. Duncan and the
other trustees Lot #8 in the town of Liberty on the west of Main
Street and north of South Street being seventy yards in length
and thirty-five in width for the benefit of Smith's Fork Circuit
to be a residence for the married preachers from time to time.
11 Mar 1837. (P. 198)

Articles of agreement between Mereda Watson and Baxter B.
Dickins in which she enters into a trust deed. 13 Mar 1837.

(P. 199)

Alexander Petty to Elizabeth Curtis 280 acres. 13 Mar 1837. (P. 200)

Alexander Petty, Administrator of Ambrose Petty, to James L. Assary 13 acres. 10 Mar 1837. (P. 201)

Alexander Petty to James L. Essary 65 acres. 13 Mar 1837. (P. 202)

Alexander Petty to James Sisson the land lying in Cannon County on the waters of Stone's River including what is called the High Cove. 11 Mar 1837. (P. 203)

William Sullivan to Richard Vincent a tract of land in Warren County on the east fork of Stone's River. 14 Jul 1826. (P. 204)

Samuel Bell to L. B. Moore some personal property. 13 Mar 1837. (P. 205)

James Barkley to Nathan Neeley a tract of land in Warren County on the south side of Stone's River in the town of Danville. 24 Jan 1832. (P. 206)

Alexander Petty to Marchel Stroud a negro man named Michel and his wife Nancy. 27 May 1836. (P. 207)

Sheriff John Graves of Warren County to William Williams a tract of land. 6 Mar 1837. (Pp. 207-208)

John W. Pearson of Fountain County, Indiana to John Rogers a tract of land in Rutherford County on the waters of the middle fork of the three forks of the east fork of Stone's River. 24 Jul 1834. (P. 209)

Joseph Young of Rutherford County to Margaret Lenox of the same place 50 acres on Carson's Fork of Stone's River. 10 Sep 1835. (P. 210)

Commissioners to Robert C. Price Lot #57 in the town of Woodbury. 13 Jun 1836. (P. 211)

William B. Stokes to John Reynolds a trust deed. 19 Jul 1836. (P. 212)

Stephen Murphy of Warren County to Washington Cameron of the same place 220 acres in Warren County on Pine Creek. 23 Feb 1835. (Pp. 213-214)

James D. Holt to Fielding Holt a gray horse. 7 Mar 1837. (Pp. 214-215)

A. F. McFerrin and B. L. McFerrin to James Mitchell 50 acres on Brally's Creek. 17 May 1837. (Pp. 215-216)

James Mitchell to David Caughanour 121 acres on Brally's Fork of the east fork of Stone's River. 10 Jan 1837. (Pp. 216-217)

William Meadleton is bound to John St. John in the sum of $530. 9 Apr 1831. (P. 217)

Joel Cherry to John Witt 42 acres on the waters of the Horse Spring Fork of Stone's River beginning in Rutherford County. 17 Nov 1835. (P. 218)

John Witt to Joel Cherry the tract of land in Warren County where the said John Witt now lives. 17 Oct 1835. (P. 219)

John Witt to Hugh Reed 42 acres. Bounded: the heirs of Thomas Hopkins. 5 Sep 1836. (P. 220)

Joel Cherry to Lewis Lemay 15 acres. Entry entered in the name of William Craft. 25 Mar 1837. (P. 221)

John H. Wood to James Wood 20 acres on the east fork of Stone's River. 20 Jul 1836. (P. 222)

John McClarin to John Witt a trust deed. 7 Nov 1835. (P. 223)

Woodson Northcutt to Jeremiah Elrod 21½ acres on the east fork of Stone's River. 24 Aug 1836. (Pp. 223-224)

Parmenas Williams to James Sisson 50 acres on Stone's River. 11 Jun 1836. (P. 224)

John Petty to Marshall Stroud a negro woman named Betsy for $500. 3 Nov 1835. (P. 225)

Trott & McBroom of Rutherford County to James Taylor Lot #5 in the town of Danville. 3 Nov 1818. (P. 225)

Trott & McBroom to David W. Anglin Lot #2 in the town of Danville. 30 Nov 1818. (P. 226)

Solomon Briant to Joseph A. Brandon 50 acres in Warren County. 21 Dec 1828. (Pp. 226-227)

Samuel Tittle to Henry Dennis 22 acres on the west side of the Camel Creek of the Clear Fork. 24 Mar 1837. (P. 227)

Joshua W. Briant to Richard Vinson 120 acres on the east fork of Stone's River. 20 Jun 1829. (P. 228)

Hamon Barrett to Richard Vinson 36 acres in Warren County. 23 Nov 1831. (PP. 228-229)

David Carver to John Young 47 acres on Clear Fork of Smith's Fork. 31 Dec 1836. (Pp. 229-230)

Robert L. Shaw to Joseph Turney 100 acres in the 10th District. 6 Apr 1837. (P. 230)

Henry Fork to William B. Evans of Warren County 50 acres in Warren County. 26 Oct 1831. (Pp. 230-231)

Obadiah Rich to Joseph Adamson 50 acres on Clear Fork of Smith's Fork. 1 Sep 1836. (P. 231)

John Fite to Tilman Bethel 95 acres. 30 Nov 1824. (P. 232)

Clinton B. Reynolds to Jonathan Griffith a negro woman named Jans, about 36, and her child named Lucy, about 4 months, for

$625. 14 Nov 1836. (P. 232)

Eliza Witherspoon to Enos T. Witherspoon all of her part of her father's land which was left to her by dowery. 20 Apr 1837. (P. 233)

Alexander Petty to Nicholas Gooding 50 acres in one of the forks of what is known by the name of the Line Hill Hollow. 16 Mar 1837. (Pp. 233-234)

Thomas T. Armstrong to Baxter B. Dickins 100 acres. 26 Jan 1837. (Pp. 234-235)

Baxter B. Dickins to Joseph Nivens 100 acres. 6 Apr 1836. (P. 235)

Oran Stroud to Jesse Miligan 200 acres. 21 Dec 1836. (Pp. 235-236)

David Crowder to Thomas Bradford some personal property. 2 May 1837. (P. 236)

Joseph Ramsey to Hugh Reed a negro girl named Mary for $650. 2 May 1837. (P. 237)

John Brown to William Thompson Lot #2 in the town of Woodbury. 12 May 1837. (P. 237)

Saldon Brashears to John Milton a tract of land in Warren County. 30 Oct 1828. (Pp. 238-239)

Alexander Petty to Joshua Barton a negro man named Green. 27 Dec 1836. (P. 239)

John Melton, Sr. to John Melton, Jr. a tract of land in Warren County. 6 Nov 1829. (Pp. 239-240)

James Melton of Warren County to John Melton, Jr. of the same place 20 acres in the 1st District of Warren County. 9 Oct 1828. (Pp. 240-242)

John H. Smith to Samuel E. Burger 1000 acres on Sink Creek and Dry Fork. 3 Aug 1836. (Pp. 242-243)

Cantrell Bethell to James Allen 120 acres above Smith's Fork. 24 Oct 1836. (Pp. 243-244)

Henry Fite to Joseph Clark 35 acres on the waters of Smith's Fork of the Caney Fork. 4 Feb 1837. (Pp. 244-245)

John M. McKnight to Drewry Matthews two and one half acres on Stone's River. 23 Jan 1837. (P. 245)

John Pendleton of Warren County to Benjamin Pendleton 150 acres in the 1st District of Warren County. 1 Jul 1834. (Pp. 245-246)

Blackman C. Thomas to H. R. Jarrett some personal property. 5 Jun 1837. (P. 246)

Benjamin Pendleton to William West 119½ acres on the east fork of Stone's River. 5 Jun 1837. (Pp. 246-247)

Henry Trott, Jr. to James J. Trott Lot #9 in the town of Woodbury. 7 Jun 1837. (P. 247)

Thomas West to E. T. Goggin two half acre lots in the town of Liberty. 26 May 1837. (P. 248)

Gabriel Lance and James H. Lance to Henry Wallace 200 acres on the head waters of Charles' Creek. 19 Jun 1837. (Pp. 248-249)

Greenberry Sapp to Henry Warren 125 acres on the head waters of Charles' Creek, the place whereon the said Warren now lives. 3 Jul 1837. (Pp. 249-250)

James Taylor to Joseph Pinkerton Lot #2 in the town of Woodbury. 4 Jul 1837. (P. 250)

James Taylor to Joseph Pinkerton a tract of land in the 6th District. 4 Jul 1837. (Pp. 250-251)

William Wood and Elijah Neeley are bound to Benjamin Sapp and Henry D. McBroom. 8 Apr 1837. (P. 251)

James Evans of Smith County to German Gossett of the same place a lot of land in Smith County. Bounded: Brick Store House. 3 Jan 1831. Witnesses: William J. Givan and George L. Givan. (Pp. 251-252)

John Fisher to Eason, Webb & Company a negro woman named Vilet for $500 to satisfy a lien that the heirs of Jacob Jennings has. 14 Jul 1837. (Pp. 252-253)

Hugh Reed to Thomas Williams a tract of land on Carson's Fork of Stone's River. 24 Aug 1836. (P. 253)

Almon Rigsby to Moses Cummings of Warren County 120 acres in Warren County on the head waters of Mountain Creek. 30 Sep 1830. (P. 254)

Daniel Cherry of Wilson County to Benjamin Cummings of Warren County 100 acres. 22 Nov 1811. (P. 255)

Benjamin Cummings, Jr. to Moses Cummings 57½ acres on the head waters of the east fork of Stone's River. 23 Jan 1828. (P. 256)

Hardy Lasiter to Luke Lasiter 100 acres on Brally's Fork of Stone's River. 3 Nov 1836. (Pp. 257-258)

Milton Fowler of Rutherford County to Charles P. Alexander of Warren County 130 acres on Dry Creek. 13 Nov 1834. (Pp. 258-259)

James Goodner to Thomas Bradford two negroes, to wit, Dua, about 26, and Aggy, about 20 months. 6 Aug 1831. (P. 259)

James Soap and wife Elizabeth to Robert Vinson 50 acres on Dry Creek in Rutherford and Warren Counties. 30 Mar 1835. (P. 260)

Jacob Overall to John Webb 93½ acres. 24 Jun 1826. (Pp.

261-262)

Parson Dill to James C. McGee a bay horse. 9 Apr 1837.
(P. 263)

Benjamin Pendleton of Warren County to Benjamin H. F. Phillips 104 acres in Warren County on Hill's Creek. 3 Sep 1832.
(Pp. 265-266)

Tarver Martin to David Crowder 60 acres on Engine Creek in the 11th District. 1 Jan 1837. (P. 266)

David Crowder to Thomas Bradford 60 acres. 1 May 1837.
(P. 267)

Luke McDowell to Thomas Bradford a tract of land on Dry Creek on the main road leading from Sparta to Nashville. 27 May 1836. (P. 268)

Richard Hancock to Fountain Owens a tract of land on the Harricane Fork of Sanders' Fork waters of Smith's Fork. 20 Jul 1837. (Pp. 268-269)

James (also written as Isaac) Beaty to Elizabeth Beaty 20 acres. 24 Jun 1837. (P. 269)

John Wood, Sr. of Warren County to James Barkley and the other trustees a tract of land on the head waters of the east fork of Stone's River in Warren County for a meeting house. 7 Aug 1837. (Pp. 269-270)

Joseph Soape of Tipton County to Joseph Warren 100 acres on Fowler's Creek. 7 Oct 1836. (Pp. 270-271)

Beverly Pearce of Warren County to James Taylor one half acre on the east fork of Stone's River in Warren County. 9 Nov 1829. (P. 271)

Joseph Soape to Charles P. Alexander 100 acres on Fowler's Creek. 7 Oct 1836. (P. 272)

Frances Cooper to Enos Witherspoon 58 acres. 5 Aug 1837.
(Pp. 272-273)

Samuel Garrison to John S. Vaughan 1000 acres on Hurricane Creek. 8 Aug 1837. (P. 273)

John A. Dunn to Allen R. Stone a trust deed. 28 Aug 1837.
(P. 274)

James Mitchell to his nephew, Jesse Gilliam, 50 acres on Brawley's Fork. 15 Jun 1837. (P. 275)

James Ferrell to John H. Wood 300 acres. 2 Sep 1837. (P. 276)

Thomas Glover to Jacob Fite 88 acres. 20 Aug 1836. (P. 277)

William Dale to John Vantrease 25 acres on Helton's Creek of Smith's Fork. 31 Aug 1837. (Pp. 277-278)

James A. Wilson to William Floyd 60 acres. 3 Sep 1837.

(Pp. 278-279)

Henry Warren to Arthur Warren, his son, for love and affection 85 acres on the east fork of Stone's River. 8 Sep 1837. (Pp. 279-280)

Henry Warren, Sr. to his son, David Warren, for love and affection 183 acres on the east fork of Stone's River. 8 Sep 1837. (P. 280)

William Denton, attorney for Isaac C. Denton, Hugh L. Denton, Telford Denton, Richard H. Bean in right of his wife Elizabeth, formerly Elizabeth Denton, and Daniel Thomason in right of his wife Mary, formerly Mary Denton, all of the State of Arkansas, to William Wood 182 acres. 13 Sep 1837. (Pp. 281-282)

James McKnight to David Wendell of Murfreesborough 115 acres. 1 Sep 1837. (Pp. 282-283)

James Ferrell to James J. Trott Lot #63 in the town of Woodbury. 16 Sep 1837. (P. 283)

Isaac Brunston and Daniel M. Brunston to Daniel Coggin 65 acres on Helton's Creek. 18 Sep 1837. (P. 284)

William Phillips to Alexander Finley 50 acres. 20 Mar 1837. (P. 285)

Isaac Beaty to Richard Webber 50 acres. 18 Sep 1837. (P. 286)

Robert Desha, Barnett Henderson and wife Lucinda, Thomas Fearn and wife Sally to James S. Odum 320 acres in Wilson County on Smith's Fork of the Caney Fork. 19 Aug 1836. (Pp. 287-288)

Alexander Petty to Nicholas Gooding 50 acres on Lime Hill Hollow of Stone's River. 20 Sep 1837. (Pp. 288-289)

William Brown to John M. Bennett his interest in the estate of his father James Brown. Said Brown is a resident of Smith County. 6 Aug 1829. (P. 289)

Jesse Todd to Edmund P. Stokes a tract of land on Brawley's Fork of the east fork of Stone's River. 25 Sep 1837. (P. 290)

Edmund P. Stokes to John Witt 40 acres. 4 Oct 1837. (P. 291)

Thomas Woodall to Joseph Turney 50 acres. 27 Jul 1837. (P. 292)

Benjamin Bennett to Taylor Bennett 40 acres on Dismal Creek. 27 Dec 1836. (P. 293)

James Williams to William Young 100 acres on the Barren Fork of Collins River. 25 Jul 1836. (P. 294)

Joseph A. Brandon to Margaret Dennis 50 acres in the 6th District. 30 Sep 1837. (P. 295)

Daniel Coggin to Thomas Trammel 65 acres on Helton's Creek. 21 Sep 1837. (P. 296)

Joshua Brown to John M. Bennett his interest in the land willed to him by his father, James Brown. 2 Oct 1837. (P. 297)

John Higgins to Solomon Travis 162½ acres on the east fork of Stone's River. 4 Aug 1837. (P. 298)

Hezekiah B. Newby of Jefferson County, Illinois and wife Nancy to Joab Patterson, husband of Elizabeth Bennett, daughter of John M. Bennett deceased. William Patterson, husband of Nancy Bennett, Benjamin Bennett, William Bennett, Thad Bennett, Rebecca Bennett, and Richard Bennett are heirs of said John M. Bennett. 17 Mar 1837. (Pp. 299-301)

Robert Espy to George Espy his bond. 22 Oct 1837. (P. 302)

Joseph Graham of Washington County, Arkansas to Onedimus Evans of the same place his power of attorney to receive that which is owed him by Henry Hart in Tennessee. 9 Sep 1837. (Pp. (Pp. 302-305)

John Wooldridge of Rutherford County to Thomas Wilson a trust deed. 17 Oct 1837. (Pp. 305-306)

John Wooldridge to G. W. Cantrell a trust deed. 17 Oct 1837. (Pp. 306-307)

Joseph D. Morgan of Warren County to Bates and Hoodenpile his power of attorney. 9 Sep 1837. (Pp. 307-308)

Onedimus Evans, Attorney for Joseph Graham, to Samson Braswell 133 acres on Dry Creek of Smith's Fork. 14 Oct 1837. (Pp. 304-305)

John Wooldridge of Rutherford County to Thomas Wilson a trust deed. 17 Oct 1837. (P. 305)

William Smith of Rutherford County to Alexander Orr of the same place 35 acres on the north side of the main Stone's River in Rutherford County. 4 Nov 1825. (Pp. 308-309)

Joshua Barton to his son, Dale Barton, 250 acres. 15 Aug 1837. (Pp. 309-310)

Hale Barton to Lewis Jetton 250 acres on the east fork of Stone's River. 28 Aug 1837. (Pp. 310-311)

Samuel Bogle and wife Isabel to James Odum 33 acres, it being their share as heirs of Thomas Bogle. 6 Feb 1837. (Pp. 311-312)

William Phillips to Jonathan Wimberly a trust deed. 3 Nov 1837. (Pp. 313-314)

Anuel Rains to John Espy 75 acres on Stone's River. 7 Oct 1837. (Pp. 314-315)

Thomas Hickman to Andrew Pickett 47 acres on Hickman's Creek. 10 Aug 1836. (Pp. 315-316)

Alexander Orr of Rutherford County to John Bartley 47 acres on the east fork of Stone's River. 3 Dec 1831. (Pp. 316-317)

Lemuel Dunkin to James Essary 235½ acres on the waters of the Barren Fork of Collins' River. 14 Aug 1837. (Pp. 317-318)

Thomas Whaley and wife Henrietta to Wills Adamson the tract of land formerly owned by Josiah Duncan, it being the land that the said Adamson now lives. 19 Oct 1837. (PP. 318-319)

Joshua Barton to George Crockett 133 acres on Brally's Fork and the Dry Fork. 20 Nov 1837. (P. 319)

John Barkley of Rutherford County to Greenberry Sapp six acres on the east fork of Stone's River. 20 Mar 1837. (P. 320)

Edmund Davenport to Auley Davenport 75 acres on the head waters of Stone's River. 14 Nov 1837. (Pp. 320-321)

George St. John and Catharine St. John relinquish their rights to slaves to Robert G. Spicer, David O. Spicer, and Lucy W. Spicer for the consideration of promoting peace and preserving that friendship that is desirable among relations. The slaves are to remain in the peaceable possession of George and Catharine St. John during the life of the latter or wife. 18 Nov 1837. (Pp. 321-322)

Henry Warren to Greenberry Sapp 50 acres on the north side of the east fork of Stone's River. 11 Feb 1837. (Pp. 322-323)

Ambrose Petty to Parker F. Stone five acres on the Barren Fork of Collins River. 1 Dec 1837. (PP. 323-324)

Lewis Lemay to Parker F. Stone 252 acres on the waters of the east fork of Stone's River. 25 Nov 1837. (Pp. 324-325)

Joseph Pinkerton to Parker F. Stone 121 acres on Stone's River. 5 Jul 1837. (P. 326)

Joseph Pinkerton to Parker F. Stone a tract of land adjoining the town of Woodbury. 5 Jul 1837. (P. 327)

Thomas Wood to Barnard Richardson 175 acres on Fall Creek. 10 Jun 1837. (P. 328)

William Bennett to John M. Bennett 100 acres in Smith County on Smith's Fork of the Caney Fork. 17 Feb 1824. (P. 329)

Nancy Bennett, William A. Pratt, James Bennett, James Crook, G. W. Bennett, and Collin Bennett to John M. Bennett the tract of land on Dismal Creek whereon the said Henry Bennett and wife now live. 10 Nov 1834. (Pp. 329-330)

Commissioners to Thomas St. John Lot #20 in the town of Woodberry. 13 Jun 1836. (Pp. 330-331)

Nathan Woods to Richard A. Lemay a tract of land on the east fork of Stone's River. 26 Dec 1837. (Pp. 331-332)

Ward Barrett to John Andrews a trust deed. 1 Nov 1837. (Pp. 332-333)

Winphrey Witherspoon to William Haney 120 acres. 15 Nov 1837. (Pp. 333-334)

Thomas Felton, Jr. and Thomas Felton, Sr. to Thomas Bradford 20 acres on the north side of Helton's Creek. 20 Jun 1828. (Pp. 334-335)

Benjamin Knott of Rutherford County to Alexander McKnight 220 acres. 20 Nov 1837. (Pp. 335-336)

Benjamin Knott and Knott Armstrong to John M. McKnight 105 acres on the east fork of Stone's River. 16 NOv 1837. (Pp. 336-337)

Templeton Moore to John Hollis some livestock. 23 Nov 1837. (P. 337)

Joseph Knott and George W. Knott to Cyrus L. Roberts a tract of land on both sides of Brally's Fork on west fork of the main east fork of Stone's River. 25 Oct 1836. (P. 338)

Jesse Sullins to John Young ten acres in Warren County on the west of the Short Mountain. 27 Nov 1835. (P. 339)

Silas Cooper to Tilman Bethel and Thomas Allen 75 acres on Dismal Creek. 16 Jan 1838. (Pp. 339-340)

Lewis Lemay to Richard A. Lemay 130 acres on the Barren Fork of Collins' River. 20 Mar 1837. (Pp. 340-341)

John Hays, Peter Hays, Henry Hays, Edmund T. Goggin and wife Nancy, formerly Nancy Hays to William Hays 39 acres that Hugh Hays bought of James Stanford in his life time. 10 Oct 1836. (Pp. 341-342)

Brice M. Richardson to Wiley Devenport 50 acres on Sanders' Fork. 26 Sep 1836. (Pp. 342-343)

Hale Reed to Robert J. Summers 50 acres in the 17th District. 28 Nov 1837. (Pp. 343-344)

Thomas Hopkins to Elizabeth Byford a bond. Said Elizabeth is the widow of Henry Byford. 15 Mar 1830. (P. 344)

Nathan Wood to George D. Wood 100 acres on the east fork of Stone's River. 22 Dec 1837. (Pp. 344-345)

Nathan Wood to G. W. Wood 62½ acres on the east fork of Stone's River. 26 Dec 1837. (Pp. 345-346)

Joshua Barton to James F. Brown two tracts of land on Brally's Fork of Stone's River. 27 Dec 1837. (Pp. 346-347)

William Cummings and William Stone of Warren County to Nathan Wood 50 acres in Warren County on Stone's River. 12 Jan 1830. (P. 346)

Daniel Manes to Eldridge Campbell 100 acres on the east fork of Stone's River. 12 Aug 1837. (Pp. 346-347)

Anderson Barnett to Nathan Finley a trust deed. 25 Dec 1837. (P. 347)

Zachariah Lefever to Thomas Leek 110 acres. 10 Jun 1837. (P. 348)

John Wood to Nathan Wood 62½ acres in Warren County on the east fork of Stone's River. 5 Jul 1828. (Pp. 348-349)

Nathan Wood to George W. Wood a tract of land on Hill's Fork of Stone's River. 1 Jan 1837. (Pp. 349-350)

Solomon Travis to Moses Elkins eight and one fourth acres on the ridge between my plantation and said Elkins'. 16 Dec 1837. (P. 350)

Solomon Travis to Joseph Bryson 100 acres in the 17th District. 20 Jan 1838. (P. 351)

Commissioners to A. C. Penn Lot #14 in the town of Woodberry. 18 Jun 1836. (Pp. 352-353)

Alexander Petty to Elizabeth Curtis 100 acres. 20 Jun 1837. (P. 353)

Joseph Clark and the other commissioners to John M. McKnight Lot #39 in the town of Woodbury. 20 Nov 1837. (Pp. 353)

Robert L. Fagan of Warren County to James Y. Bradford of the same place 100 acres on the west side of Brally's Fork of Stone's River. 1 Jan 1838. (P. 354)

James Mitchell and Jesse Gilliam to David Caughnor 50 acres on Brally's Fork of the east fork of Stone's River. 25 Nov 1837. (P. 355)

James L. Essary to James Sisson 210 acres on the Horse Springs Fork of Stone's River. 4 Jan 1838. (P. 356)

William Boyd to Robert Boyd and Robert L. Boyd a trust deed. 21 Dec 1837. (Pp. 357-358)

Parker F. Stone to his daughter, Sarah Word, and her husband Thomas Word, a deed of gift of a negro woman named Leath and her three children, to wit, Creape, Amey, and one infant at the brest. 8 Jan 1838. (P. 358)

John Brown to Henry Young Lot #58 in the town of Woodbury. 23 Dec 1837. (Pp. 358-359)

Commissioners to Parker F. Stone a town lot in the town of Woodbury. 21 Dec 1837. (Pp. 359-360)

Commissioners to Parker F. Stone Lot #8 in the town of Woodbury. 20 Dec 1837. (Pp. 360-361)

John K. Sauls to Parker F. Stone a trust deed. 11 Dec 1836. (Pp. 361-362)

Henry Byford of Rutherford County to Aaron Byford 50 acres in Rutherford County. 20 Jan 1838. (Pp. 362-363)

Hardy Byford to Washington Leigh 50 acres in Rutherford County on Carson's Fork of Stone's River. 30 Jan 1835. (Pp. 363-364)

Parker F. Stone to Allen R. Stone, his son, a tract of land known as Lot #6 in the town of Woodbury. 18 Jan 1838. (P. 364)

John Gunter of Smith County to John Halpain 50 acres on the Rock House of Stone's River. 24 Aug 1829. (P. 365)

Daniel Harpoole to John Melton 25 acres on the Rockhouse Fork of Stone's River. 18 Jan 1838. (Pp. 365-366)

William Stone to John Melton five acres on Rock House Fork of Stone's River. Bounded: Widow Halpain. 18 Jan 1838. (PP. 366-367)

Daniel Harpole to William Stone 15 acres on the east fork of Stone's River. 15 Jan 1838. (P. 367)

John Barkley, Jr. to John L. Moore some livestock. 30 Jan 1838. (Pp. 367-368)

John Barkley, Jr. to John L. Moore 102 acres. 12 Sep 1837. (P. 368)

Milus F. Travis to John Barkley 33 acres in Rutherford County on the east fork of Stone's River. 1 Jan 1838. (P. 369)

Allen R. Stone to Parker F. Stone a tract of land adjacent to the town of Woodbury. 3 Feb 1838. (Pp. 369-370)

Parker F. Stone to Gabriel Hume a trust deed. 5 Feb 1838. (Pp. 370-372)

David Scott to P. M. Wade a trust deed. 11 Aug 1837. (P. 373)

Mitchell Daniel to Richard A. Lemay a tract of land on Barren Fork. 7 Dec 1836. (Pp. 373-374)

William Falkenberry, Maxwell Caruthers, and Joseph Simpson to David Tenpenny 16 acres in the 2nd District. 2 Oct 1837. (PP. 374-375)

Eldridge Campbell to Benjamin H. F. Philips 100 acres on Hill's Bank of the east fork of Stone's River. 23 Jan 1838. (P. 375)

Josiah Youngblood to George T. Ford 140 acres in the 7th District. 3 Feb 1838. (P. 376)

Arthur Warren and Henry Warren to Thomas Thompson a tract of land in Warren County on the head waters of the east fork of Stone's River. 30 Jul 1818. (Pp. 376-377)

Solomon Briant to William Givins 71 acres in Rutherford County on the head waters of Rush Creek. 19 Dec 1828. (Pp. 377-378)

Louis G. Martin to John H. Wood a trust deed with a slave as security. 13 Feb 1838. (P. 378)

Parker F. Stone to Allen R. Stone a lot adjacent to the town of Woodbury. 25 Feb 1838. (P. 379)

Micajah Petty to Joseph Ramsey his interest in the following negroes (riginally belonging to the estate of Jesse Gipson and E. Jane Moore) viz. Vine, Lucy, Lewis, Peter, Wesley,
Isaac, and a girl child that Lucy has about two years old. 21
Feb 1838. (Pp. 379-380)

Elijah Whaley and Seth Whaley to their mother, Margaret
Whaley, a tract of land that Thomas Whaley died seized and possessed of. 10 Feb 1838. (P. 380)

Margaret Whaley, relict of Thomas Whaley; Seth Whaley;
Polly Goggin and William Goggin to Elijah Whaley 100 acres.
21 Feb 1838. (Pp. 380-381)

Margaret Whaley and others to Seth Whaley 125 acres on
Clear Fork. 10 Feb 1838. (Pp. 381-382)

S. H. Duncan of (Maury) County to Wills Adamson his interest in a tract of land that Josiah Duncan died seized and
possessed of. 6 Feb 1838. (P. 383)

Thomas Whaley to Seth Whaley his interest in the estate of
his father Thomas Whaley. 1 Feb 1838. (P. 384)

George W. Mears to Nathan Finley 45 acres in the east fork
of Stone's River. 28 Feb 1838. (Pp. 384-385)

Nathan (Neely) to Henry Trott, Jr. a trust deed. 2 Mar
1838. (P. 384)

William Bryson to John L. Moore 100 acres in the 11th District. 27 Feb 1838. (P. 385)

Thomas S. Todd to William Todd a mortgage. 12 Mar 1838.
(Pp. 385-386)

Samuel P. Russell to John Hollis a trust deed. 19 Feb
1838. (P. 386)

William Moore to John D. McBroom a tract of land on Stone's
River. 26 Jan 1838. (Pp. 386-387)

John Eddings to John Brown a trust deed. 15 Mar 1838.
(Pp. 387-388)

Hardy Byford to Archebald Lewis a tract of land on Bralley's
Fork of the east fork of Stone's River. 9 Jan 1837. (Pp. 388-
389)

Alsa Jones and wife Levenia to William Moore their interest
in a tract of land that was left to Elizabeth Jane Moore by
Jesse G. Moore deceased. 10 Aug 1835. (Pp. (PP. 389-390)

Matthew Edwards to Cyrus L. Roberts a tract of land on Bralley's Fork. 24 Jan 1837. (P. 390)

Alvis Holt and wife Lilly to William Moore their interest
in a tract of land that was left to Elizabeth Jane Moore by
Jesse G. Moore. 10 Oct 1838. (P. 391)

William T. Almond and James Ramsey to Elizabeth Haas Lot

#21 in the town of Woodbury. 7 Mar 1838. (Pp. 391-392)

William Rea of Rutherford County to Jacob Thomas of Wilson County 101 acres in Wilson County on Sanders' Fork. 29 Nov 1836. (P. 392)

Russell Lewis and wife Delilah to William Moore their interest in a tract of land that was left to Elizabeth Jane Moore. 7 Aug 1835. (Pp. 392-393)

Joseph Eledge, Sr. to William F. Eledge and Joseph L. L. Eledge 101 acres. 9 Aug 1837. (Pp. 393-394)

William Bryson to Stephen Wilson 150 acres on Sanders' Fork. 14 Feb 1838. (P. 394)

Matthew Edwards to Robert Pallett 25 acres on Bralley's Fork. 5 Mar 1838. (Pp. 394-395)

James Essary to William Wharton 125 acres in the 5th District. 6 Mar 1838. (P. 395)

Moses Shelby to James Essary 300 acres on the Barren Fork of Collins' River. 5 Mar 1838. (P. 396)

John A. Spurlock to Francis Turner 300 acres on Clear Fork of Smith's Fork. 5 Mar 1838. (Pp. 396-397)

Commissioners to Josiah Ferris of Rutherford County Lot # 36 in the town of Woodbury. 26 Jun 1836. (P. 398)

George T. Ford to Elijah Neeley 25 acres. Bounded: Josiah Youngblood. 3 Mar 1838. (P. 399)

Frances Turner to Francis Spurlock 35 acres in a 350 acre tract transferred to Francis Garner from Joseph Spurlock. 2 Jan 1838. (Pp. 399-400)

Elisabeth Halpain, widow of John Halpain; William Halpain, Joseph Halpain, John Halpain, and Margaret Halpain of Cannon County; John Frazer and wife Sally, Robert F. Frazier and wife Elizabeth of Coffee County, heirs of John Halpain to John Milton 50 acres on Stone's River. 12 Jan 1838. (Pp. 400-401)

Commissioners to Nathan Neeley Lot #25 in the town of Woodbury. 13 Jun 1836. (Pp. 401-402)

Aaron Ratcliff of Lawrence County to Cullin Carter 153 acres, it being a part of a 1064 acre tract granted to Jenkins Whiteside. 4 Feb 1833. (Pp. 402-403)

Jacob Spangler of Warren County to Samuel Spangler of Montgomery County, Virginia 50 acres in Warren County. 30 Sep 1828. (Pp. 403-404)

John Eddings to C. Reed Davis, trustee for the use of John Brown, a trust deed. 16 Mar 1838. (Pp. 404-405)

George W. Mears to Nathan Finley 45 acres on Past Fork of Stone's River. 17 Mar 1838. (Pp. 405-406)

William L. Alman to Joseph Ramsey Lot #32 in the town of

Woodbury. 8 Mar 1838. (PP. 406-407)

John Witt to Joseph H. Smith 40 acres in the 3rd District. 16 Nov 1837. (P. 407)

Leanner Watson to Luke Lasiter 100 acres on Clear Fork of Stone's River. 19 Mar 1838. (P. 408)

John Standley to William C. Odom 50 acres. 29 Dec 1837. (Pp. 408-409)

John Standley to William C. Odom some livestock. 19 Mar 1838. (Pp. 409-410)

John Willard to William Willard 25 acres on Harricane Creek of Sanders' Fork. 18 Feb 1837. (P. 410)

Highram Rossen to James L. Essary 50 acres on Stone's River. 19 Mar 1838. (Pp. 410-411)

Commissioners to William West Lot #53 in the town of Woodbury. 18 Jun 1836. (Pp. 411-412)

William Bates to the County Court Commissioners Lot #37 in the town of Woodbury. 18 Jun 1836. (Pp. 412-413)

William West to Francis Cooper Lot #37 in the town of Woodbury. 20 Mar 1838. (Pp. 413-414)

Jesse Todd to the heirs of David Faulkenberry 25 acres on Dry Creek. 30 Sep 1837. (P. 414)

Elizabeth Curtis to Joel Cherry 100 acres on Stone's River. 23 Mar 1838. (Pp. 414-416)

Commissioners to Edward Bragg Lot #59 in the town of Woodbury. 13 Jun 1836. (Pp. 416-417)

Leonard George of Rutherford County to Samuel H. Laughlin a tract of land formerly in Warren County. 30 Sep 1837. (Pp. 417-418)

Robert L. Fagan to John W. Stroud 76 acres in the 3rd District. 4 Dec 1837. (Pp. 418-419)

Peter J. Thomas to Herrod Holt three tracts of land. 1 Mar 1837. (Pp. 419-420)

Commissioners to Martin Stewart and John Hollis Lot #35 in the town of Woodbury. 18 Jun 1836. (Pp. 420-421)

Richard Eddings to William G. Henderson 25 acres in Distrists 2 and 6. 3 Apr 1838. (Pp. 421-422)

Pleasant W. Tucker and William Thompson to Bates & Humes a trust deed. 9 Apr 1838. (Pp. 422-423)

Joseph H. Haas to William Y. Henderson a trust deed. 14 Apr 1838. (P. 424)

Samuel Richardson to Hugh Robinson 224 acres on Brawley's Fork of Stone's River. 22 Aug 1835. (Pp. 424-425)

Hugh Allen to Randall Pafford his power of attorney. 30

Aug 1836. (Pp. 425-426)

James McAdow to James W. McAdow two negroes, one by the name of Isaac, about 24; the other, a negro woman, about 58, for $1000. 23 Mar 1838. (P. 426)

John H. Stoneman to William C. Odom a mortgage. 24 Mar 1838. (P. 426)

James McAdow, Sr. to James McAdow, Jr. 153 acres on both sides of Harrison's Creek of Sanders' Fork. 23 Mar 1838. (P. 427)

William Preston to William Mears a tract of land on east fork of Stone's River. 24 Mar 1838. (Pp. 427-428)

William Sullins to Robert Bailey a tract of land on the head waters of Stone's River. 30 Dec 1837. (Pp. 428-429)

James McDonald to Alexander McKnight and Robert Marshall his power of attorney to sell his interest in the estate of James Greer. 28 Dec 1837. (P. 429)

David Smith to David Carder 97 acres on Clear Fork of Stone's River. 17 Apr 1838. (Pp. 429-430)

Dosher Bragg to Edward Bragg 13 acres on Locke's Creek. 2 Apr 1836. (Pp. 430-431)

William C. Johnson to Joseph Moore a trust deed. 5 Apr 1838. (P. 431)

Samuel Bell to Lewis Bell a trust deed. 17 Apr 1838. (P. 432)

Clabourn Gunter of Warren County to J. G. W. Rose of the same place a tract of land in Warren County on Dry Fork of Smith's Fork. 6 Apr 1838. (Pp. 432-433)

John Estes to James W. Stewart a trust deed. 19 Apr 1838. (Pp. 433-434)

Allen R. Stone to Parker F. Stone 1000 acres on Stone's River. 30 Apr 1838. (P. 434)

Parker F. Stone to Allen R. Stone a negro boy, Bannister, of a light coulor or mulatto, about 17. 22 Apr 1838. (P. 435)

Charles P. Alexander to James McBroom 47 acres where the said Alexander now lives. 17 Oct 1833. (Pp. 435-436)

Ambrose Petty to Edmund M. Chahill a mortgage. 7 May 1835. (P. 436)

John D. McBroom to Henry D. McBroom a trust deed. 18 Apr 1838. (Pp. 437-439)

Elijah Higgins of Warren County to John Higgins 50 acres on Harricane Creek. 2 May 1835. (P. 440)

Lazarus Holman to Richard L. McKnight 120 acres. 7 May 1838. (P. 441)

Johnathan Wherry to Lewis Jetton ten acres on the east side of the east fork of Stone's River. 7 May 1838. (Pp. 441-442)

John Tucker to John Pendleton 30 acres on the head waters of Stone's River. 21 Jun 1836. (Pp. 442-443)

George W. Mears to Goldsbury Mears a mortgage. 25 Apr 1838. (Pp. 443-444)

James D. Morgan of Warren County to Phillip Hoodenpyle LOt #23 in the town of Woodbury. 27 Apr 1838. (P. 444)

William Bates and the other commissioners to Nathan Neeley Lot #3 in the town of Woodbury. 22 Nov 1837. (Pp. 444-445)

Nathan Neeley to Henry Trott, Jr. 81 square poles on the Public Square of Woodbury. 12 May 1838. (P. 446)

Calvin Sullivan to John Brown his interest in two tracts of land sold by a decree of the Circuit Court. 28 May 1838. (P. 447)

Henry Sauls to Jacob Wright a trust deed. 7 May 1838. (P. 447)

Benjamin B. Cooper to Cosby, Marshall, & Company of Rutherford County a tract of land on Sanders' Fork. 7 Apr 1838. (P. 448)

Samuel Moore to William Moore a peace or parcel of land that was let to Elizabeth Jane Moore by Jesse G. Moore deceased and at the decease of Elizabeth Moore a part fell to me. 18 Jan 1834. (P. 448)

Richard Eddings to Joseph Ramsey a trust deed. 18 May 1838. (P. 449)

William Bryson to Fanny Bryson his interest in two negro slaves. 15 May 1838. (Pp. 449-450)

Blake Sagely to William Stacy a tract of land that Susanah Thompson, widow of Jason Thompson, obtained as her dower and conveyed to Ira C. Kneeland who conveyed it to the said Blake Sagely. 9 Mar 1838. (Pp. 450-451)

John R. Sullivan to Thomas C. Word a trust deed. 15 May 1838. (Pp. 451-452)

Samuel Moore to Joseph Harper a tract of land on the head waters of Burges' Creek. 12 May 1838. (P. 452)

Susanah Bell to William D. Gowan 14½ acres on the east fork of Stone's River. 22 Sep 1839. (P. 453)

Joseph Knott to Joseph Pinkerton 78½ acres on Brally's Fork of the east fork of Stone's River. 3 Jan 1838. (P. 454)

Alford Whitfield to Silas A. Robinson 170 acres on Brally's Fork of the east fork of Stone's River. 10 May 1838. (P. 455)

Eli Whitfield to John McCrary the tract of land on which Willis Whitfield lived and died. 17 May 1838. (Pp. 455-456)

Josiah Youngblood to Robert K. Stephens (also written as Sampson Stephens) a trust deed. 25 May 1838. (Pp. 456-478)

State of Tennessee Grant #14038. 250 acres on the Clear Fork of Sanders' Fork to Zachariah Thomason. 4 Feb 1837. (P. 459)

Valentine Simpson to David McGill ten acres on Carson's Fork of the east fork of Stone's River. 21 May 1838. (P. 459)

Solomon Brents of Perry County to Gabriel Hume three acres in the 6th District. 1 Jun 1838. (Pp. 459-460)

Johnson Brents of Perry County to Gabriel Hume 37 acres on the east fork of Stone's River. 1 Jun 1838. (Pp. 460-461)

Anthony Tittle and Nancy Tittle to Joseph H. Bogle a slave named Mariah, age 19. 29 May 1838. (P. 461)

Isham Adams to Henry, Trott, Jr. 71 acres. 17 May 1838. (P. 462)

Henry Kurby to George Grizzell a trust deed. 25 May 1838. (P. 463)

George St. John, Catharine St. John, Joseph Ramsey, and Robert G. Spicer to Jacob Wright a negro man named Kit, about 25. 28 May 1838. (Pp. 463-464)

James P. Thompson to James Cherry 50 acres in Warren County on the Barren Fork of Collins' River. 17 Aug 1837. (Pp. 464-465)

Whereas by descent from Isaac Turney deceased, Pleasant Turney, John C. Turney, Elizabeth Taylor, Polly Adams, Sally S. Campbell, Frances Turney, George Turney, Lemuel Turney, and Bowman Turney have title to a tract of land in the 10th District. 9 Oct 1837. (P. 464)

Thomas (Whylvent) to James Coit a tract of land on Barren Fork of Collins' River. 25 Nov 1842. (P. 464)

James Wilson to Anderson J. Thomas a trust deed. 18 Jun 1838. (Pp. 1-2)

Samuel C. Bryant to Blake Sagely 126 acres on Brasley's Fork of the east fork of Stone's River. 28 May 1838. (Pp. 2-3)

John Wright to Samuel C. Bryant 128 acres on Brawley's Fork. 8 Mar 1836. (Pp. 3-5)

Hardy Spicer to Abel and Henry D. McBroom 50 acres on the east fork of Stone's River. 2 Jul 1838. Mentions the Graveyard Hollow. (P. 5)

Thomas St. John to Henry Trott, Jr. Lot #20 in the town of Woodbury. 14 Jun 1838. (Pp. 5-6)

Jacob Wright to Caleb Sullivan 50 acres. (Pp. 6-8)

Trott and McBroom to Pompey Daniels of Warren County Lot #26 in the town of Danville. 30 Nov 1818. (Pp. 8-9)

Solomon Brients and Elizabeth Brients, his wife, to Harmon Barrett a tract of land. 9 Jun 1838. (Pp. 9-10)

Rizen Fowler to A. F. and B. L. McFerrin a trust deed. 10 Jul 1838. (Pp. 12-13)

Elijah Armstrong to John Higgins 25 acres on Hurricane Creek in Wilson County. 18 Oct 1830. (Pp. 13-15)

William Moore to John D. McBroom a trust deed. 8 Aug 1838. (Pp. 15-16)

(Pages are misnumbered)

Pompey Daniels of Hardin County to James M. Brown, guardian of Frances Ann and Henry Wiley, minor heirs of Henry Wiley, Lot #26 in the town of Danville. 9 Jun 1838. (Pp. 19-21)

William Moore to Abel McBroom and Jesse McBroom 113 acres on the east fork of Stone's River. 11 Aug 1838. (Pp. 21-22)

Judge C. Campbell to John Pendleton 250 acres on the head waters of the Barren Fork of Collins' River. 15 Aug 1838. (Pp. 22-23)

John Morgan of Warren County to John Pendleton 100 acres on Barren Fork of Collins' River. 20 Dec 1836. (Pp. 23-25)

Sheriff H. R. Jarratt to Joseph Ramsey a town lot in the town of Woodbury, it being a lot of land belonging to the heirs of Henry Wiley. 21 Aug 1838. (Pp. 25-26)

Henry Trott, Jr. to William Bates a trust deed. 19 Aug 1838. (Pp. 26-32)

Thomas Brients to Thomas Vance 30 acres. 28 May 1838. (Pp. 32-33)

B. L. McFerrin to Johnson Rayburn & Company two tracts of land on Bralley's Fork of Stone's River. 23 Aug 1838. (Pp. 33-

34)

John Brown to Benjamin C. Stephens seven and one fourth acres in the 6th District. 13 Jul 1838. (Pp. 35-36)

William Phillips to James Essary of Warren County a trust deed. 25 Aug 1838. (PP. 36-38)

William Simpson and wife Nancy of Randolph County, Illinois to William Pike a tract of land. 2 Sep 1837. (Pp. 38-40)

James C. King to George D. Gordon 5000 acres. Bounded: Washington Britton. 27 Aug 1838. (Pp. 40-41)

James Higgins to Archebald Stone a certain negro man of yellow color named George, about 26. 27 Aug 1838. (P. 42)

Britton Moore to John H. Wood 25 acres. 29 Aug 1838. (Pp. 43-44)

B. L. McFerrin to William Holt 53 acres on Brawley's Fork of Stone's River. 30 Aug 1838. (Pp. 45-46)

Samuel Edmondson to James C. King 5000 acres. Bounded: Washington Britton. 27 Aug 1838. (Pp. 46-47)

James Mitchell to John H. Wood a trust deed. 8 Sep 1838. (Pp. 47-49)

Robert Vinson to James Taylor 50 acres. 3 Sep 1838. (Pp. 49-50)

A. C. Penn to J. Ferris half of Lot #14 in the town of Woodbury. 5 Sep 1838. (Pp. 50-51)

William Norton of Bedford County to Jeremiah Cleveland 185 acres. 19 Sep 1837. (Pp. 51-53)

Hezekiah Oaks to William Norton of Bedford County a tract of land on Bralley's Fork. 17 Jul 1837. (PP. 53-55)

William Parton to William West 100 acres on the east fork of Stone's River. 7 Sep 1838. (PP. 55-57)

John L. Shaw and James Spurlock to Frances Spurlock a tract of land on Clear Fork. 21 Apr 1838. (Pp. 57-59)

Thomas Cavett to Medford Caffy 115 acres on the east fork of Stone's River. Said Caffy is a resident of Rutherford County. 10 Sep 1838. (Pp. 60-61)

Jacob Berger to Samuel Dinby 143 acres on Dry Fork of Smith's Fork. 23 Aug 1837. (PP. 61-63)

P. F. Stone to Allen R. Stone a black boy named Nelson and a little girl named Martha of light collour. 30 Aug 1838. (P. 63)

Merrit Givins to Margaret Dennis 16 acres. 14 Sep 1838. (P. 64)

Isham Adams to William Bates 115 acres on Stone's River. 20 Sep 1838. (P. 65)

John Willard to Abraham Cooper a trust deed. 21 Sep 1838. (P. 66)

Thomas L. Turner to John B. Stone a trust deed. 15 Sep 1838. (Pp. 67-69)

Thomas Merit to William Y. Henderson a trust deed. 28 Sep 1838. (Pp. 69-70)

Milton Fowler to Benjamin Hayes 100 acres. 2 Jan 1837. (Pp. 70-72)

Oran B. Stroud to John Petty a trust deed. 3 Oct 1838. (Pp. 72-73)

John St. John to Thomas Cooper 50 acres in Warren County in the mountain district. 8 Oct 1838. (Pp. 74-75)

Daniel Parkhurst to Joseph Clark 65 acres in Warren County on Mountain Creek. 1 Oct 1838. (Pp. 75-76)

Robert Tittle to Peter Adams his interest in the tract of land whereon Samuel Tittle deceased lived. 27 Sep 1838. (Pp. 77-78)

Samuel Lance to Jonathan Wherry 262 acres in the 8th District on the east fork of Stone's River. 19 Oct 1838. (Pp. 78-79)

George Bynum to John Bynum, Sr. a mortgage. 20 Oct 1838. (Pp. 79-80)

Ambrose Petty to William Young a trust deed. 25 Oct 1838. (Pp. 80-82)

Oran Stroud to Micajah Petty 35 acres on Carson's Fork of the east fork of Stone's River. 25 Oct 1838. (Pp. 82-83)

John B. Stone to Thomas Cavett 57 acres on the east fork of Stone's River. 24 Sep 1838. (Pp. 83-84)

Wila Willis of Rutherford County to Hezekiah Oaks of the same place a tract of land on the east fork of Stone's River in Rutherford County. 2 Dec 1835. (Pp. 84-86)

George Bryson to James Reed 25 acres in the 11th District. 17 Sep 1838. (Pp. 86-87)

Milton Fowler of Coffee County to Achilles Alexander 60 acres on Fowler's Creek. 25 Sep 1838. (Pp. 88-89)

Thomas St. John to Ezekiel (Mullins) 30½ acres on the east fork of Stone's River. 22 Dec 1836. (Pp. 89-90)

George Bogle of Wilson County to William Higgins 50 acres on Harricane Creek of Sanders' Fork. 13 Feb 1837. (Pp. 90-91)

James West of Warren County to Adam J. Moore of the same place 90 acres. Bounded: by said Moore. 16 Apr 1838. (P. 92)

Frances Cooper to Franklin Coleman Lot #37 in the town of

DEED BOOK B

Woodbury. 11 Oct 1838. (P. 93)

Robert J. Summers to Elihu Witherspoon 50 acres. Bounded: Ezekiel Alexander. 30 Oct 1838. (Pp. 93-95)

George Bogle to William Higgins 50 acres on the north side of a small ridge. 18 Feb 1837. (Pp. 95-96)

William Hollis to James Taylor 50 acres on the south side of the east fork of Stone's River. 5 Nov 1838. (Pp. 96-98)

Francis Bryson to James Thomas a trust deed. 25 May 1838. (Pp. 98-100)

Archebald Stone to James Higgins a quit claim deed to a negro boy of yellow complexion named Bob. 14 Nov 1838. (Pp. 100-101)

James W. Stover of Philadelphia, Pennsylvania to William H. Tomlinson and others 5000 acres on the head waters of the east fork of Stone's River. 11 Jun 1838. (Pp. 101-105)

Oliver Hale, Jr. to Solomon Hart 5000 acres on the head waters of the east fork of Stone's River. Said Hale is a resident of Philadelphia. 24 Apr 1838. (Pp. 106-108)

Oliver Hale, Jr. of Philadelphia to James Stover 5000 acres. 24 Apr 1838. (Pp. 108-110)

John Elam to William Preston 21½ acres on the east fork of Stone's River. 6 Nov 1838. (Pp. 111-112)

William and William H. Middleton to John and Henry Elam 90½ acres in the 6th District. 10 Nov 1838. (Pp. 112-113)

Green B. Sapp to Benjamin Sapp 106 acres in the 6th District on the north side of the east fork of Stone's River. 28 Oct 1838. (Pp. 113-115)

Zachariah Bush to Jane Lambert and her children 191 acres on Brawley's Fork of the east fork of Stone's River. 21 Nov 1838. (Pp. 115-117)

William Milligan to Thomas Thompson 52 acres on Stone's River in the 6th District. 19 Nov 1838. (Pp. 117-118)

Zachariah Bush to Jesse B. Robertson 160 acres in the 4th District. 28 Nov 1838. (Pp. 118-119)

Zachariah Bush to Dabney Ewell a negro woman named Winney and a boy named Washington. 22 Nov 1838. (Pp. 119-120)

Mark Adcock to H. D. Duncan a tract of land in what was Warren County. Said Mark is the son of John Adcock. 15 Oct 1838. (Pp. 120-122)

C. Reed Davis to William Preston a trust deed. 14 Mar 1838. (Pp. 122-124)

Epaphaditus Francis to Armsted Francis a tract of land. 16 Jun 1838. (P. 124)

Joseph Young to Thomas Sadler. 1831. (PP. 125-127)

Hugh Porter to Thomas Sadler 25 acres in Rutherford County on Brawley's Fork on the east fork of Stone's River. 23 Sep 1833. (Pp. 127-128)

C. R. Davis to Jesse Hollis 139 acres. 14 Mar 1838. (Pp. 128-130)

G. R. T. Blount of Beaufort County, North Carolina to James Stone 380 acres on the east side of the Rock House Fork. 22 Aug 1832. (PP. 130-132)

Joseph Knox and William A. Knox to Albert T. Fagan 150 acres on the east side of Brawley's Fork of Stone's River. 6 Jun 1838. (Pp. 132-133)

James Higgins to John W. Summers a negro boy named George of yellow complexion. 20 Nov 1838. (Pp. 133-134)

John W. Stroud to John McClain 76 acres in the 3rd District. 3 Nov 1838. (Pp. 134-135)

Benjamin Pendleton to John Brown 50 acres in the 6th District. 5 Sep 1838. (Pp. 135-136)

Matthew Edwards to James J. McElroy six acres. 13 Aug 1838. (Pp. 136-137)

Matthew Edwards to James J. McElroy a tract of land. 24 Dec 1838. (Pp. 136-138)

Archebald McDougle to Hiram Dodd 350 acres on the east side of Wilmett's Camp Creek. 12 Dec 1838. (Pp. 139-140)

William Haney to Willis W. Haney a trust deed. 27 Dec 1838. (Pp. 140-141)

William Haney to Willis W. Haney 120 acres. 25 Dec 1838. (Pp. 141-142)

James A. Steel to John A. Travis a trust deed. 1 Jan 1839. (Pp. 143-144)

Josiah Youngblood to John Brown 143 acres in the 6th District. 31 Dec 1838. (Pp. 144-145)

Sheriff H. R. Jarratt to John Fisher two town lots in the town of Woodbury. 23 Apr 1838. (Pp. 146-148)

Richard Eddings to Adam Elrod 25 acres. Bounded: John Eddings. 3 Jan 1839. (Pp. 148-150)

George T. Ford to Robert Walkup 87½ acres on Stone's River. 19 Dec 1837. (Pp. 150-151)

Henry H. Clifton to George Walker 44 acres on the east fork of Stone's River. 24 Aug 1836. (Pp. 152-153)

Melchideck Williams and other trustees to William Bates and Gabriel Hume two two lots in the town of Woodbury. 22 Dec 1838. (Pp. 153-155)

Andrew J. Wood to Thomas G. Wood a trust deed. 10 Jan 1839. (Pp. 155-158)

DEED BOOK B

Henry Trott, Jr. to John Webb, James K. Eason, and John Fisher a trust deed. 12 Jan 1859. (Pp. 158-159)

George Crockett to Joshua Barton 133 acres in the forks between Brawley's Fork and the Dry Fork. 23 Nov 1838. (Pp. 159-160)

James Essary of Warren County to Richard M. Lemay 200 acres on Barren Fork of Collins' River. 11 Jun 1838. (Pp. 161-162)

Andrew Morrison to George Peebles and John L. Chaney 50 acres in the 17th District. 22 Dec 1837. (Pp. 162-164)

Albert T. Fagan to Asariah Gaither 150 acres on Brawley's Fork of the east prong of Stone's River. 28 Dec 1838. (Pp. 164-165)

Received of Henry Trott, Jr. on a note for the redemption of Lot #38 in the town of Woodbury. 14 Jan 1839. (Pp. 165-166)

H. R. Jarratt, Sheriff, to William Bates a tract of land. 14 Jan 1839. (Pp. 166-167)

Luke Lasiter to Lewis Pumphrey 100 acres. Bounded: Hardy Lasiter. 18 Dec 1838. (P. 168)

John Chaney to Joseph H. Bogle a man slave named Sandy, age 25. 26 Dec 1838. (P. 169)

James Y. Bradford to William A. Knox 100 acres on Bralley's Fork of Stone's River. 14 Jan 1839. (Pp. 169-170)

H. Yoakum to Jesse Jarnigan 55 acres on Bralley's Fork of the east fork of Stone's River. 11 Jan 1839. (Pp. 171-172)

Archebald Stone to William Stone 57 acres in Warren County on the east fork of Stone's River. 5 Jul 1828. (Pp. 172-174)

Moses Cummins to William Stone 32½ acres. 24 Dec 1838. (Pp. 174-175)

James H. Stone to Thomas Cavett one or two acres. 24 Sep 1838. (Pp. 175-176)

Thomas Sadler to Valentine Simpson a bond. 25 Dec 1839. (Pp. 177-178)

Abraham Berger to John C. Cannady six acres on Dry Creek of Smith's Fork. 29 Sep 1838. (Pp. 178-179)

James M. Roberts to Granville Roberts a trust deed. 17 Jan 1839. (Pp. 179-180)

Robert Vinson to David M. Stewart a trust deed. 17 Jan 1839. (Pp. 180-183)

Joseph Harper to Lathan Finley a trust deed. 17 Jan 1839. (Pp. 184-185)

H. R. Jarratt to Albert McKnight a trust deed. 11 Aug 1838. (Pp. 185-188)

37

C. Reed Davis to John Pendleton a trust deed. 14 Mar 1838. (Pp. 188-189)

John Jones to William Brownfield 15 acres in Warren County on the east fork of Stone's River. 3 Oct 1829. (Pp. 190-191)

William Brownfield to Harmon Barret 62½ acres in Warren County on the head waters of the east fork of Stone's River. 3 Sep 1832. (Pp. 192-193)

Jacob Faulkenberry to Joseph Simpson 74 acres on the west side of the middle fork of Stone's River. 28 Sep 1837. (Pp. 193-194)

Peter Simpson to his son, Joseph Simpson, 34 acres in the 3rd District. 16 Jan 1839. (Pp. 195-196)

Matthew Patton to B. B. Dickins a quit claim deed to 150 acres. 3 Dec 1838. (Pp. 196-197)

Abraham Berger to John C. Cannady three quarter's of an acre in the mountain district on the head waters of Dry Creek of Smith's Fork. 19 Mar 1838. (Pp. 197-198)

David T. Warren to George Gannon 63 acres on the waters of the east fork of Stone's River. 21 Jan 1839. (Pp. 199-200)

Thomas D. Young of Hardeman County to Robert L. Fagan a tract of land in Rutherford County. 3 Feb 1836. (Pp. 200-201)

Robert Bailey to Nathan Neeley a bond. 20 May 1834. (Pp. 201-202)

Archebald Stone of Warren County to William Grimes 100 acres in Warren County on the east fork of Stone's River. 4 Nov 1835. (Pp. 203-204)

George T. Ford to William B. Evans 60 acres in the 7th District. 18 Jan 1839. (Pp. 204-205)

William Hollis to Joseph Spurlock a certain negro boy named Henry, about 15. 17 Jan 1839. (Pp. 205-206)

Joseph Whitely and wife Elizabeth to Henry Trott, Jr. their interest in Lots #61 and 62 in the town of Woodbury. 28 Jan 1839. (Pp. 206-207)

John B. Stone, Trustee of Cannon County, to Thomas L. Turner three tracts of land. 29 Jan 1839. (Pp. 207-208)

Thomas L. Turner to Thomas Elkins 50 acres in the 6th District. 29 Jan 1839. (Pp. 208-210)

James D. Holt to Fielding Holt a trust deed. 30 Jan 1839. (P. 210)

Johnathan Wimberly to James J. Trott 50 acres on the north side of Bullpen Creek. 4 Feb 1839. (Pp. 210-212)

Johnathan Wimberly to Henry Trott, Jr. 100 acres in the 5th

District. 4 Feb 1839. (Pp. 212-213)

Sheriff H. R. Jarratt to William Word four negroes, to wit, Leatha and her four children, Virginia, Anna, and Eleanor. 12 Jan 1839. (P. 215)

Charles C. Evans to John Rigsby 15 acres in Evans' Hollow. 4 Feb 1839. (Pp. 215-216)

John Rigsby to C. C. Evans a tract of land on Rock House Fork of Stone's River. 14 Sep 1838. (P. 217)

Patsy Gannon, widow of Mark Gannon; William Young and wife Uffy who is one of the heirs of the said Mark Gannon and Patsy Gannon; Joseph Whitely and wife Elizabeth who is one of the heirs of the said Mark Gannon and Patsy Gannon; and Polly or Mary Gannon who is also an heir of the said Mark Gannon and Patsy Gannon to Henry Trott, Jr. the land in the town of Woodbury whereon the said Patsy Gannon now lives and the same that was deeded to her by James Taylor on 3 Jun 1838. 8 Feb 1839. (Pp. 218-221)

Henry Trott, Jr. to Patsy Gannon et al 65 acres in the 6th District. 8 Feb 1839. (Pp. 221-222)

Robert Marshall to Robert W. Lansden 100 acres in the 17th District. I reserve one and a half acres for the benefit of a school house. 1 Feb 1839. (Pp. 222-224)

C. R. Davis to Jesse Hollis 129 acres. 14 Mar 1838. (Pp. 224-225)

James Williams to John Brewer a tract on Barren Fork of Collins' Creek. 1 Apr 1837. (Pp. 225-227)

Moses Cummings to William Gilly 220 acres on Mountain Creek. 4 Feb 1839. (Pp. 227-228)

Hugh Reed to William Stroud 95 acres on the east fork of Stone's River. 1 Feb 1839. (PP. 228-230)

James O. George to John A. George a boy slave named Dick. 12 Oct 1838. (P. 230)

Caswell Sullivan and wife Cadijah, Rezin Fowler, and Jemima Soape to Benjamin Hayes 100 acres on which Thomas Fowler lived and died. 5 Feb 1839. (Pp. 231-232)

Aleathy Fowler, by statute of dower, to Benjamin Hayes 100 acres in the 2nd District. 9 Feb 1839. (Pp. 232-233)

The heirs of Thomas Fowler to Achilles Alexander a tract of land on Fowler's Creek. 5 Feb 1839. (Pp. 234-236)

J. G. W. Rose to Jonathan Hendrickson several tracts of land on Dry Fork of Smith's Fork. 9 Jan 1839. (Pp. 237-238)

David D. Hipp to Joel Farris 150 acres in the 5th District. 18 Sep 1838. (Pp. 238-239)

Merit Givins to Solomon J. Givins a trust deed. 18 Feb

1839. (Pp. 240-241)

Benjamin Allen to William Stone 100 acres on the east fork of Stone's River. 13 Feb 1839. (Pp. 241-242)

John A. George to James O. George a negro boy named Dick, about 12. 26 Feb 1839. (Pp. 242-243)

James O. George to James M. Brown a trust deed. 27 Feb 1839. (PP. 243-247)

Mumford Tenpenny to Richard Tenpenny a trust deed. 1 Mar 1839. (P. 248)

Brachus Gannon to James M. Brown a trust deed. 1 Mar 1839. (Pp. 249-251)

Robert to Nathan Neeley a town lot in the town of Woodbury. 23 Feb 1839. (PP. 251-254)

Joshua Barton to William Barton a negro boy named Tom. 15 Jan 1839. (Pp. 254-255)

Andrew J. Wood and Abraham Burger to John Wood, Sr. a tract of land in the 9th District. 11 Feb 1839. (Pp. 255-256)

George T. Ford to Isaiah Neeley 15 acres on Cavender's Branch. 13 Dec 1837. (Pp. 257-258)

Thomas Thompson to his grandson, Thomas Smith Scott, a cow and calf. 4 Mar 1839. (Pp. 258-259)

Nicholas Gooding to William Byford 50 acres. 26 Oct 1838. (Pp. 259-260)

William Middleton and Joseph Morgan to John and Henry Elum 115½ acres in the 6th District. 11 Mar 1839. (Pp. 261-262)

George W. Conley to L. C. McLin a trust deed. 18 Mar 1839. (Pp. 262-263)

John Brown to Thomas G. Wood a trust deed. 14 Mar 1839. (Pp. 263-265)

John H. Wood to John Childrup a quit claim deed. 15 Mar 1839. (Pp. 265-266)

John Childrup to George Walker a tract of land on the east fork of Stone's River. 15 Mar 1839. (Pp. 266-267)

Pleasant Cothran to Dabney Ewell 250 acres on Brawley's Fork of Stone's River. 23 Feb 1839. (PP. 267-268)

James Ferrell to Thomas Bowen 50 acres in Rutherford County on the east fork of Stone's River. 29 Jan 1835. (PP. 268-269)

Robert Fagan to B. L. McFerrin 100 acres on the east side of Brawley's Fork of Stone's River. 12 Mar 1839. (PP. 270-271)

Valentine Simpson to Elisha B. Rose 100 acres in the 3rd District. 22 Nov 1838. (Pp. 271-272)

DEED BOOK B

William Anderson to S. H. D. Duncan 150 acres on Barren Fork of Collins' River. 28 Mar 1839. (Pp. 272-274)

Josiah Ferris to Allen R. Stone Lot #36 in the town of Woodbury. 12 Jan 1838. (Pp. 274-275)

Josiah Ferris to Thomas and William Word Lot #36 in the town of Woodbury. 12 Jan 1838. (Pp. (Pp. 275-277)

Jacob Wright to Levin Jones 85 acres on the south side of the middle fork of the east fork of Stone's River. 17 Feb 1837. (Pp. 277-278)

Nathan J. Norris to Anderson S. Davis a trust deed. 15 Apr 1839. (Pp. 278-279)

John Bashaw to Edmund Finley a tract of land on the east fork of Stone's River, it being a part of the Thomas Fowler land. 4 Apr 1839. (PP. 279-281)

Joseph D. Morgan to Thomas R. Young a title bond. 21 May 1838. (Pp. 281-282)

John Brown to William Bates 100 acres on the east fork of Stone's River. 25 Mar 1839. (Pp. 282-283)

John L. Chaney to George Peeples of Rutherford County his interest in 50 acres on Sanders' Fork in the 11th District. 27 Mar 1839. (Pp. 283-285)

John Brown to Caleb Early 50 acres in the 6th District. 13 Apr 1839. (Pp. 285-286)

Mark A. Pope to John W. Summers a mortgage. 16 Apr 1839. (Pp. 286-287)

Cosby, Marshall, & Company to James McKnight 50 acres on Sanders' Fork. 16 Apr 1839. (PP. 287-288)

William Mears to Thomas L. Turner 25 acres in the 6th District. 26 Apr 1839. (Pp. 288-291)

Aaron Bryford to Thomas Hopkins of Warren County 50 acres in Rutherford County on Carson's Fork of Stone's River. 22 Aug 1835. Said Bryford is a resident of Rutherford County. (Pp. 291-292)

Albert G. Campbell to William Barton, Jr. 2000 acres on the waters of Camel and Hericane Creeks. 21 Jan 1839. (Pp. 292-294)

Albert Smithson to Thomas L. Turner 100 acres on the east fork of Stone's River, it being the place where the said Smithson now lives. 13 May 1833. (PP. 294-297)

Nathan Williams to Joseph Willard 5000 acres on Charles Creek, waters of Collins' Creek. Said Williams is a resident of Philadelphia. Joseph Willard is a resident of Suffolk County, Massachusetts. 31 Jan 1839. (Pp. 297-300)

Joseph Willard of Boston, Massachusetts to Joseph Libbey

5000 acres on Charles Creek of Collins' River. 9 Apr 1839.
(Pp. 300-302)

George Davenport to John W. Summers 25 acres in the 1st
District. 4 May 1839. (Pp. 302-304)

Joseph Ramsey to John Brown the following slaves, to wit,
Vina, Lucy, Lewis, Peter, Mary. Said negroes formerly belonged
to the estate of Jesse G. Moore. 4 May 1839. (Pp. 304-305)

Joseph Douls to William E. Evans 5000 acres on Charles
Creek. 23 May 1838. (Pp. 306-307)

William E. Evans to Nelson Scovil 5000 acres on the east
fork of Stone's River. 14 May 1839. (Pp. 308-314)

Nelson Scovil to Ashley Scovil 5000 acres on the east fork
of Stone's River. 18 Oct 1838. (Pp. 315-317)

C. Reed Davis to A. Barnett 600 acres. 14 Mar 1838. (Pp.
317-318)

Joseph Spurlock and John L. Shaw to Frances Turner five
acres on the Clear Fork. 21 Apr 1838. (Pp. 319-320)

Johnathan Paris to Sampson Stephens 85 acres on Mountain
Creek. 3 Jan 1839. (Pp. 321-323)

Jacob Faulkenberry to Abner Adams 150 acres on the east
side of the middle fork of Stone's River. 8 Jan 1839. (Pp. 324-
325)

Henry Kirsey of Warren County to Ruben Blew a negro boy
named Henry, supposed to be five years old. 3 Jul 1838. (Pp.
325-326)

John Brown to Ruben Blew a slave. 15 Dec 1838. (P. 326)

Sheriff H. R. Jarratt to A. F. and B. L. McFerrin a tract
of land in the 2nd District. 4 May 1839. (Pp. 327-328)

Solomon C. Paris to William L. Covington 69 acres in the
9th District. 14 May 1839. (Pp. 328-329)

Richard Vinson to Richard Tenpenny 53 acres in the 6th District. 14 May 1839. (P. 330)

William Cummins and William Stone to Anderson Barnett 150
acres in the 6th District. 16 May 1839. (Pp. 331-332)

Sheriff H. R. Jarratt to Joseph Ramsey Lot #32 in the town
of Woodbury. 14 May 1839. (Pp. 332-333)

Richard Vinson to John H. Wood a mulatto girl named Lutecia
as a trust deed. 15 May 1839. (P. 334)

John Whitfield to Jacob A. Lain his power of attorney to
sell a tract of land in Coffee County. 16 May 1839. (Pp. 335-
337)

William Faulkenberry to James B. Hollis, both of Rutherford

County, 26½ acres on Bralley's Fork of Stone's River. 10 May 1834. (Pp. 337-338)

James O. George, James M. Brown, John A. George, William F. George, and John Finley to James Wood a trust deed. 24 May 1839. (P. 339)

Joseph H. Smith to A. F. McFerrin a trust deed. 29 May 1839. (Pp. 340-341)

Richard Vinson to Nathan Neeley a title bond. 5 Jun 1839. (Pp. 341-343)

Thomas Sadler to Jacob A. Lane his power of attorney to sell four tracts of lae in Coffee County. 15 Jun 1839. (Pp. 343-345)

William Patton to A. F. McFerrin a trust deed. 20 Jun 1839. (Pp. 345-346)

Richard Vinson to Nathan Neeley a mortgage. 5 Jun 1839. (Pp. 347-349)

Alexander Orr to James D. Orr 100 acres on the east fork of Stone's River. 13 Jun 1839. (PP. 349-350)

Alexander Orr to E. A. Orr 35 acres on the east fork of Stone's River. 4 Dec 1838. (Pp. 351-352)

Samuel Gunter to William F. Elledge a trust deed. 18 Jun 1839. (Pp. 352-355)

Kelin Felps to John N. Bailey a tract of land on the head waters of the east fork of Stone's River in the 7th District. 28 Jun 1839. (Pp. 355-356)

Nathan Neeley, trustee of Robert Vinson, to Joseph Warren Lot #34 in the town of Woodbury. 28 May 1839. (PP. 357-358)

Richard Vinson to Archebald Stone a mortgage. 6 Jul 1839. (Pp. 358-360)

Jonathan Wharry to Alexander Lawrence five acres on the east fork of Stone's River. 18 Jul 1839. (Pp. 360-361)

Alexander Lawrence to Louis Jetton five acres on the east fork of Stone's River. 19 Jul 1839. (Pp. 362-363)

Benjamin G. Stephens to Gabriel Hume 83½ acres in the 6th District. 16 Jul 1839. (Pp. 363-365)

Benjamin F. Reynolds to Joseph Willard of Massachusetts 5000 acres on Charles Creek of Collins' River. 21 Feb 1839. (Pp. 365-367)

David Lane of Rockingham County, New Hampshire to Benjamin F. Weymouth 5000 acres on Charles Creek of Collins' River. 12 Feb 1839. (Pp. 367-370)

Joseph Willard to John Perry 5000 acres on Charles Creek of Collins' River. 13 Apr 1839. (Pp. 370-372)

John Brown to Thomas G. Wood a title bond. 7 Aug 1839. (Pp. 373-374)

John Fisher and James K. Eason to John Webb Lot #3 in the town of Woodbury. 3 Aug 1839. (Pp. 374-375)

John Webb to James Ewing and Thomas Richmond Lot #3 in the town of Woodbury. 3 Aug 1839. (Pp. 375-377)

Arthur A. Whitfield to Blake Sagely his interest in a tract of land belonging to the heirs of Willis Whitfield. 25 Jul 1839. (Pp. 377-378)

Ansel Whitfield to Silas A. Robinson his interest in a tract of land owned by Willis Whitfield deceased. Witness: Allen Whitfield. 27 Apr 1839. (Pp. 378-379)

James M. Mitchell to Robert Mitchell a trust deed. 27 Aug 1839. (Pp. 380-381)

William Todd to Henry Good some personal property. 31 Aug 1839. (Pp. 381-382)

John Brown to Thomas Cooper 227 acres in the 6th District. 16 Aug 1838. (PP. 382-384)

Thomas G. Wood to John Wood a trust deed. 10 Jan 1839. (Pp. 384-385)

James Patrick of Williamson County to Jacob Wright 67 acres in Warren County on the north side of the east fork of Stone's River. 23 May 1814. (PP. 386-388)

John Jones to William Brownfield of Warren County 15 acres in Warren County on the east fork of Stone's River. Said Jones is a resident of White County. 3 Oct 1829. (Pp. 388-390)

Caleb Sullivan of Warren County to Joseph Jones of the same place 81 acres on a north branch of the east fork of the three forks of Stone's River. 2 Dec 1817. (PP. 391-393)

Gabriel Hume to Thomas C. Word two negroes as a trust deed. 10 Sep 1839. (Pp. 393-394)

William James of Warren County to Buckhannon James 81 acres on the south side of the east fork of Stone's River. 16 Jan 1832. (Pp. 394-396)

William Smith of Rutherford County to Joseph C. McGee of the same place a tract of land in Rutherford County containing 23 acres. 17 Aug 1839. (Pp. 396-398)

James Allen to James Essary a trust deed. 25 Sep 1839. (Pp. 398-399)

Woodson Northcutt to Robert A. Campbell 582 acres on the waters of Barren Fork of Collins' River. 26 Sep 1839. (Pp. 399-403)

Lewis Pumphrey to Luke Lasiter 100 acres on the west side of Brawley's fork of Stone's River. 16 Sep 1839. (Pp. 403-405)

DEED BOOK B

Susannah and Elisha Bell, administrators for James Bell, to William Bell a tract of land in Rutherford County where the same James Bell lived. 28 Jan 1831. (Pp. 405-406)

William W. Milligan to Medford Caffey 62 acres on Cavenor's Branch. 27 May 1839. (Pp. 407-408)

T. F. Maxey to Thurston Daniel an agreement on a dividing line. 7 Jan 1839. (Pp. 408-409)

Joseph Harper to Woodson Northcutt 200 acres on the east fork of Stone's River. 30 Sep 1839. (Pp. 409-411)

State of Tennessee Grant No. 1526. 5000 acres to David Lane on Charles Creek of Collins' River. 19 Nov 1838. (Pp. 411-412)

Richard Tenpenny to Mary Sutton seven acres on the east fork of Stone's River. 4 May 1839. (Pp. 412-413)

Sheriff H. R. Jarratt to Joseph C. McGee 21 acres in the 1st District. 28 Sep 1839. (Pp. 414-415)

Brice M. Richardson to Abner C. Alexander 100 acres in the 11th District. 12 Oct 1839. (Pp. 415-416)

Richard Foster to Reuben Elem 30 acres in the 8th District. 8 Oct 1839. (Pp. 416-417)

Joseph C. McGee to James Mitchell 18 acres in the 1st District. 12 Oct 1839. (Pp. 418-419)

William Bell to John B. Jetton a tract of land in the 2nd District. 5 Oct 1839. (Pp. 419-421)

Sampson Stephens to Luke Sherley 20 acres on the south side of the Short Mountain. 12 Oct 1839. (Pp. 421-422)

Daniel Parkhurst to Luke Sherley 20 acres on the head waters of Mountain Creek. Said Parkhurst is a resident of Johnson County, Indiana. 27 Sep 1837. (Pp. 422-424)

Samuel Bryson to James B. Summers of Wilson County a title bond on two tracts of land in Wilson County. 12 Oct 1839. (Pp. 424-425)

Frederick G. St. John to John B. Stone a trust deed. 22 Oct 1839. (Pp. 425-427)

Henry Hart of Philadelphia to Seth J. North and others 2000 acres. 17 Aug 1838. (Pp. 427-430)

Samuel B. Marshall, U. S. Marshall for the Middle District of Tennessee, to Godfrey M. Fagg and Thomas Washington recovery of a judgment. 22 Oct 1839. (Pp. 430-434)

Thomas Cavett to William H. Murray of Rutherford County 107 acres on the east fork of Stone's River. 24 Sep 1839. (Pp. 434-436)

Westley Higgins, one of the heirs of John Higgins deceased, to George Bogle his interest in the land of his mother, Mary Higgins. 31 Oct 1839. (PP. 436-437)

Sheriff H. R. Jarratt to David M. Jarratt all the rights that Parker F. Stone has in a slave boy named Nelson. 29 Nov 1838. (PP. 437-438)

Zachariah Bush to Thomas Adams, the son of Henry Adams, 60 acres on Brawley's fork of the east fork of Stone's River. 5 Nov 1839. (Pp. 439-440)

Thomas Sadler to Valentine Simpson ten acres on Brawley's fork of the east fork of Stone's River. 10 Sep 1839. (PP. 440-442)

John Rogers to Alexander Inglish 50 acres on Stone's River. 27 Feb 1839. (Pp. 443-444)

Samuel Gunter to William Stone 100 acres on Smith's Fork. 4 May 1839. (Pp. 444-446)

Claburn Gunter to William Stone, both of Warren County, 158 acres on the dry fork of Smith's Fork. 22 Mar 1834. (Pp. 446-448)

John Brown to Joseph Ramsey 149 acres in the 6th District. 20 Apr 1839. (Pp. 448-450)

Joel Cherry to Ambrose Petty 25 acres on Barren Fork of Collins' River. 15 Dec 1836. (Pp. 450-451)

Moses H. Glascock of Jackson County, Alabama to Joseph Nivens 17 acres on Bralley's Fork of the east fork of Stone's River. 12 Mar 1839. (PP. 451-453)

James Taylor of Warren County to Thomas St. John of the same place his interest in 50 acres in Warren County on the south side of the east fork of Stone's River. 2 Oct 1836. (Pp.453-454)

Commissioners to Clement R. Davis Lots #52 and 53 in the town of Woodbury. 8 Oct 1839. (Pp. 455-456)

Richard Hancock to Lewis Hancock 36 acres for one dollar. 10 Sep 1839. (Pp. 456-457)

Zachariah Thomason of DeKalb County, Alabama to Lewis Hancock 174 acres on the head waters of Sycamore Creek waters of the Clear Fork. 17 Sep 1838. (Pp. 457-459)

Robert Tittle to William Collins 200 acres on Canell Fork of the Clear Fork. 7 Aug 1839. (Pp. 460-461)

John Higgins of Warren County to Samuel Tittle of Smith County 50 acres on the Kenel Fork of the Clear Fork of Smith's Fork beginning in Wilson County. 29 May 1829. (Pp. 461-462)

John Brown to Thomas G. Wood four acres in the 6th District. 24 Oct 1838. (Pp. 463-464)

Hiram Bryson to Wiley Davenport some personal property. 9 Nov 1839. (Pp. 464-465)

William Mears to Goldsborough Mears 67 acres on the east fork of Stone's River. 2 Jan 1839. (Pp. 465-466)

DEED BOOK B

William Elkins to John B. Stone a trust deed. 19 Nov 1839. (Pp. 467-468)

John Childress to George Walker 70 acres on the east fork of Stone's River. 8 Nov 1839. (Pp. 468-470)

Augustin S. Gunter of Warren County to John Patterson a tract of land in Warren County on the waters of Dry Fork of the Caney Fork. 25 Dec 1829. (Pp. 470-471)

James Gunter of Warren County to John Patterson 30 acres that Augustin S. Gunter now lives on, it being a part of a 140 acre tract that Clabourn Gunter now lives on. 4 Oct 1827. (Pp. 471-473)

Alyette Turnley to Benjamin Sapp 158 acres in Warren County where both parties live. 24 Mar 1830. (Pp. 473-475)

Robert Marshall to Thomas D. Summers 150 acres in the 11th District. 1 Mar 1839. (Pp. 475-476)

Thomas Merritt to John Elum a trust deed. 7 Dec 1839. (Pp. 476-478)

John Elum to John N. Mitchell a trust deed. 5 Dec 1839. (Pp. 478-480)

John Pendleton to William Elkins 125 acres on the waters of the east fork of Stone's River. 5 Dec 1829. (Pp. 480-482)

Joseph Ramsey to James Wood 109½ acres on the east fork of Stone's River. 10 Dec 1839. (Pp. 482-485)

Benjamin Pendleton, Executor of John Brown, to Jesse Lawrence 40 acres in the 6th District. 6 Dec 1839. (Pp. 485-486)

Joseph H. Smith to Joseph F. Brown 40 acres in the 3rd District. 4 Dec 1839. (PP. 486-488)

Jesse Todd to Jacob Faulkenberry 50 acres on Brawley's Fork of the east fork of Stone's River. 26 Jul 1839. (Pp. 488-489)

State of Tennessee Grant. 5000 acres on Charles Creek. 9 Jan 1830. (Pp. 490-491)

William E. Evans to David Davis 5000 acres on Charles Creek. 20 Dec 1838. (Pp. 491-493)

David Davis to Marcus A. Metcalf 5000 acres on Charles Creek. 22 Jan 1839. (Pp. 493-495)

Joseph Evans of Philadelphia to Matthew Matthews 5000 acres on Sanders' Fork and Hurricane Fork of Smith's Fork. 13 Mar 1839. (Pp. 496-498)

William Lowell of Philadelphia to Matthew Matthews 4500 acres on Charles Creek waters of Collins River. 25 Apr 1839. (Pp. 498-501)

Nathan Williams of Philadelphia to Matthew Matthews 5000 acres on Charles Creek. 23 May 1839. (Pp. 501-503)

John M. Mears to Elijah Mears 40½ acres in the 6th District. 21 Dec 1839. (Pp. 503-505)

Micajah F. Todd to James P. Todd a trust deed. 23 Dec 1839. (Pp. 505-506)

Gabriel Lance to Samuel Elam a trust deed. 26 Dec 1839. (Pp. 506-508)

Milas F. Travis to Andrew M. Alexander 80 acres in the 1st District. 27 Dec 1839. (Pp. 508-509)

Solomon J. Givins to Merit Givins a trust deed. 3 Jan 1840. (Pp. 509-510)

Richard Vinson to Nathan Neeley a trust deed. 11 Jan 1840. (Pp. 511-512)

Eleazar Orr to Phillip Maxey 116 acres on the east fork of Stone's River. 14 Oct 1839. (Pp. 512-513)

Richard Vincent to W. H. Sneed of Rutherford County a certain mulatto girl named Latitia, about 9. 31 Nov 1839. (Pp. 513-514)

Isaac Young to E. A. Orr 225 acres on Banin Fork of Collins River. 13 Jan 1840. (Pp. 515-516)

John C. Martin to Alexander Orr 16 acres in the 1st District. 28 Jan 1839. (Pp. 516-517)

Gideon Rucker to John C. Martin 100 acres. 3 Jan 1840. (Pp. 517-518)

Sheriff H. R. Jarratt to David M. Jarratt two town lots in the town of Woodbury belonging to Henry Trott, Jr. 6 Jan 1840. (Pp. 518-519)

Gideon Rucker to John C. Martin 100 acres on the east fork of Stone's River. 3 Jan 1840. (Pp. 517-518)

Joseph Warren to James M. Brown 130 acres. 6 Jan 1840. (Pp. 520-521)

Ruben Elem to William West 30 acres in the 8th District. 14 Jan 1840. (Pp. 521-522)

Gideon Rucker to John C. Martin 113 acres in the 1st District. 6 Dec 1839. (Pp. 522-523)

Benjamin Pendleton, Executor of John Brown, to Jesse Lawrence 40 acres in the 6th District. 11 Nov 1840. (Pp. 523-524)

A. Stougthonbourgh to B. L. McFerrin a negro girl named Tilda, about 12 or 13. Said party of the first part is a resident of Bibb County, Alabama. 3 Oct 1839. (P. 525)

Robert Bailey to Nathan Neeley 133 acres in the 6th District. 19 Oct 1839. (Pp. 525-526)

John B. Stone to Arthur Youngblood a trust deed. 15 Jan 1840. (Pp. 527-528)

DEED BOOK B

Cullin Curler to Joseph Simpson 55 acres. 20 Jan 1832. (Pp. 528-530)

William B. Stokes to James Wood a negro man of yellow color by the name of Washington, not exceeding 20 years of age. 29 May 1838. (P. 530)

Thomas Whitfield to Armstrong Carter 15 acres in the 12th District. 12 Apr 1839. (Pp. 531-531)

Commissioners to William Cummings Lot #11 in the town of Woodbury. 13 Jun 1836. (Pp. 531-532)

(Pages are misnumbered)

James Todd, Jr. to A. F. and B. L. McFerrin a tract of land in the 4th District. 16 Jan 1840. (Pp. 534-535)

A. F. Todd to A. F. McFerrin a trust deed. 16 Jan 1840. (Pp. 536-537)

Elijah Stephens to James Smith a trust deed. 18 Jan 1840. (Pp. 537-539)

Levi Pillow to William Y. Henderson a trust deed. 20 Jan 1840. (Pp. 539-540)

Allen Beaty to Joseph S. Elledge a trust deed. 18 Jan 1840. (Pp. 541-543)

Elizabeth Beaty to Joseph S. Elledge a trust deed. 18 Jan 1840. (Pp. 543-546)

Robert A. Smith to John A. George a girl slave named Nelly, about 13. 24 Jan 1840. (Pp. 546-547)

Robert A. Smith to John A. George some personal property. 24 Jan 1840. (Pp. 547-548)

Henry Sauls to Moses McKnight 160 acres in the 1st District. 28 Jan 1840. (Pp. 549-550)

Clement R. Davis from Nathan Neeley a trust deed. 27 Jan 1840. (Pp. 550-552)

Joseph Warren to Andrew M. Alexander a town lot in the town of Woodbury. 28 Jan 1840. (P. 553)

Richard C. Price to James Raines of Warren County a trust deed. 16 Jan 1840. (Pp. 554-555)

Henry Trott, Jr. to Charles T. New the lot in the town of Woodbury on which the said New now lives. 28 Jan 1840. (Pp. 555-556)

Hezekiah Clement to Benjamin Webber 50 acres in the 4th District. 28 Nov 1839. (Pp. 556-557)

Harmon Barrett to William West 468 acres on the north side of the east fork of Stone's River. 27 Jan 1840. (Pp. 557-559)

Fanny Cogwell, widow of Frederick Cogwell; Richard Cogwell, Meshac Tassey and wife Nancy, all heirs of Frederick Cogwell, to

Ezekiel Hays 40 acres in the 2nd District. 27 May 1839. (Pp. 559-561)

Samuel J. Garrison and Joseph Ramsey to Robert Bailey a negro boy named Joe. 30 Jan 1840. (P. 561)

George W. Conley to William L. Covington a mortgage. 8 Feb 1840. (Pp. 562-564)

Buchanan James of Wilson County to James L. James 81 acres in the 6th District. 18 Feb 1840. (Pp. 564-566)

William Rolston to Moses Cummings a trust deed. 18 Feb 1840. Witness: Sinclair Cummings. (Pp. 566-568)

Samuel Phillips to William West a trust deed. 28 Dec 1840. (Pp. 568-569)

William Bates to Ramsey and Jarratt a negro woman named Abby, about 22; and her four children namely Eliza, about 8, Stephen, about 6, Peter, about 3, and a sucking child named Pomp; also a mulatto girl by the name of Patsey, about 18, and her child Elizabeth, about 4. 18 Feb 1840. (P. 570)

John J. McElroy to Cyrus L. Roberts a tract of land in the 13th District. 28 Feb 1840. (Pp. 571-572)

Thomas L. Turner to William Cummings a trust deed. 21 Feb 1840. (Pp. 572-574)

John S. Bowen to Milas Saffle 200 acres. 10 Mar 1840. (Pp. 574-575)

Harmon Barrett to J. J. Trott a mortgage. 17 Mar 1840. (PP. 575-577)

Michael West, Executor of Abraham Sauls, to Henry Sauls 166 acres in the 1st District. 24 Jan 1840. (Pp. 577-578)

John St. John to Thomas G. Wood some livestock. 23 Mar 1840. (PP. 579-580)

Joseph Knox, Sr. to B. L. McFerrin 78 acres in the 12th District. 20 Mar 1840. (PP. 580-581)

Joseph Knox, Jr. to A. F. and B. L. McFerrin a trust deed. 20 Mar 1840. (Pp. 581-582)

Richard J. Conn to Gideon Rucker 122 acres in the 3rd District. 5 Feb 1840. (Pp. 583-584)

Caleb Earley to Thomas L. Todd and wife Nancy Ann 50 acres. 12 Mar 1840. (Pp. 585-586)

Henry Warren to Henry Enos of Warren County certain tracts of land. 17 Mar 1840. (Pp. 587-589)

Helton Smith to John Hollingsworth seven and a half acres on the south branch of Canell Creek. 28 Mar 1840. (Pp. 590)

Helton Smith to John Hollingsworth 20 acres in the 10th District. 15 Nov 1839. (P. 591)

DEED BOOK B

Samuel Richardson to David Patton two acres in the 12th District. 11 Feb 1839. (Pp. 592-593)

Hugh Robinson to Henry Thrower 30 acres on Carson's Fork of Stone's River. 9 Mar 1839. (Pp. 593-594)

Mary and Patience Edwards to Joseph Knox, Jr. a tract of land on Brally's Fork of Stone's River. 11 Aug 1838. (Pp. 594-596)

David M. Jarratt and Joseph Ramsey to Josiah Youngblood 41 acres. 5 Apr 1844. (Pp. 597-598)

Peter Adams to Thomas Womack 50 acres on Canal Creek. 21 Sep 1844. (Pp. 598-599)

DEED BOOK C

James Miller of Marshall County, Mississippi to Everett K. Dodge of Boston, Massachusetts 369 acres on Hurricane Creek. 1 Nov 1839. (P. 1)

William Partin to Gabriel Lance a trust deed on 300 acres. 29 Feb 1840. (Pp. 2-3)

John Wood departed this life leaving property to his children. A portion of them believe it is not his last will and testament for the want of a deposing mind and memory on the part of the said Wood. William Wood, James Wood, John H. Wood, Benjamin F. Wood, Andrew J. Wood, Jackson Wherry and wife Elizabeth, Archebald Stone and wife Sarah, (French) G. St. John and wife Ann, heirs of the said John Wood seek to settle the dispute. 1 Jan 1840. (Pp. 3-7)

Anthony Summers to James S. Odom 20 acres on the north branch of Sanders' Fork. 15 Jan 1840. (Pp. 7-9)

William Kirk to Joseph Bailey 138 acres in the 7th District on the east fork of Stone's River. 26 Mar 1840. (Pp. 9-11)

Henry Trott, Jr. to James J. Trott a trust deed. 3 Apr 1840. (Pp. 11-12)

Jesse Todd to A. Alexander 60 acres on Fowler's Creek. 25 Nov 1839. (Pp. 12-13)

Henry Trott, Jr. and Nathan Newby to Patsy Gannon, William Young and wife Uffy, Joseph Whitely and wife Elizabeth 85 acres in the 6th District. 22 Feb 1840. (Pp. 13-15)

Dawson McGlocklin to Ezekiel Hays a trust deed. 2 Apr 1840. (Pp. 15-16)

Dabney Ewell to Zachariah Bush two negro slaves. 3 Feb 1840. (P. 16)

James Wood to his nephews and nieces, to wit, Cynthia A. L. Wherry, Levesta Wherry, Oliver H. Wherry, Jackson L. Wherry, and Mira Wherry. 24 Mar 1840. (P. 17)

J. C. Martin to Edward Bragg 72½ acres in the 1st District. 22 Jun 1838. (P. 18)

Henry Trott Jr. to Martin Cox 61 acres in the 5th District. 31 Mar 1840. (P. 19)

John H. Stroud to Martin Cox 22 acres on Horse Spring Fork of Stone's River. 12 Sep 1837. (Pp. 20-21)

William Stroud to Martin Cox 75 acres on Horse Spring of Stone's River. 12 Sep 1837. (Pp. 21-22)

James Price to John McClain a trust deed. 13 Apr 1840. (Pp. 22-23)

Melvay Brashears to Aneil Melton ten acres in the 7th District. 20 Apr 1840. (Pp. 23-24)

Arthur Warren to James Sullivan 35 acres on the east fork of Stone's River. 16 Apr 1840. (P. 24)

DEED BOOK C

William Lack and wife Elizabeth to Armsted Francis 37 acres in the 11th District. 22 Sep 1838. (Pp. 25-27)

John P. Walker of Franklin County to Luke Sherley five acres on the south side of Short Mountain. 16 Oct 1839. (Pp. 27-28)

Willis W. Haney to Zachariah Bush 120 acres. 24 Mar 1840. (Pp. 28-29)

Archebald Stone to Cynthia A. L. Wherry, Levetta B. Wherry, Oliver Henry Perry Wherry, Jackson L. Wherry, and Mira P. Wherry, his nephews and nieces a deed of gift of ten acres. 21 Mar 1840. (Pp. 30-31)

George T. Ford to Archebald Stone 70 acres. 6 May 1840. (Pp. 31-32)

John H. Porterfield to Lemuel A. Reed 200 acres on the middle fork of the east fork of Stone's River. 4 May 1840. (Pp. 32-33)

James Manahan to Alexander Espey 30 acres on Brawley's Fork of the east fork of Stone's River. 21 May 1838. (Pp. 33-34)

Elizabeth Brown to John D. Alexander of Rutherford County a negro boy named James, between the age of 9 and 10, for $320. 6 Nov 1839. (P. 35)

Augustus Oliver to Samuel Underhill a tract of land in the 1st District. 18 Nov 1837. (Pp. 35-36)

Richard Vincent to John Williams 100 acres in the 6th District. 13 Sep 1839. (Pp. 36-37)

Charles Esley to William Pace 72½ acres on Brawley's Fork of the east fork of Stone's River. 25 Oct 1838. (Pp. 37-38)

Marshal Stroud to John Petty a negro man named Mike, 50; and a woman slave named Nancy, about 50. 14 Feb 1839. (Pp. 38-39)

Hugh Robinson to Jesse Jarnegan 74 acres. 27 May 1839. (P. 39)

Robert Fagan to Thomas Hopkins 60 acres on Brawley's Fork of Stone's River. 10 Mar 1836. (Pp. 40-41)

Alfred Gannon to John Rogers a negro girl named Caroline, about 16, for $500. (P. 41)

Alexander McKnight to John Blair 42 poles. 14 May 1840. (Pp. 41-42)

William A. Knox to Vincent Gaither 100 acres on Brawley's Fork of Stone's River. 27 Dec 1838. (P. 43)

Jonathan Farris of Warren County to Edith Warley 204 acres on Stone's River. 9 Mar 1839. (PP. 44-45)

Jacob Burger to Samuel Denby one acre on Dry Creek. 19 Feb 1839. (P. 45)

William Hollis, Sr. of Warren County to Jesse Hollis 30

acres on Dry Creek of the East fork of Stone's River in Warren County. 15 Jan 1833. (Pp. 46-47)

John Mullins to J. D. Orr a trust deed. 3 May 1840. (Pp. 47-48)

Amy Burge, Henry Burge, John M. Hill, Wright Burge, Elisha Bell, and William Burge, legal representatives of Brevard Burge, to Burwell Walker, all of Rutherford County, a tract of land on the East Fork of Stone's River in Rutherford County, 20 Dec 1830. (Pp. 48-49)

WILLIAM B. EWING and RANDALL EWING versus JAMES EWING, 10 Feb 1840. (P. 50)

Allen Beaty to Joseph L. Elledge 50 acres in the dark hollow. 26 May 1840. (P. 51)

Oran Stroud of Warren County to Martin Cox 50 acres, 3 Sep 1832. (P. 52)

William Craft to Gideon Duke 50 acres on the barren fork of Collins River. 10 Jun 1832. (P. 53)

William Craft to Gideon Duke 50 acres on the barren fork of Collins River. 10 Jun 1832. (Pp. 53-54)

Samuel Burnett to John H. Wood a trust deed. 29 May 1840. (Pp. 55-56)

Thomas H. Hopkins to William Gooding 50 acres on Carson's Fork of Stone's River. 23 Sep 1841. (P. 56)

John Craft to his son, Hugh Craft, 144 acres. 25 Jul 1842. (P. 57)

William Howard to Frankey Howard 70 acres on Brawley's Fork of the East Fork of Stone's River. 30 May 1840. (Pp. 57-58)

Gideon Duke to Martin Cox 100 acres. 26 May 1840. (Pp. 59-60)

John Mullins to John Childers 100 acres on Locke's Creek, 7 Mar 1840. (Pp. 60-61)

Sheriff James George to Juie Haynes 640 acres. 8 Jun 1840. (Pp. 61-62)

William Bryson to Michael Jones 100 acres in the 11th District. 11 Jun 1840. (Pp. 62-63)

Henry Kearsey to George Grizzle a trust deed. 12 Jun 1840, (Pp. 63-65)

Martin Cox to John H. Wood 250 acres. 13 Jun 1840. (Pp. 65-67)

William Gunter to George Grizzle a trust deed. 16 Jun 1840, (Pp. 67-68)

William Bates to Thomas G. Able of Fredonia County, New York 2000 acres. 9 Jun 1840. (Pp. 69-70)

Gabriel Hume to A. R. Stone a negro boy named John. 8 Sep 1838. (Pp. 70-71)

Thomas G. Abel to William Bates a patent deed. 9 Jun 1840. (Pp. 71-72)

William Bates to Horace Foster 1250 acres. Said Foster is a resident of Franklin County, New York. 9 Jun 1840. (Pp. 72-73)

William Bates to Thomas G. Abel 3000 acres. 9 Jun 1840. (Pp. 74-75)

F. G. St. John to B. F. Wood a trust deed. 19 Jun 1840. (Pp. 75-76)

Sheriff H. R. Jarratt to Mathew Pinkston 600 acres. 8 May 1839. (Pp. 77-78)

Calvin H. Alexander to John Toliver 100 acres on barren fork of Collins' River. 7 Oct 1839. (Pp. 78-79)

William Bates to Thomas G. Abel 5000 acres. 25 Jun 1840. (Pp. 79-82)

Arthur Warren to James Taylor 75 acres on the south side of the east fork of Stone's River. 29 Jun 1840. (Pp. 82-83)

William Bates to Horace Foster 12,950 acres. 25 Jun 1840. (Pp. 84-85)

Iverson J. Thomas to Moses (Bowen) a trust deed. 1 Jul 1840. (Pp. 85-86)

John Porterfield and Lemuel A. Reed to James M. Roberts 180 acres on Stone's River. 27 May 1840. (Pp. 86-88)

William Whitemare to William Howard 70 acres on Brawley's Fork of the East Fork of Stone's River. 1 Dec 1838. (Pp. 88-89)

Benjamin Webber to B. B. Dickins a trust deed. 6 Jul 1840. (Pp. 90-91)

William Howard and Frankey Howard to Aron Byford 70 acres on Brawley's Fork of the East Fork of Stone's River. 29 Jun 1840. (Pp. 91-92)

Herod Holt to Aron Byford 200 acres on the head waters of Carson's Fork of Stone's River. 19 Oct 1838. (Pp. 92-94)

Thomas St. John to Nathan Finley 15 acres on Stone's River. 7 Jul 1840. (P. 94)

Andrew J. Wood to Joshua M. Coffee his interest in the estate of John Wood deceased. 8 Jul 1840. (P. 95)

Henry C. Summers to Benjamin B. Cooper a trust deed. 27 Jun 1840. (Pp. 95-96)

Allen Morgan to William Bates and Charles P. Alexander 200 acres in the 5th District. 6 Jul 1840. (Pp. 96-97)

John Basham to James A. George and John A. George, Executors of Robert George, four acres on the waters of the dry fork of the east fork of Stone's River. 11 Jul 1840. (Pp. 97-98)

Alfred P. Gowen of Rutherford County to John D. Fulk and William Gillim of the same place 518 acres. 2 Jul 1840. (Pp. 98-101)

Francis Bryson to James Thomas his power of attorney to receive any thing that might be due him as guardian of Lacky Bryson, minor heir of Samuel Bryson. 4 Jul 1840. (P. 102)

Richard Butcher to Henry Kersey 30 acres. 9 Jul 1840. (Pp. 102-103)

John Witt to A. F. McFerrin a trust deed. 18 Jul 1840. (P. 104)

Andrew J. Bogle to Abraham Cropper a trust deed. 18 Jul 1840. (Pp. 105-106)

James Wood, Executor of John Wood, to John Finger 250 acres as an act of compromise. 22 Jul 1840. (Pp. 106-107)

Joseph Ramsey to Eliza Neely ten acres on the north side of Stone's River. 22 Jul 1840. (Pp. 107-108)

Abner S. Leash to Thomas Leach a brown mare. 3 Aug 1840. (Pp. 108-109)

Joseph H. Cann to Martin Cox 125 acres in the 3rd District. 5 Aug 1840. (Pp. 109-110)

James Manahan to John Ring 160 acres on Brawley's Fork of Stone's River. 8 Aug 1840. (Pp. 110-111)

Elizabeth Beaty sold to Isaac W. Elledge 100 acres on Horse Spring Fork of Stone's River in the 4th District. 12 Aug 1840. (Pp. 111-113)

Edmond Taylor to his daughter, Agnes T. Cannon, a deed of gift for her and her children of a negro woman, to wit, Louisa, about 21, and her three children, Martha, William John, and Jessee. 12 Aug 1840. (Pp. 113-114)

Daniel C. Mullins to Job Stephens 15 acres on the head waters of the east fork of Stone's River. 20 Feb 1840. (Pp. 114-115)

Henry Dasher to Rebecca Dasher 50 acres on the dry fork of the east fork. 6 Apr 1840. (Pp. 115-116)

Benjamin Pendleton to James M. Brown three negroes, to wit, Lewis, about 20; Lucy, about 26, and her child, about six months. 29 Jul 1840. (Pp. 116-117)

James M. Brown to Logan Henderson a negro slave of black color named Lewis, about 20. 22 Aug 1840. (P. 117)

John Martin to Robert K. Stephens 282 acres. 25 Aug 1840. (Pp. 118-119)

Mary Esley to William Pace 50 acres in the 4th District.

Mary Esley is the wife of George Esley. 11 May 1840. (Pp. 119-120)

Thomas Rigsby to Claiborne C. Gunter of Pickens County, Alabama 75 acres. 26 Aug 1840. (Pp. 120-122)

James Smith to Joseph Trimble 368 acres. 7 Sep 1840. (Pp. 122-123)

Erasmus Jones to Judy Cox 100 acres on the head waters of Haricane Creek. 22 Aug 1840. (Pp. 124-125)

Adam Elrod to Jesse Sewell town lot #50 in the town of Woodbury. 3 Sep 1840. (Pp. 125-126)

Jesse Sewell to Thomas C. Word town lot #50 in the town of Woodbury. 5 Sep 1840. (Pp. 126-127)

Alexander Finley to Charles Espey 250 acres on Barren Fork of Collins River. 1 Nov 1838. (Pp. 127-128)

Alexander Finley to George Espey 193 acres on Barren Fork of Collins River. 1 Nov 1838. (Pp. 128-129)

Benjamin F. Wood to his nephews, Thomas Jefferson Todd and John Alexander Todd, a deed of gift. 24 Jul 1840. (Pp. 129-130)

John H. Wood to Charles P. Alexander 40 acres. 19 Oct 1833. (Pp. 130-131)

James M. Brown to Benjamin Pendleton a negro woman named Lucy, about 26, and her child, about 6 months. 19 Sep 1840. (Pp. 131-132)

Charles P. Alexander to James M. Brown 40 acres in the 6th District. 18 Sep 1840. (Pp. 132-133)

Henry D. McBroom and Abel McBroom to James M. Brown 89¼ acres in the 6th District. 17 Sep 1840. (Pp. 133-134)

Richard P. Johnson to J. J. Jones a trust deed. 18 Sep 1840. (Pp. 134-135)

James Cherry to Joseph Hollis, both of Rutherford County, a tract of land in Rutherford County on the east fork of Stone's River. 7 Feb 1825. (Pp. 135-136)

Robert King to Richard Hancock 22 acres in the 10th District. 19 Sep 1840. (P. 137)

John Hollis and wife, Esther, to Joseph Hollis 21 acres on dry creek of the east fork of Stone's River. 30 Sep 1840. (Pp. 138-139)

John Clark of Marshall County, Henry Lance and wife Zilpha of Cannon County to Thomas Rigsby their interest in the estate of their father Joseph Clarke deceased. 20 Feb 1837. (Pp. 139-140)

James Bell to David Hollis, both of Rutherford County, 150 acres in Rutherford County on Stone's River. 12 Aug 1824. (Pp.

140-141)

John Bryson to L. B. Moore 50 acres in the 11th District. 23 Sep 1840. (P. 142)

James M. Brown to Benjamin Pendleton, Executor of John Brown, a trust deed. 19 Sep 1840. (Pp. 143-144)

Henry Dasher to William Young 99 acres in the 2nd District. 22 Sep 1840. (Pp. 145-146)

James M. Brown to Joseph Ramsey 69 acres on the east fork of Stone's River. 19 Sep 1840. (Pp. 146-147)

William Evans of Philadelphia, Pennsylvania to John B. Champion of the same place 5000 acres on the waters of Charles Creek and Stone's River. 12 Jan 1839. (Pp. 147-149)

John B. Champion and wife, Catherine F., of Philadelphia to Benjamin Free 5000 acres. 2 Oct 1840. (Pp. 149-152)

Jobe Stephens to Sampson Stephens a tract of land near the east fork of Stone's River. 1 Oct 1840. (Pp. 152-153)

John Daniel and Solomon C. Paris to William Wood 100 acres on Mountain Creek. 8 Mar 1830. (Pp. 154-155)

Jesse Johnson to William Wood 54 acres on the east fork of Stone's River. 28 Sep 1839. (Pp. 155-156)

John Melton to Thomas Elkins 252¼ acres. 5 Oct 1840. (Pp. 156-160)

Sampson Stephens and Robert H. Stephens to William Lee a negro woman named Malinda. 8 Oct 1840. (Pp. 160-161)

Richard L. McKnight to William E. McLin 120 acres. 9 Feb 1840. (Pp. 161-163)

Commissioners to James J. Trott town lot #40 in the town of Woodbury. 10 Mar 18__. (Pp. 163-164)

Thomas Nokes to Alfred S. Hancock 50 acres in the 10th District. 26 Oct 1840. (P. 165)

Joseph Warren to Joseph Ramsey 110 acres in the 2nd District. 31 Jan 1840. (Pp. 166-167)

Robert Lack and Charles R. Abbot to William Bates 150 acres on Stone's River. 19 Sep 1840. (Pp. 167-168)

William Bates to Calvin Curles 115 acres on Stone's River. 26 Oct 1840. (Pp. 168-169)

James A. George to Thomas Elkins a slave named Sarah belonging to the heirs of William Sullivan deceased. 20 Oct 1840. (Pp. 169-170)

Katherine Taylor to Thomas Nokes 50 acres on Sickamore Fork of the Clear Fork of Smith Fork, it being the land on which the said Katherine now liveth. 14 Oct 1839. (Pp. 171-172)

Lemuel Turney to John W. Haley 357 acres in the 10th District. 12 Sep 1840. (Pp. 172-174)

Nathan Williams of Philadelphia to James S. Keith and others
of the State of Maine 5000 acres on Barren fork of Collins River.
1 May 1839. (Pp. 174-176)

Augustine Oliver to Samuel Underhill 50 acres on Lock's
Creek. 29 Sep 1840. (Pp. 176-177)

Enoch Ferrell to Robert K. Stephens 117 acres. 26 Nov 1840.
(Pp. 177-179)

David McKinght to John M. McKnight 20 acres on McKnight's
Creek. 20 Sep 1840. (Pp. 179-180)

William Pace to John Haney 72 acres on Brawley's Fork. 30
Nov 1840. (Pp. 180-182)

William E. Watts to William E. Melvin a trust deed. 19 Dec
1840. (Pp. 182-183)

Thomas G. Abel to Ludlam M. Parsons of Roland County, Ver-
mont 5000 acres in Cannon County. 26 Nov 1840. (Pp. 183-185)

Benjamin Pendleton to Edmond Pendleton 153½ acres. 29 Dec
1840. (Pp. 185-186)

Isaac Finley to Benjamin Hays a trust deed. 30 Dec 1840.
(Pp. 187-188)

Isaac Finley to John Finley 140 acres on dry fork of the
east fork of Stone's River. 23 Dec 1840. (Pp. 188-190)

Jacob Moore to Henry Warren 98 acres. 1 Jan 1841. (Pp.
190-191)

William Cummins to David Cummins his power of attorney to
sell three tracts of land. 1 Jan 1841. (Pp. 191-192)

Thomas Wendel to John P. Hare 50 acres, it being a tract
of land granted to Joseph Hendricks by the State of North Carolina. 10 Nov 1840. (Pp. 193-195)

Isaac Finley to Benjamin Hayes, both of Rutherford County,
123½ acres in Rutherford County on the dry fork of the east fork
of Stone's River. 31 Dec 1835. (Pp. 195-196)

Acheles Alexander to Benjamin Hayes 60 acres on Fowler's
Creek. 26 Nov 1839. (Pp. 196-197)

Jacob Faulkenberry to Joseph F. Brown a trust deed. 7 Jan
1841. (Pp. 197-198)

William Bates to William Wharton lot #6 in the town of
Woodbury. 3 Nov 1840. (Pp. 199-200)

William Bryson and Christopher Owen to Joseph Bogle 40 acres.
17 Oct 1840. (Pp. 200-201)

Robert McNary, Administrator, to Hugh Robinson 224 acres
on Brawley's Fork of Stone's River. 22 Aug 1840. (Pp. 201-202)

Willis Cannon and wife Letsey to Hugh Robinson 270 acres on

Brawley's Fork of the east fork of Stone's River. 7 Nov 1825. (Pp. 203-204)

Woodson Northcut to Robert A. Campbell of Warren County a trust deed. 11 Jan 1841. (Pp. 204-207)

Hugh Robinson to Jesse Robinson 121 acres on Brawley's Fork of the east fork of Stone's River in the 12th District. 9 Oct 1840. (Pp. 207-208)

William Pace to Hugh Robinson 50 acres in the 12th District. 11 Jan 1841. (Pp. 208-209)

Sheriff James A. George to James W. Burger 50 acres. 1 Oct 1840. (Pp. 209-213)

Daniel M. Stuart to James T. Bowman 261 acres14 Jan 1841. (Pp. 213-215)

The heirs of James Robertson, late of Davidson County, to wit, Felix Robertson, John B. Craighead, Levenia Craighead, Delilah Bosley, James R. Robertson, R. C. Napier, John Bosley, L. P. Cheatham, Elizabeth Cheatham, John M. Robertson, and F. D. Robertson to William B. Robertson of Abbeville Parish, Louisiana, himself an heir, several tracts of land for a large sum of money. 20 Jul 1825. (Pp. 216-218)

William B. Robertson of Louisiana to Leonard P. Cheatham of Davidson County 500 acres in Dyer County. 2 Nov 1825. (Pp. 218-219)

William L. Sullivan to David T. Warren a tract of land. 1841. (P. 220)

James Hogg of Orange County, North Carolina to James Robertson of Sumner County 666 acres on the east fork of Stone's River. 19 May 1797. (Pp. 221-222)

Richard Butcher to his daughter, Patsey Martin, wife of John Martin, a deed of gift of a negro man named Jo, a negro boy named Elijah, a negro girl named Mehalah Jack. 19 Jan 1841. (Pp. 222-223)

Samuel Moore to John Petty a trust deed. 19 Jan 1841. (Pp. 223-224)

Isaac Finley to William Hollis, both of Warren County, 60 acres in Warren County on the dry fork of the east fork of Stone's River. 15 Oct 1835. (Pp. 224-225)

Archebald Lewis to William Williams 50 acres on Brawley's Fork of Stone's River. 25 Oct 1840. (Pp. 226-227)

Aniel Rains to John Petty a trust deed. 21 Jan 1841. (Pp. 227-228)

Joseph F. Brown to David Coinghour a tract of land in the 3rd District. 6 Jan 1841. (Pp. 229-230)

Samuel Moore to Stanford Smith 15 acres. 1 Jan 1841. (Pp. 230-231)

DEED BOOK C

State of Tennessee Grant #14716. 191 acres to Jesse G. Moore. 24 Oct 1837. (P. 231)

William West to Henderson Jackson 300 acres. 23 Jan 1841. (P. 232)

Robert B. Williams to Alexander W. Hogwood a trust deed. 23 Jan 1841. (Pp. 233-234)

Zachariah Thomason to Isaac Keaton 52 acres on Sickamore fork of the clear fork. 21 Sep 1838. (Pp. 234-235)

Jesse Johnson to Marcum 25 acres on Mountain Creek. 25 Sep 1839. (Pp. 235-236)

Joseph Clark to William Marcum 65 acres on Mountain Creek. 26 Sep 1839. (Pp. 236-238)

Daniel C. Mullins to Robert K. Stephens 50 acres. 3 Dec 1840. (Pp. 238-239)

David Carder to J. Mullins 97 acres. 26 Jan 1841. (Pp. 239-240)

Vincent Gaither to John H. Wood 57 acres. 27 Dec 1838. (Pp. 240-241)

Iverson J. Thomas to Henry Thomas a certain negro man of a black colour by the name of Silas and not exceeding 32 years of age. 1 Jan 1841. (Pp. 241-242)

Cyril Durham to James W. Stewart a trust deed. 19 Feb 1841. (Pp. 242-243)

Henry Thomas of Wilson County to Higdon R. Jarratt a trust deed. 23 Feb 1841. (P. 244)

John J. McElroy to Cyrus L. Roberts 25 acres in the 12th District. 25 Feb 1841. (P. 245)

Cyrus L. Roberts to John J. McElroy 20½ acres in the 12th District. 25 Feb 1841. (P. 246)

William Sullivan died seized and possessed of two tracts of land on the east fork of Stone's River. The land was sold to John Brown who has departed this life. Minty Sullivan, one of the heirs of decedent, agrees to convey land to James M. Brown. Aug 1840. (P. 247)

John Martin to Archebald Hicks a negro man named Joseph, about 23. 16 Jan 1841. (P. 248)

James Stone of Warren County to Samuel C. Evans of the same place 80 acres in Warren County. 19 Sep 1833. (Pp. 248-249)

Samuel C. Evans to William Covington 80 acres on the head waters of the Rock House Fork of Stone's River. 25 Jan 1841. (P. 250)

John Fisher to John Estes a trust deed. 3 Mar 1841. (Pp. 251-252)

Elijah Stephens to William Young a mortgage. 9 Mar 1841. (Pp. 252-253)

William McGlocklin to Ezekiel Hays a trust deed. 8 Mar 1841. (Pp. 253-254)

State of Tennessee Grant #7449. 12 acres to Stephen Mitchell. 29 Jul 1815. (Pp. 254-255)

John Berry to E. M. Armstrong four negroes, to wit, Maria, about 25, of a black colour; Louisa, about 20, of a yellow colour; Lucinda, about 7, of a black colour; Nely, about 2, of a yellow colour. 21 Jan 1841. (Pp. 255-256)

Abraham Leonard Walker to Samuel Young 260 acres on the head waters of the east fork of Stone's River on the south side of Short Mountain, it being land granted to Alfred Walker deceased. 3 Oct 1839. (Pp. 256-257)

William Nichols of Rutherford County to Robert Mitchell 30 acres in Rutherford County on the east fork of Stone's River. 17 Sep 1829. (P. 258)

Samuel Young to Joseph Bailey 200 acres in the 7th District. 20 Mar 1841. (P. 259)

Elijah Pittard to Benjamin Hays a trust deed. 15 Mar 1841. (P. 260)

William Cummings to William Bates 46 acres on the east fork of Stone's River (viz) Hill's Creek. 5 Dec 1839. (P. 261)

James Higgins, one of the heirs of John Higgins, to William Higgins his interest in the estate of his father, John Higgins, and his mother, Mary Higgins at her death. 26 Mar 1841. (P. 262)

Abner Moore to Anthony Summers 100 acres in the 11th District. 2 Apr 1841. (Pp. 262-263)

William Cummings to Joseph Bailey 144 acres on the east fork of Stone's River. 13 Apr 1839. (Pp. 263-265)

Joseph Knox to Edmund Lambert 69 acres in the 12th District. 5 Apr 1841. (Pp. 265-266)

John M. Denton to Edward Bragg a trust deed. 18 Feb 1841. (Pp. 266-267)

Peter Huntsucker to Elijah Mears 24 acres in Warren County on the east fork of Stone's River. 15 Sep 1824. (Pp. 267-268)

Henry Trott, Jr. to S. H. Laughlin of Warren County a trust deed. 1 Jan 1841. (Pp. 269-272)

James Mears to Elijah Mears 14 acres in the 6th District. 8 Apr 1841. (P. 273)

David Coughinour to John A. Jacobs a title bond. 13 Apr 1841. (Pp. 273-275)

Samuel B. Boles to Thomas Brevard a trust deed. 14 Apr

1841. (P. 275)

Absolom Davenport to Willie Davenport 19 acres in the 10th District for $81. 8 Aug 1840. (P. 276)

Wallis Estill, Jr., Executor of Wallis Estill of Franklin County, to David McKnight 300 acres on McKnight's Creek. 6 Feb 1841. Witnesses: John M. McKnight and James T. C. McKnight. (Pp. 276-277)

Alexander Higgins to Frances Turner a woman slave named Clary, 16 years of age. 6 Apr 1841. (Pp. 277-278)

Richard C. Price to John Young a trust deed. 1 Mar 1841. (P. 278)

John Anderson to Higdon R. Jarratt 137 acres in the 1st District. 27 Apr 1841. (P. 279)

Simpson Gilly and wife Sarah to John Bynum 130 acres in the 12th District. 21 Oct 1840. (P. 280)

Abraham Burger to William J. Dawson a town lot in the village of Machanic adjoining Short Mountain Campground. 28 Feb 1838. (P. 281)

George Grizzle a deed of gift to his nephew, Isaac Gunter, of a sorrel mare. 14 May 1841. (P. 282)

Jackson Wherry and wife Elizabeth (Betsy) to Jonathan Wherry their interest in the estate of John Wood. 17 May 1841. (Pp. 282-283)

Jubelee and Joseph Mullins to Harrison Smith 97 acres on clear fork of Smith Fork. 15 Jan 1841. (Pp. 283-285)

Baxter B. Dickins to Armstrong Carter 15 acres on Brawley's Fork of Stone's River. 1 Mar 1839. (Pp. 285-286)

John C. Martin and Daniel M. Stuart to Jesse Q. Seawell town lot #35 in the town of Woodbury. 19 May 1841. (Pp. 286-287)

Archebald Stone to Stanford Smith a title bond. 21 May 1841. (Pp. 287-288)

Thomas Washington and Godfrey M. Fogg to Jesse Brewer and Benjamin Brewer one acre adjoining the town of Woodbury. 11 May 1841. (Pp. 289-290)

B. L. McFerrin to Edmund Lambert 69 acres in the 12th District. 11 Mar 1841. (P. 290)

John P. Hare to Richard L. McKnight 100 acres on the first creek that empties into the east fork of Stone's River. 21 Nov 1840. (P. 291)

William Todd to James D. Good and Robert M. Good a trust deed. 8 Jun 1891. (P. 292)

Joseph F. Brown and Jacob Faulkenberry to Richard Jones 187 acres on Bralley's Fork of Stone's River. 11 Jun 1841.

(P. 293)

Hiram Morris to Daniel C. Mullins 22 acres on Sycamore Fork of the Clear Fork. 30 Dec 1840. (P. 294)

John Andrews to Perses Andrews 137 acres in the 1st District. 29 May 1841. (Pp. 294-295)

Jesse Sullins a deed of gift to John Young for the maintainance of myself so long as life should last. 4 Jan 1841. (P. 295)

Jesse Sullins to Joseph Mullins 66 acres on the east fork of Stone's River. 23 Jun 1841. (P. 296)

Samuel Gray of Rutherford County to John Williams 63 acres in Rutherford County on Brawley's Fork of Stone's River. 8 Sep 1829. (Pp. 297-298)

Matthew Edwards and Pasha Edwards to John J. McElroy 53 acres on the east fork of Stone's River. 30 Aug 1838. (Pp. 298-299)

John Andrews and Samuel H. Andrews to Ephraim Andrews a trust deed. 12 Jul 1841. (P. 299)

Perses Andrews to Milas F. Francis a trust deed. 16 Jul 1841. (Pp. 300-301)

Erasmus Jones to Richard J. Bond 60 acres in the 11sth District. 19 Oct 1840. (Pp. 301-302)

Samuel Gray to John Williams 70 acres on Bralley's Fork of Stone's River. 21 Jul 1841. (Pp. 302-303)

Samuel Gray to John G. Keele 150 acres on Bralley's Fork of Stone's River. 14 May 1841. (P. 303)

Henry Kersey to William Wilson 50 acres on Sink Creek. 10 Mar 1841. (P. 304)

Edmund Taylor to George W. Young of Marshall County, Mississippi a negro boy named Benjamin Franklin for $400. 27 Jul 1841. (Pp. 304-305)

H. D. McBroom to Benjamin T. McBroom 129 acres on the east fork of Stone's River. 18 Jun 1841. (Pp. 305-306)

Commissioners to James Wood town lot #31 in the town of Woodbury. 9 Mar 1841. (P. 306)

Joseph Ramsey to Henry Hays 112 acres in the 2nd District. 3 Aug 1841. (P. 307)

Asa Smith to Samuel Spears 50 acres on clear fork of Smith's Fork. 5 Aug 1841. (P. 308)

A. M. Alexander to William H. Faire 80 acres in the 1st District. 25 Jun 1841. (P. 309)

Francis G. Hamilton and wife Jane E. to Milas F. Travis their interest in the estate of Daniel Travis. 9 Aug 1841. (P. 310)

Meredith Thompson to grandson, Willie Adams, a deed of gift a sorrel mare. Said Willie Adams is the son of Isham Adams. 4 Aug 1841. (P. 311)

John Haney to Allen Thomas 72½ acres on Bralley's Fork of the east fork of Stone's River. 11 Aug 1841. (Pp. 311-312)

Barton W. S. Travis to Milas F. Travis his interest in the estate of Daniel Travis. 20 Nov 1838. (Pp. 312-313)

William D. Carnes to Milas F. Travers 110 acres in Rutherford County. 4 Sep 1833. (Pp. 313-314)

Samuel Moore to William H. Peyton 75 acres on Burges' Creek. 3 Aug 1841. (Pp. 314-315)

Alexander Tassey to Henry Hays a trust deed. 3 Sep 1841. (P. 315)

David Coughinour to Elizabeth Jacobs a slave named Madison, about ten. 4 Sep 1841. (P. 316)

Commissioners to James Wood, Executor of John Wood, town lot #41 in the town of Woodbury. 9 Mar 1841. (Pp. 316-317)

Rolin Lee to Campbell Company 150 acres. 6 Sep 1841. (Pp. 317-319)

Abraham L. Bell, William Jamison and wife Nancy Emaline, Martha Bell, and Susannah Bell, all of Cannon County, to Maxwell Chambers of Rowan County, North Carolina their interest in the estate of James Bell deceased. 11 Sep 1841. (Pp. 319-320)

Martin Stewart to Jesse Q. Seawell (three) acres. 15 Sep 1841. (P. 320)

Samuel Underhill to Archebald Stone his interest in 50 acres. 26 Jan 1837. (P. 321)

Susannah Adams to Benjamin Webber 60 acres on Bralley's Fork of Stone's River. 30 Mar 1841. (Pp. 321-322)

Thomas H. Hopkins to Baxter B. Dickins two slaves, to wit, Delia, about 8, and Ellen, about 7. 14 Dec 1840. (P. 323)

John McClain to John Rogers a tract of land on Carson's Fork of Stone's River. 19 Jun 1841. (Pp. 323-324)

Edmond Taylor to Joseph Mason of Rutherford County a certain negro girl slave named Lucy, about 12. 10 Apr 1839. (P. 324)

John C. Martin to Joshua Barton 100 acres in the 1st District. 17 Sep 1841. (Pp. 324-325)

Henry Warren to Jacob Moore 98 acres. 4 Oct 1841. (Pp. 326-328)

Benjamin Weymouth of Philadelphia to John M. Still of the same place a tract of land in Cannon County. 9 Mar 1839. (Pp. 328-332)

Alexander Higgins to John Milton 12 acres in the 7th District. 29 Oct 1841. (P. 333)

Thomas Elkins to John Milton 15 acres in the 7th District. 2 Nov 1841. (Pp. 334-338)

John Andrews to Ephraim Andrews a trust deed. 20 Nov 1841. (Pp. 338-339)

Benjamin Weymouth to Uriah Iverson 5000 acres on the east fork of Stone's River and Sanders' Fork of Smith's Fork. 13 Sep 1841. (Pp. 339-340)

T. G. Wood to Edmund Pendleton 153 acres. 5 Oct 1841. (Pp. 340-341)

Sheriff James O. George to James K. Eason a tract of land. 6 Aug 1841. (Pp. 341-342)

State of Tennessee Grant #1207. 142 acres to William Nichols. 9 Dec 1840. (Pp. 342-343)

Samuel H. Andrews to Ephraim Andrews a trust deed. 4 Dec 1841. (Pp. 343-344)

James Odom of Monroe County, Mississippi to James Gray a negro boy named Jackson, about 22. 7 Dec 1841. (Pp. 344-345)

Barbary McConnegal to Abraham Gooding a trust deed. 25 Jan 1838. (Pp. 345-347)

Daniel C. Mullins to William B. Nokes 20 acres on the Cyemore fork of the clear fork. 1 Sep 1841. (Pp. 347-348)

Samuel Tittle to Elijah Higgins 50 acres. 10 Mar 1838. (P. 349)

William Preston to Eli Preston 75 acres on the east fork of Stone's River. 5 Dec 1836. (P. 350)

William Willard to James McAdow 25 acres on Harricane Creek. 21 Dec 1841. (P. 351)

Nathaniel Finley to Edmund Finley 185 acres in the 6th District. 5 Jan 1842. (Pp. 352-353)

Valentine Simpson to William Justine Williams 25 acres. 28 Dec 1841. (P. 353)

John C. Martin to Alexander Martin of Lincoln County the following slaves, to wit, John, about 27; Frank, about 23; a man, about 21; Dave, about 12; Elenor, about 25; May, about 19; Nancy, about 20; Judy, about 16; Liza, about 4; Caron, about 3; Emeline, about 12 months; Harriet, about 8 months. 12 Jan 1842. (P. 354)

John C. Martin to Gideon Rucker 219 acres on the north side of the east fork of Stone's River. 12 Jan 1842. (P. 355)

John C. Martin to Gideon Rucker 115 acres on the north side of the east fork of Stone's River. 12 Jan 1842. (P. 356)

Milas F. Travis to William Nichols a trust deed. 14 Jan 1842. (Pp. 357-358)

Hyram Z. Tittle to John A. Standley 104 acres in the 10th

District. 12 Jan 1842. (Pp. 358-359)

William E. McLin to James S. McLin a trust deed. Said
James S. McLin is a resident of Rutherford County. 14 Jan 1842.
(Pp. 359-360)

William E. McLin to E. H. Jones of Rutherford County 190
acres. 14 Jan 1842. (Pp. 360-362)

John Barkley of Rutherford County for love and affection
to Sarah Barkley, Henry C. Barkley, William A. Barkley, Nancy
Ann Barkley, Mary Barkley, and Robert A. Barkley, heirs of John
Barkley a certain negro girl named Agnes, 10. 4 Jan 1842. (P.
362)

John Redin to Ward Barret, Sr. 200 acres. 17 Jan 1842.
(PP. 362-363)

William F. George to Daniel Tenpenny 84 acres on Dry Creek.
17 Jan 1842. (Pp. 363-364)

Ezekiel Hays to James Taylor 40 acres incluging the plantation on which Richard Cogwell now lives. 29 Dec 1841. (Pp. 364-
365)

Anuel Rains to John Petty a trust deed. 18 Jan 1842. (Pp.
365-366)

John Bryson to Melcesdic Francis 250 acres in the 11th District. 3 Jan 1842. (Pp. 366-367)

Micajah Petty to Jesse Lawrence 43 acres. 19 Jan 1842.
(Pp. 367-368)

Joseph Spurlock to Frances Spurlock 75 acres in the 10th
District. 10 Apr 1841. (Pp. 368-369)

Benjamin Pendleton to Eason and Webb a title bond. Said
Pendleton is executor of John Brown. 6 Jan 1840. (Pp. 369-371)

James M. Burger to William Stone 200 acres. 21 Jan 1842.
(Pp. 371-372)

John D. Elkins to James H. Kennedy, Executor of William B.
Kennedy deceased and Drucilla Kennedy a woman slave named Lucy,
about 23. 20 Jan 1842. (Pp. 372-373)

Solomon Travis to William West 162 acres on the east fork
of Stone's River. 21 Jan 1842. (Pp. 373-374)

Milas F. Travis to James Kellough 197 acres in the 1st
District. Bounded: the heirs of Guy Smith. 16 Jul 1841. (Pp.
374-375)

Jesse Moore heirs to H. D. McBroom 20¼ acres. 24 Jan 1842.
(Pp. 375-376)

L. R. Cheatham of Davidson County to Laner Watson a tract
of land on the east fork of Stone's River. 18 Jan 1842. (Pp.
377-378)

William Bates to Temple Tumby a woman slave named Delay.

27 Jan 1842. (P. 379)

Jacob Moore to Elizabeth Soap a trust deed. 27 Jan 1842. (Pp. 379-380)

Benjamin Webber to Patton and Dickins a trust deed. 4 Feb 1842. (Pp. 380-381)

Benjamin Webber to David Patton and B. B. Dickins a trust deed. 5 Feb 1842. (Pp. 382-383)

Jesse B. Williams to John Williams three tracts of land on Carson's Fork of Stone's River. 4 Feb 1842. (Pp. 383-384)

R. W. Odom and wife Lucy to James S. Odom a girl slave named Perthenia. 4 Jan 1842. (P. 384)

Melchesdick Williams to William West a title bond. 7 Feb 1842. (P. 385)

Jacob Moore to Elizabeth Soap 98 acres in the 2nd District. 18 Feb 1842. (Pp. 385-386)

Benjamin Webber to David Patton 50 acres in the 12th District. 22 Feb 1842. (Pp. 386-387)

Sheriff James O. George to David McGill 500 acres in the 9th District. 7 Feb 1842. (Pp. 387-388)

Josiah McEwen, Jr. to Joseph Vance a trust deed. 8 Mar 1842. (P. 389)

James Price to Thomas J. Williams a trust deed. 24 Dec 1841. (P. 390)

B. L. McFerrin to Joseph Knox a tract of land in the 3rd District. 21 Dec 1841. (P. 391)

Lance Watson and James N. Watson to Joseph Knox, Sr. 80½ acres. 18 Mar 1842. (Pp. 391-392)

Drury Spurlock to Thomas Nokes 86 acres on Kerby's branch of the clear fork. 28 Oct 1841. (Pp. 392-393)

Joseph Bogle to Abraham Cooper a trust deed. 22 Mar 1842. (Pp. 394-395)

Joseph Bogle to Sarah Bogle 90 acres for $500. 17 Jan 1842. (P. 395)

Henry Medford to James K. Eason a trust deed. 25 Mar 1842. (PP. 396-397)

Drury Spurlock of Warren County to Thomas Nokes 60 acres on Kerby's Creek, a branch of the clear fork. 20 Jun 1837. (Pp. 397-398)

Peterson Gilley to Irey Blair 22 acres on Brawley's Fork of the east fork of Stone's River. 30 Apr 1840. (Pp. 398-399)

State of Tennessee Grant #8183. 5000 acres to William E. Evans. 25 Mar 1841. (Pp. 399-400)

William E. Evans to Louis Auguste Morin 5000 acres. 3 Jan

1842. (Pp. 400-402)

John Reglasbooks to Samuel Lance a trust deed. 21 Mar 1842. (Pp. 402-403)

Thomas Lance to William H. Travis a trust deed. 27 Mar 1842. (Pp. 403-404)

Thomas Vance to William H. Travis 324 acres in the 6th District. 29 Mar 1842. (Pp. 405-406)

Thomas Nokes to Hiram N. Dodd 150 acres in the 10th District. 31 Oct 1841. (Pp. 406-407)

James Wood, Executor of John Wood, to James O. George his interest in town lot #31 in the town of Woodbury. 29 Jul 1841. (P. 407)

James O. George to Frances Coleman a town lot on the extreme east end of the town of Woodbury. 28 Mar 1842. (P. 408)

Wilie Davenport to Lawrence Stone 75 acres in the 11th District. 18 Nov 1843. (Pp. 408-409)

Abel McBroom and Benjamin T. McBroom to William Wharton town lot #15 in the town of Danville. 6 Oct 1840. (P. 409)

John A. George to Charles Alexander a trust deed. 5 Apr 1842. (Pp. 409-410)

James Whitmore to Hugh Robertson and others a trust deed. 6 Apr 1842. (Pp. 410-411)

William Wharton to Richard Lemay 125 acres in the 5th District. 9 Feb 1842. (P. 412)

Moses Owens to Samuel Burk a trust deed. 5 Apr 1842. (Pp. 412-413)

Eleazar Reed to Thomas J. Williams 640 acres in the 5th District. 23 Mar 1842. (Pp. 414-415)

Elijah Pittard to Acheles Alexander a trust deed. 5 Apr 1842. (Pp. 414-415)

Henry Trott, Jr. to Franklin Coalman town lots #20 and #30 in the town of Woodbury. 28 Mar 1842. (P. 415)

Jacob Moore to Elizabeth Soap 98 acres in the 2nd District. 18 Feb 1842. (P. 416)

John H. Wood to Thomas J. Wood a lease agreement. 15 Sep 1840. (P. 417)

John Fisher to Thomas G. Wood 150 acres. 16 Jan 1841. (Pp. 417-418)

William Higgins to Judith Cox the tract of land on Hericane Creek which I executed a title bond to James Cox in his lifetime. 15 Mar 1842. (Pp. 418-419)

Jesse Q. Seawell to David M. Jarrett of Rutherford County town lot #35 in the town of Woodbury. 4 Apr 1842. (Pp. 419-420)

Samuel Richardson and wife Elizabeth of Gibson County to Hiram Tennison 115 acres on Bralley's Fork of Stone's River. 21 Jan 1842. (Pp. 420-421)

Thomas H. Hopkins of Warren County to Hiram Tennison of Rutherford County several tracts of land. 8 Apr 1842. (Pp. 421-423)

Peterson Gilly to Ira L. Blair 50 acres on Brawley's Fork of Stone's River. 30 Apr 1840. (Pp. 423-424)

Sheriff James O. George to William West a trust of land. 8 Apr 1842. (Pp. 424-425)

Saderick Kelly to A. J. Philips 50 acres on the clear fork of Smith's Fork. 23 Jun 1840. Said Kelly is a resident of Smith County. 21 May 1842. (Pp. 425-427)

Sheriff James O. George to Jesse Q. Seawell the tract of land in the 2nd District on which Bechum Gannon now lives. 27 Apr 1842. (Pp. 427-428)

Jesse Q. Seawell to Benjamin T. McBroom 75 acres. 10 May 1842. (Pp. 428-429)

Eliza Peden to Turner B. Smith 43 acres in the 2nd District. 14 Jan 1843. (P. 429)

Benjamin Hays to Daniel Tenpenny 130 acres in the 2nd District. 7 Aug 1842. (P. 430)

William Nichols to Ephraim Andrews a trust deed on 150 acres in the 1st District. 11 May 1842. (Pp. 1-2)

Edmund Finley to John Finley 180 acres in the 6th District. ¢ may 1852. (Pp. 3-4)

Michel Jones to (Rannel) Jones a mortgage on some personal property. 10 May 1842. (PP. 4-5)

John L. Moore to Michel Jones 100 acres in the 11th District. 2 Jul 1839. (Pp. 5-6)

Michel Jones to Robert W. Lansden 130 acres in the 11th District. 10 May 1842. (Pp. 7-8)

James D. Orr to Ephraim Andrews 100 acres on the east fork of Stone's River. 12 May 1842. (PP. 8-12)

John Daniel to Jeptha Halcom 100 acres. 25 May 1841. (Pp. 12-13)

William R. Bogle to Mary Jones 66 acres. 13 May 1842. (Pp. 13-14)

William R. Bogle to Abraham Cooper a trust deed on a mare. 13 May 1842. (Pp. 14-15)

William Givens to William A. Givens 266 acres in the 6th District. 12 May 1842. (Pp. 16-17)

John C. Martin to Hardy M. Burton a mortgage. 16 May 1842. (Pp. 17-19)

Archable Stone to Lemuel M. Baird two slaves, to wit, Mary, not exceeding 22 years, and her child named Agnes, 7. 30 Mar 1842. (P. 19)

John A. Stanley to William Bogle 104 acres in the 11th District. 28 Apr 1842. (Pp. 20-21)

John C. Martin to James M. Avant a trust deed. 10 May 1842. (Pp. 21-22)

John C. Martin and wife Winney to Asa Smith their interest in the tract of land that Henry Youngblood died seized and possessed of. 4 Oct 1841. (PP. 23-24)

Aaron Byford to B. B. Dickens 70 acres in Brawley's Creek. 18 May 1842. (Pp. 24-26)

James Milligan to George Bogle 25 acres, it being a part of a tract of land belonging to John Higgins. 28 Mar 1842. (Pp. 26-28)

Baxter B. Dickens to Andrew M. Alexander 50 acres in the 12th District. 4 May 1842. (Pp. 29-30)

Sampson Stephens to Job Stephens 183 acres in the 9th District. 28 Feb 1842. (Pp. 30-32)

Mary C. Sanders to William A. Travis 200 acres belonging to the heirs of Daniel Travis. 9 Feb 1842. (Pp. 32-33)

James Marchbanks to John Bickel a trust deed on some personal property. 26 May 1842. (Pp. 33-35)

Thomas K. Williams to B. T. McFerrin 25 acres in the 16th District. 2 Jun 1842. (Pp. 35-36)

John L. Shaw to Alfred L. Hancock 294 acres in the 10th District. 28 May 1842. (Pp. 36-37)

Elizabeth Jacobs to David Coughamour a slave named Madison, about 11, for $600. 31 May 1842. (P. 38)

Nelson Cowen to Anderson Travis some personal property as a trust deed. 10 jun 1842. (Pp. 39-40)

Richard Vinson to Erasmus S. Kies town lot #43 in the town of Woodbury, it being the place on which Nathan Neely now lives. 24 NOv 1842. (Pp. 40-41)

James Stone for love and affection to Peggy Ann Elkins and Elizabeth Josaphine some personal property. 11 Jun 1842. (Pp. 41-42)

Andrew H. Young to James Young a trust deed on 100 acres on Brawley'sFork. 13 Jun 1842. (Pp. 42-43)

James Bogle to Elbert Owen 50 acres in the 17th District. 20 Feb 1837. (Pp. 43-44)

George Bogle to Elbert Owen 32 acres in the 17th District. 20 Feb 1837. (Pp. 45-46)

James W. McAdow to Nelson Owen 75 acres in the 11th District. 13 Jun 1842. (Pp. 46-47)

Nelson Owen and Elbert Owen to B. F. Odom and James S. Odom 107 acres. 14 Jun 1842. (Pp. 47-49)

Nelson Owen to Fountain Owen 140 acres on Hurricane Creek. 13 Jun 1842. (Pp. 49-51)

Ivery J. Haynes to Franklin Coalman 60 acres in the 15th District. 16 Jun 1841. (Pp. 51-52)

Edmond Lambert to John McClain a trust deed on 89 acres in the 12th District. 21 Jun 1842. (Pp. 52-53)

John A. Jacobs to David Coughamour 217 acres on Brawley's Fork of the east fork of Stone's River. 21 Jun 1842. (Pp. 53-54)

John Travis to his daughter Eleanor Travis a deed of gift of 100 acres on Lock's Creek. 5 Jan 1842. (P. 56)

Stanford Smith to Joseph Ramsey a trust deed on some cattle. 17 Jun 1842. (Pp. 57-58)

Martin Cox to B. T. McFerrin 235 acres in the 4th District. 23 Jun 1842. (Pp. 58-60)

Martin Cox to Peter Cox 125 acres in the 3rd District. 19 Apr 1842. (Pp. 60-61)

DEED BOOK D

James Lamberth to James Roberts a trust deed on some personal property. 25 Jun 1842. (Pp. 61-62)

James Gooding departed this life having purchased of the legal heirs of David Ross 100 acres in Rutherford County. Said heirs to Martha Gooding, the widow of James Gooding, a deed. James McClain and Susannah McClain are heirs of James Gooding. 16 Dec 1826. (Pp. 62-64)

Abraham Gooding, John Cooper and wife Levisy, Nicholas Gooding, Lucindy Gooding, Malinda Gooding, Martha Gooding, James McClain and wife Susannah, Joseph Gooding, and William Gooding to James Gooding their interest in a tract of land in the 12th District. 25 Jun 1842. (Pp. 65-66)

Samuel Laswell of Alabama to C. C. Davis 70 acres belonging to the heirs of Jesse (Dramon). 6 May 1842. (Pp. 66-68)

James Mears to Daniel F. Weeden 260 acres on Stone's River. 2 Jul 1842. (Pp. 68-70)

James S. Odom to R. W. Odom a woman slave named Parthena. 4 Jul 1842. (P. 71)

John Bragg to Edward Bragg and Dozier Bragg 38 acres as a trust deed. 4 Jul 1842. (Pp. 71-73)

Abraham Davenport to Joseph Bryson 20 acres in the 11th District. 28 May 1842. (Pp. 47-75)

J. S. Owen and others to Nelson Owen 138 acres. 19 Jul 1836. (Pp. 75-77)

Joseph Ramsey to James T. Bowen a negro woman named Vilet of dark complexion and about 40 years of age. Also three cows. 6 Jul 1842. (P. 77)

John Fisher to James T. Bowman a mortgage. 6 Jul 1842. (Pp. 78-79)

Susannah Bell, Sarah Deloach, John Hollis and wife Esther, Abraham L. Bell, and Martha Bell of Cannon County and Martin Tennison and wife Margaret of Illinois, Samuel J. Russell and wife Mary of Hinderhook, Missouri, and William Jamison and Nancy E. Jamison of Missouri to Maxwell Chambers of Roan County, North Carolina 270 acres in the 21st District. 6 May 1842. (Pp. 79-86)

M. D. Brown and wife Elizabeth to David McJarret a negro girl named Elvia, about 14. 16 Jul 1842. (Pp. 87-88)

Benjamin B. Cooper to Abraham Cooper three negroes, to wit, Nancy, about 20, and her two children, Elizabeth, about 2, and Hannah, about 4 months. 16 Jul 1842. (Pp. 88-89)

Otis. H. Weed to Joseph Smith his interest in 1200 acres. 28 May 1842. (Pp. 89-91)

Marcus A. Metcalf of Boston, Massachusetts to Otis H. Weed of the same place his interest in 1200 acres. 13 Jan 1841. (Pp. 91-95)

Hiram Tennison to William King a title bond. 4 Feb 1842.
(Pp. 95-97)

William Williams to B. L. McFerrin 50 acres on Bralley's
Fork of Stone's River. 3 Aug 1842. (Pp. 98-99)

John Williams to Willis H. Robinson 202 acres on Carson's
Fork of Stone's River. 3 Aug 1842. (Pp. 99-101)

Joseph Hale to William B. Bryson a boy slave named Isaac
for $127. 30 Jun 1842. (P. 101)

James Wood, Executor of John Wood, to James J. Trott town
lot #41 in the town of Woodbury. 18 Jul 1840. (Pp. 102-103)

Aron Duggan and Henry S. Duggan to George Bogle 50 acres
in the 11th District. 14 Jan 1842. (Pp. 103-104)

E. Francis to Armstead Francis a negro girl slave named
Sarah. 6 Aug 1842. (Pp. 104-105)

William McAdow to James Milligan 280 acres on Duncan Creek.
19 Mar 1838. (Pp. 105-108)

Eprophraditus E. Francis to John W. Summers 140 acres on
Sanders Fork. 5 Aug 1842. (Pp. 108-109)

Eleazar Beaty to Samuel Grissom a trust deed on some livestock. (Pp. 110-111)

John C. Ransom to T. C. Word a tract of land on Barren Fork
of Collons River. 10 Aug 1842. (Pp. 111-113)

Ephraim Anders to Thurston Daniel 111 acres. 10 Aug 1842.
(Pp. 113-114)

James D. Orr to Ephraim Anders 14 acres. 1 Aug 1842. (Pp.
116)

Melchesidick Francis to George Bogle 22 acres in the 12th
District. 13 Aug 1842. (Pp. 116-118)

Melchesidick Francis to Armstead Francis 20 acres. 13 Aug
1842. (P. 118)

Melchesidick Francis to George Bogle a man slave named
Richarg, age 28. 13 Aug 1842. (Pp. 118-120)

James Wood to Joshua M. Coffee two acres in the 9th District.
20 Jul 1842. (Pp. 120-121)

Baxter M. Dickens, Sr. and David Patton to Aaron Byford
617½ acres. 8 Jun 1842. (Pp. 121-122)

Aaron Byford to B. B. Dickens 618½ acres in the 12th District. 22 Jun 1842. (Pp. 123-124)

Zachariah Bush to B. B. Dickens 269 acres in the 12th District. 17 Aug 1842. (Pp. 124-125)

Aron Duggan to Nelson Owen and B. B. Cooper a trust deed.
19 Aug 1842. (Pp. 126-127)

David McKnight to Robert Boyd of Rutherford County a tract

of land on McKnight's Creek. 9 Aug 1842. (Pp. 128-129)

John L. Shaw to John W. Haley two and one half acres in the 10th District. 28 May 1842. (Pp. 129-130)

James S. Odom and wife Mary, the daughter of Micajah Francis, to Little B. Moore 20 acres in the 11th District. 27 Jul 1842. (Pp. 130-132)

Hiram Brandon to Cornelius Brandon a trust deed on some livestock. 22 Aug 1842. (Pp. 133-134)

Robert A. Campbell of Warren County to Adrian Northcut of the same place 250 acres on Stone's River. 1 Aug 1842. (Pp. 134-137)

John R. Sullivan to Benjamin Fowler town lot #29 in the town of Woodbury. 24 Aug 1842. (Pp. 137-138)

Abel McBroom to William Barton and Benjamin T. McBroom a trust deed. Sary McBroom is the wife of Henry D. McBroom, brother of the said Abel McBroom. Sally Jane Barton, daughter of Sarah and Henry D. McBroom is the wife of William Barton, Jr. 2 Aug 1842. (Pp. 138-142)

Jacob Burger to Samuel Denby 187 acres in the 9th District. 8 Oct 1841. (Pp. 142-143)

Abel McBroom to William Barton, Jr. and Benjamin F. McBroom a trust deed. 2 Aug 1842. (Pp. 144-149)

William Bates to Samuel Edmonson 1700 acres. 5 Sep 1842. (Pp. 149-151)

John A. George and Charles P. Alexander to James Taylor 177 acres on the south side of the east fork of Stone's River. 7 Sep 1842. (Pp. 152-154)

Joseph Ramsay to Abel McBroom a town lot in the town of Woodbury. 2 Aug 1842. (Pp. 154-155)

Abraham Brandon to George W. Thurston a trust deed. 6 Sep 1842. (Pp. 155-157)

James Taylor to John A. George 100 acres on the south side of the east fork of Stone's River. 7 Sep 1842. (Pp. 157-159)

Gabriel Williams and Melchesadick Williams to John T. Wale town lot #22 in the town of Woodbury. Bounded: Elizabeth Brent, now the wife of Solomon Brent and formerly known by the name of Elizabeth Broonfield. 16 Aug 1842. (Pp. 159-160)

Samuel McDaniel to Abner Thomas a girl slave named Celia. 18 Feb 1842. (Pp. 160-161)

Thomas H. Hopkins of Warren County to Fielden Holt a mortgage. 5 Aug 1840. (Pp. 161-162)

James Sisson to Daniel Finley 40 acres on Carson's Fork of Stone's River. 25 Jan 1840. (Pp. 163-164)

Andrew H. Youree to Joseph Trimble 124 acres. 9 Sep 1842. (Pp. 164-166)

James Gooding of (Barry) County, Missouri to John Finley 100 acres on Brawley's Fork of Stone's River. 2 Jul 1842. (Pp. 166-167)

L. B. Moore to Samuel C. Odom 75 acres. 20 Sep 1842. (Pp. 168-169)

John McMin and George Bogle, Executors of John Higgins, to Aaron Duggan and Henry S. Duggan 50 acres on Harricane Creek. 27 Apr 1840. (Pp. 169-170)

John Estes to D. M. Jarrett a negro slave named Jefferson, about 26. 9 Sep 1842. (Pp. 170-171)

Francis Cooper to William C. Leach seven acres in the 11th District. 19 Sep 1842. (Pp. 171-172)

Anthony Summers to Francis Cooper six acres in the 11th District. 20 Jun 1837. (Pp. 172-174)

Abenon Moore to Francis Cooper one acre in the 11th District. 25 Jun 1842. (Pp. 174-175)

James Ewing, trustee of James McAdow, his interest to the heirs of James W. McAdow, namely Ann, Eliza, Marshall, J. W., Madison, N. McAdow, minor heirs of Nubern S. McAdow. 3 Sep 1842. (Pp. 175-177)

H. R. Jarrett to A. M. Alexander a negro boy named Aron for $450. 3 Oct 1842. (P. 177)

H. R. Jarrett to Enos McKnight a girl named (Nancy), about 25. 3 Oct 1842. (P. 178)

Elijah Mears to Isaac McBroom 100 acres in the 6th District. 31 May 1842. (Pp. 178-180)

John Stump of Davidson County to John J. Rusworm 5000 acres on Stone's River and the Barren Fork of Collins River. 20 Sep 1842. (Pp. 180-181)

Christopher Owen and Permelia Owen to Michel Jones their interest in a tract of land formerly owned by Samuel Bryson. Also their interest in the widow's dower. 6 Apr 1839. (Pp. 182-183)

Eliza Witherspoon to Robert Wilson her interest in the estate of Ebenezer A. Witherspoon and in the estate of James C. Witherspoon. 19 Oct 1842. (P. 184)

H. R. Jarrett to James McKee a boy slave named Alford for $550. 26 Jan 1842. (Pp. 184-185)

Joseph Ramsey to Goldberg Mears 22 acres on Stone's River. 7 Nov 1842. (Pp. 185-186)

Marcus A. Metcalf of Suffolk County, Massachusetts to John Tuttle 1200 acres. 1 Feb 1841. (Pp. 187-189)

David Coughenour and Malinda Coughenour were intermarried. Some circumstances have occurred which prevent them from living together. They agree to a deed of separation. 25 Nov 1842.

(Pp. 189-191)

John C. Martin and Daniel F. Weaden to Hardy M. Burton a negro boy slave, about 12. 29 Nov 1842. (Pp. 191-192)

John Bragg to Dozier Bragg 190 acres in the 1st District. 3 Dec 1842. (Pp. 192-193)

Hugh Robinson to Asa Todd 163 acres in the 12th District. 25 Aug 1842. (Pp. 193-195)

John Bragg to Jacob Wright a trust deed. 4 Jul 1842. (Pp. 195-196)

Joseph Williard of Boston, Massachusetts to Daniel B. Whiterly 5000 acres on the Barren Fork of Collins River. 20 Aug 1839. (Pp. 196-198)

Marcus A. Metcalf to Amos Sweetsen 2400 acres. 15 Jan 1842. (Pp. 199-200)

Hugh Robison to Wilie H. Robison 42 acres in the 12th District. 26 Aug 1842. (Pp. 201-202)

James Manakin and John King to Alexander Espey 13 acres. 1 Apr 1841. (Pp. 202-203)

Annual Rains to John Petty a trust deed. 9 Dec 1842. (Pp. 203-204)

John C. Martin to Daniel Weeden a trust deed. 29 Nov 1842. (Pp. 205-206)

Zachariah Bush to Ivy Bush a boy slave supposed to be named Washington, about 8. 12 Dec 1842. (Pp. 206-207)

John C. Keele to Jonathan Smith 150 acres on Bralley's Fork. Said Smith is a resident of Coffee County. 30 Jun 1842. (Pp. 207-208)

L. D. Panken to Ewell Pankey a trust deed. 27 Dec 1842. (Pp. 209-210)

Parker F. Stone and A. R. Stone to H. W. Briggs of Giles County 640 acres. Said Alen R. Stone is a resident of Craford County, Arkansas. 8 Dec 1842. (Pp. 210-212)

Alexander Inglish to John Rodgers a trust deed. 21 Jan 1843. (Pp. 212-214)

Alexander McKnight to William Boyd a trust deed. 6 Jan 1843. (Pp. 214-217)

Ephraim Andrews to A. M. Alexander a trust deed. 5 Jan 1843. (Pp. 217-222)

David Mitchell to Robert Mitchell a trust deed. 14 Jan 1843. (Pp. 222-223)

John Weber and Philip Weber to Zachariah Bush a trust deed. 16 Jan 1843. (Pp. 224-227)

William Daley to James Esary 156 acres in the 4th District.

10 Oct 1842. (Pp. 227-228)

John Bragg to Jacob Wright 180 acres in the 1st District. 28 Dec 1842. (Pp. 228-230)

A. M. Alexander to H. R. Jarratt a boy slave named Aron for $290. 17 Jan 1843. (P. 230)

William C. Odom to Abner Alexander 30 acres on Leach's Creek. 5 Jan 1843. (Pp. 231-232)

John K. Sauls and Alexander McKnight to Jacob Wright 40 acres near the Smith County line. 5 Jan 1843. (Pp. 232-233)

Samuel H. Laughlin of Warren County to Cave Johnson of Montgomery County 500 acres about six miles from the town of Woodbury. 18 Jan 1843. (Pp. 233-235)

John Morgan to Samuel H. Laughlin 190 acres, it being a tract of land given by the State of Tennessee to the said John Morgan by Grant #4425 in 1830. 24 Nov 1838. (Pp. 236-237)

James Wood, Executor of John Wood, to John (F) a tract of land on the east fork of Stone's River. 18 Jan 1843. (Pp. 238-240)

Thomas G. Wood to John H. Wood a mortgage. 19 Dec 1842. (Pp. 240-241)

James T. Bowman to Abner Fisher a negro woman by the name of Leale, about 40 of dark complexion. 28 Dec 1842. (P. 242)

Mordacai J. Duke to William Smith 220 acres on the Barren Fork of Stone's River. 20 Jan 1843. (Pp. 242-243)

Samuel L. Bryson to Alman Mullinax 100 acres in the 4th District. 29 Jul 1839. (P. 244)

John Martin, Sr. to Manson M. Brien a negro man slave named Elijah, about 15. 6 Feb 1843. (Pp. 245-246)

Wiley Davenport to Joseph Bryson 19 acres in the 11th District. 3 Feb 1843. (Pp. 247-248)

Josiah McEwen to William D. Beaty a trust deed. 10 Feb 1843. (Pp. 248-250)

James K. Eason to Warren Cummings a slave named Anderson, 6, and a girl slave named Emaly. 10 Feb 1843. (Pp. 250-251)

Isaac W. Elledge to Thomas C. Word two negro women, to wit, Easther and Aggy, they being the same negroes levied on and sold by Parker F. Stone. 8 Nov 1842. (P. 251)

Jesse Q. Seawell to Thomas C. Wood a town lot known as lot #50 in the town of Woodbury. 3 Aug 1841. (Pp. 252-253)

William Duncan to William Smith a trust deed. 13 Feb 1843. (P. 253)

James K. Eason to Archebald Stone a boy slave named (Henry), 15. 7 Feb 1843. (P. 254)

Josiah McEwen, Sr. to Joseph Tenpenny a trust deed. 14 Feb 1843. (Pp. 254-255)

James Smith to Stanford Smith 31 acres in the 1st District. 16 Feb 1843. (Pp. 255-256)

James M. Brown to James Smith a title bond. 25 Aug 1835. (Pp. 257-258)

John Fisher to Adam Elrod a trust deed. 22 Feb 1843. (Pp. 258-259)

Abel McBroom to Jesse and Benjamin Brewer town lot #1 in the town of Woodbury. 23 Feb 1843. (Pp. 259-260)

Charles B. Walker to Burwell J. Walker a carding machine. 2 Jan 1843. (Pp. 260-261)

Charles B. Walker to Robert M. Stewart 44 acres on the east fork of Stone's River. 22 Feb 1843. (Pp. 261-262)

James K. Eason to W. J. Whithorne a negro man named Robert, between 30 and 40. 27 Feb 1843. (P. 263)

Joseph A. Brandon to Tobias Tenpenny a trust deed. 27 Feb 1843. (Pp. 263-265)

Benjamin Hays to Alexander H. Sutton 85 acres in the 2nd District. 15 Aug 1842. (Pp. 265-266)

Hiram Tennison to John P. Walker of Coffee County 371 acres. 8 Mar 1843. (Pp. 266-267)

William Duncan to Clary Duncan 640 acres in the 5th District. 13 Feb 1843. (Pp. 267-268)

Henry Warren to Alexander McBroom 20 acres on the east fork of Stone's River. 2 Mar 1843. (Pp. 268-269)

Ephraim Andrews to the President and Directors of the Bank of Tennessee a trust deed. 1 May 1843. (Pp. 270-271)

William C. Bowen to Brinkley Lasater 200 acres. 3 May 1843. (Pp. 271-272)

Isaac Adcock to Samuel Denby a man slave named Henry, about 30, for $500. 3 Jan 1843. (P. 273)

David Patton to Blake Sagely a trust deed. 9 May 1843. (Pp. 273-276)

William Moore to Blake Sagely a trust deed. 10 May 1843. (Pp. 276-278)

John W. Summers to Armstead Francis 140 acres on Dry Fork. 19 Apr 1843. (Pp. 278-279)

Augustus Toliver to Samuel Underhill 50 acres. 18 Apr 1843. (Pp. 280-281)

Richard Hancock to Fountain Owen 320 acres in the 10th District. 5 Aug 1842. (Pp. 281-282)

Jesse Hollis to John H. Wood 2250 acres in the 2nd District.

19 May 1843. (Pp. 283-286)

Thomas Whybreul to the President and Directors of the Long Island Bank. 7 Oct 1842. (Pp. 286-288)

Richard L. McKnight to William W. McKnight 100 acres in the 1st District. 5 Aug 1841. (Pp. 288-289)

Richard Vinson to David M. Jarratt 250 acres. 16 May 1843. (Pp. 289-290)

William Young to Thomas G. Wood a trust deed. 27 May 1843. (Pp. 291-292)

Caleb H. Gilley to John H. Lawrence 292 acres in Coffee County on Bralley's Creek. 12 Jan 1843. (P. 292)

James Hollis to John H. Wood 250 acres. 19 May 1843. (Misnumbered)

Thomas St. John to Thomas G. Wood 100 acres on the east fork of Stone's River. 27 Aug 1838. (Pp. 293-294)

Ezekiel Bass to Thomas St. John 100 acres on the east fork of Stone's River. 13 Sep 1837. (Pp. 294-295)

Elizabeth McKnight to James Watts a certain black cow. 18 Feb 1843. (P. 296)

Eli Preston to H. M. T. Walls 100 acres in the 5th District. (Pp. 296-297)

Akelus Alexander to George W. Thurston 60 acres on Fowler's Creek. 26 Jun 1843. (PP. 297-298)

William Preston to John Preston 150 acres on the east fork of Stone's River. 26 Mar 1843. (Pp. 299-300)

Samuel Tittle, Robert Tittle and wife Susannah, James Nokes and wife (Sophrona) to Peter Daniel a tract of land bought of brother Anthony Tittle. 14 May 1843. (Pp. 300-302)

Eleazar Beaty to John Cooper a trust deed. 16 Jul 1843. (Pp. 302-303)

Josiah McEwen, Sr. to Joseph Vance 150 acres on Locke's Creek. 24 Mar 1843. (Pp. 303-305)

Sarah Bogle to William McKnight 30 acres on Leach's Creek. 16 Feb 1843. (Pp. 306-307)

Frank Howard to Henderson Yoakum a negro boy named Anderson, 6, for $175. 20 May 1843. (P. 307)

Charles B. Walker to James T. Bowman 44 acres. 24 Jul 1843. (P. 308)

William Gunter to Enock Ferrell a trust deed. 30 May 1843. (P. 309)

Woodson Northcut to Robert Carson 317 acres. 16 Oct 1842. (Pp. 310-311)

James K. Eason to William B. Ewing a town lot in the town of Woodbury. Bounded: H. D. McBroom. 25 Aug 1843. (Pp. 311-312)

Robert Carson to Swinfield Smith 317 acres in the 5th District. 15 Aug 1843. (Pp. 312-313)

Ambrose Petty to Swinfield Smith 100 acres in the 5th District. 15 Aug 1843. (Pp. 313-314)

A. M. Weeden and wife Paulina J. to Higdon R. Jarratt a negro woman named Mariah, 27. 29 Jun 1843. (Pp. 314-315)

Edmond Walls to Thomas C. Word a trust deed. 22 Aug 1843. (Pp. 316-317)

Mordacai J. Duke to Jackson Lynn 200 acres. 9 Sep 1843. (Pp. 318-319)

William L. Covington to Eli Young 80 acres on the head waters of the Rock House Fork of Stone's River. 4 Sep 1843. (Pp. 319-320)

Erasmus Jones, Sr. to Erasmus Jones, Jr. 104 acres in the 11th District. 10 Dec 1842. (Pp. 320-321)

Michael Jones to Richard J. Bond and Hugh B. Lanson, trustees, for the love and affection he has for the worship of Almighty God one acre in the 11th District for the use of the Baptist Church, the Methodist Church, and the Cumberland Presbyterian Church which churches are entitled to equal rights and privileges. 30 Apr 1842. (Pp. 321-322)

Stephen A. Mitchell to Jonathan Basham a trust deed. 10 Sep 1843. (Pp. 322-323)

John M. McKnight for love and affection to his two sons, Andrew McKnight and James D. McKnight 159 acres in the 1st District. 9 Sep 1843. (Pp. 324-325)

H. R. Jarratt to W. B. Byrs a negro man named Dave for $360. 1 Sep 1843. (P. 325)

Joseph Bryson to W. B. Byrs a man slave named Erasmus for $500. 11 Sep 1843. (P. 326)

Lewis T. Foster to John Paterson 28 acres in the 9th District. 14 Sep 1843. (Pp. 326-327)

John K. Eason to John Estes a trust deed. 19 Sep 1843. (Pp. 328-329)

Jesse Jernigan to Peter (Dowell) 47 acres. 8 Dec 1841. (P. 330)

Gideon Gilley to his sons, Spencer and Isaac, a deed of gift several tracts of land on Mountain Creek. 1 Jul 1842. (Pp. 331-333)

Isaac W. Elledge to John W. Hall a trust deed. 22 Sep 1843. (Pp. 333-335)

Samuel Edmonson to Josiah F. Morford of Warren County a trust deed. 25 Sep 1843. (Pp. 335-337)

James B. Summers to Rutty Vasser 100 acres in the 112th District. (Pp. 337-338)

Joel Cherry to William Williams 150 a cres on Smith's Creek of Collins River. 25 Jan 1843. (Pp. 338-339)

James Sullivan to Warren Cummings 80 acres in the 2nd District. 29 Sep 1843. (Pp. 339-340)

James Sullivan to Joseph Ramsey a trust deed. 29 Sep 1843. (Pp. 340-341)

Lewis F. Witherspoon, Enos S. Witherspoon, and Elihu Witherspoon to Tirza E. Witherspoon 50 acres on Sanders Fork. 21 Sep 1843. (Pp. 342-343)

John G. Thomas to Enos S. Witherspoon a girl slave named Letha. 26 Apr 1842. (P. 343)

Ancil Melton to John Melton a title bond. 3 Oct 1843. (Pp. 344-345)

Sullivan heirs to Thomas G. Wood 55 acres. Ex Parte the lands of William Sullivan. Bounded: Hanna Sullivan and Harry Sullivan. 22 Sep 1843. (Pp. 345-347)

Abram C. Penn to Alfred T. Gowan town lot #14 in the town of Woodbury. 20 Aug 1843. (P. 347)

Elihu L. Witherspoon and Lewis F. Witherspoon to Emos S. Witherspoon their interest in the estate of Alexander Witherspoon. 10 Oct 1843. (Pp. 348-349)

H. R. Jarratt to Joseph Bryson, Sr. a negro man slave named Pleasant, about 38. 12 Oct 1843. (P. 349)

Robert Carson to Jonathan Jones two acres in the 4th District. 5 Aug 1843. (Pp. 350-351)

John Melton, Executor of Ancil Melton, to Thomas Elkins 34½ acres in the 7th District. 29 Sep 1843. (Pp. 351-353)

John Melton, Executor of Ancil Melton, to Joel D. Melton 346 acres in the 7th District. 21 Oct 1843. (Pp. 353-354)

Baxter B. Dickens for love and affection to George Washington Webber and Francis M. Webber, sons of Benjamin Webber, a deed of gift of some livestock. 8 Oct 1843. (Pp. 355-356)

Reuben Elam to William West 470 acres in the 8th District. 2 Oct 1843. (Pp. 356-358)

Luke Sherley to Thomas Nokes 24 acres on the south side of Short Mountain. 23 Oct 1841. (Pp. 358-360)

C. R. Davis to Samuel Laswell of Alabama town lots #52 and 53 in the town of Woodbury, it being the place where the said Davis now lives. 6 May 1842. (Pp. 360-361)

William Gooding to Martha Gooding a trust deed. 10 Nov 1843. (Pp. 361-362)

John Bryson to Robert Bryson 127 acres in the 11th District. 18 Nov 1843. (Pp. 363-364)

George C. Barrett to Benjamin Sapp a trust deed. 20 Nov 1843. (Pp. 365-366)

Henry Warren to C. R. Davis 55 acres on the east fork of Stone's River. 14 Mar 1843. (Pp. 366-367)

C. R. Davis to Samuel Moore 55 acres in the 2nd District. 21 Nov 1843. (Pp. 367-368)

Benton L. McFerrin to Martin Cox a quit claim to the land where the said Cox now lives. 9 Nov 1843. (P. 368)

John P. Hopkins to Caleb Cox 100 acres in the 4th District. 21 Nov 1843. (Pp. 369-372)

James D. McKnight to Andrew M. McKnight a quit claim deed to a tract of land that the said James M. McKnight conveyed to the the said Andrew M. McKnight. 9 Sep 1843. (Pp. 372-373)

Ralph Knight to Abner Adams a trust deed. 30 Nov 1843. (Pp. 373-374)

H. R. Jarratt to Knox Armstrong 137 acres in the 1st District. 9 Aug 1843. (P. 375)

Joseph Mullins to John Young 38 acres in the 7th District. 17 Aug 1843. (Pp. 376-377)

John Pendleton to his son, James Pendleton, a deed of gift of 250 acres in the 8th District. 18 Feb 1841. (Pp. 377-378)

Edmond Walls to William Wilsher 100 acres in the 6th District. 21 May 1843. (Pp. 378-379)

Jacob Wright of Rutherford County to Jesse Carter 106 acres on Locke's Creek. 25 Dec 1843. (Pp. 379-381)

James H. Elam to Jacob Wright 186 acres in Warren County. 14 Sep 1843. (Pp. 381-382)

Stephen Childress to Thomas Barnes a revocation of his power of attorney to receive from the estate of Robert Mitchell. 30 Dec 1843. (Pp. 383-385)

Thomas J. Patton to Blake Sagely a trust deed. 1 Jan 1844. (Pp. 385-386)

James O. George to Zachariah Thomason 200 acres. 29 Aug 1840. (Pp. 387-388)

Joseph Clark to John Young 268½ acres in the 7th District. 17 Jan 1843. (Pp. 388-389)

Rebecca E. Owen to Fountain Owen the dowery of which I am now possessed. 8 Dec 1843. (Pp. 389-390)

Thomas J. Williams to Wilson Sisson 100 acres on Carson's

Fork of Stone's River. 1 Jan 1844. (Pp. 390-391)

Daniel Pearson to Albert Fagan and William A. Knox 131 acres. 14 Oct 1839. (Pp. 391-392)

Benjamin Webber to Robert A. Fagan 50 acres in the 12th District. 11 Dec 1843. (P. 393)

A. M. Alexander to Robert A. Fagan 50 acres in the 12th District. 12 Dec 1843. (P. 394)

James S. Bowman to Daniel Bowman 90 acres in the 2nd District. 25 Feb 1843. (Pp. 395-396)

Ezekiel Mullins to John A. Mullins 46½ acres on the east fork of Stone's River, it being the tract where I now live. 4 Jan 1844. (Pp. 396-397)

Thomas G. Abel to John B. Hawthorn 250 acres in what was Warren County. 18 Oct 1841. (Pp. 398-400)

Thomas G. Abel to Joseph D. Summer of Winchester in Frederick County, Virginia 150 acres. 18 Oct 1841. (Pp. 400-402)

John M. Hawthron to Joseph D. Summer 250 acres. 16 Dec 1842. (Pp. 402-405)

Richard Webber to Samuel Burke a trust deed. 11 Jan 1844. (Pp. 405-406)

Annual Rains to John Petty a trust deed. 13 Jan 1844. (Pp. 406-408)

Moses Hopper to Archebald Hicks a woman slave named Fillis, about 18. 14 Feb 1842. (Pp. 408-409)

A. M. Weeden to W. B. Byrn a negro boy named William. 4 Dec 1843. (P. 409)

William Bryson to George (Pettes) five acres in the 15th District. 13 Jan 1844. (P. 410)

Thomas Nokes to William C. Nokes 30 acres in the 10th District. 16 Jan 1844. (P. 411)

John Martin, Jr. to Berry P. Magness a trust deed. 8 Jan 1844. (Pp. 412-413)

Edmund Lamberth and Jane Lamberth to Armstrong Carter 42 acres in the 12th District. 23 Apr 1840. (Pp. 413-414)

Sheriff Isaac W. Elledge to Henderson Yoakum a town lot in the town of Woodbury. 15 Jan 1844. (Pp. 415-416)

Henderson Yoakum to Solomon Travis a lease of 200 acres for the term of five years. 15 Jan 1844. (Pp. 416-417)

John Ring to James Manahan 160 acres in the 12th District. 12 Oct 1842. (Pp. 417-418)

Jacob Wright to Eleazar A. Orr 80 acres on the east fork of Stone's River. 29 Dec 1843. (Pp. 419-420)

Larkin Keaton to Zachariah Thomason 200 acres in the 10th District. 21 Jun 1842. (Pp. 420-421)

William B. Nokes to Thomas A. Adamson 30 acres in the 10th District. 18 Jan 1844. (Pp. 421-422)

Samuel Richardson and wife Elizabeth P. to Thomas H. Hopkins several tracts of land. 23 Oct 1839. (Pp. 423-425)

Thomas H. Hopkins of Warren County to John P. Hopkins of the same place 250 acres on Spring Fork of Stone's River. 30 Jan 1841. (Pp. 425-428)

Sheriff Isaac W. Elledge to the President and Directors of the Bank of Tennessee 150 acres. 20 Jan 1844. (Pp. 428-432)

Aaron Byford to Armstrong Carter 70 acres on Bralley's Fork of Stone's River. 18 Jan 1844. (Pp. 432-433)

Thomas Nokes to Asa Smith 40 acres in the 9th District. 19 Jan 1844. (Pp. 433-434)

Peter Adams to Fountain Owen a tract of land on Canal Creek of the Clear Fork, it being nine shares out of nine in Susan Tittle's dower, the widow of Samuel Tittle. 9 Oct 1843. (Pp. 434-436)

Dozier Mullins to James T. Bowman a trust deed. 14 Jan 1844. (P. 436)

Benjamin Hays to Samuel Duke 70 acres in the 2nd District. 9 Aug 1842. (Pp. 437-438)

Elijah Higgins to John D. Elkins his interest in the estate of his father, John Higgins, and his mother's (Mary) dower. 18 Jan 1843. (P. 438)

James T. Bowman to John B. Jetton 44 acres in the 9th District. 31 Oct 1843. (PP. 439-440)

James McElroy to Cyrus L. Roberts six acres on Brally's Fork of Stone's River. 9 Apr 1842. (Pp. 440-441)

James Esary to James L. Esary 300 acres on Barren Fork of Stone's River. 20 Apr 1843. (Pp. 441-443)

Hugh Reed of Jefferson County, Alabama to James Williams 263 acres on Carson's Fork of Stone's River. 14 Aug 1841. (Pp. 443-445)

Sheriff Isaac W. Elledge to George Walker 270 acres in the 12th District. 20 Jan 1844. (Pp. 445-446)

John C. Martin to Daniel F. Weeden a mortgage. 15 May 1832. (Pp. 446-447)

Cullen Curlee to John McClain 31 acres on dry fork of the east fork of Stone's River. 29 Dec 1830. (Pp. 447-448)

John Petty to John Espey ten acres on the horse spring fork of Stone's River. 13 Oct 1842. (Pp. 448-449)

Meredith Akers to Mary (Patten) 16 acres on Bralley's Fork. 3 Sep 1842. (P. 450)

Rezin Fowler and Nathan Finley to Benjamin Hays 85 acres in the 2nd District. 17 Feb 1843. (Pp. 451-452)

James C. Martin to Daniel F. Weeden 115 acres in the 1st District. 15 May 1843. (P. 453)

H. R. Jarratt to Enos McKnight a girl slave named Nancy. 19 Sep 1843. (P. 454)

Wyatt A. Brown and wife Elizabeth to Joice Rucker a mortgage. 16 Jan 1843. (Pp. 454-455)

Ezekiel Hammons to William West 240 acres on the East Fork of Stone's River. 31 Dec 1842. (Pp. 455-456)

Thomas Elkins to William S. Melton 65 acres in the 7th District. 2 Oct 1843. (Pp. 456-458)

George Espey to Larkin Rains 227 acres. Bounded: Annual Rains. 14 Oct 1841. (Pp. 458-460)

Richard Butcher to his wife Martha a deed of gift of 100 acres, it being a part of my farm. 1 Nov 1841. (Pp. 460-461)

James Smith to Joseph Trimble a tract of land in the 6th District. 12 Oct 1843. (Pp. 461-462)

Henry Thomas to Samuel N. Thomas 213 acres in the 11th District. 26 Jan 1843. (Pp. 463-464)

Moses Owen to Charles P. Alexander a trust deed. 4 Dec 1843. (Pp. 464-465)

Elisha Reynolds to Joseph Ramsey town lot #57 in the town of Woodbury. 10 Aug 1843. (Pp. 465-467)

Medford Caffey to Thomas Nokes a title bond. 19 Dec 1843. (Pp. 467-468)

David T. Warren to Zachariah Warren 120 acres in the 2nd District. 15 Mar 1842. (Pp. 468-469)

Allen Hopkins to Hugh Robinson 30 acres in the 4th District. 4 Nov 1843. (Pp. 469-470)

Jesse Sullins, Sr. to Joseph Mullins a title bond. 17 Aug 1843. (Pp. 470-472)

Jonathan Marchbanks to John Bickle 100 acres on Barren Fork of Collins River. 20 Sep 1842. (Pp. 472-473)

Jonathan Marchbanks to Michael Bickle 150 acres on the Barren Fork of Collins River. 6 Oct 1842. (Pp. 473-475)

Absalom Davenport to John W. Summer 55 acres in the 11th District. 2 Feb 1844. (Pp. 475-476)

John Mullins to Dozier Mullins 75 acres in the 2nd District. 8 Feb 1844. (Pp. 477-478)

John Espey to John Petty ten acres on Horse Spring Fork of

Stone's River. 27 Jan 1841. (Pp. 478-480)

William Whitemore to Jesse H. Gilley 200 acres on Barren Fork of Collins River. 3 Oct 1843. (Pp. 480-481)

Sampson Mathis to John McClain a trust deed. 30 Jan 1844. (Pp. 482-483)

James L. Esary to Annual Rains 15 acres in the 4th District. 15 Jan 1844. (Pp. 483-484)

Samuel Lance to John Pendleton 250 acres in the 8th District. 18 Dec 1842. (Pp. 484-485)

John Pendleton to William A. (Pettiff) 108 acres on Stone's River. 12 Sep 1841. (Pp. 485-487)

Henry Dennis to James G. Fuston of Wilson County 140 acres on Canal Creek of the Clear Fork. 15 Oct 1842. (Pp. 488-489)

John Fisher to John Mullins 140 acres in the 1st District. 14 Jan 1843. (Pp. 489-490)

Williamson Smith of Madison County appoints J. W. Webb his power of attorney to receive his share from the sale of two negro men sold out of the working jail for jail fees and other expenses. 14 Feb 1844. (Pp. 498-499)

Samuel Edmondson to John S. Young 500 acres on Barren Fork of Collins River. Said Young is a resident of Davidson County. (Pp. 499-500)

Clabourn Gunter to Joseph Ramsey 55 acres in the 9th District. 9 Dec 1841. (misnumbered)

Thomas Thompson to Medford Coffee three acres on Cavanor's Branch. 6 Aug 1844. (Misnumbered)

P. D. Cummins to William Bates 470 acres in the 8th District. 18 Jan 1844. (Misnumbered)

John P. Hopkins to William Stroud ten acres on Horse Spring Fork of Stone's River. 14 Dec 1843. (Misnumbered)

Micager Petty to John P. Hopkins 35 acres on Carson's Fork of the east fork of Stone's River. 17 Jan 1844. (misnumbered)

Levi Parker to John Vance 105 acres on Bralley's Fork of Stone's River. 3 Aug 1837. (Pp. 500-503)

Jonathan Smith to John Nelson 100 acres on Bralley's Fork of Stone's River. 9 Nov 1842. (Pp. 503-505)

Campbell Akers of Rutherford County to Newton C. Carnahan 150 acres on Barren Fork of Collins River. 10 Jan 1843. (Pp. 505-507)

Samuel Moore to William T. McBroom 150 acres in the 2nd District. 18 Mar 1842. (Pp. 507-508)

Campbell Wallace and Richard H. Wallace to Abel McBroom and Benjamin T. McBroom town lot #15 in the town of Woodbury. 8 Sep 1837. (Pp. 508-510)

Isaac Hutt to John Bundervant 130 acres in Warren County in the 1st District. 30 Jun 1832. (Pp. 510-512)

John Bundervant to Wilson Turner 420 acres in the 9th District. 12 Mar 1842. (Pp. 512-514)

Jesse Gillim of Rutherford County to James Mitchell a deed of gift. 15 Jun 1837. (Pp. 514-515)

Gabriel Lance, James H. Lance, and Samuel Lance to Churchwell B. Randles 313 acres on the east fork of Stone's River. 24 May 1837. (Pp. 516-518)

William Whitamore to Albert G. Millikin and Jesse Millikin a trust deed. 4 Mar 1844. (Pp. 518-520)

Luaner Stone to Joseph Bryson 75 acres on Sanders Fork. 15 Feb 1844. (Pp. 520-521)

Temperance Willis, Administrator of Willie Willis and wife of the deceased, to Jesse Gilley and Jesse Gordon, the Deacons of the Hopewell Baptist Church at (Maxwell), for a term of ninety nine years, commencing 20 Aug 1843, a lease of the spring for the purpose of baptizing into the Separate Baptist Church. 2 Mar 1844. (Pp. 521-522)

Johnson Thompson to William Burton 80 acres in the 6th District. 11 Mar 1844. (Pp. 522-524)

Isaac Soap to William Ring 75 acres where Matthew B. Ford formerly lived. 25 Jan 1844. (Pp. 524-525)

State of Tennessee Grant #2871. 75 acres to William Preston. 2 Mar 1836. (Pp. 525-526)

Francis Cooper to Mark Alexander and Andrew J. Bogle, Elders of the Presbyterian Church on Sanders Fork, a deed of one half acre to be used for a meetinghouse and schoolhouse. Said church is to be used by the Cumberland Presbyterians. 4 Jan 1830. (Pp. 525-527)

Henry M. T. Walls and Edmund Walls to William Preston 100 acres on the east fork of Stone's River. 22 Mar 1844. (Pp. 527-528)

William H. Murry to William H. Murry 107 acres on the east fork of Stone's River. 4 Mar 1844. (Pp. 528-529)

James T. Bowman to Lewis Jetton 160 acres in the 4th District. 27 Mar 1844. (Pp. 530-531)

Lewis Jetton to James T. Bowman a negro girl, about 14. 27 Mar 1844. (P. 531)

H. R. Jarratt to T. C. McKnight a man slave. 2 Oct 1843. (P. 532)

Judgment against William White, assignee of John Martin, Jr., was rendered void. Also mentioned William C. Martin, Robert Martin, James Martin, Micajah Martin. 1 Apr 1844. (Pp. 532-534)

William C. Odom to James Higgins two tracts of land in the 11th District. 8 Nov 1843. (Pp. 534-535)

John C. Ransom to Henderson Yoakum 144 acres. 16 Apr 1844. (Pp. 535-537)

Thomas C. Word to Jesse Brewer a negro woman named Agnes, about 50. 21 Feb 1844. (P. 537)

Sheriff Samuel Vance to George W. Sherrill 200 acres. 17 Mar 1842. (Pp. 538-539)

Robert J. Summers to F. Coleman a trust deed. 15 May 1844. (Pp. 539-540)

Frederick Reed to Newton C. Carnahan a trust deed. 14 May 1844. (Pp. 540-541)

William Stroud to John Petty a trust deed. 25 Apr 1844. (Pp. 542-543)

Thomas Hopkins to James Whitemore 40 acres on the west branch of the east fork of Stone's River. 11 Mar 1830. (Pp. 543-544)

William Whitemore to James Whitemore 50 acres in the 12th District. 31 May 1844. (P. 545)

James Whitemore to Hiram Todd 200 acres in the 12th District. 21 May 1844. (Pp. 546-547)

Benjamin Weymouth of Philadelphia to P. Sullivan Whitley of the same place 5001 acres. 1 May 1843. (Pp. 547-549)

Mary Elam to Murfrey G. Elkins 125 acres on Stone's River. 11 Jun 1844. (Pp. 550-551)

Samuel Underhill to William Stroud and John W. Stroud 50 acres on Locke's Creek. 13 Jan 1844. (Pp. 551-552)

State of Tennessee Grant #2060. 5000 acres to Frederick Stump. 9 Jan 1830. (Pp. 552-553)

William Stroud to Jane H. Oliver 50 acres on Horse Spring Fork. The land is for love and affection to the said Jane and her children, J. N. Oliver and Daniel M. Oliver. 27 Jan 1844. (Pp. 553-554)

Isaac Young for love and affection to his wife, Mary Young, a deed of gift of a negro girl named Mary of rather copper complexion, about five years old. 1 Mar 1844. (Pp. 554-555)

Alexander Inglis to John B. Rodgers 80 acres in the 4th District. 11 Jul 1844. (Pp. 555-556)

David Patton to B. B. Dickens and others 120 poles for the Bradyville Academy at Pleasant Grove. 29 Jun 1844. (P. 557)

Alfred P. Gowan of Rutherford County to David Patton two acres for the Thyatira Congregation of the Cumberland Presbyterian Church. Bounded: north side of the road leading to Murfreesboro. 4 Nov 1843. (Pp. 558-559)

Hugh Robinson for love and affection to his daughter

Phany, the wife of George W. Sadler, 40 acres in the 12th District conveyed to me by James Britton and his wife. 11 May 1846. (Pp. 559-560)

George T. Ford to Edmund W. Vaughan 50 acres in the 7th District. 8 Feb 1851. (Pp. 560-561)

William Cummings to George Pebles 28 acres in the 8th District. 1 Mar 1847. (P. 1)

Micajah Marcum to William Marcum 120 acres in the 9th District. 8 Aug 1837. Witness: Watson Cantrell. (Pp. 1-2)

Moses McKnight to A. W. Martin 106 acres as a trust deed. 31 Jul 1842. (Pp. 2-3)

Ann W. Martin to Moses McKnight a quit claim to 166 acres in the 1st District. 5 Aug 1844. (Pp. 4-5)

A. D. Alexander to William Sauls 100 acres in the 11th District. 10 Jul 1844. (Pp. 5-6)

Richard Vinson to Nathan Neeley 150 acres in the 18th District. 2 Nov 1841. (Pp. 6-7)

J. Y. D. Wall to Thomas Elkins a trust deed. 7 Sep 1844. (Pp. 8-9)

Samuel Richardson and wife Elizabeth of Gibson County to their beloved son, Thomas W. Richardson, their power of attorney to receive their share of the estate of Thomas Hopkins, late of Warren County. 22 Jun 1841. (Pp. 9-10)

Moses McKnight to David M. Jarratt a trust deed. 5 Sep 1844. (Pp. 11-12)

Leven Jones to Milus Saffel 85 acres on the south side of the middle fork of the east fork of Stone's River. 17 Aug 1844. (Pp. 12-13)

William Wilcher to Elijah Stephens 100 acres in the 3rd District. 7 Sep 1844. (Pp. 13-14)

Robert Marshall to Thomas D. Summers, one of the deacons in the Baptist Church four acres for the Sanders Fork Baptist Church. 28 Aug 1844. (Pp. 14-15)

John B. Parris to William Elledge 110 acres in the 7th District. 7 Oct 1844. (Pp. 16-17)

Hiram Smithson to Richard H. Lemay 41¼ acres on the head waters of the Barren Fork of Collins River. 19 Oct 1844. (Pp. 17-18)

Hardy Wimbly to Zachariah Warren a trust deed. 5 Nov 1844. (Pp. 18-19)

William Stroud to B. L. McFerrin 95 acres on Horse Spring Fork of the East Fork of Stone's River. 5 Nov 1844. (Pp. 20-21)

Mary Thompson, Anson Thompson, James Ferguson and wife Mary, heirs of Thomas Thompson, to Joseph Young 80 acres in the 6th District. 12 Dec 1844. (Pp. 21-23)

John H. Lawrence to Caleb M. Gilley 270 acres in Coffee County. 21 Dec 1843. (Pp. 23-24)

Jane Travis to David Caldwell 66 acres in the 14th District.

27 Dec 1844. (Pp. 24-25)

John B. Parris and wife Jane to Jonathan Parris of Dade
County, Missouri their power of attorney to sell the land that
I purchased from Robert Hopper in the County of Dade. 3 Dec
1844. (Pp. 25-27)

Hiram Tittle, Adam Tittle, and Elizabeth Reese to Benjamin
Hall their interest as heirs at law of Samuel Tittle. 10 Oct
1843. (Pp. 27-29)

Clerk & Master to Robert T. Cannon several tracts of land
in Perry and Hickman Counties. 5 Dec 1844. (Pp. 29-31)

B. B. Dickens to Blake Sagely a tract of land in the 12th
District. 12 Jan 1844. (Pp. 31-33)

State of Tennessee Grant to Edward Gatten. 2 Dec 1836.
(Pp. 33-35)

Jacob Wright to Joseph Pinkerton five negroes, to wit,
Polly, 22; Rebecca, 5; George, 4; (ada, 2; King. 12 Jun
1844. (Pp. 35-36)

An agreement between (   ) heirs and William (   ). 25
Apr 1844. (Pp. 36-38)

Stephen Cantrell to James P. Perry 134 acres in the 7th District. 27 Dec 1844. (Pp. 38-40)

Thomas Elkins and wife Polly to Jesse Melton their interest
in the estate of Ancil Melton. 22 Dec 1844. (P. 40)

Stephen A. Mitchell to James Mitchell a trust deed. 2 Jan
1845. (Pp. 41-42)

Ancil Melton to Samuel Young 164 acres on the waters of
the Rock House Fork waters of the East Fork of Stone's River.
13 Nov 1841. (Pp. 42-43)

Joseph Elledge to Lewis Hancock 30 acres on Stone's River.
12 Apr 1835. (Pp. 44-45)

Sheriff Samuel Vance to Zachariah Thompson 200 acres in
the 10th District. 28 Dec 1844. (Pp. 45-46)

James Manahan to W. H. Mc) 160 acres in the 12th District. 30 Dec 1843. (Pp. 47-48)

L. M. Robison to B. B. Dickens a trust deed. 16 Jan 1845.
(Pp. 48-50)

Annual Rains to John Petty a trust deed. 14 Jan 1845. (Pp.
50-51)

Allen Thomas to Thomas H. Roughton 72½ acres on Brawley's
Fork of the east fork of Stone's River. Said Roughton is a
resident of Coffee County. 19 Nov 1844. (Pp. 52-53)

James M. Roberts to Allen Thomas 191 acres in the 4th District. 25 Nov 1844. (Pp. 53-54)

William C. Odom to S. J. Odom 175 acres in the 11th District. (Pp. 54-55)

William E. McLin to William W. McKnight 190 acres. 22 Jan 1844. (Pp. 56-57)

John P. Hare to William W. McKnight a tract of land. 22 Jan 1845. (Pp. 57-59)

John P. Hare to John K. Sauls 75 acres. 25 Jan 1845. (Pp. 59-60)

David M. Jarratt, Administrator of Elihu Sanders, to Thomas Cooper 63½ acres in the 6th District. 4 Feb 1845. (Pp. 61-62)

C. W. Nance of Davidson County to William Blair 85 acres on Sycamore Creek. 14 Feb 1845. (Pp. 62-64)

Hardin P. Bostic of Davidson County to C. W. Nance 800 acres. 15 Apr 1843. (Pp. 64-66)

Robert Vinson to Samuel Vance a negro man of a black complexion, about 64, named Hall. 13 Feb 1845. (Pp. 66-67)

Sheriff Samuel Vance to John H. Wood 37 acres. 6 Jan 1845. (Pp. 67-69)

Sheriff Samuel Vance to John W. Wood 90 acres. 6 Jan 1845. (Pp. 69-72)

Joseph Ramsey to Franklin Coleman town lot #27 in the town of Woodbury. 25 Feb 1845. (Pp. 72-73)

Elizabeth Soap and Henry Warren to Joseph Ramsey 107 acres in the 2nd District. 3 Feb 1845. (Pp. 74-75)

John Herman to John P. McDougal 140 acres in the 10th District. 23 Jul 1844. (P. 76)

John Q. Weatherford to John Herman 142 acres in the 10th District. 22 Jul 1844. (Pp. 77-78)

Richard C. Price to Walter Stroud a trust deed. 5 Mar 1845. (Pp. 78-79)

William Preston to Archebald Stone 30 acres in the 6th District. 15 Feb 1845. (P. 80)

Silas A. Robison to David Patton and the other trustees of the Thyatira Congregation of the Cumberland Presbyterian Church two acres. 23 Nov 1844. (Pp. 81-82)

John P. Walker to Albert G. Millikin 371 acres. 5 Aug 1844. (Pp. 82-83)

Hugh Reed by his attorney to Henderson Yoakum 640 acres. 30 Nov 1844. (Pp. 83-84)

Benjamin Pendleton to John Wheelin a tract of land on the east fork of Stone's River. 4 Mar 1845. (Pp. 84-85)

William Gunter to Thomas G. Wood a trust deed. 4 Apr 1843. (Pp. 85-87)

William Stacy to (Johnathan). Lasater 40 acres in the 12th District. 21 Nov 1844. (P. 87)

Zachariah Bush to Aaron Byford 120 acres in the 12th District. 2 May 1845. (Pp. 88-89)

Arthur Warren of Bontitoc County, Mississippi to Agnes W. Henderson 50 acres on the south side of the East Fork of Stone's River. 5 Feb 1845. (Pp. 89-90)

Frankey Parks to Thomas J. Wood a trust deed. 12 May 1845. (Pp. 91-92)

Joseph Washington Hopkins from his father, John P. Hopkins, a deed of gift of 125 acres in the 5th District. 23 May 1845. (Pp. 92-93)

Sheriff Samuel Vance to Benjamin B. Cooper 75 acres. 4 Apr 1845. (Pp. 93-95)

John P. Hopkins to A. F. and B. L. McFerrin 201 acres in the 4th District. 2 Jun 1845. (Pp. 95-97)

John P. Hopkins to Hiram Wilson 60 acres on Carson's Fork of the east fork of Stone's River. 5 May 1845. (Pp. 97-98)

John P. Hopkins of Cannon County; George W. Hopkins and Thomas H. Hopkins of Warren County to John Petty a tract of land on the waters of the Horse Spring Fork of Stone's River. 5 Jun 1845. (Pp. 98-100)

John Petty to James Petty a man slave named Allen, about 20. 10 Feb 1845. (P. 100)

Jackson G. Cummings to William Cummings 470 acres on the waters of Mountain Creek. 11 Jun 1845. (Pp. 100-102)

Erasmus Kees to Nathan F. Frogden town lot #43 in the town of Woodbury. Said Kees is a resident of Rutherford County. (Pp. 102-103)

M. G. Elkins to Henry Elam 125 acres in the 6th District. 20 Dec 1844. (Pp. 103-104)

Zachariah Thomason to William W. Adams 125 acres in the 10th District. 15 Feb 1845. (Pp. 104-105)

Achelus Alexander to Benjamin Mays 25 acres in the 2nd District. 12 Jun 1845. (P. 106)

George W. Hopkins to B. F. McFerrin three tracts of land. 30 Jan 1844. (Pp. 107-109)

John Williams to John Ogles 500 acres on Barren Fork of Collins River. 4 Mar 1843. (Pp. 109-110)

John McClain to John Rogers 20 acres. 25 Jul 1844. (Pp. 110-112)

John Fisher to Adam Elrod a trust deed. 18 Jun 1845. (Pp. 112-113)

DEED BOOK E

James Williams to John McClain 200 acres on Carson's Fork of Collins Creek. 25 Jul 1844. (Pp. 113-114)

Samuel Laswell to Adam Elrod town lot #52 and 53 in the town of Woodbury. 14 Dec 1844. (Pp. 114-115)

John P. Hopkins to John W. Stroud one acre below said Stroud's house on the creek. 25 Apr 1844. (P. 116)

Willie H. Robison to John Williams 202 acres on Brawley's Fork and Carson's Fork of Stone's River. 29 Nov 1844. (Pp. 116-118)

Joshua Barton to Johnathan Wharey two acres on the south side of Stone's River. 2 Feb 1836. (Pp. 118-119)

David McGill and John McCrary, Executors of Nancy McGill, to James McGill 298 acres in pursuant to the last will and testament of the said Nancy. (See Will Book A, pages 27 and 28.) 26 May 1845. (Pp. 119-121)

John Petty to Amos Gatter 50 acres. 4 Dec 1844. (Pp. 121-122)

James Stone to Isaiah Neeley 150 acres on the waters of Cavenor's Branch. 17 Aug 1844. (Pp. 122-123)

William Stroud, Sr. to William Stroud, Jr. 90 acres on the Horse Spring Fork of the East Fork of Stone's River. 23 May 1844. (Pp. 124-125)

Samuel E. Burger to Willy M. Freeman 500 acres in Cannon and DeKalb Counties. 21 Jan 1845. (Pp. 125-126)

Andrew Phillips to Benjamin Cummings 50 acres on Cedar Fork of Smith's Fork. 4 Dec 1844. (Pp. 126-127)

Stanfield Smith to John H. Smith 18 acres in the 1st District. 4 Apr 1845. (Pp. 127-128)

William H. Peyton to Hiram Wilson, Sr. 45 acres on Bug's Creek. 4 Aug 1845. (Pp. 128-130)

Willy M. Freeman to John W. Wall 100 acres in the 9th District. 9 Jul 1845. (Pp. 130-131)

Polly Bynum, the widow and heir of William Bynum, to B. B. Dickens 15 acres. 14 May 1842. (Pp. 131-132)

Joel Farris to David D. Hipp 150 acres in the 5th District. 28 Feb 1840. (Pp. 132-134)

Elizabeth Brown to John H. Wood the following negroes, viz. Sippie, about 10; Rebecca, about 8; Lucinda, about 6; and Isaac, about 4. 26 Aug 1845. (Pp. 134-135)

Elizabeth Brown to John H. Wood a slave named Agnes, about 35, and her child named Martha, about 18 months. 13 Aug 1845. (P. 136)

David McGill to Robert A. Fagan four acres on Carson's Fork of the East Fork of Stone's River. 17 Jan 1845. (Pp. 136-138)

George St. John, Sr. to Frederick A. St. John 52 acres in the 6th District as a deed of gift for my grandson, the said Frederick A. St. John. 17 Feb 1845. (Pp. 138-139)

Richard Webber to Daniel Tenpenny a trust deed. 14 Dec 1844. (Pp. 139-140)

Larkin Rains to Isaac Rains 277 acres in the 5th District. 15 Oct 1844. (Pp. 140-142)

James Bell of Rutherford County to Boykin Deloach 25 acres in Rutherford County on the East Fork of Stone's River. 7 Feb 1825. (Pp. 142-143)

Sarah Deloach; Templeton Moore and wife Pamelia; William C. Hollis and wife Patsy; and James Deloach, heirs of Boykin Deloach to David Hollis, Sr. 75 acres in the 2nd District. 1 Sep 1842. (Pp. 144-147)

Martha Bell to Abner Alexander ten acres in the 11th District. 17 Oct 1844. (Pp. 147-148)

Partition of the lands of Henry Wiley deceased. Mentions Mary Wiley. John A. Baird and Frances Ann Baird, his wife, received a portion. 20 Sep 1845. (Pp. 149-150)

William Bryson of Green County, Missouri to William Adamson his interest in a negro girl named Christina, about 18, of a dark complexion now in the possession of Frances Bryson. 4 Aug 1845. (Pp. 150-151)

James Esary to William Smith 150 acres on Barren Fork of Collins River. 25 Aug 1845. (Pp. 151-152)

Sheriff Samuel Vance to Alexander McKnight 50 acres. 28 Aug 1845. (Pp. 153-154)

Joseph Bryson to William E. McLin a negro boy named Pleasant, about 39. 1 Apr 1845. (Pp. 154-155)

Benjamin Webber to William Sisson a trust deed. 1 Oct 1845. (Pp. 155-156)

James Carnahan to Newton C. Carnahan 104 acres in Cannon and Rutherford Counties. 27 Aug 1845. (Pp. 156-157)

Zachariah Thomason to Burton Jackson 50 acres in the 10th District. 23 Jun 1845. (Pp. 158-159)

Burton Jackson to James Milligan 50 acres in the 11th District. 25 Aug 1845. (Pp. 159-160)

Micajah Marcum to Charles G. Foster 150 acres in the 9th District. 7 Oct 1845. (Pp. 160-161)

William Elkins to William S. Melton 67 acres in the 7th District. 11 Aug 1845. (Pp. 162-163)

Nathan F. Frogdon to Erasmus S. Kees twon lot #43 in the town of Woodbury. (Pp. 163-164)

William Stroud to Ephraim Nesbit 100 acres on Stone's River.

30 Oct 1845. (Pp. 164-166)

John Bryson to Samuel Bryson 11 acres in the 11th District. 14 Mar 1844. (Pp. 166-167)

Abner Alexander to Mary Alexander 304 acres in the 11th District. 1 Feb 1845. (Pp. 168-170)

A. R. Stone to James C. Word town lot #36 in the town of Woodbury. 17 Nov 1845. (Pp. 170-172)

A. M. Weeden to John P. Hare a negro girl named Harratt for $150. 16 Jan 1844. (P. 172)

Lewis Stare to James H. Walker 65 acres. 16 Dec 1844. (Pp. 173-174)

James H. Walker to William Campbell 65 acres on Mountain Creek. 20 Nov 1845. (Pp. 174-175)

John P. Gandy to A. F. McFerrin a trust deed. 20 Nov 1845. (Pp. 176-177)

Joseph Ramsey to William Ring 115 acres known as the Moore Tract. 25 Nov 1845. (Pp. 177-178)

Samuel Edmondson to Thomas Edmondson of Warren County a negro girl named Eliza to be used for the support of Martha Ann Cain, wife of W. L. Cain of Cherokee County, Alabama. Said Martha Ann is the daughter of said Samuel. 16 Dec 1845. (Pp. 178-180)

Jesse Q. Sewell to William C. Miller a trust deed. 23 Dec 1845. (Pp. 180-182)

Commissioners to the trustees of the Methodist Episcopal Church South town lot #45 in the town of Woodbury, containing three-fourth's of an acre. 2 Dec 1845. (Pp. 182-183)

B. R. Ryan to A. Stone a negro girl named Milly. 25 Sep 1845. (Pp. 183-184)

John Martin to Richard Hancock a man slave named Daniel, 20. 30 Dec 1845. (P. 184)

George Walker to John Hays 97 acres on the East Fork of Stone's River. 29 Dec 1845. (Pp. 184-185)

Sheriff Samuel Vance to David Caldwell 200 acres. 6 Feb 1843. (Pp. 186-188)

Jesse H. Gilley to Hiram Carnahan 1000 acres. Said Hiram was attorney for Elizabeth Carnahan, John M. A. England and wife Jane, formerly Carnahan, Sterling England and wife Mary, Jacob Baughman and wife Nancy, John Vance and wife Elizabeth, and Hiram Carnahan. Said land is in Coffee County. 7 Jan 1846. (Pp. 188-190)

William A. Travis to David Caldwell of Rutherford County his two seventh's interest in a tract of land. Said Travis is a resident of Madison County, Mississippi. 24 Dec 1844. (Pp.

190-193)

James Esary to Henry Trott, Jr. 1152 acres in the 5th District. 29 Aug 1845. (Pp. 193-194)

Alexander McKnight to James K. Sauls 43 acres on McKnight's Creek. 1 Jan 1846. (Pp. 194-195)

John P. Hopkins to Caleb Cox 50 acres in the 4th District. 24 Jan 1844. (Pp. 195-196)

Jacob Spangler to Johnathan Marchbanks 200 acres on the Barren Fork of Collins River. 8 Sep 1839. (Pp. 196-199)

Richard Webber to Daniel Tenpenny a trust deed. 31 Jan 1846. (Pp. 200-201)

Brinkley Lasater to Calvin Curlee five acres on Stone's River. 2 Feb 1846. (Pp. 201-202)

Thomas Thompson to Medford Coffee of Rutherford County a tract of land. 11 Feb 1846. (Pp. 202-203)

Benjamin Cummings to Benjamin A. Stone his one tenth interest in the estate of Moses Cummings deceased. Also his interest in that part which descended to his brother John Cummings. 17 Nov 1845. (Pp. 203-205)

William R. and James Ibby, and James D. Willard to William Willard their interest in a tract of land that descended to the heirs of Elijah Willard deceased. 9 Oct 1839. (Pp. 205-206)

Elijah Stephens to Edward C. Seal 200 acres in the 8th District. 13 Feb 1846. (P. 207)

Beverly Willard to Samuel C. Odom his interest in a tract of land originally belonging to Beverly Willard, Sr. 10 Feb 1846. (Pp. 207-208)

Elijah Higgins and wife Nancy A. to Benjamin Hale their one ninth part of a tract of land belonging to Susan Tittle as the widow of Samuel Tittle. 15 Oct 1842. (Pp. 208-210)

William Bates to Joseph Ramsey a trust deed. 10 Feb 1846. (Pp. 210-212)

William R. James and wife Isbel, John Williard, William Williard, and Martha Edwards to Nelson Odom & Samuel C. Odom their interest in a tract of land. 18 Feb 1846. (Pp. 212-214)

H. M. McKnight, Andrew M. McKnight, and Abagail McKnight to William R. Acres 37 acres belonging to John M. McKnight deceased. 11 Feb 1846. (Pp. 214-216)

Isaac W. Elledge to Jacob M. Kerkendall 100 acres in the 5th District. (Pp. 217-218)

David M. Jarratt and Joseph Ramsey to Thomas B. Brevard town lot #25 in the town of Woodbury. 23 Dec 1845. (Pp. 218-219)

Isaiah Neeley to George T. Ford 62 acres in the 6th District. 10 Feb 1846. (Pp. 219-220)

William Capshaw to John Ferrell 75 acres in the 10th District. 7 Nov 184_. (Pp. 221-222)

D. M. Jarratt and Joseph Ramsey to William Bates the following negroes, to wit, Fanny, Patsy, Stephen, Peter, Pompey, and Mary, these being all the negroes that were formerly conveyed unto us by S. Bates and the latter of which was born since. 10 Feb 1846. (P. 222)

Elizabeth Brown to D. M. Jarratt a certain negro boy named Nelson, 16. 23 May 1844. (P. 223)

Stephen Moore to Alfred L. Hancock 75 acres in the 10th District. 11 Apr 1846. (Pp. 223-224)

Benjamin Hale, Sr. to Fountain Owen 80 acres, it being the four shares I have in the dower of Susannah Tittle, the widow of Samuel Tittle. 13 Apr 1846. (Pp. 224-225)

Richard L. McKnight to Bennett Rucker 45 acres in the 1st District. 13 Jan 1842. (P. 226)

Bennett Rucker to Richard L. McKnight 30¼ acres in the 1st District. 13 Jan 1842. (P. 226)

Hugh Ledbetter to William Morris a title bond. 5 Oct 1843. (Pp. 227-228)

William B. Nokes to William Dodd 20 acres in the 10th District. 1 May 1846. (Pp. 228-229)

Anderson Burnett to Hamon St. John 75 acres in the 6th District. 2 Aug 1845. (Pp. 229-231)

Joseph Ramsey to Henry Perry town lot #6 in the town of Woodbury. 9 Feb 1846. (Pp. 231-232)

Edmund Taylor to Samuel Edmundson a negro man named Anthony. 24 Mar 1846. (Pp. 232-233)

H. D. McBroom to Elijah Neeley a title bond. 27 Mar 1841. (Pp. 233-234)

Benjamin Pendleton to A. F. Todd ten acres in the 8th District. 30 May 1846. (P. 234)

Dozier Mullins to James Medlin 70 acres where I now live. 27 May 1846. (Pp. 235-236)

Andrew Bogle to Michael Wilson 150 acres in the 11th District. 30 May 1846. (P. 236)

Solomon Travis to Andrew Bogle 100 acres in the 1st District. 22 Sep 1840. (Pp. 237-238)

Adam Tittle, Hiram Tittle, Elizabeth Reeves, Salvina Nokes, Salina Destiny, Mary Ann Higgins to George W. Reeves 50 acres belonging to our father Samuel Tittle. 23 Jun 1846. (Pp. 238-240)

Rizen Fowler to John R. Sullivan town lot #29 in the town of Woodbury. 1 Oct 1845. (Pp. 240-241)

James Taylor to Benjamin Sapp 45 acres on (Hollace) Creek. 23 Oct 1845. (Pp. 242-243)

Eleazar Orr to John Henderson 16 acres on the East Fork of Stone's River. 27 Jun 1846. (Pp. 243-244)

John G. W. Rose to Samson Stephens 25 acres as a trust deed. 24 Jul 1846. (Pp. 244-246)

John McClane to Calvin Curlee 76 acres in the 3rd District. 8 May 1845. (Pp. 246-247)

Margaret Dennis to James Tenpenny 50 acres in the 6th District. 30 Jul 1840. (Pp. 247-248)

David McGill to George Peebles 500 acres in the 9th District. 15 Jun 1846. (P. 249)

Joseph Youngblood of DeKalb County to James Wood 81 acres to be held in trust for the use of Nancy Ann Milligan, Elizabeth Milligan, William Thompson, Thomas J. Thompson, Polly Thompson, Caroline Thompson, and James A. Thompson, all of the above are the sons and daughters of Sarah Thompson, wife of Anson Thompson, the said Sarah Thompson being allowed her life estate in said land. 21 Aug 1846. (Pp. 250-252)

Richard McKnight to James H. Byrns 69 acres in the 1st District. 24 Aug 1846. (Pp. 252-253)

William West to Benjamin Fugett of Bedford County 700 acres as a trust deed. 3 Sep 1846. (Pp. 253-254)

Benjamin Fugett to William West the following negroes, to wit, Lile, about 30; Jenney, her daughter, about 3; Hannah, her daughter, about 9 months; and Harriet which is about 9 years old. 30 Jul 1846. (P. 255)

Annual Rains to John Petty a trust deed. 9 Sep 1846. (Pp. 255-257)

William W. Adams to Lewis Hancock 53 acres in the 10th District. 4 Sep 1846. (Pp. 257-258)

Isham Pelham and Levi Pelham to Mitchel Daniel 100 acres on the Barren Fork of Collins River. 9 May 1845. (Pp. 258-259)

Joseph Ramsey to James Wood 37 acres in the 6th District. 10 Sep 1846. (Pp. 260-261)

Joseph Ramsey to James Hawkins 55 acres in the 9th District. 14 Dec 1844. (Pp. 261-262)

John W. Mullins to John Young 54 acres on the East Fork of Stone's River. 26 Sep 1846. (Pp. 263-264)

George W. Myers of Warren County to Allen Wilson of Wilson County 25 acres in Wilson County on Smith Fork between the Canal Creek and Wilmuth Creek. 17 Apr 1829. (Pp. 264-266)

DEED BOOK E

Harmon St. John to William Cathey 75 acres in the 6th District.   31 Sep 1846. (Pp. 266-267)

James O. George to John Martin 75 acres in the 2nd District. 3 Oct 1840. (Pp. 268-269)

Daniel C. Mullins to James Smithson and William S. Clark 50 acres in the 9th District.   23 Oct 1846. (Pp. 269-270)

John W. Stroud to Jane H. Oliver and then to her two heirs, Ibby N. Oliver and Daniel M. Oliver, a parcel of land on Horse Springs Fork.   30 May 1846. (P. 271)

John Kellough to John K. Witherspoon and William E. Witherspoon 137 acres in the 1st District. 11 Jan 1843. (P. 1)

Samuel Moore to Winney Peyton 75 acres on Burge's Creek. 7 Sep 1846. (P. 2)

David Cloyd to Eliza J. Marshall a negro man named Allen. 2 Nov 1866. (Pp. 2-3)

George C. Barrett to William Bates a trust deed. 5 Nov 1846. (Pp. 3-4)

Berry Vinson to Jesse Brewer and Benjamin Brewer his interest in the real estate of Richard Vinson and the dower set a part to the widow. 8 Nov 1845. (P. 4)

George Walker and John Hays object to the above deed which is objected to in the Register's Office in Book E, pages 184-186. 18 Nov 1846. (Pp. 4-5)

William West to Benjamin Fuget 834¼ acres. 17 Nov 1846. (Pp. 5-6)

William West to Thomas Keel 21 acres in the 6th District. 3 Sep 1846. (Pp. 6-7)

Nathan Neely to William West 150 acres in the 6th District. 24 Jan 1844. (Pp. 7-8)

John Daniel to Peter Daniel 259½ acres in the 9th District. 30 Oct 1846. (Pp. 8-9)

James Taylor to John A. George a tract of land on the south side of the East Fork of Stone's River. 5 Nov 1846. (Pp. 9-10)

James Medlin to E. A. Orr a trust deed. 18 Dec 1846. (Pp. 10-11)

T. B. Brevard to A. M. Weeden town lot #6 in the town of Woodbury. 12 Dec 1846. (Pp. 11-12)

James Goodin departed this life, previous to 10 Dec 1836, having purchased of the legal representatives of David Ross deceased 100 acres in Rutherford County on Carson's Fork of Stone's River. Martha Gooding, the widow of James Gooding; Nicholas Goodin, John Cooper and wife Visa, and Martha Gooding, Jr., heirs of James Gooding, to Joseph Gooding their interest in the said tract of land. 19 Dec 1846. (Pp. 12-13)

William West to Warren Cummings 150 acres on the East Fork of Stone's River. 4 Jan 1847. (P. 14)

Samuel Vance to Thomas C. Word 115 acres as a trust deed. 19 Dec 1846. (Pp. 14-18)

Benjamin Fugett and Rizen Fowler enter into an agreement to divide a tract of land. 7 Jan 1847. (P. 19)

James Taylor to Edmond Taylor a negro woman named Aggie. 29 Dec 1846. (P. 19)

Brinkley Lasater to James L. Esary 200 acres. 17 Oct 1846.

DEED BOOK F

(P. 20)

Robert K. Stephens to Micager Markham 175 acres in the 9th District. 26 Dec 1846. (P. 21)

William Moss to Gabriel Moss 130 acres in the 8th District. 3 Sep 1846. (Pp. 22-23)

Henry Sisson to Thomas Sisson his interest in the estate of James Sisson. 14 Mar 1846. (P. 24)

Elbert Owen to Nelson Owen a trust deed. 1 Feb 1847. (Pp. 24-25)

George Gannon to Zachariah Warren three acres in the 2nd District. 1 Feb 1847. (Pp. 25-26)

H. P. Bostick to John Witt a tract of land. 16 Jun 1843. (Pp. 26-31)

John Witt to A. F. and B. L. McFerrin 50 acres in the 3rd District. 16 Aug 1845. (Pp. 31-34)

Willis M. Freeman to H. W. Richardson 25 acres in the 9th District. 7 Oct 1846. (Pp. 34-35)

Henry Trott to Bryan Johnson a boy slave named Moses, going on 14 years. 30 Jan 1847. (P. 35)

Ira L. Blair to William Soap 50 acres in the 12th District. 10 Dec 1846. (Pp. 35-36)

James Taylor to his nephew, Nathaniel M. Taylor, a deed of gift of 220 acres. 8 Feb 1847. (Pp. 36-37)

Lemuel Duncan to William Cummings 135 acres on Barren Fork of Stone's River. 29 Jan 1838. (Pp. 37-38)

Robert K. Stephens to Frances Turner a boy slave named Jacob of dark complexion and about 23 or 24 years of age. 16 Feb 1847. (P. 38)

James Todd to A. F. and B. L. McFerrin 66 acres in the 4th District. 17 Jan 1846. (P. 39)

Charles Poff to A. F. and B. L. McFerrin 100 acres in the 3rd District, it being the land that Jas. Poff lived and died. 15 Jun 1846. (P. 40)

James Read and wife Mary, formerly Mary Ann Poff, to A. F. and B. L. McFerrin their interest in the tract of land that James Poff died seized and possessed of. Said interest is one seventh. 6 Feb 1847. (Pp. 40-41)

James Todd to A. F. and B. L. McFerrin a tract of land. 16 Feb 1847. (P. 42)

Samuel Spangler to William Groose 100 acres in the 4th District. 29 Apr 1846. (Pp. 42-43)

Leroy Rose, Administrator of ?G. W. Rose, to Sampson Stephens 25 acres on Mountain Creek. 10 Aug 1846. (Pp. 43-44)

David M. Jarratt to Henry Trott, Jr. 28½ acres in the 6th District. 9 Feb 1847. (Pp. 44-46)

Robert W. Lansdon to William M. Hooker 100 acres in the 11th District. 25 Jan 1847. (P. 46)

John C. Martin to Daniel Weeden a release of warranty. 14 Oct 1846. (P. 47)

Henry Trott and Nathan Neely to William Grimes 58 acres in the 6th District. 21 Sep 1843. (Pp. 47-48)

William and Britton Grimes to Turner B. Smith 52 acres, it being a deed of gift from William Grimes to the heirs of Britton Grimes. Said deed was registered in Cannon County in Book A, page 408. (Pp. 48-49)

James Taylor to James Taylor Henderson a deed of gift 200 acres, it being the south part where I now live. 31 Mar 1846. (Pp. 49-50)

David M. Jarratt to Stanford Smith 35 acres in the 2nd District. 15 Oct 1846. (Pp. 50-51)

James S. James to David M. Jarrett 30 acres in the 6th District. 10 Feb 1847. (Pp. 51-52)

Elizabeth Boyd, David T. Tassy, P. W. Boyd, Isbel Boyd, Dosamur Tassy, Robert L. Boyd, William T. Boyd, Elizabeth Abston, and William Boyd, to James T. McKnight, Executor of David McKnight and guardian to the heirs of said estate, a man slave named Aron for $550. 14 Feb 1846. (P. 52)

James Taylor to Agnes W. Henderson 226 acres for love and affection during her life and then to Pleasant Henderson. If said Pleasant should die before the said Agnes W. Henderson, then to Baulding and Robert C. Henderson. 25 Apr 1845. (P. 53)

Aron Byford to Richard Holt a trust deed. 25 Feb 1847. (Pp. 53-54)

Johnathan Marchbanks to Jacob M. Kerkendall 50 acres on Barren Fork of Collins River. 30 Jan 1846. (P. 55)

Nicholas Smith and wife Penelope to Joseph H. Bogle 122 acres in the 11th District. 3 Jan 1847. (Pp. 56-57)

John Mullins and James Medley to John Bragg ten acres in the 1st District. 38 Oct 1846. (P. 57)

John Frazer to William McAdow 261 acres in the 6th District. 6 Mar 1847. (Pp. 58-59)

William H. Travis to Samuel C. Travis 40 acres in the 1st District. 24 Feb 1847. (Pp. 59-60)

William H. Travis to Thomas Vance 224 acres in the 6th District. 8 Mar 1847. (P. 60)

David Hays and Britton Grimes to Henry Hays a trust deed. 13 Mar 1847. (P. 61)

John A. George to William Crane 46 acres on Barren Fork of Stone's River. 5 Mar 1847. (Pp. 61-62)

Thomas Elkins for love and affection to Dillard Elkins 60 acres in the 7th District. 7 Apr 1846. (Pp. 62-63)

Martha Sullivan, formerly Roberts, Sarah Carnahan, formerly Roberts, James Roberts, Granville Roberts, William N. Moore and wife Eletha L., heirs of C. L. Roberts, to Granville Roberts a tract of land in the 12th District. 1 Jun 1846. (Pp. 63-64)

Samuel D. Person to Thomas S. Eells of Bucks, Pennsylvania 1500 acres. Said Person is a resident of New York. 6 Dec 1840. (Pp. 64-66)

Samuel Edmonson to Henry Manning 40 acres on Barren Fork of Stone's River. 8 Sep 1846. (Pp. 66-68)

John J. McCleroy to Calvin Roberts 94 acres in the 12th District. 31 Jan 1845. (Pp. 68-69)

Thomas Nokes to William Nokes a title bond. 14 Sep 1846. (P. 69)

A. M. Weeden to Thomas B. Brevard town lot #35 in the town of Woodbury. 1 Apr 1847. (P. 70)

Mary Jones to William R. Bogle 66 acres. 26 Sep 1846. (P. 71)

William McKnight to Joseph Bogle 90 acres. 7 Apr 1847. (P. 72)

Richard Webber to Thomas Lowe 25 acres on Brawley's Fork of Stone's River. 18 Dec 1844. (Pp. 73-74)

Jacob Adcock to Abner Mulinax a negro girl named Martha, 6, for $300. 7 Apr 1847. (P. 74)

Richard Webber to John Webb, Jr. 50 acres. 20 Jan 1847. (Pp. 74-75)

Joseph Hall to Charles J. Hancock 775 acres in the 10th District. 14 Apr 1847. (Pp. 75-76)

Lexington Asher to John B. Ward 148 acres in the 8th District. 12 Apr 1847. (P. 77)

A. F. and B. L. McFerrin to William Stroud 175 acres in the 4th District. 21 Apr 1847. (P. 78)

Benjamin Sapp to William N. Foster 220 acres in the 6th District. 5 Apr 1847. (P. 79)

Roda Whitfield for love and affection to her son, Alford Whitfield, some personal property. 23 Apr 1844. (P. 80)

Mary Thompson, Ason Thompson, James Ferguson and wife Mary, Joseph Youngblood, James C. Youngblood and wife, all heirs of Thomas Thompson, to Jacob Adcock 122¼ acres in the 6th District. 12 Nov 1844. (Pp. 81-82)

Jacob Adcock to Samuel Gunter 122½ acres in the 6th District.

5 Apr 1847. (Pp. 82-83)

Edmund Pendleton to John O. Elkins 153 acres in the 8th District. 15 Mar 1847. (Pp. 53-54)

William Bates to George T. Ford and the other trustees of the Methodist Episcopal Church one acre of land on which a church house now stands known as Prospect Meeting House. 24 May 1847. (Pp. 84-85)

William Rogers to William P. Hickerson a trust deed. 25 May 1847. (P. 85)

John Barry to Rizen Fowler a trust deed. 5 Jun 1847. (P. 86)

Joseph Beason to Joseph M. Anderson his interest in a family of slaves now in the possession of my mother, Peggy Neely Beason, in the County of Walker, State of Georgia, consisting of one old woman, Susey, her children, Nancy and Vina, and grandchildren of Susey, to wit, Wade, Julia, Hanah, Sam, Stephen, and several others who are grandchildren of Susey, the family in all numbering about twelve. The said family of slaves were a deed of gift from James G. (Beetly) of North Carolina to the said Peggy Neely Person and her children. I, being a child of said Peggy, have an interest in said family. Mentions my deceased father Solomon Beason. 29 Mar 1847. (Pp. 87-88)

William Rogers to Alexander Morgan his interest in the estate of his father, John Rogers, which is a one seventh interest. 26 Sep 1846. (Pp. 88-89)

Harrison Smith to George (Grimes) 97 acres on the clear fork of Smith's Fork on the west side of Short Mountain. 15 Jun 1847. (Pp. 89-90)

Samuel E. Burger to H. W. Richardson certain lots in the town of Mechanicksville. 15 Jun 1847. (P. 90)

Turner B. Smith and Joseph Ramsey to George Gannon 43 acres in the 4th District. 16 Jun 1847. (P. 91)

Elizabeth Brashears to James L. Brashears 25 acres on the East Fork of Stone's River. 25 Jun 1846. (Pp. 91-92)

Joseph Ramsey to William Justis 707 acres in the 2nd District. 15 Jun 1847. (Pp. 92-93)

Walter Stroud and Richard Price to Isaac Brooks, Jr. 266½ acres in the 5th District. 7 Apr 1847. (P. 94)

John McCrary and wife Sary M., Silas A. Robinson and wife Elizabeth, and Blake Sagely to Thomas Whitfield their interest in 200 acres in the 12th District. 27 Jul 1841. (Pp. 95-96)

John McCrary to George Whitfield his interest in a tract of land which may be allotted to him as an heir of Willis Whitfield. 3 Oct 1847. (Pp. 96-97)

Willis Whitfield, Jr., heir of Willis Whitfield, Sr., his

interest in a tract of land in the 12th District. 8 Jul 1846. (Pp. 97-98)

David Jones to C. R. Davis two tracts of land in the 3rd District. 10 Jul 1847. (Pp. 98-99)

William Rogers to Alexander Morgan his interest in the estate of his father, John B. Rogers. 6 Apr 1847. (Pp. 99-100)

B. H. F. Philips to Peter Philips 138 acres in the 5th District. 22 Jul 1847. (Pp. 100-102)

Henry A. Bratton of Wright County, Missouri to William Bratton 100 acres at the Stage Road where it crosses the south boundary of a tract of land lately owned by Dillard Greenstaff. 27 Mar 1847. (Pp. 102-103)

David McGill a deed of gift to Jessey B. Robinson a negro girl named Clery. 14 Apr 1847. (Pp. 103-104)

William D. Stroud to John W. Stroud 150 acres that I bought of A. F. and B. L. McFerrin. 28 Feb 1847. (Pp. 104-105)

David McGill to his son, James McGill, a deed of gift of 74½ acres in the 4th District. 14 Apr 1847. (Pp. 105-106)

Hezekiah Clements to James Lambert 30 acres on Brawley's Creek. 7 Aug 1847. (Pp. 106-107)

Thomas Sisson, Administrator of James Sisson, to A. P. Inglis 197 acres as a trust deed. 2 Nov 1846. (Pp. 107-108)

Jesse Sisson, William Sisson, Benjamin Creson and wife Sarah, Thomas Sisson, and Henry Sisson, heirs of James Sisson, to A. J. Inglis 278 acres in the 4th District. 2 Nov 1846. (Pp. 108-109)

Hezekiah Clements to William C. Soap 23 acres in the 12th District. 9 Aug 1847. (P. 110)

Richard Gibson to F. A. Edwards 60 acres in the 5th District. 12 Jul 1847. (P. 111)

James O. George to Enoch Jones 30 acres in the 9th District. 7 Sep 1840. (Pp. 111-112)

Jonathan Paris of Warren County to Enoch Jones 185 acres on Mountain Creek. 21 Feb 1839. (Pp. 113-114)

Austin S. Millikin to John Epley a trust deed. 11 Aug 1847. (Pp. 114-115)

Austin S. Millikin to Samuel Jamison a trust deed. 10 Aug 1847. (Pp. 115-116)

Moses McKnight to W. W. McKnight 65 acres in the 8th District. 20 Nov 1845. (Pp. 116-117)

Joshua Vassar to Stephen A. Mitchell a tract of land on Horse Spring Fork of Stone's River. 17 Aug 1847. (Pp. 118-119)

Bennett Rucker to Henry Goodloe 380 acres. 25 Jun 1847. (Pp. 118-119)

Bennett Rucker to Henry Goodloe a trust deed on a negro man named Harry, 100 years old; a negro man named Charles, about 60; a man named George, about 65; Caley, about 45; Henry, about 21; Jim, about 15, all of dark complextion; and the following negro women, to wit, Delpha, about 60; Fanny, about 70; Crisy, about 55; Nancy, about 40, and her five children, Reuben, about 3, Susana, about 5, Ann, about 20, and her child, Edmund, about one month. 25 Jun 1847. (Pp. 120-121)

John Q. Weatherford to Albert G. Millikin 300 acres. 25 Aug 1847. (Pp. 121-123)

Albert G. Millikin to John W. Millikin 300 acres in the 5th District. 25 Aug 1847. (Pp. 123-124)

John W. Stone to C. C. Hancock a woman slave named Milly, 25. 2 Sep 1847. (Pp. 124-125)

A. M. McKnight to William W. McKnight 16 acres in the 1st District. 25 Jul 1847. (Pp. 125-126)

Thomas D. Summers to Melchisidic Francis 60 acres in the 11th District. 27 Jul 1847. (Pp. 126-127)

Thomas D. Summers to Armstead Francis 90 acres in the 11th District. 27 Jul 1847. (P. 127)

John McClane to Walker Dodd 100 acres in the 4th District. 10 Sep 1847. (P. 128)

Charles C. Evans to John H. Evans 75 acres on Rock House Fork of Stone's River. 10 Sep 1847. (Pp. 128-129)

Samuel Moore to William H. Peyton 50 acres on Horse Spring Fork. 5 Dec 1846. (Pp. 129-130)

James Stone to William Nokes 90 acres, it being a part of a 100 acre tract of land granted to John Montgomery. 1 Jun 1846. (Pp. 130-131)

Henry Morris to Fountain Owen a tract of land on Clear Fork of Smith's Fork. 1 Jul 1846. (Pp. 131-132)

Ephraim Nesbitt to William Stroud, Jr. 100 acres on Burger's Creek. 15 Sep 1847. (Pp. 133-134)

A. Stone to J. W. Orrand a boy slave named (Allen). 30 Sep 1847. (Pp. 134-135)

James Taylor for love and affection to Mary Jane Weeden, daughter of Elizabeth W. Ferrell and granddaughter of Edmond Taylor, lot #7 in the town of Danville. 16 Apr 1845. (P. 135)

William Stroud to Norris Kerkendall a title bond. 3 May 1847. (P. 136)

Larkin Rains to Charles Espy 150 acres on Barren Fork of Collins River. 16 Sep 1847. (Pp. 136-137)

Margaret Dennis to James Tenpenny 61 acres in the 6th District. 21 Sep 1847. (Pp. 137-138)

John Rodgers to Elizabeth Rodgers his interest in the estate
of his father John B. Rodgers, which share is one eighth. 30
Sep 1847. (Pp. 138-139)

W. W. Cummings and William Stone to Gabriel Hume two acres
in the 6th District. 19 Oct 1847. (Pp. 139-140)

James T. Henderson and James Taylor to William L. Covington
150 acres in the 6th District. 16 Mar 1847. (Pp. 140-141)

Henry Ford, Jr. to G. B. Mars and William Stone 100 acres.
7 Nov 1846. (P. 141)

Isaiah Neely to John W. Mullins 175 acres in the 6th District. 5 May 1847. (Pp. 142-143)

Mitchel Daniel to A. M. Alexander ten acres in the 5 District. 11 Oct 1847. (P. 143)

A. M. Alexander to Benjamin Fugett a town lot in the town
of Woodbury. 7 Oct 1847. (P. 144)

Henry M. Ford to G. B. Mars and William Stone 100 acres in
the 6th District. Said Henry M. Ford is a resident of Benton
County, Arkansas. 7 Nov 1846. (Pp. 144-146)

Erin Chery to Oliver C. Duncan a trust deed. 4 Nov 1847.
(Pp. 146-147)

William Nokes to Thomas Barrett 50 acres in the 8th District.
3 Aug 1846. (Pp. 148-149)

John H. Witherspoon and William E. Witherspoon 86 acres in
the 1st District. 31 Oct 1846. (P. 149)

John H. Witherspoon and William E. Witherspoon to Joseph
Dement, Eleanor Andrews, and Jane Andrews 112 acres in the 1st
District. 31 Oct 1846. (P. 150)

Jemima Patrick to M. F. Todd 30 acres in the 4th District,
it being "all my wright of dower as willed to me by Jesse Patrick.
5 Nov 1847. (P. 151)

Abraham Gooding to Isaiah Parker 80 acres on Carson's Fork
of Stone's River. 12 Jan 1843. (Pp. 152-153)

John Fisher to R. Fowler a trust deed. 11 Nov 1847. (Pp.
153-155)

Leanar Orr to T. G. Sullivan 53 acres. Bounded: Thomas
Bragg deceased. 7 Nov 1847. (P. 155)

Philip Harris to Micajah Petty a trust deed. 26 Nov 1847.
(P. 156)

John Cross of Rutherford County to John Pedon 137 acres
on Lose Creek, a branch of East Fork of Stone's River. 31 Dec
1838. (Pp. 155-158)

James Taylor for love and affection to Nathaniel M. Taylor,
a son of Edmond Taylor and Mary Taylor, lot #2 in the town of
Woodbury. 18 Apr 1845. (P. 158)

James Taylor for love and affection to Nathaniel M. Taylor a deed of gift of town lot #2 in the town of Danville. 18 Apr 1845. (P. 158)

Elizabeth Norris, Thomas Norris, Isaac Norris, and Almira Norris to L. F. Porterfield 230 acres in the 9th District. 3 Sep 1847. (P. 159)

Thomas C. Word to Thomas G. Wood 125 acres in the 5th District. 23 Dec 1846. (Pp. 160-161)

Thomas Leech a deed of gift to his son, Thomas K. Leech, of 160 acres in the 11th District. 8 Dec 1847. (Pp. 161-162)

Thomas Leech a deed of gift to his son Abner S. Leech, of 60 acres in the 11th District. 8 Dec 1847. (P. 162)

Thomas Leech to William C. Leech the following slaves, to wit, Tabby, about 60; Ben, about 35; Jake, about 32; Sidney, about 28; Teresa, about 26; Dick, about 9, for $2000. 8 Dec 1847. (P. 163)

Joseph Youngblood to John W. Bryant 50 acres in the 6th District. 27 Sep 1847. (Pp. 163-164)

William Cathey to William F. Mers 75 acres in the 6th District. 23 Dec 1847. (Pp. 164-165)

John A. George to Elevean Jones 100 acres on Hollis' Creek. 12 Aug 1844. (Pp. 165-167)

Samuel Vance to Stanford Smith 50 acres. 4 Jan 1847. (Pp. 167-169)

James Sisson and wife Ann to John Bowen and other trustees the land where the Rocky Point Meeting House is located. 24 Dec 1841. (Pp. 169-170)

Benton McFerrin to Milton Todd 35 acres in the 4th District. 8 Jan 1848. (P. 171)

B. L. McFerrin to Nathan F. Norris 30 acres in the 4th District. 8 Jan 1848. (Pp. 171-172)

Nathan J. Norris to Robison L. Fagan a trust deed. 8 Jan 1848. (Pp. 172-173)

B. L. McFerrin to William (Todd), Jr. 35 acres in the 4th District. 8 Jan 1848. (Pp. 173-174)

B. L. McFerrin to Mary Sheppard 50 acres in the 4th District. 11 Jan 1848. (Pp. 174-175)

William Willis to Jesse Gilley, Sr., Jessey Jernigan, and Silas A. Robinson one acre in the 12th District including Hopewell Meeting House, called by some persons Willis' Meeting House. 12 Nov 1847. (Pp. 175-176)

Peter Cox to Alexander McBroom 125 acres in the 3rd District for $325. Bounded: the land conveyed to Burrel Walker. 21 Jan 1847. (Pp. 176-177)

Henry R. Perry to Gabriel Hume town lot #5 in the town of Woodbury. 14 Jan 1848. (P. 177)

Joseph Trimble to Robert Gordon a trust deed. 27 Nov 1843. (Pp. 178-179)

Robert Carson to William Price 40 acres in the 4th District. 29 Dec 1847. (P. 179)

Richard W. Lemay to B. B. Haley 110 acres in the 5th District. 27 Dec 1847. (P. 180)

John H. Wood to Armstrong Brandon six acres in the 3rd District. 2 May 1846. (Pp. 180-181)

Cornelius Brandon to Joseph A. Brandon 55 acres in Rutherford County. 17 Jun 1835. (Pp. 181-182)

Benjamin Sapp to Larkin W. Hammond 42 acres in the 6th District. 25 Dec 1847. (Pp. 182-183)

John Pedon to John Fann 30 acres in the 1st District. 29 Nov 1847. (Pp. 183-184)

Richard W. Lemay to Henry Trott a man slave named Aron, about 32. 15 Dec 1845. (P. 184)

George Sherrill to Uriah B. Bush 200 acres on the dividing ridge between the waters of Brawley's Fork and Carson's Fork of Stone's River. 5 Mar 1846. (Pp. 184-185)

David M. Jarratt to John C. Smithson 201 acres in the 5th District. (Pp. 185-186)

Sheriff Samuel Vance to John Hollinsworth 100 acres. 15 Oct 1847. (Pp. 186-188)

Thomas Sisson, Administrator of James Sisson, to William Williams 50 acres in the 4th District. 13 Jan 1845. (Pp. 188-189)

Hezekiah Clements to James Lambert 15 acres on Brawley's Fork. 13 Sep 1847. (Pp. 189-190)

Richard Price to Richard W. Lemay a trust deed. 110 acres in the 4th District. 29 Jan 1848. (P. 190)

Claton Lance and wife Matilda; William Young and wife Jane of Warren County to Wilford Littrel their interest in 48 acres that Silas Littrel was seized and possessed of in his lifetime and the tract that Allen Miles now lives on. 7 Feb 1848. (P. 191)

William Whitamore to William P. Jackson a title bond. 19 Jan 1848. (P. 192)

Joseph W. Pendleton, the surviving Executor of Richard Sandridg of Louisa County, Virginia of the one part and Damer Sandridge, Mela Sandridge, Louiza Sandridge, and (Hallah) Sandridge, free persons of color, emancipated and set free by the Last Will and Testament of the said Richard Sandridge of the other part. Party of the first part to the parties of the second part. 31 Dec 1847. (Pp. 192-195)

Alexander McBroom to Britton W. Snipes 20 acres in the 2nd District. 9 Feb 1848. (Pp. 195-196)

David Hollis to John Hollis 75 acres in the 2nd District. 2 Feb 1848. (Pp. 196-197)

John Hollis to Alexander McBroom 75 acres in the 2nd District. 7 Feb 1848. (Pp. 197-198)

Jane Rucker for love and affection to her children, to wit, Thomas S. Rucker, James H. Rucker, Samuel Rucker, John C. Martin and wife Sophia B., Daniel F. Weeden and wife Mariah L., Claburn R. Jarratt and wife Catharine, Pleasant (Labby) and wife Elizabeth, Eli Bell and wife Sarah her interest in the estate of her late husband Gideon Rucker. The following slaves are given to the children, to wit, Caleb, Aggy, Rachel, Clabern, Amanda, Elon, Isaac, Jacob, Homell, Jo, Edmond, Rhody, Amy, and all their increase. 14 Feb 1848. (Pp. 198-199)

John Smith and William Smith to Henry Hays a trust deed. 16 Feb 1848. (Pp. 199-200)

William Ring, Sr. to Noah W. Lain 54 acres where Matthew B. Ford formerly lived and where Aaron Byford now lives. 4 Feb 1848. (Pp. 200-201)

James T. Henderson to William Barton a trust deed. 19 Feb 1848. (Pp. 201-202)

Joseph Trimble to James R. Tolbert 124 acres in the 12th District. 14 Feb 1848. (Pp. 202-203)

David Hollis for love and affection to the Baptist Church at Brawley's Fork one acre to be used by the church and also for erecting an academy. 25 Dec 1847. (Pp. 203-204)

Allen Thomas to P. J. Thomas 100 acres on Stone's River for $500. 10 Nov 1847. (Pp. 204-205)

William Bates, Executor of Moses Shelby, to Joab Brooks 50 acres as a title bond. 22 Dec 1846. (P. 205)

Levin Jones to Abraham Creson 100 acres on Hollis' Creek. 10 Dec 1847. (Pp. 206-208)

Henry Davenport, Elizabeth Bryson, formerly Davenport, and Joseph Davenport, all being the legal heirs of Hardy Davenport deceased, to William Davenport their interest in 120 acres in the 11th District. 1 Sep 1847. (Pp. 208-209)

Ephraim Andrews to James L. Kelton 175 acres in the 1st District. 11 Aug 1847. (Pp. 209-210)

Baxter B. Dickens to Ivy Bush 149 acres on Brawley's Fork of Stone's River. 27 Jan 1844. (P. 210)

Mark Gannon of Warren County to Daniel Tenpenny 44½ acres in Warren County on the south side of Stone's River. 8 Feb 1825. (P. 211)

John Young to Archebald Edwards 35 acres on the dry fork of the east fork of Stone's River. 30 Oct 1829. (Pp. 212-213)

William Stone to William S. Melton a tract of land in the 7th District. 15 Feb 1848. (P. 213)

William S. Melton to William Stone a tract of land in the 7th District. 15 Feb 1848. (P. 214)

John W. Summer, Executor of Matthew Summer, to Alexander Higgins 135 acres in the 7th District. 19 Feb 1848. (Pp. 214-215)

Jesse B. Robinson to Zachariah Bush 160 acres in the 12th District and on Brawley's Fork of Stone's River. 7 Dec 1846. (Pp. 215-216)

Zachariah Bush to Jesse H. Gilley and Harvey Bush 160 acres in the 12th District. 9 Oct 1847. (Pp. 216-217)

H. D. McBroom and James Taylor to B. L. McBroom a trust deed. 26 Apr 1848. (Pp. 217-218)

John W. Summer, Armstead Francis, Nicholas Smith, and Thomas D. Summer, the heirs of Matthew Summer, to Armstead G. Odom a girl slave named Louisey, age 8, for $420. 22 Dec 1847. (Pp. 218-219)

John W. Summer, Nicholas Smith, Thomas D. Summer, Armstead Francis, and Armstead G. Odom to John N. Bailey a slave named Mary, age 10. 22 Dec 1847. (P. 219)

Emmey Summer, widow of Matthew Summer, to John W. Summer, Penelope J. Smith, Elizabeth H. Francis, Thomas D. Summer, and Matthew Bogle, and Eliza J. Odom a family of negroes, consisting of five, to wit, Sintha, 26; Mary, 10; Louisa, 8; Hannah, 5; and Rachel. 21 Dec 1847. (Pp. 219-220)

John W. Summer, Thomas D. Summer, Nicholas Smith, Armstead Francis, and Armstead G. Odom to William H. Grimmitt a woman slave named Sintha, a girl slave named Hannah, and a girl slave named Rachel. 22 Dec 1847. (Pp. 220-221)

B. B. Dickens to Thomas Holt 25 acres in the 12th District. 15 Jan 1848. (P. 221)

B. B. Dickens to John Webber 617½ acres. 30 Dec 1847. (P. 222)

Benjamin Webber to Thomas Holt 60 acres. 23 Sep 1846. (P. 223)

Ann Sisson for love and affection to her daughter, Jane Byford, 75 acres in the 4th District. 11 May 1847. (P. 224)

George Bogle to Malcisidic Francis 250 acres in the 11th District. 20 Jan 1845. (P. 225)

John M. Banks to Jefferson Todd 139½ acres in the 4th District. 13 Mar 1848. (Pp. 226-227)

George Bogle to Malcisidic Francis a man slave named Richard, age 30. 20 Jan 1845. (P. 227)

Josiah Fouston to Isaac T. Blair 30 acres in the 10th District. 31 Jan 1848. (Pp. 227-228)

Henderson Yoakum to Franklin Coleman the north half of town lot #14 in the town of Woodbury. 11 Nov 1847. (P. 229)

Josiah Ferris to Franklin Coleman a town lot in the town of Woodbury. Bounded: A. C. Penn. 8 Feb 1848. (Pp. 229-230)

John McClain to John M. Banks a tract of land in the 4th District. 13 Mar 1848. (P. 230)

Maxwell Caruthers and wife Mary to Allen Godwin 45 acres in the 3rd District. 29 Dec 1847. (P. 230)

James Sisson to Joel Cherry 110 acres in the 4th District. 24 Jan 1844. (Pp. 231-232)

John Hollinsworth to Josiah Fouston 30 acres in the 16th District. 31 Jan 1848. (Pp. 232-233)

Thomas Parker to John McClain 20 acres in the 4th District. 8 Sep 1838. (P. 234)

Green W. Whitfield to Thomas Y. Whitfield his interest in the land of his brother Wright Whitfield. Also, his interest in the estate of his grandfather, Willis Whitfield. 13 Dec 1844. (Pp. 234-235)

Calvin W. Roberts to Joseph Pinkerton 71 acres in the 12th District. 2 Nov 1846. (Pp. 236-237)

David Hollis to James R. Taylor 12 acres in the 3rd District. 7 Mar 1848. (Pp. 237-238)

Jesse B. Robinson to Hugh Robinson 194½ acres in the 12th District. 27 May 1846. (Pp. 238-239)

John Barton to his daughter Elizabeth Taylor 130 acres on Dry Fork. 2 Oct 1848. (Pp. 239-240)

Joshua Barton to the deacons of the Brawley's Fork Baptist Church 324 poles. 10 Jun 1847. (Pp. 240-241)

Peter Adams to Thomas Womack 250 acres on Wilmouth Fork of the Clear Fork of Smith's Fork. 12 Feb 1848. (Pp. 241-242)

William Melton to John Melton his interest in the estate of Ancil Melton. 17 Mar 1848. (P. 242)

Daniel Faulkenberry and Hugh P. Faulkenberry of Lawrence County; Joshua Billingsley and wife Elizabeth Catharine of Fulton County, Arkansas appoint William Faulkenberry their power of attorney to sell 25 acres transferred by William Nash to David Faulkenberry. Said William Faulkenberry is also a resident of Fulton County, Arkansas. 12 Nov 1847. (Pp. 242-244)

William Faulkenberry to Maxwell Caruthers 135 acres in the 3rd District. 30 Dec 1847. (Pp. 244-245)

DEED BOOK F

James Sisson for love and affection to Jesse Sisson, Sr. a saw mill in the 4th District. 23 Nov 1844. (Pp. 245-246)

Willis F. Couch to Richard Lemay 125 acres in the 5th District. 27 Dec 1847. (Pp. 246-247)

James L. Kelton and John M. Andrews to James T. C. McKnight their interest in a negro man named Aaron, 27 or 28, which formerly belonged to the heirs of Robert Boyd and was purchased from said heirs by James T. C. McKnight in the year 1846. 5 Aug 1847. (Pp. 247-248)

Jesse Gilley to James Cawthorn 235 acres on Bralley's Fork of Stone's River. 24 May 1847. (PP. 248-249)

Joseph Ramsey of Warren County to Richard Tenpenny his interest in five acres in the 6th District. 16 Jun 1847. (Pp. 249-250)

John Mullins to William D. Gowen a trust deed. 5 Nov 1847. (Pp. 250-251)

Erasmus Jones to Ephraim Andrew J. M. Jones and William B. Byrn a trust deed. 23 Mar 1848. (Pp. 251-254)

James K. Eason and John Webb to Alfred D. Fugett 32 acres in the 6th District. 17 Apr 1847. (Pp. 254-255)

John W. Stroud, Robert J. Good, and George B. Good 175 acres to Christopher C. Good. 17 Apr 1848. (Pp. 255-256)

David Coughamour to Thomas H. Roughton his power of attorney to act in his name. 14 Apr 1848. (Pp. 256-258)

Byrd Lusk to John Petty a trust deed. 15 May 1848. (Pp. 258-259)

John J. Smith to Thomas B. Brevard a woman named Charrity, age 30. 20 May 1848. (Pp. 259-260)

Joseph Ramsey of Warren County to Henry R. Perry three acres in the 6th District. 20 May 1848. (Pp. 260-261)

Annual Rains to John Petty a trust deed. 24 May 1848. (Pp. 261-262)

Allen Godwin to Benjamin Hayes 45 acres in the 3rd District. 24 May 1846. (P. 263)

Henry Trott to Joseph Sherlock 28½ acres in the 6th District. 27 May 1848. (Pp. 264-265)

William Nichol to Lucretia Ready 140 acres in the 1st District. 5 Jun 1848. (Pp. 265-266)

Henry Trott to John J. Smith a title bond. 12 Oct 1847. (Pp. 266-267)

Robert W. Brandon to A. M. Weeden nine acres in the 5th District. 12 Jun 1848. (Pp. 267-268)

Hugh B. Landsden to William C. Donnell 130 acres in the 11th District. 1 Feb 1848. (Pp. 268-269)

Dozier Mullins to James Medlin 30 acres on Lock's Creek. 2 Nov 1846. (Pp. 269-271)

Hugh Robinson to Martin S. Hoover 30 acres in the 12th District. 3 Nov 1846. (Pp. 271-272)

Robert A. Smith to William McKee a trust deed. 17 Jun 1848. (Pp. 272-273)

Keeton Smith to William McKee 172½ acres on which I now live. 3 Nov 1838. (P. 273)

James T. Henderson to William Barton a trust deed. 16 Jun 1848. (Pp. 274-275)

David Jones, one of the heirs of Jonathan Jones, to C. R. Davis his interest in the land on which the said Jonathan Jones lived including the mansion house. 14 Oct 1847. (Pp. 275-276)

David Jones to C. R. Davis a man slave named Simon. 12 Oct 184_. (P. 276)

Robert S. Ferrell to C. R. Davis his power of attorney the receive his share of the estate of his grandfather, Jonathan Jones. 7 Feb 1848. (Pp. 276-277)

William Bates to Daniel F. Manus a title bond. 28 Feb 1846. (P. 278)

R. H. Mason to C. T. New a title bond. 15 Jun 1848. (Pp. 279-280)

R. H. Mason to J. B. Brewer a title bond. 15 Jun 1848. (Pp. 280-281)

Thomas W. Richardson to John Kirsey 25 acres in the 9th District. k6 Jun 1848. (Pp. 281-282)

John Kirsey to John Patterson eight acres in the 9th District. 16 Jun 1848. (Pp. 282-283)

Lemuel G. Moore and wife Drufina, formerly Adams, to William Patrick 160 acres in the 11th District, it being the land on which James Adams lived before his death and which descended to the said Drufina together with the other heirs. 15 Jun 1848. (Pp. 284-285)

Shadrack J. Odom to William Patrick 460 acres his one share interest in the estate of James Odom. 7 Aug 1845. (Pp. 285-286)

John Teague to F. G. St. John a trust deed. 17 Jun 1848. (Pp. 286-287)

Thomas G. Abel of New York to Frederick P. Stephens of Buffalo, New York 5150 acres in Cannon and DeKalb Counties. 6 May 1842. (Pp. 288-291)

John B. Jetton to Robert W. Brandon 152 acres in the 2nd District. 6 Nov 1847. (Pp. 291-293)

Nancy Brown and A. M. Weeden have an undivided interest in

the following slaves, to wit, Moses, Grant, Caroline, William, Dave, Susan, Benjamin, and Aggy. Said parties agree to divide the slaves between themselves. The said Augustine M. Weeden is to receive Moses, Grant, Caroline, William, amounting to $1750. The said Nancy Brown is to receive Dave, Benjamin, and Aggy. 8 Jul 1848. (Pp. 293-294)

Meredith Akers to Mitchel Daniel a title bond. 1 Aug 1848. (Pp. 294-296)

James T. Odom, Samuel C. Odom, and R. W. Odom to Jehue M. Odom their interest in 460 acres belonging to the children and heirs of James Odom deceased. 22 Dec 1848. (Pp. 296-298)

Henry Moffitt to Richard C. Price a trust deed. 7 Jul 1848. (Pp. 298-301)

Henry Trott to William R. Akers town lot #38 in the town of Woodbury on the southeast corner of the public square. 15 Aug 1848. (Pp. 301-302)

Alexander Nesbitt and John Chappell enter into an agreement in which the said Chappell agrees to repair the mill on the main east fork of Stone's River. 14 Jul 1848. (Pp. 302-303)

William C. Odom to William C. Patrick his interest in the estate of James Odom. 10 Aug 1848. (Pp. 303-304)

John Y. Smith to A. D. Fugett a trust deed. 19 Aug 1848. (Pp. 305-306)

William McAdow for love and affection to his daughter, Eliza Pendleton, wife of Benjamin Pendleton, three slaves, to wit, Mary, about 23; Violet, about 4; and Martha, two years old. 18 Aug 1848. (Pp. 306-307)

James Ready to John Pedon a trust deed. 24 Aug 1848. (Pp. 307-308)

Jacob Burger to Robert Patterson 60 acres in the 9th District. 18 Aug 1848. (Pp. 308-309)

John W. Mullins to Robert Bailey a negro woman named Charlotte, 32, for $400. 2 Sep 1848. (Pp. 309-310)

James Medlin to Grundy Fann and Cornelias Parker 110 acres in the 1st District. Bounded: by the tract that I once lived on, now occupied by Mr. Mullins. 18 Aug 1848. (Pp. 310-311)

John Hollis to Joseph Simpson 35 acres in the 3rd District. 1 Sep 1848. (Pp. 311-312)

William Stacy to Pinkney Todd seven acres in the 12th District. 7 Mar 1848. (P. 313)

James McGill to Peter Simpson 18 acres in the 3rd District. 30 Aug 1848. (Pp. 313-314)

H. R. Jarratt to P. C. Tally a negro boy named Willoby, 11, for $290. 4 Oct 1842. (P. 315)

John B. Rogers to John M. Banks ten acres. 3 Mar 1848. (Pp. 315-316)

Parker F. Stone to Thomas C. Word 5000 acres gramted bu the State of Tennessee Grant No. 14750 on 28 Nov 1837. Said Word is a resident of Wilson County. 22 Feb 1847. (Pp. 316-317)

Abner Adams to John Hollis 150 acres in the 3rd District. 1 Sep 1848. (Pp. 317-318)

Frances Turner to Fountain Owen 700 acres on the Clear Fork. 13 Jun 1848. (Pp. 319-320)

Pryor Grissom to James Hall 300 acres in the 5th District. 12 Jan 1842. (Pp. 320-321)

Joseph Ramsey to Alman Rigsby a tract of land in the 7th District. 12 Oct 1847. (Po. 321-322)

Alexander Finley to Dr. Daniel Spangler 140 acres on the Barren Fork of Collins River. 24 Sep 1847. (Pp. 322-323)

Hiram Tittle of Wilson County to Henry Dennis of the same place 30 acres in Wilson County. 1 Mar 1847. (Pp. 323-324)

James R. Taylor to Maxwell Caruthers 20 acres in the 3rd District. 15 Mar 1848. (Pp. 325-326)

Maxwell Caruthers and wife Mary to Elizabeth Taylor 25 acres in the 3rd District. 18 Sep 1848. (Pp. 326-327)

George Tittle of Warren County to Henry Powell 300 acres on the Clear Fork of Smith's, it being the land that said Powell now lives on. 28 Jan 1839. (Pp. 327-329)

Stephen Harriman to John W. Mullins a trust deed. 31 Aug 1848. (Pp. 329-330)

C. B. Davis to Thomas G. Wood a trust deed. 7 Sep 1848. (Pp. 330-332)

Armstead Carter to Joseph Carter 70 acres on Brawley's Fork of the East Fork of Stone's River for $250. 28 Jan 1848. (Pp. 332-333)

Richard D. Eddings to J. D. Weatherford a trust deed. 29 Sep 1848. (Pp. 333-334)

Henry Trott to H. M. Burton a trust deed. 9 Oct 1848. (Pp. 334-335)

Abraham Cooper to Joseph Bryson a trust deed. 10 Nov 1845. (Pp. 335-337)

Adam (Hofer) to John Pendleton 275 acres on the Barren Fork of Stone's River. 10 Apr 1832. (Pp. 337-338)

James Pendleton to John Pendleton 250 acres in the 8th District. 12 Oct 1848. (Pp. 338-339)

Henry Howerston to his son, Philip Howerston, 200 acres in the 5th District. 18 Oct 1848. (Pp. 339-340)

John A. Webber and Benjamin Webber to Zachariah Bush a trust deed. 17 Apr 1848. (Pp. 340-341)

William Stacy to Pinkney Todd 115 acres in the 12th District. 5 Jan 1848. (Pp. 342-343)

T. S. Rucker and C. R. Jarratt to Daniel F. Weeden a girl slave named Susan, about 5, for $265. 12 Oct 1848. (P. 343)

Joseph H. Bogle to William G. Bratten 225 acres in the 11th District. 11 Oct 1848. (Pp. 343-344)

A. M. Weeden to J. and B. Brewer a negro girl named Siller Susan for $350. 9 Oct 1848. (Pp. 344-345)

E. A. Orr to R. H. Rogers 100 acres. 21 Oct 1848. (Pp. 345-346)

James T. Moore to Elizabeth R. Taylor a negro man named Young George. Said negro was bequeathed to me by James Taylor deceaaed. This transaction is in consideration of the compromise of two suits in the Circuit Court of Cannon County. 13 Oct 1848. (P. 346)

John F. Weeden to James Henderson a negro girl named Mary and one named Laura. This transaction is in consideration of a compromise of two suits in the Circuit Court of Cannon County concerning the will of James Taylor. 1 Nov 1848. (P. 347)

William Ferrell to John F. Weeden one and a half acres in the 6th District. 23 Sep 1848. (Pp. 348-349)

John F. Weeden to William Ferrell a town lot in the town of Woodbury. Also to the said Ferrell the interest of the said John F. Weeden and wife Mary in the following slaves, to wit, Jordan, Huldy, Temperance, Araminta, Ruth, Julian and her five children and their names are Mary, Laura, John, Frances, and Henry. Said Weedens are also transferring all their interest in the estate of Edmond Taylor deceased as heirs at law of Elizabeth Ferrell deceased. Also our interest in the estate of Ligston Ferrell. 8 Sep 1848. (Pp. 349-350)

John Melton to John Cummings 150 acres in the 7th District. 26 Sep 1848. (Pp. 350-352)

Joel Cherry a deed of goft to John Parker 100 acres in the 4th District. 10 Jun 1847. (Pp. 352-353)

Campbell C. Akers to Mitchel Daniel 15 acres in the 5th District. 19 Aug 1848. (Pp. 353-354)

Elizabeth R. Taylor, J. T. Henderson, James T. Moore, James R. Taylor, J. F. Weeden, and Agnes M. Henderson enter into an agreement concerning the estate of James Taylor deceased. 18 Oct 1848. (Pp. 354-356)

Procession of the lands of William Bynum. Mentions land owned by Jason Thompson and devised to John McNairy. 9 Sep 1848. (Pp. 356-358)

John McNairy Thompson to procession of land. 2 Oct 1848. (Pp. 358-361)

John Hollingsworth to Fountain Owen 75 acres on Canal Fork

of Clear Fork in the 10th District. 13 Oct 1848. (Pp. 362-363)

Mary Thompson, Anson Thompson, James Ferguson and wife Mary, James C. Youngblood and wife Cyreny, all heirs of Thomas Thompson, to Vincent Bayley 81½ acres in the 6th District. 12 Nov 1844. (Pp. 363-365)

T. S. Rucker, Eli Bell, C. H. Jarratt, S. W. Rucker, and D. F. Weeden, the children and heirs of Gideon Rucker, to John C. Martin their interest in 219 acres in the 1st District. 9 Oct 1848. (P. 365)

Hugh Robison to Hiram Todd 14 acres in the 12th District. 27 Mar 1848. (P. 366)

Joel Melton to R. Fowler a trust deed. 29 Nov 1848. (Pp. 367-368)

James T. Henderson to Elizabeth R. Taylor, in consideration of the Last Will and Testament of James Taylor, the following negro slaves, to wit, Old George, Susan, Elvira, Martha, Daniel, William, Jirdan, and Nancy. 13 Oct 1848. (Pp. 368-371)

Valentine Simpson to Joseph Simpson 18 acres in the 12th District. 6 Dec 1848. (Pp. 371-372)

B. F. Odom to Jehu M. Odom and William Patrick 460 acres, it being his interest in one share as one of the children of James Odom deceased. 4 Jan 1848. (Pp. 373-374)

G. B. Mears to William Stone, Sr. his interest to take effect after the death of Mary Ford who has a life estate in 100 acres in the 6th District. 11 Dec 1848. (Pp. 374-375)

John M. Odom and William C. Patrick agree to a deed oa partition of 460 acres which the derived by descent from James Odom. 12 Oct 1848. (Pp. 376-377)

William A. Knox to Albert Fagan 131 acres on Crawley's Fork of Stone's River. 18 Dec 1848. (Pp. 377-378)

Valentine Simpson to Jesse Millikin ten acres in the 12th District. 6 Dec 1848. (Pp. 379-380)

Wiley Rackley to George Ashford 55 acres on Canal Creek, it being the place where said Rackley now lives. 17 Jan 1844. (Pp. 380-381)

Samuel C. Evans to George Ashford 50 acres in the 6th District. 6 Dec 1848. (Pp. 381-382)

Robert W. Brandon to Arthur Warren 65 acres in the 12th District. 9 Nov 1848. (Pp. 382-383)

Peyton Sheppard and wife Mary to A. F. McFerrin 50 acres in the 4th District. 26 Dec 1848. (Pp. 383-385)

Henry Maney to John McIver 484 acres. 26 Sep 1846. (Pp. 385-386)

Benjamin Bates of Warren County to William Bates 5000 acres on Dry Creek of Smith's Fork. 28 Jan 1840. (Pp. 386-388)

Henry Lance and C. C. Gunter to John Nokes 150 acres on the head waters of the East Fork of Stone's River. 6 Oct 1846. (Pp. 388-389)

William Elkins to Jacob Adcock 100 acres in the 7th District. 11 Nov 1848. (Pp. 389-391)

William C. Parish to Isaac M. Gowen a trust deed. 5 Jan 1849. (P. 391)

James Cawthron to John Nelson 32 acres on Brawley's Fork of Stone's River. 26 May 1846. (Pp. 392-393)

Elizabeth R. Taylor for love and affection to her mother, Ann M. Wharton, a negro woman named Elvira, about 15. 9 Jan 1849. (P. 393)

John Melton to Squire Warren seven and one fourth acres in the 7th District. 21 Dec 1848. (Pp. 393-396)

William W. McKnight to Oswin Alexander a title bond. 11 Jan 1849. (Pp. 397-398)

R. W. Brandon to John H. Wood three boy slaves, one by the name of Philip, about 14; one by the name of Squire, 10; and one by the name of James, about 3, for $682. 19 Jan 1849. (Pp. 398-399)

Robert W. Brandon to A. M. Weeden 152 acres in the 2nd District. 18 Jan 1849. (Pp. 399-400)

Albert G. Millikin to John McClain a trust deed. 25 Dec 1848. (Pp. 401-404)

Benjamin Pendleton to John R. Sullivan a trust deed. 3 Feb 1849. (Pp. 404-405)

Samuel Gunter to J. S. Keith a negro girl named Fanny, 9, for $350. 3 Feb 1849. (Pp. 405-406)

Samuel Gunter to Stith Hays 122½ acres in the 6th District. 5 Feb 1849. (Pp. 406-407)

Epaproditus Francis to T. T. Johnson a trust deed. 6 Feb 1849. (Pp. 407-408)

Epaproditus Francis to M. Francis a trust deed. 6 Feb 1849. (Pp. 408-409)

George Ashford to Ira Hollandsworth 300 acres in the 10th District. 13 Oct 1848. (Pp. 409-410)

Robertson L. Fagan to A. F. and B. L. McFerrin a negro boy named Alford of yellow complexion now in his 12th year, and a negro girl named Eliza of yellow complexion now in her 12th year. 12 Feb 1849. (Pp. 410-411)

David M. Jarratt to S. H. A. McKnight two negroes, Jim, about 73, and his wife Celia, about 60. 14 Feb 1849. (P. 411)

Leonard Lamberson to William Blair a negro man of a black color named Jim, 40 or 41. 8 Dec 1840. (Pp. 412-413)

Samuel Gunter to William Blair a negro girl named Cloe. 7 Jun 1838. (P. 413)

Thomas Nokes and Archebald Stone to David M. Jarratt a title bond. 28 Jan 1846. (Pp. 413-414)

Thomas B. Sanford and Elizabeth R. Taylor, widow, enter into a marriage contract. 14 Feb 1849. (Pp. 414-416)

Joseph Melton to William Melton a trust deed. 15 Feb 1849. (Pp. 416-418)

John W. Bryant to Alexander S. Moore a title bond. 5 Feb 1849. (Pp. 418-419)

Michael Bickel to Jacob M. Keykendoll 150 acres on Barren Fork of Collins River. 11 Nov 1845. (Pp. 419-420)

Azariah Gaither and wife Elizabeth, Albert G. Millikin and wife Sarah to Bozel Gaither their interest in a tract of land in the 3rd District that Brice Gaither purchased from Prior Bralley and died seized and possessed of. 5 Jul 1847. (Pp. 420-421)

Bozel Gaither, Robertson L. Fagan and wife Sintha to Isaac B. Young 145 acres in the 3rd District. 22 Aug 1848. (Pp. 422-423)

Henry Trott to Eldridge H. Campbell 184½ acres in the 5th District. 1 Dec 1846. (Pp. 423-424)

William Travis to Henderson Campbell 50 acres on the Barren Fork of Collins River. 11 Dec 1847. (Pp. 424-425)

William Ferrell to John F. Weedon his interest in the following negroes, to wit, John and Frances. The said negroes were willed to Mary Jane Weedon by James Taylor deceased. 23 Feb 1849. (Pp. 425-426)

John F. Weedon relinquishes his interest in the following negroes, to wit, Julia and Henry to William Ferrell. The said negroes were willed by Mary Jane Weedon by James Taylor. 23 Feb 1849. (P. 426)

John Espey to Amos Gaither 30 acres in the 4th District. 15 Dec 1845. (Pp. 427-428)

Richard Hancock to Christopher C. Hancock a man slave named Spencer, age 21. 7 Jan 1849. (P. 428)

John Petty to Amos Gaither 75 acres in the 4th District. 15 Jan 1849. (Pp. 428-429)

D. F. Weedon to Henry Hays a negro boy named Claborn, about 19. 9 Nov 1848. (Pp. 429-430)

Eli Bailey to John R. Sullivan, R. Fowler, and others a mortgage. 7 Feb 1849. (Pp. 430-431)

Thomas J. Williams to James Williams and John McClain a trust deed. 17 Feb 1849. (Pp. 431-432)

Archebald Stone to C. M. Miller of Rutherford County a negro boy named Sam of a yellow complexion, aged 15 years and 2 months. 26 Apr 1850. (P. 433)

John Melton to his son, John D. Melton, for love and affection 126 acres which is his seven ninth's interest in the dowery tract whereon Mary Melton, the widow of Ancil Melton, now lives. Six of said interests were purchased from the other heirs and one by hership. 5 Mar 1849. (Pp. 1-3)

Nathan M. Taylor to R. Fowler lot #2 in the town of Woodbury. 2 Mar 1849. (Pp. 3-4)

Annual Rains to Amos Gaither 25 acres in the 4th District. 15 Jan 1849. (Pp. 5-6)

Evan Eddings to Lewis Hollis a trust deed. 24 Feb 1849. (Pp. 6-7)

Joseph Ramsey to Daniel Tenpenny a mulatto girl named Fanny and her child, John. Fanny is about 17 years of age and John is about 18 months. 13 Jun 1848. (Pp. 7-8)

Henry Maney to John Woods a negro man named Alfred of a copper color, about 33, for $500. 31 Jan 1849. (Pp. 8-9)

William M. Hooker to George H. Keaton 100 acres in the 11th District. 9 Mar 1849. (Pp. 9-10)

John Leiper to John McIver 164 acres. 19 Oct 1847. (Pp. 10-13)

Edmund Davenport to Joseph Bryson, Sr. 40 acres in the 11th District. 7 Oct 1844. (Pp. 13-14)

William Bond to R. J. Bond a trust deed. 3 Mar 1849. (Pp. 14-15)

Jesse B. Robinson, son of Hugh Robinson, to William Carson 100 acres on Carson Fork of Stone's River. 19 Aug 1837. (Pp. 16-18)

James Saunders of Sumner County to Thomas Bragg of Rutherford County 82 acres in Rutherford County on Lock's Creek. 21 Aug 1833. (Pp. 18-20)

Jacob Adcock to Calvin Curlee a negro boy named David, about 11. 30 Apr 1847. (P. 20)

Jacob Adcock to William Blair a negro boy named Isaac. 12 Mar 1849. (Pp. 20-21)

The widow and heirs of Wiley H. Robinson. Ex Parte. One of the heirs is Jesse B. Robinson. 19 Mar 1849. (Pp. 21-22)

William Elkins to Thomas Elkins 25 acres in the 7th District. 29 Jun 1847. (Pp. 22-24)

John S. Young to John McIver of Rutherford County 500 acres. 27 Feb 1846. (Pp. 24-25)

William G. McCullough to Joseph Horn 25 acres in the 12th District. 1 Feb 1849. (Pp. 25-26)

John McClain to Everett Haynes 110 acres in the 4th District. 24 Mar 1849. (Pp. 27-28)

DEED BOOK G

William Crane and wife Mary A., formerly Mary A. Alexander, to John A. George a quit claim to 275 acres, it being their interest in the estate of Charles P. Alexander. Said land descended to the said Mary A. by descent from the Estate of her deceased father, Charles P. Alexander, he having died intestate and leaving fourteen children. 27 Mar 1847. (Pp. 28-30)

Circuit Court decree. Lewis Jetton and C. J. Martin, Administrators of Levi Parker, to R. Fowler, guardian of the heirs of the said deceased. Mentions the dower of Sarah Parker. See Circuit Court Book K, page 483. 10 Mar 1849. (Pp. 30-31)

Isaac M. Elledge, William F. Elledge, Joseph L. Elledge, James Melton and wife Polly, James H. Stone and wife Susan, John B. Paris and wife Jane, Samuel Vance and wife Sarah, heirs of Joseph Elledge, 70 acres. Bounded: Joseph L. Elledge and Samuel Vance. 6 Feb 1844. (Pp. 31-35)

Ira Hollandsworth to John Hollandsworth, Sr. ten acres in the 10th District. 5 Mar 1849. (Pp. 36-37)

Hugh Ledbetter to John Hollandsworth 47 acres in the 10th District. 5 Mar 1849. (Pp. 37-38)

John McIver to Charles L. Nelson 500 acres, Said Nelson is a resident of Rutherford County. 22 Mar 1849. (Pp. 38-41)

Milton E. Watts to Joseph A. Dement 86 acres in the 1st District. 31 Jan 1849. (Pp.41-43)

Moses McKnight to Samuel H. McKnight 100 acres in the 1st District for $300. 1 Feb 1844. (Pp. 43-44)

Joseph Ramsey to Jesse and Benjamin Brewer a negro boy named Edmund, about 9, of a yellow complexion. 12 Jun 1848. (P. 44)

Thomas Leech for the love and affection I have for my child, Thomas K. Leech, a negro boy named Henry, about 9. 15 Jan 1848. (P. 45)

George Gannon to Benjamin Sapp 45 acres in the 2nd District. 10 Mar 1849. (Pp. 45-46)

Asa Smith to William Barton a negro man named Luke, about 30. 12 Feb 1849. (P. 47)

Gabriel Hume to John Ward 86½ acres in the 6th District. 10 Feb 1849. (Pp. 48-49)

John W. Mullins to A. D. Fugett a trust deed. 20 Apr 1849. (Pp. 49-51)

William Todd to Martha Norris 30 acres in the 4th District. 5 Apr 1849. (Pp. 51-52)

John Young to Joseph Bailey 65 acres in the 7th District on the head waters of the east fork of Stone's River. 21 Apr 1849. (Pp. 52-53)

Nathan L. Norris to William Todd 30 acres. 5 Apr 1849. (Pp. 53-54)

James Cawthon and Jonathan Smith to John Nelson 100 acres on Brawley's Fork of Stone's River. 10 Jan 1844. (Pp. 55-56)

Benjamin Bowman to Alexander Nesbit 90 acres belonging to the estate of Daniel Bowman, the said Benjamin being the Executor. 3 Feb 1846. (Pp. 56-58)

Sarah McEwen to John Barrett 45 acres in the 1st District. 30 Mar 1849. (Pp. 58-59)

Peter Adams to Josiah Fuston a tract of land in the 10th District. 21 Feb 1849. (Pp. 60-61)

James W. Tenpenny to Benjamin Fugett 62 acres in the 6th District. 31 Jan 1849. (Pp. 61-62)

Thomas Wammack to Josiah Fuston 50 acres in the 10th District. 27 Feb 1849. (Pp. 62-63)

Westley Harriman to A. D. Fugett a trust deed. 24 Feb 1849. (Pp. 63-64)

John W. Mullins to John Davis 15 acres in the 7th District. 4 Nov 1848. (Pp. 65-66)

F. D. Wrather to J. L. Fare a boy slave named Josephus and a woman slave named Ann as a trust deed. 21 Apr 1844. (Pp. 66-67)

John W. Mullins to George Ashford a title bond. 24 Mar 1844. (Pp. 67-68)

Martha Walls to William Preston his interest in the estate of Edmond Walls (who was my father). 20 Apr 1849. (Pp. 68-69)

James Connelly and wife Caroline to William Preston their interest in the estate of Edmond Walls. 30 Apr 1844. (Pp. 69-70)

Eli Preston and wife Mary to William Preston their interest in the estate of Edmond Walls who was the father of the said Mary. 28 Apr 1849. (Pp. 70-71)

Lemuel J. Duncan to Caleb Cox 25 acres in the 2nd District. 5 Jun 1848. (Pp. 72-73)

John B. Stone to John R. Sullivan a trust deed. 26 Mar 1849. (Pp. 73-74)

Allen Wilson of Wilson County to Hugh Ledbetter 25 acres in the 10th District. 16 Nov 1846. (Pp. 74-76)

Caleb B. Davis to George W. Thompson all his library of books as a trust deed. 3 May 1849. (Pp. 76-77)

William R. Akers to James W. Byrns 87½ acres in the 1st District. 15 Jan 1849. (Pp. 77-79)

Vincent Bailey to John K. Rigsby and William T. Rigsby 81 acres in the 6th District. 27 Nov 1848. (Pp. 79-80)

John McClain to Bozzell Gaither 160 acres in the 4th District.

12 Jan 1849. (Pp. 80-82)

Luke Lasater to Joseph Knox, Sr. 100 acres on Brawley's Fork of Stone's River. 3 May 1849. (Pp. 82-83)

Absolom Bowen to James B. Hollis ten acres on Brawley's Fork of Stone's River. 20 Apr 1841. (Pp. 83-84)

Albert T. Fagan to William A. Knox 100 acres in the 12th District. 24 Apr 1848. (Pp. 85-88)

Joseph Knox to William A. Knox 65 acres for $395. 3 May 1849. (Pp. 88-90)

William A. Knox to John F. Curlee 65 acres on Brawley's Fork of Stone's River. 3 May 1849. (Pp. 90-91)

Josiah Spurlock to Henry Dennis 47 acres on the Clear Fork of Stone's River. Said Spurlock is a resident of Smith County. 20 Oct 1823. (Pp. 91-93)

William F. Mears to Upha Edwards and Alfred Edwards 75 acres in the 6th District. 11 Nov 1848. (Pp. 93-94)

John N. Bailey to Thomas D. Summers a girl slave named Mary, 10. 1 Sep 1848. (Pp. 94-95)

John W. Stone to Abel McBroom a negro girl named Juda, 17, for $550. 18 May 1849. (P. 95)

Isaac A. Keaton to Richard Hancock 52 acres in the 10th District. 17 May 1849. (Pp. 96-97)

Pleasant Libby and wife Elizabeth of Lynchburg, Virginia to John C. Martin a tract of land in Cannon County. 15 Mar 1849. (Pp. 97-100)

Thomas Tedder and wife Rhoda, formerly Sauls, to A. D. Alexander their interest in 68½ acres which John K. Sauls died seized and possessed of. 29 May 1849. (Pp. 100-101)

Elizabeth Carnahan, John Carnahan, M. A. England and wife Jane, formerly Carnahan, James Carnahan, T. E. England and wife Mary, formerly Carnahan, Jacob Baughman and wife Nancy, formerly Carnahan, John Vance and wife Elizabeth, formerly Carnahan, and Hiram Carnahan to Elijah Athey 50 acres. 17 Jan 1846. (PP. 101-102)

Solomon Spicer to William McFerrin a trust deed. 6 Jun 1849. (Pp. 103-104)

Eli Barrett to John Barrett a trust deed. 14 May 1849. (Pp. 105-106)

John Fisher to Samuel Vance a trust deed. 28 May 1849. (Pp. 106-108)

John Finley to Dawson McGlockin ten acres on the east fork of Stone's River. 5 Feb 1839. (Pp. 108-109)

James T. Henderson to James A. Taylor a negro man named Allen, about 25. 1 Jan 1849. (Pp. 109-110)

John H. Wood to Robert W. Brandon three negroes, to wit, Phillis, Oceola, and James. 19 Jan 1849. (Pp. 111-112)

Robert W. Brandon to William Barton three negroes, to wit, Phillis, about 15; Oceola, about 12; and James, about 4. 13 Jun 1849. (Pp. 112-113)

A. J. Wood to Joseph H. Bogle a woman slave named Mariah, 19. 22 Jun 1849. (P. 113)

Pleasant Cawthon to John Robinson 15 acres in Coffee County. 7 Oct 1848. Witness: James McCullough. 7 Oct 1848. (P. 113)

James W. Hamilton to A. M. Weedon the tract of land where the said Weedon now lives. Said Hamilton is a resident of Davidson County. 7 Feb 1849. (Pp. 123-124) (The pages are misnumbered)

William Scurlock to Robert M. Jones 30 acres on Sink Creek. 2 Mar 1848. (Pp. 124-127)

John W. Mullins to Bazel Ashford a title bond. 20 Sep 1848. (Pp. 127-128)

James J. Trott to John Fisher lot #2 in the town of Woodbury. Bounded: on the east by the Female Academy lot. 16 Jan 1847. (Pp. 128-129)

William C. Miller to Isaac M. Gowen a title bond. 10 Mar 1849. (Pp. 129-130)

Franklin Coleman to William C. Miller town lot #30 in the town of Woodbury. 28 Feb 1849. (Pp. 130-131)

James A. Vinson to James W. Tenpenny his interest in 42 acres in the 6th District, it being a part of the lands that Richard Vinson died seized and possessed of. 12 May 1849. (Pp. 132-133)

Daniel S. Ford to Abram Hathaway 20 acres on the Clear Fork. 16 Mar 1849. (Pp. 133-135)

James Sisson to William Gooding a tract of land on Carson's Fork of Stone's River. Bounded: Martha Gooding and Jesse Sisson. 12 Oct 1849. (Pp. 135-136)

Samuel Vance, Administrator of Richard Vinson, to William West 273 acres. 2 Jul 1849. (Pp. 136-138)

Henry Moffet to Richard C. Price a trust deed. 2 Jul 1849. (Pp. 138-139)

S. B. Spurlock to A. J. Wood a negro woman named Minta, about 32 or 33, and her two children, Margaret, about 3, and Reuben, about 7 or 8 months. 9 Jul 1849. (P. 140)

State of Tennessee Grant #537. 74½ acres to John Farley. 9 Jan 1830. (Pp. 141-142)

Jesse B. Robinson to James McGill a title bond. 14 Dec 1849. (Pp. 142-143)

James McGill to William McGill 74 acres in the 4th District. 28 Mar 1848. (Pp. 143-144)

J. C. Martin to Daniel F. Weedon 20 acres in the 1st District. 2 Jul 1849. (Pp. 144-145)

Huldy Sandridge to her daughter Caroline Sandridge a deed of gift of 1200 acres. Bounded: Dabney Sandridge. 23 Jul 1849. (Pp. 146-147)

Isaiah Parker of Coffee County to John Finley 100 acres on Carson's Fork of Stone's River in the 4th District. 8 Nov 1847. (Pp. 147-149)

Q. A. Capps to Richard Holt and Joseph Holt 65 acres in the 12th District. 19 Dec 1846. (Pp. 149-151)

Richard C. Price to A. F. and B. L. McFerrin 100 acres in the 5th District. 14 Aug 1849. (Pp. 151-152)

Isaac B. Young to James Cook and John W. Cook 145 acres in the 3rd District. 13 Aug 1849. (Pp. 153-154)

Richard C. Price to John Mitchel 200 acres in the 5th District. 21 Jul 1848. (Pp. 154-155)

Robert Bailey to Lewis Stair 18½ acres on the east fork of Stone's River. 13 Feb 1837. (Pp. 155-158)

John H. T. Bell to William S. Bell a trust deed. 12 Jul 1849. (Pp. 158-159)

R. A. Smith to Jacob Wright a tract of land. 12 Jun 1848. (Pp. 160-161)

Thomas Bowen to John H. Wood 50 acres in the 3rd District. 7 Sep 1849. (Pp. 162-163)

Albert G. Millikin to John W. Millikin a trust deed. 12 Sep 1849. (Pp. 163-165)

Daniel Manus to John R. Sullivan and F. D. Wrather 150 acres in the 8th District. 12 Sep 1849. (Pp. 165-166)

Robert Marshall to William Bogle 80½ acres in the 11th District. 29 Jul 1849. (Pp. 166-167)

Augustine M. Weedon to Joshua Barton 26 acres. 14 Sep 1849. (P. 168)

Articles of agreement between Lewis Stair and M. G. Elkins. 6 Mar 1849. (Pp. 169-170)

Joseph Ramsey to A. M. Weedon 210 acres in the 3rd District. 7 Sep 1849. (Pp. 170-172)

Hugh Ledbetter to William Morris 70 acres in the 10th District. 12 Oct 1848. (PP. 172-173)

William Morris to Cullen E. Jacobs 200 acres on Wilmouth Creek. 13 Sep 1849. (Pp. 173-175)

Alexander Orr to E. A. Orr 15 acres. 10 Jan 1849. (Pp.

175-176)

Alexander Orr to Eleazar A. Orr two acres on the east fork of Stone's River. 19 Jun 1848. (Pp. 177-178)

Martin S. Hoover to John Williams 48 acres on Brawley's Fork of the east fork of Stone's River. 11 Aug 1847. (Pp. 179-180)

Alexander Young to Joseph Ramsey 32 acres in the 6th District. 13 Jun 1849. (Pp. 180-181)

Jesse B. Robertson to Martin S. Hoover 66½ acres in the 12th District. 9 Mar 1849. (Pp. 181-183)

Abel McBroom and Henry D. McBroom to Archebald Stone 50 acres in the 6th District. 4 Jan 1849. (Pp. 183-184)

Thomas Wammack to Peter Adams 50 acres in the 10th District. 27 Feb 1849. (Pp. 184-185)

Edmond McCahill to Gabriel Hume and others 2800 acres. 4 Jul 1838. (Pp. 185-188)

Stephen Banks to Lot Banks of Coffee County a trust deed. 25 Oct 1849. (Pp. 188-190)

William McAdow to his son, James B. McAdow, 70 acres on the south bank of Hill's Creek. 6 Oct 1849. (Pp. 190-191)

William McAdow to his son, John A. McAdow, a negro man named Peter, about 80; a black woman named Mariah, 35; a woman named Matilda, 33; one named Anderson; a girl named Adney, known by the name of Puss, 10; a boy named Bob, about 18 months. 6 Oct 1849. (Pp. 191-192)

William McAdow to his son, John A. McAdow, 191 acres in the 6th District. 6 Oct 1849. (Pp. 192-194)

State of Tennessee Grant #5012. 5000 acres to William Cummings. 9 Jan 1830. (Pp. 194-197)

F. D. Wrather to William Cummings a negro girl named Lucinda, about 14, for $425. 12 Oct 1849. (P. 197)

Farman D. Wrather to A. C. Beech two negro slaves, to wit, a girl named Ibby and a boy named Lewis. 11 Oct 1849. (P. 198)

William H. Couch to John Tubb ten acres in the 5th District. 9 Nov 1844. (Pp. 198-200)

John A. McAdow to Eliza Ann Pendleton, wife of Benjamin Pendleton 65 to 80 acres in the 6th District for the love and affection that the said McAdow has for his sister, the said Eliza Ann Pendleton. 23 Oct 1849. (Pp. 200-201)

F. D. Wrather to David M. Jarratt a negro boy named Isaac, about 8, for $375. 12 Oct 1849. (Pp. 201-203)

William McAdow to his son, William S. McAdow, the following slaves, to wit, Rody, about 7, and a boy named Sandy, about 5. 5 Nov 1849. (P. 203)

William S. McAdow to Zebelon Brevard a trust deed. 5 Nov 1849. (Pp. 204-205)

R. H. Rogers to E. A. Orr 100 acres. 28 Mar 1849. (Pp. 205-206)

Gabriel Lance to Moses H. Cummins 60 acres on the East Fork of Stone's River. 19 Nov 1849. (Pp. 207-208)

Eli Bailey to John S. Brien a mortgage. 17 Nov 1849. (Pp. 208-211)

Richard Hancock and Lewis Hancock to the School Commissioners of the 10th District a tract of land on the east side of the Sycamore Fork, containing one acre. 1 Aug 1848. (Pp. 211-213)

Samuel Spears to John Blanton 50 acres in the 9th District. 17 Nov 1849. (Pp. 213-214)

Benjamin Whitfield and wife Elizabeth of Izard County, Arkansas to Mathew Whitfield of Cannon County their power of attorney to receive their share of the estate of Whitmale Herrell. 12 Oct 1849. (Pp. 215-216)

John Melton, Executor oa Ancil Melton, to James Melton 74 acres. 15 Dec 1845. (Pp. 217-219)

James Melton to George G. Melton 113 acres in the 7th District. 5 Dec 1849. (Pp. 219-221)

Leven Jones to Simeon Hollis a trust deed. 4 Dec 1849. (Pp. 222-224)

Richard Arnold to John Robinson a tract of land in the 12th District. 26 Feb 1849. (Pp. 225-226)

Archebald Stone to James T. Henderson 50 acres in the 6th District. 8 Oct 1849. (Pp. 226-227)

A. F. McFerrin and B. L. McFerrin to Samuel Grear 50 acres in the 3rd District. 11 Jan 1848. (Pp. 227-229)

Ezekiel Mullins and others to John Ward 64 acres in the 6th District. 26 Nov 1849. (Pp. 229-230)

William Willis to Hugh R. Cawthon a tract of land in the 12th District on Brawley's Fork of the East Fork of Stone's River. Mentions the partition of land between the said William Willis and Mary Willis. The one acre on which the Meeting House stands is excluded. 27 Nov 1849. (Pp. 231-232)

David Patton of Rutherford County to Silas A. Robinson of the same place six acres on Carson's Fork of the East Fork of Stone's River. 5 Feb 1833. (Pp. 233-234)

Joseph R. Dickson to John F. Patton 104 acres in the 11th District. 1 Oct 1847. (Pp. (Pp. 234-235)

William Willis to Robert W. Woodruff 309 acres which I have at the time of the death of my mother Temperance Woodruff. 18 Dec 1849. (Pp. 235-237)

C. B. Davis to Abraham Burger a trust deed. 25 Sep 1849. (Pp. 237-239)

William D. Gowen to John Hays 44 acres on the East Fork of Stone's River. 8 Dec 1849. (Pp. 239-240)

Abram Creson to James Creson 100 acres on the south side of the East Fork of Stone's River. 8 Oct 1849. (Pp. 241-243)

William Stroud, Sr. for love and affection to his daughter Jane H. Oliver 30 acres in the 4th District. John W. Stroud is to hold the land is trust. 13 Jun 1848. (Pp. 243-244)

Franklin Coleman to Wrather and Hall a town lot as a trust deed. 11 Dec 1849. (Pp. 245-246)

Frances Bryson to Iverson J. Thomas her dower of 40 acres in the 11th District. 7 Nov 1849. (Pp. 246-247)

Iverson J. Thomas to Robert W. Landsdon 40 acres in the 11th District. 19 Dec 1849. (Pp. 247-248)

William Stroud, Sr. to William D. Stroud 100 acres on Burger's Creek. 27 Mar 1848. (Pp. 248-250)

William D. Stroud to James Petty a trust deed. 15 Dec 1849. (Pp. 251-252)

A. F. McFerrin to Isaac Young 152 acres in the 4th District. 21 Mar 1846. (Pp. 252-255)

Isaac Young to his daughter Elizabeth Todd several tracts of land in the 4th District. The land is not to be under the control of her husband James Todd, Jr., but instead under the control of Isaab B. Young as trustee. 9 Oct 1849. (Pp. 255-257)

Andrew English to Joseph Hollis 80 acres on Bralley's Fork of the east fork of Stone's River. 6 Nov 1830. (Pp. 257-259)

Archebald Hicks to James B. Elledge 22 acres in the 9th District. 20 Sep 1849. (Pp. 259-260)

Elisha B. Rose to Samuel Grear 100 acres in the 4th District. 8 Oct 1849. (Pp. 261-262)

Benjamin Pendleton to M. C. Cummins a trust deed. 28 Nov 1849. (Pp. 262-263)

William Young to John H. Young 96 acres in the 2nd District. 3 Sep 1849. (Pp. 263-264)

John L. Taylor to Thomas B. Brevard a trust deed. 14 Dec 1849. (Pp. 265-266)

Albert G. Millikin to Isaac W. Elledge and Azariah Gaither his interest in the Hugh Porter place as a trust deed. 16 Jan 1850. (Pp. 266-269)

Bazzel Gaither to John McClain 160 acres in the 4th District. 28 Sep 1849. (Pp. 269-270)

David Patton for love and affection to Nancy Patton and her bodily heirs by John Patton some personal property. 26 Sep 1849. (Pp. 270-271)

Thomas Wamack to Peter Adams 50 acres in the 10th District. 10 Feb 1849. (Pp. 272-273)

Jesse Sisson to Andrew English three acres in the 4th District. 31 Jul 1848. (Pp. 273-274)

William C. Donnell to Hugh B. Lansden 130 acres. 13 Mar 1849. (Pp. 274-276)

William Wood to Lewis Starr 138 acres on the East Fork of Stone's River. 5 Mar 1839. (Pp. 276-278)

Edmund Walls and Willis F. Couch enter into an agreement. 10 Nov 1845. (Pp. 278-279)

Dudley Graham to S. J. Goodlow a man slave named Savery. 28 Jan 1850. (Pp. 279-280)

W. M. Bragg to Dozier Bragg 66 acres in the 1st District. 6 Nov 1849. (Pp. 280-281)

Samuel Denby to William W. Prim and the other trustees of the Campground of the Methodist Church one acre in the 9th District. 28 Apr 1848. (Pp. 281-283)

William Bogle to William H. Cox 100 acres in the 11th District. 28 Dec 1849. (Pp. 283-284)

Pleasant Cawthon to Redman Bynum 54 acres in the 12th District. 12 Feb 1848. (Pp. 284-286)

Jesse Gilly to James H. Whittemore 99 acres on Brawley's Fork of Stone's River. 15 Dec 1847. (Pp. 286-287)

Jesse Gilly to Simeon Gilly 99 acres on Brawley's Fork of Stone's River. 15 Dec 1847. (Pp. 287-288)

Jesse Gilly to James L. Cawthon 12 acres on Brawley's Fork of Stone's River. 25 Nov 1848. (Pp. 289-290)

F. D. Wrather to David M. Jarratt two negroes, to wit, Jinny, about 40, and her child Layett, about 5. 8 Jan 1850. (Pp. 290-291)

John C. Martin to John R. Sullivan a woman slave named Rhoda. 8 Jan 1850. (Pp. 291-292)

Dabney Ewell of Coffee County to Pleasant Cawthon a quit claim to a tract of land on Brawley's Fork of Stone's River. 2 Feb 1848. (Pp. 292-293)

Jesse B. Robinson, Silas A. Robinson, Hannah McCasline, George W. Sadler and wife Euphania, Robert Gordin and wife Levina to Pleasant Cawthon their one seventh interest in a tract of land in the 12th District. 29 Dec 1848. (Pp. 293-296)

Samuel J. Goodloe of Rutherford County to Dudley J. Graham a title bond. 4 Feb 1850. (P. 296)

Dudley J. Graham to A. M. Weedon a man slave named Save. I warrant the said slave to be sound, healthy, sensible, and a slave for life. 4 Feb 1850. (P. 297)

Dudley J. Graham to Samuel J. Goodloe a boy slave. 4 Feb 1850. (P. 298)

Thomas Sisson to Peter J. Thomas 111 acres on Carson's Fork of the East Fork of Stone's River. 31 Jan 1848. (Pp. 298-300)

H. D. McBroom and Benjamin Sapp to William Wood 50 acres in the 9th District. 27 Mar 1841. (Pp. 300-301)

Thurston Daniel to Jonathan Wherry 111 acres in the 1st District. 16 Oct 1849. (Pp. 301-303)

William Preston to John F. Preston 120 acres in the 6th District. 7 Feb 1850. (Pp. 303-304)

Micajah Petty to William C. Woodall 18 acres on Horse Springs Fork. 17 Feb 1849. (Pp. 304-306)

Jesse Sisson to Frances Spry 100 acres in the 5th District. 12 Feb 1850. (Pp. 306-307)

Joseph Ramsey to Britton W. Snipes 56 acres in the 2nd District. 1850. (Pp. 307-308)

Aaron Byford to B. B. Dickens 54 acres. 15 Jan 1850. (Pp. 309-311)

Joel Maney to James B. Hollis 141 acres in Rutherford County. 26 Feb 1848. (Pp. 311-312)

Richard M. Lemay to Mitchell Daniel 100 acres on Barren Fork of Collins River. 3 Nov 1849. (Pp. 312-314)

F. D. Wrather to J. S. Fare a trust deed. 15 Feb 1850. (Pp. 314-317)

William Preston to Benjamin Fugett a trust deed. 21 Jan 1852. (Pp. 318-319)

State of Tennessee Grant #20079. 66 acres to Micajah Petty. 9 Jan 1850. (Pp. 319-320)

William Parton to to Aaron V. Parton 230 acres in the 8th District. 29 Dec 1849. (Pp. 320-322)

R. A. Smith to Larkin Keaton 1543 acres. 13 Jan 1849. (Pp. 322-323)

Henry Enos to William Parton 500 acres in the 8th District. 10 Feb 1849. (Pp. 324-325)

George T. Ford to Jesse Lawrence 18 acres in the 7th District. 14 Feb 1850. (Pp. 325-326)

Nathan J. Norris and wife Martha to Andrew C. Dubois 30 acres in the 4th District. 20 Jul 1849. (Pp. 326-328)

Erasmus Kees to J. and B. Brien a town lot in the town of Woodbury. Bounded: Elizabeth R. Sanford. 13 Feb 1850. (Pp. 328-329)

Sampson Stephens to Stanford Smith 30 acres. 31 Dec 1849. (Pp. 329-331)

Joseph A. Gooding to Oliver C. Duncan 50 acres. 6 Mar 1847. (Pp. 331-332)

George W. Young of Lawnes County, Alabama to Isaac Young three acres on the Barren Fork of Collins River. 24 Oct 1847. (Pp. 332-334)

Joseph Ramsey to Abraham Burger 31 acres. 13 Feb 1850. (Pp. 334-335)

Abner S. Leech to William C. Leech 60 acres in the 11th District. 16 Feb 1850. (Pp. 335-336)

Samuel J. Goodloe to A. M. Weedon a negro boy named Grant for $600. 16 Feb 1850. (Pp. 336-337)

F. D. Wrather to J. L. Fare a trust deed. 18 Feb 1850. (Pp. 337-338)

William Preston to Hiram Y. Little a title bond. 25 Apr 1846. (Pp. 339-340)

William C. Woodall to William D. Stroud a trust deed. 16 Feb 1850. (Pp. 340-342)

R. A. Smith, Sheriff, to A. F. McFerrin a bill of sale. 11 Feb 1850. (Pp. 342-344)

James T. Henderson to Nathaniel M. Taylor 169 acres in the 6th District. 18 Feb 1850. (Pp. 344-346)

James Landers, Administrator of Abraham Trigg, late of Sumner County, to Patsy Gannon, Joseph Whitely and wife Betsy, William Young and wife Ufa, and Patsy Gannon, being the only lawful heirs of the late Mark Gannon a tract of land in Warren County sold by Alexander Trigg in his life time to James Taylor. 20 Feb 1830. (Pp. 346-348)

William Preston to John F. Preston 80 acres in the 6th District. 20 Feb 1850. (Pp. 348-349)

C. B. Davis to James Wood a trust deed. 22 Feb 1850. (Pp. 349-351)

J. L. Fare to Stephen Jourdan four negroes, to wit, Ann, about 18; Se), about 17; Josephus, about 14; and Rebecca, about 15. 19 Feb 1850. (Pp. 351-352)

Allen Miles and wife Delila to Wilford Literell 82 acres. 23 Feb 1850. (Pp. 352-355)

Nathaniel M. Taylor to Washington Kennedy 27½ acres in the 6th District. 25 Feb 1850. (Pp. 355-356)

Washington Kennedy to N. M. Taylor 82 acres in the 6th District. 25 Feb 1850. (Pp. 356-358)

M. C. Alexander, by descent from Charles P. Alexander, to J. A. George a tract of land in the 2nd District. 4 Mar 1850. (Pp. 358-359)

J. L. Fare to James M. Roberts four negroes, to wit, Ann, Rebecca, Sipes, and Josephus. 19 Feb 1850. (Pp. 359-360)

Joseph Bryson, Sr. to Joseph Bryson, Jr. a negro girl named Mary, 11, and of a black complexion for $400. 26 Feb 1850. (Pp. 360-361)

Benjamin H. F. Philips to Alexander Bryant ten acres to be held in trust for Susana Bryant. 7 Feb 1841. (Pp. 361-362)

William R. Akers to Richard M. Lemay town lot #38 in the town of Woodbury. 20 Sep 1848. (P. 363)

Andrew Dubois to Elias H. Dubois 30 acres in the 4th District. 28 Feb 1850. (Pp. 364-365)

A. F. McFerrin and B. L. McFerrin to Washington Leigh 82 acres in the 4th District. 18 Feb 1850. (Pp. 365-367)

Cullen E. Jacobs to George Grizzle 200 acres in the 10th District. 11 Mar 1850. (Pp. 368-369)

Elizabeth Summer and P. G. Leech to R. J. Bond 70 acres in the 11th District. 18 Feb 1850. (Pp. 370-371)

Iverson J. Thomas to G. L. W. Herndon 20 acres in the 11th District. 17 Dec 1849. (Pp. 371-372)

G. L. W. Herndon to Joseph Bogle 20 acres in the 11th District. 11 Mar 1850. (Pp. 373-374)

Ephraim, Andrew, and Thomas N. Yourie, Administrators of Joshua Nichols; Joseph Nichols, Elizabeth Jane Nichols, and Mary Elmira Nichols, minor heirs of said Joshua Nichols deceased, petition to sell a tract of land to John P. Hare. 30 Mar 1850. (Pp. 374-375)

Albert G. Millikin to Ransom Jones 200 acres in the 5th District. 13 Mar 1850. (Pp. 376-377)

Annual Rains to James Petty and Samuel Grear a trust deed. 8 Apr 1850. (Pp. 377-379)

David Colwell to William M. Bragg 200 acres in the 1st District. 11 Mar 1850. (Pp. 379-380)

John F. Weedon to Regin Fowler his one half interest in 200 acres in the 6th District. 17 Feb 1846. (Pp. 380-381)

Daniel F. Weeden to Regin Fowler his one half interest in 260 acres in the 6th District. 13 Aug 1845. (Pp. 382-383)

Benjamin Sapp and Larkin W. Hammond to Regin Fowler 106½ acres in the 6th District. 29 Dec 1849. (Pp. 383-385)

William Rea of Rutherford County to Christopher Owen 166 acres on Sanders Fork. 20 Feb 1850. (Pp. 385-386)

Joseph Knox to John W. A. Knox 100 acres in the 3rd District as a deed of gift. 29 Mar 1850. (Pp. 386-388)

F. D. Wrather to John R. Sullivan 150 acres in the 8th District. 12 Dec 1849. (Pp. 388-389)

William Travis to David Travis a title bond. 12 Apr 1850.

John W. Parker to Thomas H. Williams 275 acres on the head waters of Carson's Fork. 15 Apr 1850. (Pp. 390-391)

Thomas H. Williams to Joseph P. Holt a trust deed. 15 Apr 1850. (Pp. 392-393)

John McIver to T. G. Jones 690 acres. 6 Apr 1850. (Pp. 393-394)

Abraham C. Pallett and Agnes Dickens of Jackson County, Missouri to Thomas A. Pallett their power of attorney to receive their share of the estate of their brother James Y. Pallett. 7 Mar 1850. (Pp. 394-396)

Samuel C. Young and wife Nancy of Jackson County, Missouri to Jane Pallett five acres in Cannon County. 4 May 1846. (Pp. 396-398)

Meredith Akers and wife Elizabeth to G. W. A. Pallett their power of attorney to transfer to Jane Pallett, the mother of the said Elizabeth, a tract of land. Said Elizabeth is the sister of James Y. Pallett. Said Akers are residents of Marian County, Alabama. 2 May 1850. (Pp. 398-401)

Jane Pallett, Thomas A. Pallett, Agnes Dickinson, Abram C. Pallett to Meredith Akers, Elizabeth Akers, and Mary Y. Pallett their interest in 60 acres in the 12th District, it being a tract of land conveyed to James Y. Pallett out of a 178½ acre tract belonging to the heirs of Abraham Pallett. 18 Apr 1850. (Pp. 401-403)

Jane Pallett to Meredith Akers, Elizabeth Akers, and Mary Y. Pallett 69 acres in the 12th District, it being land deeded to me by the heirs of Abram Pallett, bearing date 18 Oct 1828. 18 Apr 1850. (Pp. 403-404)

Benjamin Sapp to John B. Paris a title bond. 15 Aug 1849. (Pp. 405-406)

S. J. Odom to B. F. Odom 200 acres in the 11th District on Hurricane Creek. 8 Jan 1850. (Pp. 406-407)

Jane Pallett to Albert G. Millikin five acres on the east side of Bralley's Fork of Stone's River. 19 Apr 1850. (Pp. 408-409)

George Rogers to Alexander Milligan 80 acres. 1845. (Pp. 409-411)

Allen Wilson to Alexander Milligan 118 acres on the waters of Harrican of Sanders Fork of Smith's Fork. 4 May 1838. (Pp. 411-412)

Alexander Milligan to John Milligan 119 acres on the waters of Harrican Fork of Sanders Fork of Smith's Fork. 3 Sep 1845. (Pp. 412-414)

Asa Smith to Manson M. Brien a negro man named Washington. 16 Apr 1850. (Pp. 414-415)

Thomas Barrett to Alexander McBroom a trust deed. 6 May

1850. (Pp. 415-416)

William Stroud to Abraham Baren 150 acres on Horse Spring Fork of Stone's River. 7 Dec 1849. (Pp. 416-418)

Elam McKnight to Abner S. McKnight 125 acres. 3 Feb 1847. (Pp. 418-419)

F. D. Wrather to J. L. Fare a trust deed. 1 May 1850. (Pp. 419-421)

F. D. Wrather to his wife, Elizabeth, a trust deed on some personal property for $300. 16 May 1850. (Pp. 421-422)

T. H. Roughton to James H. Roughton 72 acres in the 12th District. 21 May 1850. (Pp. 422-424)

Daniel F. Weedon and Maria L. Weedon to William Barton five acres in the 1st District. 25 Dec 1848. (Pp. 424-425)

Bazel Gaither to Peter Cox a man slave named Robert, 29. 29 May 1850. (Pp. 425-426)

James Stone to George T. Ford 71 acres in the 7th District. 20 Apr 1849. (Pp. 426-427)

Merritt Givens, Mary Givins, James Sullivan and wife Jane, William Moore and wife Elizabeth, John Warren, John B. Justice, all heirs of Henry Warren, to Arther Warren, Jr. the tract of land in the 2nd District which Henry Warren died seized and possessed of. 30 Nov 1849. (Pp. 428-430)

Joel Brooks and Nancy Grissom enter into an agreement in which the said Nancy is put into possession of a 500 acre tract of land. 6 Jun 1850. (Pp. 430-431)

T. J. Orrand to John Orrand a trust deed. 28 May 1850. (Pp. 432-433)

Allen Wilson to Charles Hancock 39 acres on Herican Creek of Sanders Fork of Smith's Fork. 4 May 1838. (Pp. 433-435)

Albert M. McKnight to Andrew M. McKnight 266 acres. 2 Mar 1850. (PP. 436-439)

Richard C. Price to Warren Cummins a trust deed. 10 Jun 1850. (Pp. 439-442)

David D. Hipp to John M. Banks two acres in the 5th District. 6 Apr 1850. (Pp. 442-443)

John W. Stroud to Micajah Petty one acre in the 4th District. 18 Jun 1850. (Pp. 443-444)

Shadrack Elkins, Susan Elkins, and John Deloach, heirs of Boykin Deloach, to Alexander McBroom 50 acres in the 2nd District. 21 May 1850. (Pp. 444-447)

America Arnold to Newton C. Carnahan his interest in his wife's Share of the estate of James R. Tolbert. 15 Jun 1850. (Does not give the name of the husband of America Arnold). (Pp. 447-448)

Alexander Inglis to Andrew S. Inglis 50 acres in the 4th District. 15 Apr 1850. (Pp. 448-449)

Levin Jones to William Todd 40 acres in the 4th District. 18 Jun 1850. (Pp. 449-451)

Jacob Burger to Jonathan Hendrickson five acres in the 9th District. 6 Oct 1849. (Pp. 451-452)

William Bryson to Francis Bryson, guardian of Locky Bryson, minor heir of Sam'l Bryson, my interest in the negroes belonging to the Estate of said Sam'l Bryson. Said negroes should be sold under a decree of the Circuit Court of Wilson County. 13 Jun 1838. (Pp. 452-453)

Henry Moffitt to Walter Stroud 230 acres in the 5th District. 24 Jun 1850. (Pp. 453-454)

R. H. Mason to Joseph Pinkerton a trust deed. 28 Jun 1850. (Pp. 455-457)

Sheriff R. A. Smith to Earthman and Travis 386 acres known as the property of Moses H. Glasscock. 8 Mar 1850. (Pp. 457-458)

James T. Henderson to Archebald Stone 15 acres in the 6th District. 2 Jun 1850. (Pp. 458-459)

Caleb Cox to Martin Cox 100 acres in the 4th District for $800. 19 Jun 1850. (Pp. 459-461)

Abraham Baren to Martin D. Crook 150 acres on Horse Spring Fork of Stone's River, it being the tract where William D. Stroud now lives. 22 Jul 1850. (Pp. 461-462)

F. D. Wrather to Franklin Coleman the town lot where the said Coleman formerly lived and used one room as a store house. Bounded: north by the public square and east by John R. Sullivan's grocery house. 19 Jul 1850. (PP. 462-463)

William C. Leech, Commissioner of the minor heirs of Curry Green, to David Hogwood a man slave named Harry, about 40, for $600. 18 Jul 1850. (P. 464)

Patton Farler to John Farler 75 acres on the east fork of Stone's River. 27 Jul 1850. (Pp. 464-466)

John R. Sullivan to William F. George a title bond. 23 Jan 1850. (Pp. 466-467)

Mitchel Daniel to Joseph Simpson and the other trustees of the Methodist Episcopal Church a deed of gift one acre in the 5th District on Barren Fork of Collins River. 24 Jul 1850. (Pp. 467-468)

John Bickle of Coffee County to Thomas H. Hoover 100 acres on Barren Fork of Collins River. 24 Aug 1848. (Pp. 469-470)

David D. Hipp to J. S. Keith 196 acres in the 5th District. 28 Dec 1849. (Pp. 470-472)

William Young to Rebecca Dozier three acres in the 2nd District. 3 Sep 1849. (Pp. 472-473)

Jacob Adcock to Isaac T. Blair 100 acres in the 7th District. 28 Sep 1850. (Pp. 473-475)

William Bryson to Joseph Bryson a negro boy named Erasmus, 19, of a black complexion. 2 Jan 1836. (P. 476)

Filed at office Sept. 25th 1850 at 11 o'clock A. M.

B. B. Spicer, Register

By R. Fowler, Dep. Reg.

Richard C. Price to A. F. McFerrin and B. L. McFerrin 100 acres in the 5th District. 27 Aug 1850. (P. 1)

Martin D. Crook to Micajah Petty 150 acres in the 4th District. 24 Aug 1850. (P. 2)

James L. Essary to William Byford 40 acres in the 4th District. 30 Aug 1850. (P. 3)

William S. McAdow bound to Mark Young in the penal sum of $400. 3 Sep 1850. (P. 4)

Alexander Morgan and wife Catherine, formerly Rodgers, to Daniel M. Rodgers, James H. Rodgers, and Henry D. Rodgers their interest in the estate of John Rodgers. 15 Mar 1850. (Pp. 4-5)

William C. Parrish to A. Burger a trust deed. 12 Oct 1849. (Pp. 5-7)

J. L. Colvert to A. M. Weedon a negro woman named Martha, about 33, of a copper color and her child Nancy, about 3, for $800. 29 Jan 1850. (P. 7)

Evan Eddings to Lewis Hollis a trust deed. 12 Sep 1850. (Pp. 7-8)

William C. Leech to Thomas K. Leech a negro boy named Dick, 12, for $600. 18 Sep 1850. (P. 8)

A. M. Weedon to J. L. Colvert the following negroes, to wit, Moses, about 18; America, about 17, and her child for $1600. 29 Jan 1850. (P. 9)

A. M. Weedon to Joshua Jordan a boy named Grant, about 14, and Caroline, about 12, for $1100. 21 Sep 1850. (P. 9)

A. M. Weedon to Martha Brewer a negro boy named Nick for $150. 28 Sep 1850. (P. 10)

A. M. Weedon to A. D. Fugett two negroes, to wit, Eliza, 8, and Daniel, about 3, for $550. 21 Sep 1850. (P. 10)

G. L. W. Herndon to Joseph Dill a mortgage. 15 Apr 1850. (P. 11)

Clark Hubbard to Hannah P. Vannay a negro girl named Celah for the love and affection the said Hubbard has for his daughter Hannah P. 25 Sep 1850. (Pp. 11-12)

James Taylor for love and affection to his nephew John L. Taylor one half acre. Bounded: Nathaniel M. Taylor. 6 Jun 1845. (P. 12)

John L. Taylor to Elijah Dobbs one house and lot in the town of Woodbury. Bounded: H. D. McBroom's garden. 23 Sep 1850. (Pp. 12-13)

Jesse McBroom to William T. McBroom his interest in 128 acres in the 2nd District. 28 Sep 1850. (Pp. 13-14)

William W. McKnight to Elam Alexander 190 acres in the 1st

District. 27 Sep 1850. (Pp. 14-15)

William Givins and William A. Givins to Eliza Vance 140 acres in the 6th District. 2 Oct 1850. (Pp. 15-16)

James Cook and John W. Cook to Joshua Barton 140 acres in the 3rd District. 8 Oct 1850. (Pp. 16-17)

Isaac T. Blair to Allen Jones 30 acres in the 10th District. 10 Oct 1850. (Pp. 17-18)

George Ashford to William Wilsher 88 acres in Canal Creek. 28 Aug 1850. (Pp. 18-19)

William S. McAdow to William C. Leech a negro girl named Roda, 7, and a negro boy named Sandy, about 6. 3 Sep 1850. (P. 20)

Reynea H. Mason to Nathaniel M. Taylor 89¼ acres in the 6th District. 5 Aug 1850. (Pp. 20-21)

Benjamin Hale to John Hale 50 acres in the 10th District for $200. 5 Sep 1850. (Pp. 21-22)

George Ashford to C. M. Wilsher 223 acres on Canal Creek of the Clear Fork. 28 Aug 1850. (Pp. 22-23)

William C. Leech to Jacob H. Thomas two negro slaves, one a girl named Rody, about 8, and the other a boy named Sandy, about 6. 10 Oct 1850. (P. 24)

Alexander Bryant to Warren Cummins ten acres in the 6th District. 9 Oct 1850. (Pp. 24-25)

Cornelius Parker to Grundy Fann 110 acres in the 1st District. (See Deed Book E, pages 310-311). 4 Oct 1850. (Pp. 25-26)

Mitchel Daniel to James Cook 116 acres in the 5th District. 10 Oct 1850. (Pp. 26-27)

William D. Stroud to Richard Brown 40 acres in the 4th District. 21 Sep 1850. (Pp. 27-28)

Robert T. Cannon to Asa Todd and Pinkney Todd 269½ acres in the 12th District. 10 Oct 1850. (Pp. 28-29)

William D. Stroud to Richard Brown 40 acres in the 4th District. 20 Sep 1850. (Pp. 29-30)

William Preston to Benjamin Fugett 132 acres. 17 Oct 1850. (Pp. 30-31)

A. M. Weedon to T. G. Sullivan 230 acres in the 3rd District. 19 Oct 1850. (Pp. 31-32)

R. H. Mason to Thomas B. Sanford a title bond. 24 Sep 1850. (Pp. 32-33)

James T. Henderson to T. B. Brevard a man slave named Westley for $700. 23 Oct 1850. (Pp. 33-34)

William McKee to John W. Summers, Administrator of Hector Smith, 172 acres in the 10th District. 19 Oct 1850. (Pp. 34-35)

Eleazar A. Orr to Robert Simpson 152½ acres in the 1st District. 18 Oct 1850. (Pp. 35-36)

John A. Webber to Benjamin Webber 398½ acres on Brawley's Fork of the east fork of Stone's River. 5 Oct 1850. (Pp. 36-39)

Abel McBroom to Adam Elrod a tract of land in the 6th District. 4 Nov 1850. (Pp. 39-40)

John Cummings to A. Burger a trust deed. 23 Oct 1850. (Pp. 40-41)

William D. Stroud to James Petty a trust deed. 9 Sep 1850. (Pp. 41-42)

Thomas Leech to Martha McAdow, his daughter, a negro girl named Amanda, about 7, as a deed of gift. 15 Jan 1848. (Pp. 42-43)

Thomas Leech to his child, Jane Greir, a deed of gift of a negro girl named Nancy, about 7. 15 Jan 1848. (P. 43)

Thomas Leech to his child, Nancy C. McAdow, a deed of gift of a negro girl named Mary, about 11. 15 Jan 1848. (P. 44)

William D. Stroud to James Petty 125 acres in the 4th District. 15 Oct 1850. (Pp. 44-45)

Edmond McCahill to Martin Cox ten acres on Barren Fork of Collins River. 16 Jan 1837. (Pp. 45-46)

Jesse Hollis to William Preston 15 acres in the 2nd District. 23 Jan 1849. (Pp. 46-47)

James Lambert to Willis Whitfield and Alfred Whitfield 45 acres in the 12th District. 11 Nov 1850. (Pp. 48-49)

William C. Soap to Willis Whitfield three acres on Brawley's Fork of Stone's River. 11 Nov 1850. (Pp. 49-50)

Richard W. Lemay to Samuel N. Burger 81 poles in the town of Woodbury. 16 Nov 1850. (Pp. 50-51)

Eleazar A. Orr to J. J. Woods 118 acres in the 1st District. 31 Jul 1849. (Pp. 51-52)

Nathan Finley to John H. Dasher 200 acres in the 8th District. 16 Oct 1849. (Pp. 52-53)

Albert G. Millikin to John W. Millikin a trust deed. 18 Oct 1850. (Pp. 53-54)

John L. Taylor, Nathaniel M. Taylor, and the other heirs of Edmond Taylor, to Martha Brewer a town lot in the town of Woodbury. 21 Nov 1850. (Pp. 54-55)

John Ward to John N. Mitchel 64 acres in the 6th District. 18 Nov 1850. (P. 56)

Isaac Rains to Jesse L. Douglass 157 acres in the 5th District. 3 Aug 1850. (Pp. 57-58)

John W. Bryant to William N. Foster four acres in the 6th District. 6 Nov 1850. (Pp. 58-59)

William N. Foster to Veach Crabtree 36 acres in the 6th District. 23 Nov 1850. (Pp. 59-60)

James J. Trott to Dudley J. Graham as trustee for his wife Elizabeth Graham a town lot in the town of Woodbury. 20 Nov 1850. (Pp. 60-61)

James C. Word to William Barton a town lot in the town of Woodbury. 23 Jul 1850. (Pp. 61-62)

Robert A. Smith, Sheriff, to Turner B. Smith 100 acres belonging to Abram Teague. 11 Dec 1850. (Pp. 62-63)

A. D. Fugett to Lewis Jetton two negroes, to wit, Eliza, about 8, and Daniel, about 4. 6 Nov 1850. (P. 64)

George C. Barrett to Reuben Davenport 71 acres on Sanders Fork. 18 May 1850. (Pp. 64-65)

F. D. Wrather and wife Elizabeth to David M. Jarrett a negro woman named Jinny, about 44, and her child named Wyett, about 5. 23 Nov 1850. (Pp. 65-66)

Edward Lambert to Luke Lasater 69 acres in the 12th District. 22 Nov 1850. (Pp. 66-67)

Joseph W. Hopkins to Micajah Petty 21 acres in the 6th District. 20 Nov 1850. (Pp. 67-68)

John Mullins to William P. Jackson 50 acres on Lock's Creek of the east fork of Stone's River in the 1st District. 23 May 1850. (Pp. 68-69)

James L. Essary to John Simpson 180 acres. 6 Jan 1849. (Pp. 69-70)

William C. Miller to Isaac M. Gowen a town lot known as lot #30 in the town of Woodbury. 19 Sep 1850. (Pp. 70-71)

John H. T. Bell to James Haley 100 acres in the 12th District. 8 May 1850. (Pp. 71-73)

William Cummins to John N. Doke 260 acres on the east fork of Stone's River. 23 Feb 1848. (Pp. 73-74)

A. S. McKnight to John W. Summer 50 acres in the 11th District. 4 Oct 1850. (Pp. 74-75)

Jesse H. Robinson to Hannah McCaslin 44 acres in the 12th District. 29 Mar 1849. (Pp. 75-76)

Benjamin Webber, Sr. and Benjamin F. Webber enter into an agreement in which the said Benjamin F. Webber takes possession of 398½ acres in the 12th District. 13 Dec 1850. (Pp. 76-78)

H. B. Hall to A. D. Fugett a trust deed. 24 Dec 1850. (Pp. 78-79)

Evan Eddings to John N. Doke a trust deed. 3 Jan 1851. (Pp. 79-80)

DEED BOOK H

James T. Henderson to Archebald Stone a woman slave named Letha. 23 Dec 1850. (P. 80)

Thomas Lowe to John Bynum and William Bynum 25 acres in the 4th District. 13 Jan 1851. (Pp. 80-81)

Pleasant Henderson to James T. Henderson 227 acres in the 6th District. 25 Nov 1850. (Pp. 81-82)

Jesse Sisson to John Bynum and William Bynum 15 acres in the 4th District. 13 Jan 1851. (P. 83)

Stephen A. Mitchell to William Philips 125 acres in the 4th District. 13 Jan 1851. (P. 84)

George T. Ford to James Cummins 50 acres in the 6th District. 6 Jan 1851. (Pp. 85-86)

T. G. Sullivan to William Nichols 25 acres on Locke's Creek. 3 Jan 1851. (Pp. 86-87)

George Bogle, surviving Executor of the estate of John Higgins; James Milligan and wife Elizabeth, William Higgins, Alexander Higgins, Elijah Higgins, John D. Elkins, Hiram Y. Tittle and wife Mary, Wesley Higgins, James Higgins, Joseph Marah and wife Sarah, Elijah Armstrong and wife Margaret, John Higgins, Ad. of Samuel Tittle, Carroll Anderson and wife Mary, John Tittle, Mary Tittle, Adam Tittle, Millie Jane Tittle, and Missouri M. Tittle, the last six of whom being minors petition for the sale of a tract of land. Clerk and Master to William Higgins 125 acres. 27 Oct 1846. (Pp. 87-89)

John Pendleton to William West 102¼ acres. 6 Jan 1840. (Pp. 89-90)

Benjamin Sapp to John Barry a trust deed. 15 Jan 1851. (Pp. 91-92)

John Ferrell to William Gunter 100 acres in the 11th District. 16 Jan 1851. (P. 93)

John Fisher to Adam Elrod a trust deed. 20 Jan 1851. (Pp. 93-94)

Jesse B. Robinson, Hannah McCaslin, formerly Robinson, Geroge W. Sadler and wife Euphama, formerly Robinson, Robert Gordon and wife Levina, formerly Robinson to Silas A. Robinson their interest in a tract of land in the 12th District, it being the land that Hugh Robinson lived and died on. 18 Jan 1851. (Pp. 95-98)

Pleasant Cawthon and wife Jane, formerly Robinson, to Silas A. Robinson their interest in the land that Hugh Robinson lived on at his decease. 12 Sep 1848. (Pp. 98-100)

James Loyd to T. G. Wood a trust deed. 8 Feb 1850. (Pp. 100-101)

William C. Leech to A. S. McKnight a man slave named Ben, about 38, for $700. 16 Dec 1850. (Pp. 101-102)

145

R. H. Mason to C. T. New 23 acres. 4 Dec 1850. (Pp. 102-103)

Benjamin Sapp to John Barrett 45 acres on Hollis' Creek. 15 Jan 1851. (Pp. 103-104)

John Pendleton to his son, Samuel Pendleton for love and affection 23 acres in the 2nd District. 12 Oct 1848. (Pp. 104-105)

Allen Jones to Jesse McGee 30 acres in the 10th District. 22 Oct 1850. (Pp. 105-106)

Thomas C. Word to B. F. Allen, Chairman of the County Court, one half acre in the town of Woodbury for $125. Bounded: town lot #38 and South Street. 7 Oct 1850. (Pp. 107-108)

Joel Cherry to Katharine Craft 275 acres in the 4th District. 14 Jan 1851. (Pp. 108-109)

Joel Cherry to his son, Ervin Cherry, for love and affection 110 acres in the 4th District. 14 Jan 1851. (Pp. 109-112)

John Craft to Levi Craft of Warren County 60 acres on Barren Fork of Collins River. 29 Oct 1836. (P. 112)

Levi Craft to R. Fowler 60 acres. 31 Dec 1850. (P. 113)

Regin Fowler to J. S. Keith 300 acres in the 5th District. 31 Dec 1850. (Pp. 113-114)

David Jones to Elihu Jones a trust deed. 23 Jul 1847. (Pp. 114-116)

R. S. George to William Covington a girl slave named Adaline, about 13, for $560. 24 Jan 1851. (P. 116)

Joseph A. Brandon to John Brandon 169 acres in the 5th District. 27 Jan 1851. (Pp. 116-117)

Richard C. Jones to James M. Roberts 287½ acres on Brawley's Fork of the East Fork of Stone's River. 7 Jan 1851. (Pp. 117-119)

Nathaniel M. Taylor to John Ward 89½ acres in the 6th District. 11 Jan 1851. (Pp. 119-120)

Stephen A. Mitchel to R. Fowler a trust deed. 29 Jan 1851. (Pp. 120-121)

William Holt of Ozark County, Mississippi appoints his father, Fielding Holt, his power of attorney to sell a tract of land. 28 Oct 1841. (Pp. 121-122)

Jacob Swanner to J. W. Swanner 100 acres on Barren Fork of Collins River. 3 May 1848. (Pp. 123-125)

Richard Holt to Thomas Lowe a trust deed. 3 Feb 1851. (Pp. 125-127)

Brovel Spicer to R. Fowler two acres in the 6th District. 1 Feb 1851. (Pp. 127-128)

David McGill to William McGill ten acres in the 4th District for $60. 27 Dec 1850. (Pp. 128-129)

William S. Melton to Jesse Lawrence 167 acres in the 7th District. 7 Feb 1851. (Pp. 129-130)

John Cummins to William S. Melton 150 acres in the 7th District. 7 Feb 1851. (Pp. 131-132)

Philip Webber to John Webber a tract of land in the 12th District. 7 Feb 1851. (P. 133)

William W. McKnight to A. D. Alexander two acres in the 1st District. 10 Feb 1851. (P. 134)

William Gunter to James Hankins 256 acres in the 9th District. 9 Dec 1845. (Pp. 135-136)

William Stone to James Hankins 358 acres in the 9th District. 10 Feb 1851. (Pp. 136-138)

William Bates to Edmond McCahill a tract of land. 6 Feb 1851. (Pp. 138-139)

Clerk & Master to Thomas C. Smartt and wife Sarah; Thomas Argo and wife Mary; W. J. Wetmore and wife Elen; John James; A. J. Leiper and S. H. Leiper a tract of land. 6 Feb 1851. (Pp. 140-141)

John H. Young to Mumford Tenpenny 120 acres in the 2nd District. 11 Feb 1851. (P. 142)

William Stewart to Isaac Gunter and Micajah Marcum 200 acres in the 6th District. 14 Oct 1850. (Pp. 143-144)

William Blair to his daughter Eliza Hancock, wife of N. L. Hancock, his sons James Blair, E. C. Blair, Isaac Blair, and daughter Mary Summer, wife of Baldy H. Summer, his grant of 300 acres in the 10th District. 15 Jan 1851. (Pp. 144-145)

Sarah Cooper to Nathaniel Hays a negro girl named Mary, about 18, for $500. 4 Apr 1850. (Pp. 145-146)

Dozier Bragg to Jesse Carter a title bond. 25 Sep 1848. (Pp. 146-147)

Samuel H. Laughlin to Thomas P. Argo his one sixth interest in the estate of his father Samuel H. Laughlin, it consisting of several tracts of land in Cannon and Warren Counties and several houses and lots in the City of Washington, District of Columbia. 13 Feb 1851. (Pp. 147-148)

James Sisson to Martha Gooding a part of a 75 acre tract where the said Martha now lives. 10 Feb 1838. (Pp. 148-149)

John F. Preston to Thomas B. Brevard 208 acres in the 6th District. 13 Feb 1851. (Pp. 149-150)

John A. McAdow, James B. McAdow, Ann Eliza Pendleton to Washington S. Massey a title bond. 17 Feb 1851. (Pp. 150-151)

Charles Ready to John Bynum and William Bynum a deed of

relinquishment to 25 acres in the 4th District, it being the same land which was sold by the Sheriff. 15 Feb 1851. (Pp. 151-152)

Maria L. Weeden, by her next friend Joseph G. Martin, filed for divorce and alimony from her husband, Daniel F. Weedon. The parties agree to a settlement. 3 Feb 1851. (Pp. 152-154)

Thomas G. Wood, trustee for Maria L. Weeden, to Francis Turner a bill of sale as a result of a compromise agreement the said Maria L. and Daniel F. Weeden entered into on 25 Dec 1850. (Pp. 154-155)

Thomas B. Sanford and wife E. R. to Francis Turner a negro named George, about 30. 19 Feb 1850. (Pp. 155-156)

A. Miller McKnight to John P. Hare 47 acres in the 1st District. 26 Jul 1850. (Pp. 156-157)

Alexander McKnight to John P. Hare 22 acres in the 1st District. 27 Jan 1849. (Pp. 157-158)

Andrew M. McKnight to Henry Goodlow 149 acres in the 1st District. 19 Dec 1850. (Pp. 158-159)

Noah W. Sanes to Aaron Byford 54 acres on Brawley's Fork of Stone's River. 18 Feb 1851. (PP. 159-160)

Aaron Byford to C. C. Acres 54 acres on Brawley's Fork of Stone's River. 18 Dec 1850. (Pp. 161-162)

John Bastian, Executor of Andrew Bastian, to Jesse Lawrence and Joseph Moore 228 acres in the 7th District. 1 Jan 1838. (Pp. 162-163)

Joseph Moore to L. B. Moore 112 acres in the 7th District. 25 Feb 1851. (Pp. 163-164)

William Higgins to his daughter Mary Odom, wife of Benjamin F. Odom, for love and affection 100 acres on Harrican Creek in the 11th District. 27 Feb 1851. (P. 165)

William Higgins to his daughter Mary Odom, wife of Benjamin F. Odom, for love and affection the following slaves, to wit, a woman named Rhoda, about 30, of dark complexion; a boy named Nelson, 21, of copper color; a boy named Jack, about 7, of a dark complexion. 27 Feb 1851. (P. 166)

William Higgins to his son, James Higgins, for love and affection the following negroes, to wit, a boy named Jim, about 22, of dark complexion; a girl named Lucy, about 6, of dark complexion; a boy named Henry, about 3, of dark complexion. 27 Jan 1851. (Pp. 166-168)

Josiah Fuston to William Collins 200 acres in the 10th District. 19 Oct 1850. (Pp. 168-169)

William Collins to Namen Hollandsworth 200 acres in the 10th District. 19 Oct 1850. (Pp. 169-170)

William Young, attorney for Henry Young, to James K. Eason town lot #58 in the town of Woodbury. 8 Feb 1848. (Pp. 170-171)

James K. Eson to Lewis Jetton, Trustee of Sarah E. Weedon, wife of Augustine M. Weedon, lot #58 in the town of Woodbury. 20 Dec 1850. (Pp. 171-172)

John Hollandsworth to Ira Hollandsworth 15 acres in the 10th District. 27 Feb 1851. (Pp. 172-173)

William West to George W. Thompson a portion of lot #26 in the town of Woodbury. 10 Feb 1851. (Pp. 173-174)

Armsted Carter to B. B. Dickens 81½ acres in the 12th District. 15 Jan 1851. (Pp. 174-176)

Andrew M. McKnight to Alexander McKnight 32 acres in the 1st District. 16 Jul 1850. Witnesses: John P. McKnight and Williford McKnight. (Pp. 176-177)

John Bowling of Fulton County, Arkansas to Jacob Wright of Rutherford County lot #60 in the town of Woodbury. 28 Dec 1850. (Pp. 177-178)

Joseph Ramsey to John H. Wood lot #85 in the town of Woodbury. 11 Feb 1851. (Pp. 178-179)

John W. Stroud to Sarah Good his interest in 300 acres that I bought of Walter Stroud. 13 Mar 1851. (Pp. 179-180)

Joseph Moore to Jesse Lawrence 116 acres in the 7th District. 25 Feb 1851. (Pp. 180-181)

Regin Fowler to B. M. Fugett 66 acres in the 6th District. 26 Mar 1851. (Pp. 181-182)

John A. McAdow, James B. McAdow, Eliza Ann Pendleton, and William McAdow to Washington S. Massey 261 acres in the 6th District. 31 Mar 1851. (Pp. 182-183)

Gabriel Hume to Washington S. Massey a negro boy named Harris for $700. 25 Mar 1851. (P. 184)

Washington S. Massey and A. Stone agree upon a conditional line between their tracts of land in the 6th District. 31 Mar 1851. (Pp. 184-185)

Armsted Carter to Joseph Carter seven and one half acres in the 12th District. 18 Feb 1858. (Pp. 185-186)

Clement R. Davis to Benjamin Sapp 70 acres in the 2nd District. 11 Feb 1851. (Pp. 186-187)

Jesse Lawrence to Joseph Moore 112 acres in the 7th District. (Pp. 187-188)

Robert Marshall to William C. Leech 327 acres on each side of Lick Creek. 14 Nov 1849. (Pp. 189-190)

Martha Gooding to Lucinda Gooding 12½ acres in the 4th District for $50. 19 Jul 1847. (Pp. 190-191)

Martha Gooding to Malinda Gooding 12½ acres in the 4th District on Carson's Fork of Stone's River. 19 Jul 1847. (P. 192)

J. M. Gowen to N. C. Tilford lot #30 in the town of Woodbury.

6 Mar 1851. (Pp. 192-193)

George Bogle to Hiram Gatton 75 acres in the 11th District. 4 Jan 1851. (Pp. 193-195)

Thomas Holt to W. S. Bell and John H. T. Bell 60 acres. 16 Sep 1850. (Pp. 195-199)

Mitchel Daniel to William McKnight a tract of land on Daniel's fork of Barren River containing four acres. 12 Aug 1850. (Pp. 199-200)

Silas A. Robinson to James McGill 150 acres in the 12th District. 18 Feb 1851. (Pp. 200-201)

Joel Cherry to Willis Guy 41 acres in the 5th District. 20 May 1850. (Pp. 201-202)

R. A. Smith to John F. Preston 220 acres which was recovered as a judgment against William P. McAdow. 15 Apr 1851. (Pp. 202-204)

John Hollandsworth to Ira Hollandsworth 50 acres for $900. 3 Mar 1851. (Pp. 204-205)

John Hollandsworth to Namon Hollandsworth 150 acres in the 10th District for $700. 6 Feb 1851. (Pp. 205-207)

Hugh Robinson to John A. Webber 30½ acres in the 12th District. 29 Apr 1851. (Pp. 207-208)

John A. Webber to Benjamin Webber, Sr. 30¼ acres in the 12th District. 29 Apr 1851. (Pp. 209-210)

John Hollandsworth to Aden Hollandsworth 182 acres in the 11th District. 4 Apr 1851. (Pp. 210-212)

John A. Beaird and wife Frances Ann to William F. George 34 acres where the said William F. George now lives. 29 Jan 1851. (Pp. 212-213)

A. J. Bogle to Joseph Bryson 150 acres in the 11th District. 1 Mar 1851. (Pp. 213-214)

A. M. Weedon to Sarah E. Weedon and Lewis Jetton, trustee, three negroes, to wit, Eliza, 9; Nick, 19; and one named Daniel, 4. Sarah E. Weedon, the wife of A. M. Weedon, has filed her bill of divorce against her husband. 23 May 1851. (Pp. 214-216)

Eliza Sandridge, Louisa Sandridge, Permelia Cheatham and Jack Cheatham to Thomas G. Word three fifth's of 1200 acres. 9 May 1851. (Pp. 217-219)

William Preston to Thomas J. Preston and Elijah C. Preston 65 acres in the 6th District. 2 Jan 1851. (Pp. 219-221)

Alexander Higgins to his son, John Higgins, for love and affection a negro boy named Phil, about 22. 5 Mar 1851. (P. 221)

John Young to James Sullins, Jr. 13½ acres in the 7th District. 24 May 1851. (P. 222)

J. H. Gilly to Nathan Jernigan 80 acres in Coffee County in the 1st District. 4 May 1850. (Pp. 222-223)

Ivy Bush to Robert Gordon 149 acres on Brasley's Fork of the East Fork of Stone's River. 5 Nov 1849. (Pp. 223-225)

Robert Vinson, James A. Vinson, Berry Vinson, Joseph Warren and wife Sophia, Elizabeth Barkley, Alexander Vinson, Samuel Bowen and wife Usly, Ann Vinson, all heirs of Richard Vinson to Benjamin Fugett a part of a 200 acre tract of land in the 6th District. The said Joseph Warren and wife Sophia have previously transferred their interest to James Sullivan. 24 Apr 1851. (Pp. 225-226)

Jesse Glasscock to Thomas J. Wood a tract of land known as the Negro (Gull) tract. 10 Jun 1851. (P. 227)

(Page 228 is blank)

County Court Commissioners to John Bowling lot #60 in the town of Woodbury. 6 Jan 1851. (Pp. 229-230)

John W. Summer to Aden Hollandsworth 171½ acres in the 10th District. 19 Apr 1851. (Pp. 230-231)

Abraham D. Alexander and wife Martha to A. D. Alexander their interest in 68 acres in the 1st District, it being the land that John K. Sauls died seized and possessed of. 31 May 1851. (Pp. 231-233)

Thomas B. Sanford and wife Elizabeth R. to Lewis Jetton five acres in the 6th District. 4 Jun 1851. (Pp. 233-234)

A. J. Inglis to Ervin Cherry 278 acres in the 4th District. 25 Jan 1851. (Pp. 234-235)

Micajah Petty to Willis Guy 170 acres in the 4th District. 10 Jun 1851. (P. 236)

Samuel Moore to Samuel R. Moore 500 acres in the 4th District. 7 Jun 1851. (P. 237)

William Preston to Elizabeth Phillips 30 acres in the 8th District. 5 Feb 1851. (P. 238)

Henry Young of Reeves County, Missouri appoints William Young his power of attorney to sell town lot #58 in the town of Woodbury for him. 23 Jul 1839. (PP. 239-240)

R. W. Woodruff to Mathew Whitfield a trust deed. 19 Jun 1851. (Pp. 240-242)

Elijah Higgins and Robert Higgins to Mathew Dennis 300 acres in the 10th District. 21 Aug 1850. (Pp. 242-243)

Mathew Dennis to Aaron F. Jones 300 acres in the 10th District. 21 Aug 1850. (Pp. 243-244)

William Barton to Aaron F. Jones 93 acres in the 10th and 6th Districts. 21 May 1850. (Pp. 244-245)

Henry Hayes to John Hays five acres in the 2nd District. 4

Aug 1851. (P. 245)

William P. Jackson to Jesse Carter 150 acres on the east fork of Stone's River. 8 Aug 1851. (P. 246)

Rezin Fowler to Elijah Neely a trust deed. 8 Aug 1851. (Pp. 247-249)

Rezin Fowler to G. W. Wale lot #2 in the town of Woodbury. 18 Nov 1850. (Pp. 249-250)

Samuel Moore to Reuben Hall 125 acres in the 5th District. 21 Jan 1851. (Pp. 250-251)

George W. Sadler and wife Fanny C. to Asa Todd 40 acres in the 12th District. 11 Nov 1850. (Pp. 251-253)

John W. Millikin to William J. Morton 200 acres in the 5th District. 18 Aug 1851. (Pp. 253-254)

Miles F. Travis to Ephraim Andrews a title bond. 20 Feb 1846. (Pp. 254-255)

Warren Moore and others constitute the Murfreesborough & Liberty Turnpike Company. 8 Aug 1851. (Pp. 256-259)

Lucy Smith for love and affection to Thomas H. Smith her interest in the estate of Guy Smith. 3 Apr 1849. (Pp. 259-260)

William J. A. Morton to J. J. Morton and A. W. Morton 300 acres in the 5th District. 25 Aug 1851. (Pp. 260-261)

E. R. Jones to Jesse B. Morton and R. J. Wood 200 acres. 25 Apr 1851. (Pp. 261-262)

Robert Bogle to Andrew Bogle ten acres in the 10th District. 22 Sep 1840. (P. 263)

Joseph A. Dement, Elaner Andrews, Jane Andrews to John H. Smith 56 acres in the 1st District. 4 Mar 1851. (Pp. 264-265)

James W. Tenpenny to Benjamin Fugett 60 acres in the 6th District. 1 Jan 1850. (Pp. 265-266)

Andrew Bogle to Allen R. Jones 110 acres in the 6th District. 27 Aug 1851. (Pp. 266-267)

Charles L. Nelson to William West a tract of land. 21 Jul 1851. (Pp. 267-269)

Henry Dozier to Jonathan Dozier 41 acres in the 2nd District. 2 Mar 1849. (P. 269)

Robert Bryson to Stephen Wilson 170 acres in the 11th District. 15 Feb 1850. (P. 270)

Hiram Morris to John W. Matthews 100 acres in the 10th District. 1 Sep 1851. (Pp. 271-272)

Hugh Robinson to John A. Webber 30¼ acres in the 12th District. 29 Apr 1851. (Pp. 272-273)

John A. Webber to Benjamin Webber 30¼ acres in the 12th District. 29 Apr 1851. (Misnumbered)

John Hollandsworth to Aden Hollandsworth 182 acres in the 10th District. 4 Apr 1851. (Misnumbered)

John A. Beaird and wife Francis Ann to William F. George 34 acres in the 6th District, it being the land where the said George now lives. 27 Jan 1851. (Misnumbered)

A. J. Bogle to Joseph Bryson, Jr. 150 acres in the 11th District. 1 Mar 1851. (Misnumbered)

(Pages begin again at Page 214)

A. M. Weedon to Lewis Weedon, trustee of Sarah E. Weedon three negroes, to wit, Eliza, 9; Nick, 19; and Daniel, 4. 23 May 1851. (Pp. 214-216)

Eliza Sandridge, Louisa Sandridge, Permelia Cheatham, and Jack Cheatham to Thomas G. Wood their three fifth's interest in 1200 acres. 9 May 1851. (Pp. 217-219)

William R. to William Sisson 230 acres in the 12th District. 14 Sep 1850. (Misnumbered)

John P. Hare to Wiley Davenport 75 acres. 11 Aug 1845. (Pp. 273-274)

John Witt to Caleb Cox a trust deed. 22 Aug 1851. (Pp. 275-276)

Lewis Hancock to Lewis R. Hancock 53 acres in the 10th District. 26 Jul 1850. (Pp. 276-277)

Z. Thomason to Lewis R. Hancock 15 acres in the 10th District. 26 Jul 1850. (Pp. 277-278)

Reuben Elam to John Pendleton 125 acres in the 8th District. 26 Aug 1843. (PP. 278-279)

Ervin Cherry to John Parker a trust deed. 13 Sep 1851. (Pp. 280-281)

John Parker to Ervin Cherry 100 acres in the 4th District. 1 Sep 1851. (Pp. 281-282)

Benjamin Hale to Thomas Hale 34 acres in the 10th District. 9 Mar 1849. (Pp. 282-283)

Charles J. Hancock to C. C. Hancock 77 acres in the 10th District. 17 Sep 1851. (Pp. 283-284)

Rezin Fowler to Samuel N. Burger a trust deed. 19 Sep 1851. (Pp. 285-286)

Rezin Fowler to William Cummins and Elijah Neely 260 acres in the 6th District. 19 Sep 1851. (Pp. 286-288)

Jonathan Baker to Martin D. Brown a trust deed. 24 Sep 1851. (Pp. 288-289)

Thomas E. Jones to Annett Jones a mortgage. 27 Sep 1851. (Pp. 289-290)

James A. Vinson, Robert Vinson, Joseph Warren and wife Sophia, Elizabeth Barkley, formerly Vinson, Alexander Vinson, Samuel Bowen and wife Usly Ann to T. B. Brevard their interest in a tract of land in the 6th District, it being the dower of Mary Vinson, widow of Richard Vinson. 4 Oct 1850. (Pp. 290-292)

Rezin Fowler to A. Burger a trust deed. 27 Sep 1851. (Pp. 292-293)

Samuel Cannon to Raford Cannon 100 acres on the east fork of Stone's River. 5 Mar 1844. (Pp. 293-295)

John McClain to Caleb Cox 160 acres in the 4th District. 1 Sep 1851. (Pp. 295-296)

Alexander Orr to Elam and Earthman a title bond. 18 Sep 1851. (P. 296)

William Hollis to Jesse Hollis a quit claim to 300 acres on Hollis' Creek. 12 Feb 1848. (P. 297)

William Willard to D. G. Leech a trust deed. 25 Sep 1851. (Pp. 298-299)

Aaron F. Jones, Joseph W. Jones, and D. W. Jones for love and affection to Levi D. Allen and Rufus R. Allen 100 acres in the 10th District. 10 Sep 1851. (Pp. 300-301)

Benjamin Sapp to William T. McBroom a title bond. 24 Sep 1851. (Pp. 301-302)

Eleanor Montgomery of Barra County, Missouri, the lawful sister of Robert Carson, to Samuel Carson her power of attorney to represent her in the estate of the said Robert Carson. 19 Nov 1850. Witnesses: Andrew Montgomery and William Carson. (Pp. 302-303)

James E. Winters, T. W. Adams, M. Adams, and James Dickson, the natural heirs of Margret Winters, of Gaston County, North Carolina appoint Samuel Carson their power of attorney to settle the estate of Robert Carson, Sr. 1 Dec 1849. (Pp. 303-304)

L. B. Moore to William C. Leech two tracts of land in the 10th District. 10 Mar 1851. (PP. 304-306)

Rezin Fowler to Benjamin Sapp 42 acres in the 6th District. 2 Oct 1851. (Pp. 306-307)

E. A. Orr to Franklin Fann a tract of land on the east fork of Stone's River. 19 Sep 1851. (Pp. 307-308)

Alexander Pelham to William Pelham his interest in 200 acres in the 5th District. (See Deed Book D, page 394). 2 Oct 1849. (Pp. 309-310)

G. W. Silvertooth to James Haliton of Davidson County his power of attorney to attend to the estate of his father Jacob Silvertooth of Cannon County. 28 Apr 1851. (Pp. 310-311)

James Cannon to Raford Cannon 50 acres on Stone's River. 1

Oct 1845. (Pp. 311-312)

Ervin Cherry to Neely Smoot a title bond. 27 Jan 1851. (Pp. 313-314)

Robert E. Forester to John Orran a trust deed. 8 Oct 1851. (Pp. 314-315)

Charles A. Hammons to Vincent Bailey a trust deed. 4 Oct 1851. (Pp. 315-316)

Sheriff R. A. Smith to William C. Leech 150 acres in the 11th District. 10 Jul 1851. (Pp. 316-318)

Allen Jones to Andrew Bogle 110 acres in the 6th District. 7 Oct 1851. (PP. 318-319)

William D. Gowen to Henry Hayes 130 acres on the east fork of Stone's River. 15 Oct 1851. (Pp. 319-321)

Thomas G. Jones to Rolly P. S. Kimbro 600 acres. (See Book G, pages 393-396). 23 Sep 1851. (Pp. 321-322)

A. M. Weedon to John F. Weedon a title bond. 17 May 1850. (Pp. 323-324)

Benjamin Sapp to Alexander B. Carnes 126 acres in the 6th District. 16 Oct 1851. (Pp. 324-325)

John H. Evans to Jesse Lawrence 75 acres on the Rock House Fork of Stone's River. 17 Oct 1851. (Pp. 325-326)

W. H. Peyton to James Petty 600 acres on Horse Spring Fork. 23 Sep 1851. (Pp. 326-327)

A. M. Weedon to John F. Weedon a title bond. 17 May 1850. (Misnumbered)

Benjamin Sapp to Alexander B. Carnes 126 acres in the 6th District. (Misnumbered)

John H. Evans to Jesse Lawrence 75 acres on Rock House Fork of Stone's River. 17 Oct 1851. (Misnumbered)

W. H. Peyton to James Petty a tract of land on Horse Spring Fork. 15 Oct 1851. (Misnumbered)

William Cummins and Elijah Neely to Benjamin Fugett 206 acres. 23 Oct 1851. (Pp. 328-329)

Sheriff Robert A. Smith to Ally Barnett 100 acres. 22 Oct 1851. (Pp. 330-332)

James Sullins to William Sullins 18½ acres in the 2nd District. 27 Oct 1851. (Pp. 332-333)

James M. Carson, Isabella Carson, Joseph Carson, Robert Carson, Margaret M. Carson, Mary E. Carson, and Martha Anthony, heirs of James Carson to Samuel Carson their power of attorney to settle the estate of the said James Carson. Parties of the first part are residents of Gaston County, North Carolina. 23 Apr 1851. (P. 333)

Elizabeth Jackson, the natural sister of Robert Carson, of York County, South Carolina to Samuel Carson her interest in the estate of Robert Carson. 21 Oct 1849. (P. 334)

James L. Essary to Jacob Byford 75 acres in the 4th District. 30 Aug 1850. (Pp. 335-336)

Jane Patton to Robert Patton her power of attorney to receive any money due her. 3 Nov 1851. (Pp. 336-337)

Thomas G. Wood to Robert McBroom a trust deed. 25 Oct 1850. (Pp. 337-338)

Rezin Fowler to Solomon Freeze 200 acres in the 5th District. 11 Apr 1845. (Pp. 338-339)

William Preston to William Nokes a tract of land in the 6th District. 14 Oct 1851. (Pp. 339-340)

Willis Guy to Linzy Pelar 60 acres in the 4th District. 20 Aug 1851. (Pp. 340-341)

Gabriel Hume to Henry R. Perry town lot #2 in the town of Woodbury. 14 Oct 1851. (Pp. 341-342)

William Jacobs to Alford Jacobs 100 acres. 12 Nov 1851. (Pp. 342-344)

Pleasant Cawthon to Harvey S. Cawthon 275 acres on Brawley's Fork of the east fork of Stone's River in the 12th District. 13 Oct 1851. (Pp. 344-345)

Sarah J. Good to M. A. Stroud his interest in the land I bought of John W. Stroud. 22 Nov 1851. (Pp. 345-346)

John W. Stroud to William D. Stroud a trust deed. 22 Nov 1851. (Pp. 346-347)

Elkin C. Blair to Alfred L. Hancock 60 acres in the 10th District. 22 Nov 1851. (Pp. 348-349)

Isaac T. Blair to James Blair 60 acres in the 10th District. 22 Nov 1851. (Pp. 349-350)

Thomas J. Williams, by descent from Thomas Williams, to John McClain his one eighth interest in 100 acres in the 4th District. 13 Oct 1851. (Pp. 350-351)

Washington S. Massey to James Wood three acres in the 6th District. 26 Nov 1851. (Pp. 351-353)

Hugh Craft to John Mitchel a tract of land in the 5th District. 13 Sep 1851. (Pp. 353-354)

Elizabeth Youngblood, Josiah Youngblood, Arthur Youngblood, Henderson Teasley and wife Mary, William Teasley and wife Jane, and Asa Smith, all of Warren County, to Asa Smith their interest in the dower of Elizabeth Youngblood, it being Tennessee Grant #13198 granted to Henry Youngblood. 12 Aug 1839. (Pp. 354-356)

A. M. Weedon to A. M. Goodloe 100 acres in the 2nd District. 26 Nov 1851. (Pp. 356-357)

J. M. Gowen to Joseph Pinkerton a negro girl named Mahaly, 11, of black complexion for $585. 17 Jan 1851. (Pp. 357-358)

Thomas H. Roughton to John Gordon 72½ acres on Brawley's Fork of the East Fork of Stone's River. 17 Oct 1851. (Pp. 358-359)

Peter J. Thomas to James M. Prater 110 acres in the 4th District. 28 Nov 1851. (Pp. 359-361)

John Fisher to Joseph Spurlock a trust deed. 2 Oct 1851. (Pp. 361-362)

John Petty to Marshall Sanders 500 acres in the 4th District. 15 Sep 1851. (Pp. 363-364)

John R. Sullivan to Thomas B. Sanford a woman slave named Rhoda, about 40. 3 Dec 1851. (Pp. 364-365)

James L. Essary to James Jameson 180 acres in the 4th District. 24 Sep 1851. (Pp. 365-366)

Jesse McGee to Ira Hollandsworth a tract of land in the 10th District. 4 Oct 1851. (Pp. 366-367)

Thomas B. Sanford to John R. Sullivan 12 acres in the 6th District. 3 Dec 1851. (Pp. 368-369)

Thomas G. Wood to James T. C. McKnight 175 acres, it being one half of the amount due him as an heir and legatee of David McKnight. 4 Dec 1851. (Pp. 369-370)

Joseph Simpson to Alexander F. McFerrin 35 acres in the 8th District. 9 Dec 1851. (Pp. 370-371)

John Williams to William Whitemore 100 acres in the 5th District. 16 Nov 1848. (Pp. 372-373)

Thomas B. Sanford to Joseph Spurlock 28 acres in the 6th District. 9 Dec 1851. (Pp. 373-374)

R. H. Mason to Thomas B. Sanford 52 acres in the 6th District. 9 Dec 1851. (Pp. 374-375)

Frederick P. Starnes of Buffalo, New York to Halsey R. Wing of Glen Falls, Warren County several tracts of land. 20 Aug 1850. (Pp. 376-379)

Jobe Stephens to William Blair 183 acres on the East Fork of Stone's River. 3 Sep 1851. (Pp. 379-380)

Claborn C. Gunter to M. G. Elkins and James J. Prater 75 acres in the 7th District. 9 Oct 1851. (Pp. 381-382)

Henry Lance to James J. Prater 75 acres in the 7th District. 27 Nov 1851. (Pp. 382-383)

John Nokes to Benjamin Hutchins a title bond. 10 Dec 1851. (P. 383)

Agnes W. Henderson and James T. Henderson to William Ferrell 227 acres in the 6th District. Bounded: the tract where Susan George now lives. 6 Mar 1851. (Pp. 384-385)

Adam Elrod to William D. Gowen lots #5 and 53 in the town of Woodbury. 20 Dec 1851. (Pp. 385-386)

R. H. Mason to Elizabeth R. Sanford ten acres in the 6th District. 24 Dec 1851. (Pp. 386-387)

Thomas B. Sanford and Elijah R. Sanford to R. H. Mason a tract of land in the 6th District. 23 Dec 1851. (Pp. 387-388)

Thomas B. Sanford to John F. Weedon a trust deed. 24 Dec 1851. (Pp. 388-389)

Thomas B. Sanford to William Wharton a negro woman named Rhody, about 40, for $200. 23 Dec 1851. (P. 390)

F. D. Wrather to Samuel Mottley a negro girl, about 19. 6 Jul 1850. (Pp. 390-391)

Joseph Spurlock to Thomas B. Sanford 28 acres in the 6th District. 23 Dec 1851. (P. 391)

R. A. Smith to Abraham Cooper 400 acres. 26 Dec 1851. (Pp. 392-393)

Thomas B. Sanford to John F. Weedom a trust deed. 25 Dec 1851. (Pp. 393-394)

John S. Keith to James J. Keith, his son, of Georgia his power of attorney to represent him. 1 Feb 1851. (Pp. 394-395)

John C. Martin to his daughter, Susan J. Wright, wife of William B. Wright, a deed of gift of a negro girl, about 14. 29 Dec 1851. (Pp. 395-396)

William Gunter to John L. Markum 100 acres in the 10th District. 21 Dec 1851. (Pp. 396-397)

James Keith to Adam Elrod 300 acres in the 5th District. 1 Jan 1851. (Pp. 397-398)

John S. Keith to his son, James J. Keith of Georgia, his power of attorney to represent him. 24 Dec 1851. (Pp. 398-399)

James D. Perry to John W. Melton 134 acres in the 7th District. 30 Dec 1851. (Pp. 400-401)

William H. Travis to Joseph D. McKnight 80 acres in the 1st District. 5 Jan 1852. (P. 402)

David D. Hipp to Adam Elrod 22 acres in the 5th District. 3 Jan 1852. (P. 403)

William B. Ewing to William C. Milton lot #3 in the town of Woodbury. 25 Oct 1851. (Pp. 403-404)

Archebald Stone to Gabriel Hume a title bond. 12 Dec 1851. (Pp. 404-405)

James Stone to William Gunter 25 acres on the Rock House Fork of Stone's River. 3 Oct 1851. (Pp. 405-406)

J. J. Jones to Joseph Carter 81½ acres in the 12th District. 22 Dec 1851. (Pp. 406-408)

Jesse Pierce to Warren Cummins a trust deed. 12 Jan 1852. (Pp. 408-410)

James S. Keith to Adam Elrod 196 acres in the 5th District. 2 Jan 1852. (Pp. 410-411)

John S. Keith to his son, James J. Keith of Georgia, his power of attorney to represent him. 29 Dec 1851. (Pp. 411-412)

Samuel B. Nelson to Lewis Malone as trustee for my wife, Sarah H. Nelson, a negro girl named Hannah, 6. 20 Jan 1852. (P. 413)

Samuel B. Nelson to Lewis Malone of Shelby County, Kentucky a negro woman named Mary, 24, and her two children, the oldest a girl named Dinah, about 4, and the second a boy named Levi, 14 months. 12 Jan 1852. (Pp. 413-414)

Thomas B. Brevard to Benjamin Fugett 208 acres in the 6th District. 12 Jan 1852. (Pp. 414-415)

John Orran to William H. Travis 96 acres in the 6th District. 6 Jan 1852. (Pp. 415-416)

Thomas H. Hoover to John Finley 100 acres on Barren's Fork of Collins River. 14 Jan 1852. (Pp. 416-417)

B. B. Spicer to Paralee Elkins two acres in the 6th District. 16 Jan 1852. (P. 417)

J. C. Martin and wife Sophia B. to Edward Bragg 18½ acres in the 1st District. 16 Jan 1852. (P. 418)

Samuel Carson to Clement R. Davis 200 acres in the 4th District. 10 Jan 1852. (P. 419)

Thomas G. Wood to Mark L. Young and William J. Hall 100 acres in the 5th District. 22 Jan 1852. (Pp. 420-421)

U. D. Allen to Aaron Jones 100 acres in the 10th District. 24 Nov 1851. (Pp. 421-422)

Jesse Pierce to Warren Cummins a trust deed. 31 Jan 1852. (Pp. 422-423)

James F. Foster to John W. Ware two acres in the 9th District. 24 Mar 1851. (Pp. 423-424)

Levina Ann McGee to Judith Cox her interest in 50 acres in the 10th and 11th Districts, it being the land on which the said Judith Cox now lives and was conveyed by William Higgins to James Cox now deceased. There is another tract conveyed to the said Judith Cox by Erasmus Jones now deceased. 23 Jan 1852. (P. 425)

John Patterson to John W. Ware 28 acres in the 9th District. 4 Mar 1846. (Pp. 426-427)

Everett Haynes to Charles E. Haynes one and a half acres in the 4th District. 26 Mar 1851. (Pp. 427-428)

Elijah Neely and wife Sarah; and William Wood and wife Elizabeth to Henry R. Perry 40 acres in the 6th District, it being land belonging to the heirs of James Barclay. 27 Jan 1852. (Pp. 428-430)

Mark L. Young to William T. Preston a title bond. 11 Feb 1852. (Pp. 430-431)

John W. Stroud to Ready and Keeble a trust deed. Other parties of the first part were Mary Stroud, wife of the said John W., and Sarah Jane Good. 19 Feb 1852. (Pp. 431-432)

Linsey Peeler to Sally King 23 acres in the 5th District. 16 Feb 1852. (Misnumbered)

N. C. Telford of Grayson County, Kentucky to Lewis L. Smith his power of attorney to sell a tract of land in Woodbury, known as lot #30. 22 Dec 1852. (Pp. 442-443)

N. C. Telford to Elizabeth Graham to be free from any debts of her husband, Dudley J. Graham, lot #30 in the town of Woodbury. 6 Jan 1852. (Pp. 444-445)

B. B. Spicer to John Fisher a trust deed. 18 Feb 1852. (Pp. 446-447)

William Crane to J. N. Fuller a tract of land in the 9th District. 12 Feb 1852. (PP. 447-448)

Jesse T. Douglass to Reuben Harrell 177½ acres on Barren Fork of Collins River. 1 Nov 1850. (Pp. 448-449)

Joseph P. Holt and Richard Holt to Fielding Holt 64 acres. 28 Sep 1851. (Pp. 450-451)

Jesse Sisson, Jr. to Daniel Finley 38 acres in the 4th District. 8 Feb 1850. (Pp. 451-452)

Thomas C. Ward to Joseph Bryson 26 acres in the 11th District. 27 Oct 1851. (Pp. 452-453)

Baxter B. Dickins to J. J. Jones 81 acres. 22 Dec 1851. (Pp. 453-455)

Jacob Wright to James B. Elledge 208 acres in the 6th District. 17 Feb 1852. (Pp. 455-456)

William P. Akers to Jackson Brewer, trustee of Rebecca McMahon, wife of Jonathan McMahon who was formerly before her marriage with said McMahon Rebecca Brewer, one of the heirs of the late Robert Brewer, 200 acres in the 5th District. 5 Nov 1851. (Pp. 456-458)

Richard W. Robinson to Candow S. McFaddin his interest in the estate of Jacob Silvertooth. 2 Feb 1852. (P. 458)

Joshua Barton to William Barton 100 acres in the 1st District. 16 Feb 1852. (PP. 458-459)

Joshua Barton to his daughter, Elizabeth Taylor, for love and affection a tract of land on the west side of Bralley's Fork of Stone's River. 30 Oct 1852. (Pp. 460-461)

Newman Hollandsworth to Allen R. Jones 200 acres in the 10th District. 9 Feb 1852. (Pp. 461-462)

Thomas Sisson, Jesse Sisson, William Sisson, Sally Reeves, and Polly Reeves, the heirs of James Sisson, to Anna Sisson, widow of James Sisson, 75 acres. Bounded: the school house above where the Widow Sisson now lives called Liberty School House. 25 Mar 1845. (Pp. 462-464)

Franklin Fann to Ward Barrett 39 acres in the 1st District. 2 Mar 1852. (Pp. 464-465)

Elijah Neely and wife Lidia; William Wood and wife Elizabeth to Henry D. McBroom ten acres in the 6th District. 27 Jan 1852. (Pp. 465-466)

Abraham Cooper to Veach Crabtree 416 acres in the 6th District. 27 Dec 1852. (Pp. 467-468)

Charles Ready to Alexander N. Smoot 100 acres in the 12th District. 29 Jul 1850. (Pp. 468-469)

Robert Gordon to William Ward certain negroes named as follows, to wit, Lucy and children Josiah and (Amanda). 28 Jan 1852. (P. 469)

John B. Davenport to Joel Milligan 75 acres in the 11th District. 19 Feb 1851. (Pp. 470-471)

William Smith to Daniel Finley 300 acres in the 5th District. 20 Feb 1852. (Pp. 471-472)

James Essary to King Peeler part of a 640 acre tract entered in the name of Lemuel Duncan. 19 Sep 1851. (Pp. 472-473)

John Briant to Alexander Moore 42 acres in the 6th District. 9 Mar 1852. (Pp. 474-475)

William Smith to John Miles 60 acres in the 5th District. 21 Feb 1852. (Pp. 475-476)

William Stroud to James Petty 100 acres on Berge's Creek. 13 Feb 1852. (Pp. 476-478)

Richard W. Lemay to John Miles 37 acres in the 5th District. 2 Oct 1848. (Pp. 478-479)

Daniel F. Weedon, Augustine M. Weedon, Martha Brewer, formerly Weedon, Elizabeth (Weedon), William Wharton and wife Ann, formerly Weedon, to John F. Weedon their interest in the estate of George W. Weedon who was a resident in the Republic of Texas, now State of Texas. Said deceased was formerly a resident in Warren County. Said deceased left at the time of his death nine brothers and sisters, to wit, Daniel F. Weedon, Augustine M. Weedon, William Weedon who is deceased dead and the said John F. Weedon, his brothers, and Ann M. Wharton, wife of William Wharton; Harriet Calvert, wife of William J. Calvert; Mary Shackleford, wife of Harrison Shackleford; Elizabeth Calvert, wife of William J. Calvert, Jr.; and Martha Weedon, now Martha Brewer, widow of Jesse Brewer, his sisters and Elizabeth Weedon, widow, his mother. Said parties are seeking their share of the estate. 16 Mar 1852. (Pp. 479-482)

David Travis to Margaret Earthman a title bond. 25 Nov 1844. (Pp. 482-484)

Henry R. Perry to John Webb a trust deed. 28 Mar 1852. (Pp. 484-488)

Wiley Davenport to John B. Davenport 50 acres in the 11th District. 5 Jan 1848. (Pp. 488-489)

David M. Jarratt to William Young a negro boy named Isaac, about 9. 25 Oct 1849. (Pp. 489-490)

A. S. and Lucy Emeline McKnight to James L. Odom 35 acres in the 11th District. 20 Oct 1851. (Pp. 490-492)

John McIver to Charles L. Nelson a tract of land. 12 Jan 1852. (PP. 492-493)

H. R. Perry to William Young and others the following negroes, to wit, Washington, Isaac, and Robert as a trust deed. 22 Mar 1852. (P. 494)

James T. C. McKnight to Alexander McKnight 195½ acres in the 1st District. 8 Dec 1851. (Pp. 494-495)

Fielding Holt to William Holt of Marian County, Arkansas 65 acres in the 12th District. 24 Mar 1852. (Pp. 496-497)

Clark Hubbard to his daughter, Elizabeth McAdow, my negro girl named Hannah as a deed of gift. 29 May 1850. (P. 497)

Clark Hubbard to his daughter, Martha Ann Kennedy, my negro girl Susan as a deed of gift. 29 May 1850. (P. 498)

John A. Mitchell, Administrator of John Finley; Nathan Finley, Edmond Finley and other heirs petition to sell land. 2 Jan 1852. (Pp. 498-501)

William Ferrell to R. H. Mason 227 acres in the 6th District. 5 Apr 1852. (Pp. 501-502)

William A. Givens of Grundy County and William Givens of Warren County to Merritt Givens 50 acres in the 6th District. 23 Mar 1852. (Pp. 502-504)

George Ashford and Nancy Mullins enter into a marriage contract. The said George Ashford is embarrassed in his present circumstances and is indebted to divers parties. The property now owned by the said Nancy Mullins shall not be liable for the debts of the said George Ashford. 2 Feb 1852. (Pp. 504-506)

Samuel R. James for love and affection to his two nieces, Sarah A. M. Hume and Martha Hume, the daughters of Gabriel Hume, a walnut safe. 6 Apr 1852. (Pp. 506-507)

Warren Cummins to James K. Eason a negro girl named Emily, about 16, of yellow complexion for $300. 26 Aug 1848. (P. 507)

Henry Dennis to Ira Hollandsworth 12 acres in the 10th District. 29 Mar 1852. (Pp. 508-509)

Ira Hollandsworth to Henry Dennis five acres in the 10th District. 29 Mar 1852. (Pp. 509-510)

John Peyton to Alexander Morgan 63 acres in the 1st District. 5 Apr 1852. (Pp. 510-511)

John Q. Weatherford to William Stone 178 acres belonging to the heirs of Moses Cummins. 19 Apr 1852. (Pp. 511-513)

William West to Thomas Elkins 75 acres in the 7th and 8th Districts. 19 Dec 1851. (Pp. 513-514)

Martin S. Hoover to William M. Gotcher 100 acres in the 12th District. 19 Feb 1852. (Pp. 515-516)

Sampson Stephens to Samuel Vance 179 acres in the 9th District. 5 Jan 1852. (Pp. 516-518)

David Travis and Isaac Earthman to James M. Avent a trust deed. 3 May 1852. (Pp. 518-520)

T. T. Peay to J. R. Armstrong a tract of land on the east side of the East Fork of Stone's River. 20 May 1852. (Pp. 520-521)

Jonathan Wherry to John B. Armstrong 246 acres in the 1st District. 11 May 1852. (Pp. 521-523)

Edward Gather to Arthur Gaither 100 acres in the 1st District. 7 Apr 1852. (Pp. 523-524)

Thomas G. Wood, trustee, to Francis Turner a boy slave, about 9. 4 Aug 1851. (Pp. 524-525)

John Barrett to John C. Hays a title bond. 21 May 1852. (Pp. 525-526)

R. H. Mason to Turner B. Smith ten and one half acres in the 6th District. 28 May 1852. (Pp. 526-527)

Turner B. Smith to Standford Smith 62½ acres in the 6th District. 28 May 1852. (Pp. 527-528)

(Page 529 is illegible)

Hardy Wimberly, Archebald Montgomery, and Susan Montgomery to William Gunter their interest in the estate of Hardy Wimberly. Said Susan is the wife of the said Archebald Montgomery. 9 Jun 1852. (Pp. 530-531)

James B. Elledge to Samuel Vance 23 acres in the 9th District. 20 Oct 1848. (Pp. 531-532)

R. A. Fagan to J. S. and W. T. Todd 57 acres in the 12th District. 18 Mar 1852. (Pp. 532-533)

James F. Foster to James H. Youngblood one half acre in the 9th District. 18 Dec 1849. (Pp. 533-534)

William T. Rigsby to John H. Rigsby 408 acres in the 6th District. 14 Jun 1852. (P. 535)

John Lemmons to Hiram Todd 125 acres in the 5th District. 13 Jan 1851. (Pp. 536-537)

H. M. Burton, trustee, to Morton, Smith, & Company a town lot in the town of Woodbury. 20 Mar 1852. (Pp. 537-538)

Stephen Mitchel to Daniel W. Mitchel a tract of land in the 2nd District, and in return the said Daniel W. Mitchel agrees to support me and my wife Dorothy Mitchel. 12 May 1852. (Pp. 538-540)

James B. Teneson of Dane County, Wisconsin to Thomas G. Whitfield 170 acres, it being the land that my grandfather, Willis Whitfield, died seized and possessed of. 10 Mar 1852. (Pp. 539-540)

John J. Wood to Newton C. Carnahan a woman named Nancy, 28, and her child named George, about 2. 15 Apr 1852. (Pp. 541-542)

Samuel N. Burger to A. Burger a trust deed. 17 Jun 1852. (Pp. 542-545)

Abraham Burger to Jacob Burger a trust deed. 17 Jun 1852. (Pp. 545-548)

William Jacobs of Rutherford County to John (Brewer) 55 acres on Collins River. 5 Jan 1848. (Pp. 549-550)

Thomas Banning to Thomas G. Whitfield his interest in the estate of Willis Whitfield. 6 Mar 1849. (Pp. 550-551)

Francis Cooper to Wiley Davenport 100 acres in the 11th District. 17 Jun 1852. (Pp. 551-552)

Henry R. Perry to S. B. Spurlock a trust deed. 17 Jun 1852. (Pp. 552-553)

John Murry to William Smoot a trust deed. 19 Jun 1852. (Pp. 553-554)

R. D. Eddings to J. B. Paris a trust deed. 31 May 1852. (P. 555)

Charles L. Nelson to Lewis Malone a trust deed. 25 Jan 1852. (Pp. 555-557)

Shadrach Kelly to Joseph Bogle a trust deed. 15 Apr 1852. (Pp. 1-3)

W. C. Leach to John W. Summers a trust deed. 1 Jul 1852. (Unnumbered)

Warren Davenport to George Davenport 15 acres in the 11th District. Bounded: Absolom Davenport. 20 Jun 1852. (P. 7)

William Parton to Josiah M. Crane a trust deed. 26 Jun 1852. (Pp. 7-8)

William C. Leech to John W. Summer 85 acres in the 11th District. 1 Jul 1852. (Pp. 8-9)

Jonathan Wimberly and Isaac Wimberly to William Gunter their interest in the estate of Hardy Wimberly, Sr. of Jefferson County, Alabamma. We are the lawful heirs of Isaac Wimberly who was heirs at law and brothers of the said Hardy Wimberly. 19 Jul 1852. (P. 9)

James Petty to William Stroud 50 acres belonging to Walter Maxey, Nancy Maxey, and Abey Dozier. 3 Apr 1851. (Pp. 10-11)

Thomas H. Smith to John H. Smith 18 acres in the 1st District. 27 Mar 1852. (Pp. 11-12)

Joshua Vassar to his daughter, Anna Stroud, wife of William D. Stroud, for love and affection 175 acres in the 12th District. 26 Jul 1852. (Pp. 12-13)

William D. Stroud to John Moore 25 acres in the 4th District. 24 Jul 1852. (Pp. 13-14)

John F. Weedon et al to A. M. Weedon their interest in the estate of George W. Weedon of the Republic of Texas. Elizabeth Weedon is the mother of George W. Weedon deceased. 25 Jul 1852. (Pp. 14-16)

David Caughanour to Cullen Curlee two tracts of land on Brawley's Fork of Stone's River. 3 Aug 1852. (Pp. 16-18)

William Gunter to Samuel Hays a negro gurl named Fanna, about 16, and her child named Elizabeth Frances, about 6 months. 22 Jun 1852. (P. 18)

William Wharton and Robert Vinson sto Steel and McBroom a title deed. 30 Aug 1852. (Pp. 18-20)

Ira Hollandsworth to Elizabeth Hollandsworth 40 acres in the 10th District. 19 Aug 1852. (Pp. 20-21)

Sheriff R. H. Smith to Franklin Coleman a trust deed. 31 Aug 1852. (Pp. 21-23)

Isham Pelham, Levi Pelham, Jonathan Wimberly and wife Susan, to John Pendleton 100 acres on Barren Fork of Collins River. 21 Aug 1851. (Pp. 23-25)

Robert Bailey to the Methodist Episcopal Church one acre for a church and school to be known as Bailey's Meetinghouse. 19 May 1852. (P. 25)

B. M. Fugett to T. B. Brevard 66 acres in the 6th District.
19 Jul 1852. (Pp. 26-27)

David McGill to William McGill 50 acres in the 4th District.
1 Jan 1852. (Pp. 27-28)

Joseph Simpson to Peter Simpson 32 acres in the 3rd District. 26 Aug 1852. (Pp. 28-29)

Ward Barrett, Sr. to Allen Morgan for love and affection
200 acres, and in return the said Morgan agrees to support and
keep me. 3 Sep 1852. (Pp. 29-30)

Francis Spurlock to William Kelly and William King 170 acres.
9 Mar 1850. (Pp. 30-32)

Martha Roberts, James M. Roberts, Grenville Roberts, Hampton, Sullins, Martha Sullivan, Burton L. Carnahan, and Sarah
Carnahan to Jacob W. Freas 200 acres in the 12th District. 10
Sep 1852. (Pp. 33-34)

Joseph Simpson to Clement R. Davis 133½ acres in the 3rd District. 6 Aug 1832. (Pp. 34-35)

J. J. Trott to J. M. Gowen lots #40 and 41 in the town of
Woodbury. 19 Nov 1850. (Pp. 35-36)

Travis and Earthman to James M. Avent a trust deed. 2 Sep
1852. (Pp. 36-38)

John Higgins to E. C. Jennings a boy named Philip, about 23.
13 Sep 1852. (P. 38)

Luke Lasater to Joseph Pinkerton 69 acres in the 12th District. 15 Sep 1852. (Pp. 39-40)

Jacob M. Frias to J. M. and S. G. Roberts a trust deed. 10
Sep 1852. (Pp. 40-41)

Benjamin Sapp to T. B. Brevard 42 acres in the 6th District.
18 Sep 1852. (Pp. 41-42)

Ira Hollandsworth to Alfred L. Hancock 18 acres in the
10th District. 20 Sep 1852. (P. 43)

Dozier Bragg to Jesse Carter 175 acres in the 1st District.
21 Feb 1852. (Pp. 44-45)

Aaron F. Jones to Mahaley Ann Helen Jones, the present wife
of said Aaron F. Jones, 100 acres for love and affection. 6
Aug 1852. (Pp. 45-46)

Benjamin Fugett to T. B. Brevard 260 acres in the 6th District. 26 Apr 1852. (Pp. 46-47)

W. S. Massey to G. B. Mears ten acres in the 6th District.
27 Jul 1852. (Pp. 48-49)

Daniel J. Arey and wife Mary Ann, formerly Hollis, to Luke
Lasater 163 acres in the 1st District. We are entitled to one
eighth part of all the personal property that James Hollis,
father of the said Mary Ann, died seized and possessed of. 28

Sep 1852. (Pp. 49-51)

Henry Trott to James K. Eason lot #32 in the town of Woodbury. 30 Sep 1852. (Pp. 51-52)

Lydia Price, May Price, (Reter) Price, Benjamin Webber and wife Sarah, formerly Price, to William Price a tract of land in the 3rd District known as the Peter Simpson place, our grandfather, that we have in right of our mother Jane Price, formerly Simpson, who held an undivided one seventh part in said tract of land, and we do hereby convey the ninth of a seventh part of said tract of land. 20 Sep 1852. (Pp. 52-53)

William Price to Daniel Todd and Ransom Todd 91 acres in the 3rd District. 16 Sep 1852. (Pp. 53-55)

Lewis Hancock to Isaac A. Keeton 50 acres in the 10th District. 2 Oct 1852. (Pp. 55-56)

John W. Summers to A. S. McKnight 20 acres in the 11th District. 27 Oct 1851. (Pp. 56-57)

Franklin Coleman to James Vassar his interest in 125 acres in the 2nd District, it being the land that Dawson McGlocklin died seized and possessed of. 24 Sep 1852. (P. 58)

Jacob Byford to Joshua Creson 60 acres in the 4th District. 6 Aug 1852. (Pp. 59-60)

Ervin Cherry to Joshua Creson 20 acres in the 4th District. 6 Aug 1852. (Pp. 60-61)

Elizabeth Hollandsworth to Ira Hollandsworth her interest in the estate of John Hollandsworth. 19 Aug 1852. (Pp. 61-62)

A. Burger to Jacob Burger a trust deed. 9 Oct 1852. (Pp. 62-64)

Henry R. Perry to John Webb a trust deed. 28 Jun 1852. (Pp. 64-67)

James Cook to John Pendleton 116 acres in the 5th District. 20 May 1852. (Pp. 67-68)

Benjamin F. Webber to Benjamin Webber 50 acres for $150. 1 Oct 1852. (Pp. 68-70)

Joseph Bogle to William R. Bogle 50 acres in the 11th District, it being said Joseph Bogle's undivided interest in a tract of land which fell to the heirs of Joseph Bogle, Sr. 10 Jan 1849. (Pp. 70-71)

Lemuel Owen and wife Elizabeth; Samuel B. Adams and wife Candace; and James M. Adams of Randolph County, Illinois to Samuel Carson their interest in the estate of Robert Carson. 12 Dec 1850. (Pp. 71-72)

John Brown and wife Sarah to John N. Doak their one sixth interest in a tract of land in the 2nd District. 12 Oct 1852. (Pp. 73-74)

Pinkney Todd to Asa Todd 239 acres in the 12th District. 12 Oct 1852. (Pp. 74-75)

John Hollandsworth to Ira Hollandsworth his interest in the estate of John Hollandsworth deceased for $150. 16 Sep 1852. (Pp. 75-76)

Alexander McKnight and S. T. McKnight, Executors of Moses McKnight, to W. Wilberford McKnight 15 acres in the 1st District. 24 Dec 1850. (Pp. 76-77)

William Holt, by his attorney Fielding Holt, Sr., to L. G. Tolbert 48½ acres in the 12th District. 28 Oct 1852. (Pp. 77-81)

William Price to Clement R. Davis 40 acres in the 4th District. 2 Oct 1852. (Pp. 81-83)

Clement R. Davis to William Todd 40 acres in the 4th District. 1 Nov 1852. (Pp. 83-84)

John Ward to Albert T. Fagan 86½ acres in the 6th District. 30 Oct 1852. (Pp. 84-86)

Jonathan Wherry to Gabriel Hume 262 acres in the 8th District. 3 Nov 1852. (Pp. 86-88)

Albert T. Fagan to George Lawrence 96 acres in the 6th District. 8 Nov 1852. (Pp. 88-89)

Wilson Y. Jones to John A. Whitsitt a tract of land on Barren Fork of Collins River. 5 Feb 1852. (Pp. 90-91)

John Webb and H. R. Terry to Samuel Vance 130 acres in the 6th District. 19 Nov 1852. (Pp. 92-94)

James K. Eason to Henry R. Perry lot #22 in the town of Woodbury. 20 Nov 1852. (Pp. 94-96)

John Petty to Isaac Goodright 53 acres in the 4th District. 19 Nov 1852. (Pp. 96-97)

L. B. Moore to Isaac Grizzle 112 acres in the 7th District. 24 Nov 1852. (Pp. 97-98)

Arthur Warren to Lewis Jetton 85 acres in the 3rd District. 30 Nov 1852. (Pp. 99-101)

William D. Stroud and wife Anny to James Cook 175 acres in the 4th District. 1 Dec 1852. (Pp. 101-103)

Samuel Parker to Elizabeth Mollie Bragg 50 acres on Carson's Fork of Stone's River. 3 Dec 1852. (Pp. 103-104)

Gabriel Hume to Thomas C. Smart 2800 acres. 3 Dec 1852. (Pp. 104-105)

Sampson Stephens to George Gannon ten acres in the 2nd District. 6 Dec 1852. (Pp. 105-106)

Stanford Smith to R. H. Mason ten and a half acres on the east fork of Stone's River. 20 Nov 1852. (Pp. 106-107)

Thomas G. Wood to Sarah E. Teague 100 acres on Hollis' Creek. 6 Dec 1852. (Pp. 107-109)

Sarah E. Teague and husband John to John Pendleton 100 acres in the 5th District. 6 Dec 1852. (Pp. 109-110)

William Campbell, Administrator of Reuben Hawkins, to Robert M. Fare a slave. 2 Dec 1852. (P. 111)

Sampson Stephens to Stanford Smith 30 acres in the 2nd District. 9 Dec 1852. (Pp. 111-112)

Stanford Smith to Robert K. Stephens 160 acres in the 1st District. 9 Dec 1852. (Pp. 113-114)

Frances Hancock has filed a bill for divorce and alimony against Lewis Hancock. Divorce was granted at the September Term of Court. 6 Dec 1852. (Pp. 114-115)

Stanford Smith to T. B. Brevard 52 acres in the 6th District. 11 Dec 1852. (Pp. 116-117)

Sheriff Samuel Vance to Stanford Smith 100 acres known as the Grundy Fann farm. 11 Dec 1852. (Pp. 117-122)

Benjamin F. McBroon to Isaac N. Fuller lot #46 in the town of Woodbury. 23 Oct 1852. (Pp. 122-123)

Elijah Dobbs to T. B. Brevard a house and lot in the town of Woodbury. Bounded: McBroom garden. 27 Dec 1852. (Pp. 123-124)

Isaac L. Mitchell to J. N. Fuller a trust deed. 27 Dec 1852. (Pp. 124-125)

Harmon Gatton to Almand Mullinax 75 acres in the 11th District. 2 Aug 1852. (Pp. 126-127)

John W. Mullins and B. C. Ashford to John Young their interest in a tract of land on Stone's River in the 7th District. Bounded: Widow Mullins dowery. 31 Dec 1852. (Pp. 127-129)

Gabriel Hume to Washington Kennedy 54 acres. Gabriel Hume purchased of Archebald Stone the tract of land where I now live. I was not able to make payment for said land and whereas my brothers, William C. Hume and David Hume, both citizens of Virginia made a donation of $300 to Ann L. Hume for the sole and separate use of the said Ann L. Hume, wife of the said Gabriel Hume and her children. 3 Jan 1853. (Pp. 129-131)

Stanford Smith to William Barton a trust deed. 4 Jan 1853. (Pp. 131-133)

Robert Vinson to John Ward 14 acres in the 6th District. 4 Jan 1853. (Pp. 133-134)

Josiah Hollandsworth to Aden Hollandsworth his interest in the estate of John Hollandsworth. 19 Aug 1852. (P. 135)

Daniel Finley to William Leigh 278 acres in the 4th District. 25 Nov 1852. (Pp. 135-137)

Jesse Sisson to William Leigh 50 acres on Carson's Fork of Stone's River, it being a part of a 977 acre tract surveyed in the name of James Sisson. 25 May 1850. (Pp. 157-158)

Thomas Williams to Jesse B. Williams 375 acres in the 4th

District. 7 Jan 1853. (Pp. 138-139)

William B. Evans and Samuel C. Evans to Veach Crabtree a tract of land in the 6th District. 7 Jan 1853. (Pp. 140-141)

William Cummins to Isaiah Parker 200 acres in the 4th District. 10 Jan 1853. (Pp. 141-142)

William B. Nokes to Andrew N. Johnson 80 acres in the 6th District. 8 Dec 1852. (Pp. 142-143)

Cornelius Brandon to John E. Brandon 248 acres in the 3rd District. 22 Oct 1852. (Pp. 144-145)

C. C. Akers to Robert J. Patton 54 acres on Brawley's Fork of Stone's River. 3 May 1852. (Pp. 145-146)

Samuel W. Rucker to John C. Martin 122 acres in the 3rd District. 13 Dec 1852. (Pp. 146-147)

Mayor and Aldermen of Woodbury to C. B. Davis one eighth of an acre in the town of Boodbury. Bounded: north by High Street; east by a lot formerly owned by Dr. Price with a brick building now on it. 7 Jan 1853. (Pp. 148-149)

William C. Soap to A. J. Inglis 90 acres in the 12th District. 21 Aug 1852. (Pp. 149-151)

Harrison Peyton to Peter Hunter 75 acres in the 4th District. 20 Nov 1852. (Pp. 151-152)

Cornelius Brandon to Tobias Tenpenny 80 acres in the 3rd District. 9 Sep 1852. (Pp. 152-153)

Isaac N. Fuller to R. A. Smith 50 acres in the 2nd District. 11 Jan 1853. (Pp. 154-155)

Ira Hollandsworth to Jesse McGee 25 acres in the 10th District. 6 Jan 1853. (Pp. 155-156)

William S. Melton to Jesse Lawrence 150 acres in the 8th District. 14 Jan 1853. (Pp. 156-158)

Albert G. Milligan to William Sisson 100 acres in the 12th District. 13 Jan 1853. (Pp. 158-159)

Charles L. Nelson of Rutherford County to M. S. Nelson 400 acres. 1 Aug 1852. (Pp. 159-161)

A. G. Millikin to Mary Y. Pallet ten acres in the 12th District. 30 Sep 1852. (Pp. 161-162)

Cornelius Brandon to his daughter, Louisa Gordon, 40 acres in the 3rd District. 6 Dec 1852. (Pp. 162-163)

William Nichols to Thomas G. Sullivan 25 acres in the 1st District. 15 Jan 1853. (Pp. 163-165)

John Sauls and Grundy Fann to David B. Reed 50 acres in the 1st District. 26 Jan 1853. (Pp. 165-166)

Abraham Gooding to William Leigh 50 acres on Carson's Fork of Stone's River. 15 Dec 1840. (Pp. 166-168)

John Finley to Thomas W. Moore of Coffee County two tracts of land on Carson's Fork of Stone's River. 30 Jan 1853. (Pp. 168-170)

Benjamin F. Alexander and wife Mary J. to John N. Doak a tract of land in the 2nd District on Hollis' Creek. 3 Feb 1853. (Pp. 170-171)

John Ward to R. H. Mason 103 acres in the 6th District. 5 Feb 1853. (Pp. 171-173)

Sheriff Samuel Vance to John Young 50 acres. 7 Feb 1853. (Pp. 173-174)

John Barrett to John C. Hays 45 acres in the 2nd District. 12 Feb 1853. (Pp. 175-176)

William King to Luke Lasater a negro woman named Betsy, about 25. 18 Jan 1853. (P. 176)

John A. Webber to John B. Armstrong a trust deed. 10 Feb 1853. (Pp. 176-178)

William West to William F. George a part of lot #37 in the town of Woodbury. 14 Feb 1853. (Pp. 178-179)

Richard J. Bond to William R. Bogle a title bond. 13 Oct 1852. (Pp. 179-180)

Washington Leigh to Peter Hunter 82 acres in the 4th District. 12 Jan 1852. (Pp. 180-182)

John Hollis to Clement R. Davis five acres in the 3rd District. 14 Feb 1852. (Pp. 182-183)

A. S. McKnight to Alexander Milligan one rod and 24 poles in the 11th District. 14 Feb 1853. (Pp. 183-184)

Stanford Smith to Dozier Bragg, Sr. five acres in the 10th District. 15 Feb 1853. (P. 185)

John Barrett to Alexander Morgan 45 acres in the 1st District. 15 Feb 1853. (P. 186)

Samuel Denby to his daughter Maney R. Jones and her husband William B. Jones a negro girl named Charlet, about 4, as a part of their legacy to my estate. 15 Feb 1853. (P. 189)

Samuel Denby to my daughter Nancy R. Jones and her husband William R. Jones 100 acres in the 9th District. Mentions my son William Denby. 29 Apr 1852. (Pp. 189-190)

James B. Summers to Andrew J. Bryan 125 acres in the 11th District. 5 Nov 1852. (Pp. 191-192)

John C. Smithson to Joshua Haley 200 acres in the 5th District. 11 Feb 1853. (PP. 192-194)

Henry Dennis to Ira Hollandsworth 12 acres in the 10th District. 9 Feb 1853. (Pp. 194-196)

Ira Hollandsworth to William Collins 150 acres. 14 Feb 1853. (Pp. 196-197)

J. H. Thomas to Armstead Francis a man slave named Jack, between 40 and 50, for $625. 12 Jan 1853. (Pp. 197-198)

Stanford Smith to Edward Bragg one and a half acres in the 1st District. 4 May 1849. (Pp. 198-199)

Reuben Herald to John L. Espy a tract of land in the 5th District. 17 Feb 1853. (Pp. 199-200)

James W. McAdow and William C. Leach to John W. Marshall 200 acres in the 11th District. 17 Feb 1853. (PP. 200-201)

Aaron F. Jones to E. J. Wood a trust deed. 19 Feb 1853. (Pp. 201-202)

John A. George, Administrator of Charles Alexander, to Henry Hays a tract of land. 21 Feb 1853. (Pp. 202-204)

William Bratton to William Groom 226 acres in the 11th District. 17 Jan 1853. (Pp. 204-205)

John A. George, Administrator of Charles P. Alexander, to R. A. Smith a tract of land. 21 Feb 1853. (Pp. 205-207)

Elaner Andrews and Jane Andrews to Joseph A. Dement 56 acres in the 1st District. 4 Mar 1851. (Pp. 208-209)

John Harriman to Daniel Grizzle 80 acres in the 10th District. 11 Feb 1853. (Pp. 209-210)

Stanton Smith to A. Burger a trust deed. 17 Feb 1853. (Pp. 211-212)

Henry Powell to William Powell 200 acres in the 10th District. 11 Oct 1853. (Pp. 212-213)

Henry Trott to William Wimberly a tract of land in the 5th District. 17 Feb 1853. (Pp. 214-215)

Jesse B. Williams to J. J. and A. W. Morton a tract of land in the 5th District. Bounded: Betsy Williams. 29 Jan 1853. (Pp. 215-216)

William G. Bratten to G. W. E. Wale 105 acres on the east fork of Stone's River. 21 Feb 1853. (Pp. 216-217)

John Young to John Davis 25 acres in the 7th District. 21 Feb 1853. (P. 218)

Stephen Wilson to Michael Wilson 150 acres in the 11th District. 4 Mar 1853. (P. 219)

Stephen Wilson to Michael Wilson 50 acres in the 11th District. 4 Mar 1853. (P. 220)

Shadrach J. Odom, Sarah S. Odom, W. C. Summar, Lucinda, Summer, B. B. Cooper, and Rebecca Cooper to Nelson Owen a tract of land that Jesse Owen died seized and possessed of. 18 Aug 1850. (Pp. 221-223)

John Bankhead to Robert Barton three negro slaves, to wit, Nancy, 28, Susy, daughter of Nancy, and Amy, ditto. 10 Nov 1817. (PP. 223-225)

DEED BOOK I

Jesse Sisson to William Stacy 500 acres in the 4th District. 26 Jan 1853. (Pp. 225-226)

Peter Tribble to William Campbell a negro boy named Randle, about fore. 26 Nov 1814. (Pp. 226-227)

John Hawkins, Richard Butcher, Joseph Hawkins, Reuben Hawkins, and Sarah Pitts to William Campbell a negro girl named Lucy, about 6. 10 Oct 1825. (Pp. 227-228)

James Stone to Isaac Gunter 16 acres in the 7th District. 16 Mar 1853. (Pp. 228-229)

Veach Crabtree to A. B. Carnes 36 acres in the 6th District. 17 Mar 1853. (Pp. 229-230)

Henry Dennis to Jesse McGee two acres in the 10th District. 8 Oct 1852. (Pp. 230-231)

Ira Hollandsworth to Henry Dennis five and one half acres in the 10th District. 29 Mar 1852. (P. 231)

Samuel Pendleton to Hugh Craft 150 acres in the 5th District. 15 Feb 1853. (P. 232)

A. Burger and S. N. Burger to H. L. B. Douglass a town lot in the town of Woodbury. Bounded: Southeast corner of the Public Square. 24 Mar 1853. (P. 233)

Dozier Bragg, Jr. Minford Pedon and wife Nancy J., formerly Bragg, John Whitlock and wife Sally L., formerly Bragg, and William M. Bragg to Thomas G. Sullivan 200 acres in the 1st District. 16 Mar 1853. (P. 234)

Alexander Young to John N. Mitchell 94 acres in the 2nd and 6th Districts. 25 Mar 1853. (Pp. 235-236)

Andrew J. Bogle to John Bogle 100 acres in the 11th District. 21 Aug 1852. (Pp. 237-238)

R. H. Mason to Jacob Hoover 227 acres. 31 Mar 1853. (Pp. 238-239)

Anna Smith, John M. Smith, Manerva Smith, being the widow and heirs of James Smith, to John F. Curlee their interest in 50 acres in the 3rd District. 10 Mar 1853. (Pp. 239-240)

Benjamin F. Allen to William Young 12 acres in the 8th District. 3 Apr 1853. (P. 240)

Zachariah Warren to Thomas G. Sullivan 110 acres in the 2nd District. 9 Apr 1853. (Pp. 240-241)

L. R. Hancock to Frances Hancock 50 acres in the 10th District. 20 Mar 1853. (P. 242)

L. R. Hancock to B. J. Hancock 50 acres in the 10th District. 20 Mar 1853. (P. 253)

Zachariah Warren to Thomas G. Sullivan 110 acres 110 acres in the 2nd District, 9 Apr 1853. (Misnumbered)

T. G. Sullivan to John P. Gandy 160 acres in the 3rd District. 2 May 1853. (Misnumbered)

John H. Wood and wife Roxanna P., formerly Roxanna P. Sutton, to Thomas G. Wood their interest in the estate of Edmond Sutton. 2 Dec 1851. (Pp. 246-248)

William W. McKnight and wife Elizabeth; John Teague and wife Sarah E.; Mary Sutton; Margaret T. L. Sutton; Mary Tassey; and A. Tassey, all heirs of Alexander H. Sutton, 85 acres in the 2nd District. 27 Mar 1850. (Pp. 248-250)

James H. Reed to George W. Reed 50 acres in the 12th District. 27 Mar 1850. (Pp. 250-251)

Sarah Freeze; Sarah E. Freeze; Daniel D. Lynn and wife Martha; and Benjamin Freeze, all of Cannon County; and John and Elizabeth Freeze of Coffee County, heirs of Solomon Freeze, to Daniel Finley 200 acres in the 6th District. 1 Jan 1853. (Pp. 251-254)

Thomas G. Wood to Robert C. McBroon 100 acres. 21 May 1853. (P. 255)

Stephen A. Mitchell to A. F. McFerrin 16 acres in the 4th District. 22 May 1853. (P. 255)

Thomas G. Wood to Robert C. McBroom a tract of land. 21 May 1853. (Pp. 255-256)

William Stone to Jesse Lawrence 150 acres in the 7th District. 2 May 1853. (PP. 257-258)

Isaac Markum to Henry Burket 175 acres in the 9th District. 13 Jun 1853. (Pp. 258-259)

William C. Leech to Samuel C. Odom 223 acres in the 11th District. 9 Feb 1852. (Pp. 260-261)

John A. George and R. H. Mason to Samuel Burk five acres in the 6th District. 13 Jun 1853. (Pp. 261-262)

Joseph Ramsey to John Q. Weatherford a tract of land in the 6th District. 10 Feb 1853. (Pp. 262-263)

Turner B. Smith to William Stone a trust deed. 15 Jun 1853. (Pp. 263-264)

Rezin Fowler to Elijah Neely a trust deed. 8 Aug 1851. (Pp. 264-267)

Hiram Moses to Richard Hancock a tract of land in the 10th District. 1 Jun 1853. (Pp. 267-268)

Richard Hancock to Hiram Moris 80 acres in the 10th District. 21 Jun 1853. (P. 269)

John Miles to Daniel Finley 60 acres in the 5th District. 2 Jun 1853. (Pp. 270-271)

Swinfield Smith to B. M. Hall five acres in the 5th District. 15 Apr 1853. (Pp. 271-272)

Sheriff Samuel Vance to Eakin and Company 200 acres. 20 Jun 1853. (Pp. 272-275)

Jesse Sisson, William Sisson, Thomas Sisson, and Polly Sisson, the heirs of James Sisson, to Sally Sisson 75 acres. Bounded: the school house above the Widow Sisson's called Liberty School House. 5 Apr 1845. (Pp. 275-277)

Sheriff Samuel Vance to Daniel Tenpenny 50 acres. 27 Jan 1853. (Pp. 277-278)

Thomas Sisson to William Sisson 150 acres in the 8th District. 26 Apr 1847. (Pp. 279-280)

William West to Thomas Elkins and Dillard L. Elkins 113 acres in the 7th and 8th Districts. 2 Jul 1853. (Pp. 280-281)

William Sisson to Michael Bowman 245 acres in the 4th District. 6 Jul 1853. (Pp. 282-283)

Michael Bowman to Jesse Millikin 245 acres in the 4th District. 6 Jul 1853. (Pp. 283-284)

A. D. Alexander to A. C. Alexander 165 acres. 16 Oct 1849. (P. 285)

William Stroud to C. C. Good 50 acres in the 4th District. 11 Oct 1851. (P. 286)

R. A. Smith to John H. Wood 140 acres. 7 Feb 1852. (Pp. 287-291)

John H. Wood to Stith Hays 140 acres in the 6th District. 9 Jul 1855. (Pp. 291-292)

Stith Hays to A. B. Carens 140 acres in the 6th District. 4 Jul 1853. (Pp. 292-293)

Sheriff Samuel Vance to J. T. Blair 38½ acres in the 7th District. 12 Jul 1853. (Pp. 293-295)

Henry Wiley to Warren Cummins 151 acres. 15 Jul 1853. (Pp. 295-296)

Thomas K. Leech to William C. Leech 170 acres in the 11th District. 10 Sep 1850. (Pp. 296-297)

Henry Trott to John R. Brooks 50 acres in the 5th District. 17 Feb 1853. (Pp. 298-299)

Benjamin A. Godwin and wife Rebecca to C. B. Summer 200 acres in the 3rd District. Also, the interest we have in the dower assigned to Mary Brandon, widow of Cornelius Brandon. 20 Jul 1853. (Pp. 299-300)

Alexander Warren and wife Nancy Ann to John N. Doak their interest, it being one sixth, a tract of land in the 2nd District. 2 Aug 1853. (Pp. 300-301)

John Epley to the different denominations of separate Baptists a tract of land on the waters of the Barren Fork of Collins River to be known as Liberty Meeting House and School House. 1 Aug 1853. (Pp. 301-302)

Peter Hunter to A. F. McFerrin 82 acres in the 4th District. 1 Aug 1853. (Pp. 303-304)

William C. Leech to William C. Donell 170 acres in the 11th District. 6 Aug 1853. (Pp. 304-306)

Samuel C. Young to John Hewit and wife Ann his interest in the estate of his father Joseph Young. Witness: Isaac B. Young. 17 Feb 1853. (P. 306)

Daniel G. Travis and Amos Travis to Edward Gaither 33 acres in the 1st District. 29 Jul 1853. (Pp. 306-307)

Meredith Akers and wife Elizabeth to Mary Y. Pallett 16 acres in the 12th District, it being the land allotted to the said Elizabeth out of a 175½ acre tract belonging to the heirs of Abram Pallett by grant of the State of Tennessee No. 1742. 8 Aug 1853. (Pp. 308-309)

Joseph H. Bogle to Matthew Bogle 100 acres in the 11th District. 1 Aug 1853. (Pp. 309-310)

Meredith Akers and wife Elizabeth to Mary Y. Pallett 50 acres in the 12th District. 10 Aug 1853. (Pp. 310-312)

Alexander Nesbit and Benjamin Wallace enter into an agreement in which the said Nesbitt agrees to furnish the stone for a saw mill. 2 Sep 1850. (Pp. 312-315)

Isaac Grizzle to George Turner 112 acres in the 7th District. 1 Sep 1853. (PP. 315-317)

Rhody L. Williams, Tilda P. Williams, and Nancy M. Williams, heirs of James M. Williams and Tempa Williams, to Lemuel T. Williams their power of attorney to receive their share of the estate of Willis Whitfield. Said parties of the first part are residents of Itawamby County, Mississippi. 15 Aug 1853. (Pp. 317-320)

Lemuel T. Williams, James M. Williams, Rhoda L. Williams, Tilda P. Williams, Nancy M. Williams, and Elizabeth C. Smith, formerly Williams, the legal heirs of James M. Williams and Tempa Williams, to Alford Whitfield their interest in the estate of Willis Whitfield (who was our grandfather). 2 Sep 1853. (Pp. 320-322)

William Godwin and wife Rebecca to Allen Godwin their power of attorney to receive their share of the estate of Cornelius Brandon. Said parties of the first part are residents of Hardin County. 10 Aug 1853. (Pp. 322-323)

Sheriff Samuel Vance to A. Stone and J. L. Fare 200 acres. 8 Jul 1853. (Pp. 323-325)

Sheriff Samuel Vance to William G. Bratton 100 acres. 8 Jul 1853. (Pp. 325-327)

Thomas Elkins to D. L. Elkins 40 acres in the 7th District. 5 Sep 1853. (Pp. 327-330)

Mary Clark, widow of Andrew Clark; John W. Clark, Mary A. Clark, Robert A. Clark, children of full age; Robert Clark, Jane Clark, and William Clark guardian of Archabald A. Clerk, minor heir of Robert H. and Jane Clark, all of Mecklenburg

County, North Carolina appoint John Clark of Rutherford County their power of attorney to receive their share of the estate of Robert Carson. 26 Mar 1853. (Pp. 330-332)

Margaret Clark, John W. Clark, Robert N. Clark, and William Clark as guardian through their attorney in fact John Clark of Rutherford County to Samuel Carson 200 acres in the 4th District. 17 May 1853. (Pp. 332-333)

Daniel Tenpenny to Johnathan Basham 84 acres on Dry Creek, a branch of the east fork of Stone's River. 5 Sep 1853. (Pp. 333-335)

William C. Leech to John W. Summer a trust deed. 10 Sep 1853. (Pp. 335-338)

William Godwin and wife Isabella to C. B. Summers a tract of land in the 3rd District, it being the dower assigned to Mary Brandon, widow of Cornelius Brandon. 3 Sep 1853. (Pp. 338-340)

Isaac Gunter to Micajah Marcum 100 acres in the 10th District. 1 Sep 1853. (Pp. 340-341)

Micajah Marcum to Samuel Marcum 96 acres in the 9th District. 3 Sep 1853. (Pp. 341-342)

Joseph Horn to Albert G. Millikin 25 acres in the 12th District. 25 Jan 1853. (P. 343)

Elisha B. Rose to William Denby 200 acres in the 9th District. 12 Oct 1852. (Pp. 344-345)

Francis Spurlock to Fountain Owen 300 acres in the 10th District. 22 Sep 1853. (Pp. 345-346)

James A. Spurlock to John Burkett a tract of land in the 10th District. 28 Aug 1853. (Pp. 347-348)

Henry Maney to L. M. Maney a slave named Nathan, 36, for $800. 21 Sep 1853. (Pp. 348-349)

Elizabeth Rucker to Benjamin Rucker her power of attorney to receive her share of the estate of James Taylor. 8 Mar 1853. (Pp. 349-350)

Isaac R. Young to Elizabeth Todd a negro girl slave of yellow or mulatto complexion named Judy, about 20. Said girl is a gift for my sister Elizabeth Todd, wife of James Todd. 2 Sep 1853. (Pp. 351-352)

Robert Marshall to B. F. Odom a negro woman named Charlott, a boy named Abram, and a girl named Juda, ages as follows, Charlott, 34; Abram, 4; and Juda, 3, all for $1000. 24 Nov 1849. (P. 352)

Jesse Millikin to Albert G. Millikin his power of attorney to sell 300 acres. 4 Oct 1853. (Pp. 352-353)

Robert W. Lansdon to Shadrach J. Odom 136 acres in the 11th District. 28 Nov 1853. (Pp. 353-355)

B. B. Alexander to F. C. Alexander his interest in his mother's estate. 21 Aug 1847. (Pp. 355-356)

Samuel Carson to Clement R. Davis 200 acres. 2 Aug 1853. (Pp. 356-357)

James Blair to William Ferrell 200 acres in the 9th District. 10 Oct 1853. (Pp. 358-359)

Peter Simpson to Peter Cox 100 acres in the 5th District. 14 Mar 1848. (Pp. 359-360)

James C. Creson to Lewis Creson ten acres in the 2nd District. 10 Oct 1853. (Pp. 361-363)

William C. Leech to A. P. Davis a man slave named Ben, 40, for $800. 15 Aug 1853. (P. 363)

Elam McKnight to Steven Wilson 24 acres in the 11th District. 10 Sep 1853. (Pp. 364-365)

William Todd to James S. Todd 28½ acres in the 12th District. 10 Oct 1853. (Pp. 365-366)

John Pendleton to his daughter Malinda West, the wife of Charles H. West, 50 acres on the Barren Fork of Collins River. 5 Oct 1853. (Pp. 366-367)

Mark L. Young to T. J. Preston and E. C. Preston a title bond. 7 Feb 1853. (Pp. 367-369)

A. Cooper to B. J. Hancock a tract of land in the 10th District. 3 Jun 1853. (Pp. 369-370)

Samuel Denby to his son, William Denby, a negro boy named Caleb, about 6. 30 Apr 1853. (Pp. 370-371)

Isaac Keeton to Abraham Cooper 50 acres in the 10th District. 18 Oct 1852. (Pp. 371-372)

Bluford J. Hancock to Thomas Ford 87 acres in the 10th District. 15 Oct 1853. (Pp. 373-374)

John Pendleton to M. L. Young one and a half acres in the 5th District. 12 Jan 1853. (Pp. 374-375)

William H. McCabe to Stith Hays 145 acres in the 5th District. 15 Sep 1853. (Pp. 376-377)

R. M. Hall to William Young 130 acres in the 5th District. 12 Oct 1853. (Pp. 377-378)

Uriah B. Bush to Isaac Kirkland 200 acres in the 12th District. 30 Mar 1850. (Pp. 378-380)

Edward G. Steel to L. B. Nelson a trust deed. 17 Oct 1853. (Pp. 380-381)

John Webber to Benjamin Webber 66 acres in the 12th District. 26 Oct 1853. (Pp. 381-382)

J. M. Odom to A. J. Odom a title bond. 21 Jan 1853. (Pp. 382-383)

Henry Burket to Micajah Massey 175 acres in the 10th District. 10 Oct 1853. (Pp. 383-384)

Thomas Silliman to Edmund Gaither 50 acres on the north side of the main east fork of Stone's River. 21 Oct 1853. (Pp. 385-386)

Jacob W. Frias to Joseph Pinkerton 180 acres in the 12th District. 22 Oct 1853. (Pp. 386-388)

W. W. Elledge to Joseph Pinkerton 32 acres in the 12th District. 17 Oct 1850. (Pp. 388-389)

Jacob W. Freas to Azariah Gaither 20 acres in the 3rd District. 22 Oct 1853. (Pp. 390-391)

Grundy Fann and Stanford Smith to William M. Bragg 110 acres in the 1st District. 5 Nov 1853. (Pp. 391-392)

Joshua Barton to William Barton 200 acres in the 3rd District for $1800. 2 Nov 1853. (Pp. 392-393)

Peter Hunter to R. H. Mason 75 acres in the 11th District. 22 Sep 1853. (P. 394)

Henry Maney to Delilah Bosley 500 acres except for the three acres where Alex Bryant now lives. 15 Aug 1853. (P. 395)

James Cummings to Benjamin Cummings 78 acres in the 6th and 7th Districts. 12 Nov 1853. (Pp. 396-397)

Jesse Gilliam to Lewis Jetton 200 acres in the 1st District. 23 Jul 1853. (Pp. 397-399)

Thomas Powell to Hiram Wilson a title bond. 6 Jun 1853. (Pp. 399-400)

Alexander N. Smoot to James L. Cawthon 100 acres on Brawley's Fork of Stone's River. 7 Nov 1853. (Pp. 400-402)

William M. Gotcher to A. J. Inglis 100 acres in the 12th District. 6 Oct 1853. (Pp. 402-403)

Andrew J. Bogle and wife Emily to F. C. Alexander 165 acres in the 11th District. 8 Nov 1853. (Pp. 404-405)

Abel McBroom to William Barton and Benjamin F. McBroom as trustees for the use and support of Sarah McBroom, wife of Henry D. McBroom, a tract of land during her life and at the death of the said Sarah McBroom to be equally divided between John D. McBroom, Benjamin T. McBroom, William F. McBroom, Sarah Barton, the wife of William Barton, and Abel McBroom, Jr., all the children of the said Sarah McBroom and Henry D. McBroom. 25 Nov 1853. (Pp. 405-408)

Matthew Bogle and Armstead G. Odom and wife Eliza to Joseph H. Bogle 142 acres in the 11th District. 20 May 1853. (Pp. 408-410)

Joseph Hollandsworth to Aden Hollandsworth a tract of land in the 10th District. 19 Nov 1853. (Pp. 410-411)

Aden Hollandsworth to John D. Hollandsworth 45 acres in the 10th District. 12 Nov 1853. (Pp. 412-413)

Elizabeth Sanford to Bell, Wharton, & Company one acre in the 6th District. 1 Dec 1853. (Pp. 413-414)

King S. Peeler to John C. Fowler 85 acres in the 3rd District. 5 Dec 1853. (Pp. 415-416)

Dabney Sandridge to Abraham Burger and Edward A. Keeble 277 acres on Charles Creek and Barren Fork of Collins River. 5 Dec 1853. (Pp. 416-417)

William Young to Benjamin Wilson 12 acres in the 8th District. 6 Dec 1853. (Pp. 417-418)

Alexander McKnight to Amzi W. Marlin 162 acres in the 1st District. 28 Jun 1853. (Pp. 419-420)

Elijah Stevens to Benjamin Fugett 50 acres in the 6th District. 21 Oct 1852. (Pp. 420-421)

Elijah Stevens to Benjamin Fugett 165 acres in the 6th District. 21 Oct 1852. (Pp. 421-422)

J. C. Leak appoints Joseph Nash his power of attorney to sell a tract of land. 6 Dec 1853. (Pp. 422-423)

C. W. Nance to Joseph C. Leak a tract of land on Sycamore and Canal Creeks. 21 Nov 1853. (Pp. 423-424)

Mayor and Aldermen to Joseph Spurlock lot #64 in the town of Woodbury. 31 Nov 1852. (Pp. 424-425)

Mayor and Aldermen to Joseph Spurlock three town lots in the town of Woodbury. 1 Mar 1852. (Pp. 426-427)

R. H. Mason to Jacob Hoover 240 acres in the 6th District. 1 Mar 1852. (Pp. 428-429)

Charles L. Nelson of Rutherford County to James R. Nelson 402 acres. 1 Aug 1852. (Pp. 429-430)

James L. Colvert and wife Johannah to Henry Goodlow 30 acres. 5 Dec 1853. (Pp. 431-433)

C. E. Curlee to Luke Lasater a man slave named Allen. 31 Dec 1853. (P. 433)

Alexander Orr to Robert Simpson 37 acres. 14 Sep 1853. (Pp. 433-435)

H. and B. Douglass & Company of Nashville to Zebulon L. Brevard lot #38 in the town of Woodbury. 20 Dec 1853. (Pp. 435-436)

John C. Martin to John H. Wood 122 acres in the 3rd District. 6 Jan 1854. (Pp. 436-437)

Alfred M. Goodlow and A. M. Weedon to Benjamin Wallace 105 acres in the 2nd District. 4 Jan 1854. (Pp. 437-439)

Deadamia Bowen, widow of William Bowen, to William G. Bowen her power of attorney to receive her share of the estate of John Grissam. Witness: Samuel Bowen. 10 Jan 1854. (P. 439)

Alexander S. Moore to William B. Nokes 42 acres in the 6th District. 31 Dec 1853. (Pp. 439-440)

Phillip P. Maxcy to Joseph McKnight 75 acres in the 1st District. 8 Sep 1853. (Pp. 441-442)

William W. Adams to John B. Perkins 200 acres in the 10th District. 12 Jan 1852. (Pp. 442-443)

State of Tennessee Grant #19,003. 55 acres in the 2nd District to George Gannon. 9 Jan 1830. (Pp. 443-444)

Benjamin Sapp to Mary Sutton 48 acres in the 2nd District. 31 Oct 1853. (Pp. 444-445)

Chancery Court decree. S. H. McKnight to Alexander McKnight 170 acres. James T. McKnight is executor. Legatees are John L. Kelton and wife Eliza; Eugenia, John M., Andrew and wife Sarah Jane, Samuel H. McKnight, and George D. McKnight. Said parties are heirs of Daniel McKnight. 20 Jan 1854. (Pp. 445-453)

Archebald Stone to Abel Rushing 365 acres on Hill's Creek of Stone's River, it being the premises where the said Stone now lives. 5 Nov 1853. (Pp. 454-456)

Rezin Fowler to William Cummings and Elijah Neely 260 acres in the 6th District. 19 Sep 1851. (Pp. 457-459)

Aaron F. Jones to Joel Milligan a trust deed. 19 Sep 1851. (Pp. 459-460)

John J. Wood to David N. Rolston 18 acres in the 1st District. 3 Nov 1853. (Misnumbered)

Rezin Fowler to Elijah Neely a trust deed. 8 Aug 1851. (Pp. 460-463)

L. B. Moore to Malissa Jane Elledge transfer of State of Tennessee Grant #23,120. 12 Jul 1853. (Pp. 463-465)

C. C. Gunter to M. G. Elkins his fee simple interest in 80 acres to take effect at the death of Nancy Clark who has a life estate. 2 Feb 1854. (Pp. 465-466)

William Cummings to N. G. Elkins 164½ acres in the 7th District. 6 Feb 1854. (Pp. 466-468)

Daniel Spangler to Samuel Spangler a tract of land on Barren Fork of Collins River. 2 Feb 1848. (Pp. 468-470)

Alexander McKnight and S. H. McKnight, Executors of Moses McKnight, to W. W. McKnight 146 acres in the 1st District. 1 Jun 1853. (Pp. 470-471)

Henry Swanner to John Umbarger 45 acres in the 5th District. 13 Feb 1854. (Pp. 471-472)

Micajah Petty to Matthew W. Bowling and Henry G. Bowling 300 acres in the 4th District. 3 Dec 1853. (Pp. 472-473)

Sarah Cooper for love and affection to B. B. Cooper a deed of gift of four negroes, to wit, Susan, about 60; Lane, about 18;

Rebecca, about 16; and Richard, about 14. 13 Dec 1852. (P. 474)

James Smithson to B. H. Summars 50 acres in the 7th and 9th Districts. 24 Sep 1853. (Pp. 475-476)

Joel Milligan to John L. Harris 50 acres in the 11th District. 26 Aug 1852. (Pp. 476-477)

Andrew J. Bogle to Joseph Bryson 15 acres in the 11th District. 13 Feb 1852. (Pp. 477-479)

Merrit Givens to William Nichols 80 acres. 11 Feb 1854. (Pp. 479-480)

Joseph Bryson to John Bogle seven acres in the 11th District. 6 Mar 1853. (Pp. 480-481)

Calvin Brandon to C. B. Summer 200 acres, it being the interest I have in the dower assigned to Mary Brandon, widow of Cornelius Brandon. 14 Feb 1852. (Pp. 481-483)

William C. Leech to John W. Summer 327 acres in the 11th District. 12 Feb 1854. (Pp. 483-485)

Lewis Creson to Isaac T. Hailey 50 acres in the 2nd District. 16 Dec 1853. (Pp. 485-487)

Benny Cooper and Phillip Cooper to Jane Cooper their interest in the estate of Thomas Cooper. 22 Nov 1853. (Pp. 487-488)

Sheriff Samuel Vance to Blake Sagely 70 acres belonging to John A. Webber. 16 Feb 1854. (Pp. 488-490)

Sheriff Samuel Vance to Harvy L. Bush 160 acres belonging to Zachariah Bush. 18 Feb 1854. (Pp. 491-492)

James Petty to Irvin Petty 100 acres in the 4th District. 20 Feb 1854. (Pp. 492-494)

William Wharton to P. M. Jarratt a negro woman named Rhoda for $200. 28 Jan 1853. (P. 494)

Micajah Petty to William J. Petty 170 acres in the 4th District. 28 Jun 1850. (Pp. 495-496)

William Travis to David Travis for love and affection 200 acres. Said David Travis is the nephew of the said William Travis. 20 Oct 1845. (Pp. 496-497)

B. T. McBroom and W. T. McBroom to D. M. Jarratt several town lots for the benefit of Sarah McBroom, wife of Henry D. McBroom and then to her children, to wit, John D. McBroom, Benjamin T. McBroom, William J. McBroom, Abel McBroom, Jr., and Sarah Barton, wife of William Barton. 23 Feb 1854. (Pp. 498-502)

Amandy M. Bush, daughter of William J. Trigg appoints Willis W. Bush, her husband, her power of attorney to receive her share of the estate of Mollie Taylor, widow of Charles Taylor. 28 Feb 1854. (Pp. 502-503)

Alexander McBroom and Thomas Barrett to Benjamin Fugett
50 acres in the 6th District.   1 Mar 1854.   (Pp. 503-504)

(Book begins with page 28)

John Miles to Robert S. Miles 37 acres in the 5th District. 11 Mar 1854. (Pp. 28-29)

Irvin Petty to Henry Burkett 270 acres in the 4th District. 22 Feb 1854. (Pp. 29-30)

Parker F. Stone of Crofford County, Arkansas to Thomas C. Word 300 acres 300 acres in what was Warren County. 8 Mar 1853. (Pp. 30-35)

Samuel C. Odom to Clark Hubbard 251 acres in the 11th District. 23 Jun 1848. (Pp. 35-36)

Joseph K. Dickson of Carroll County to J. H. Alexander a tract of land in Cannon and Wilson County, it being his interest in the estate of Alexander S. Dickson. 24 Dec 1853. (Pp. 36-37)

John Cannon and wife Elizabeth, formerly Dickson, of Carroll County to J. H. Alexander their interest in the estate of Alexander S. Dickson. 23 Dec 1853. (Pp. 38-39)

Thomas Dickins of Gibson County to John H. Alexander of Carroll County his interest in the estate of Alexander S. Dickson. 23 Dec 1853. (Pp. 39-40)

R. M. Hurt and wife Emily, formerly Dickson, Levi W. Dickson, and John M. Dickson, all of Carroll County, to J. H. Dickson their interest in the estate of Alexander S. Dickson. 13 Dec 1853. (Pp. 41-42)

Martin Cannon and wife Araminta, formerly Dickson, of Henry County to J. H. Alexander their interest in the estate of J. H. Dickson. 6 May 1852. (Pp. 42-44)

Ezekiel Dickson of Fayette County to J. H. Alexander their interest in the estate of Alexander S. Dickson. 9 Jun 1851. (Pp. 44-45)

Rebecca Dickson to J. M. Odom her interest in 188 acres in Cannon and Wilson County. 3 Feb 1854. (Pp. 45-47)

Daniel Jones of Warren County to Henry Powell 200 acres in the 9th District. 15 Mar 1852. (Pp. 47-48)

William T. McBroom to Benjamin T. McBroom 128 acres in the 2nd District. (Pp. 48-49)

James J. Tolbert to S. T. Tolbert 160 acres in the 12th District. 4 Feb 1854. (Pp. 50-51)

Charles Espy to Alexander Finley 20 acres on the road leading from Woodbury to Manchester. 5 Sep 1848. (Pp. 51-52_

William West of Warren County to Martha Barratt a tract of land. 4 Mar 1854. (Pp. 53-54)

W. W. McKnight to S. H. McKnight 49 acres in the 1st District. 22 Mar 1854. (Pp. 54-55)

John G. M. Cooper to Jane Cooper his interest in the estate of Thomas Cooper. 7 Mar 1854. (Pp. 55-56)

Daniel Fite to George Gannon 25 acres in the 2nd District. 30 Mar 1854. (Pp. 56-57)

John C. Martin and wife Sophia B. and J. T. Martin to William Barton six acres in the 1st District. 17 Feb 1854. (Pp. 57-58)

Daniel Fite to Mary Tassey, wife of Alexander Tassey, 105 acres 105 acres in the 2nd District. Said land is to be free from the debts and liabilities of the said Alexander Tassey. 31 Mar 1854. (Pp. 59-60)

Henry Lance to Thomas Richardson 120 acres in the 7th District. 21 Feb 1854. (Pp. 61-62)

Henry R. Perry, Ann M. Perry, Powell Perry, John W. Perry, Edmond Perry, Martha Perry, Malissa Perry, Jackson Perry, and Moses Perry to John Manus 200 acres in the 6th and 8th Districts. 6 Dec 1852. (Pp. 62-63)

Baldy H. Summer and wife Mary to William Grizzle 60 acres in the 10th District. 19 Sep 1853. (Pp. 63-65)

James A. England to John Hays a negro woman named Julia, about 22, of a copper complexion and three children, to wit, Mary, about 4 years and six months; Henry, about 2 years and six months; and John, about 9 months. 5 Apr 1854. (Pp. 65-66)

Thomas G. Sullivan to Elizabeth R. McKnight 123 acres for her separate use and benefit and to be free from the control of her husband William W. McKnight. 3 Apr 1854. (Pp. 66-67)

Benjamin T. McBroom to George W. Thompson 128 acres a tract of land to be used for Sarah McBroom, wife of Henry D. McBroom. 24 Feb 1854. (Pp. 68-69)

A. C. Alexander to F. C. Alexander 165 acres in the 11th District. 29 Jan 1852. (Pp. 70-71)

Stanford Smith to William Barton a trust deed. 11 Apr 1854. (Pp. 71-73)

Richard U. Lemay to R. H. Mason 160 acres in the 5th District. 5 Apr 1854. (P. 73)

Jesse Gilly, Sr. to John Gilly 60 acres in the 12th District. 16 Jan 1854. (Pp. 74-75)

Joshua Barton and wife Jane to Ephraim Andrews their power of attorney to sell unto Ellen R. Hagan, James Hamilton, Ridley Thomas, and Noble Wade, all of Nararro County, Texas 640 acres in Navarro County known as the Thomas Barton survey. Said Andrews is also a resident of Navarro County. 25 Apr 1854. (Pp. 75-76)

Robert K. Stephens to Anderson P. Stephens and Richard L. Stephens 560 acres in the 1st and 2nd Districts. 11 Apr 1854. (Pp. 76-78)

Robert Teal to A. Burger a trust deed. 13 May 1854. (Pp. 78-80)

Abel McBroom, by deed of gift, by deed of gift, to William Barton as trustee for Sarah McBroom a tract of land. At her death, it was to be equally divided between the children of the said Sarah and Henry D. McBroom, to wit, John D. McBroom, Benjamin T. McBroom, William McBroom, Abel McBroom, Jr., and Sarah Barton, wife of William McBroom. John D. McBroom to R. H. Mason his interest. 17 May 1854. (Pp. 80-82)

James Nicholson and wife Clementine, formerly Smith, to R. G. Smith of Rutherford County their interest in the estate of O. B. Smith. 1 May 1854. (Pp. 82-84)

William McBroom to William Barton a trust deed. 22 May 1854. (Pp. 84-87)

Alexander Higgins to Elijah N. Walkup 135 acres in the 7th District. 19 Mar 1854. (Pp. 87-88)

Baldy H. Summer to Sarah Blair 16 acres in the 9th District. 25 May 1854. (Pp. 89-90)

Sheriff W. C. Elledge to M. W. Armstrong and B. H. Bilbro 30 acres belonging to Jackson Fann. 6 Jun 1854. (Pp. 90-92)

William T. McBroom to John P. McBroom 150 acres in the 2nd District. 6 Jun 1854. (Pp. 92-93)

Charles Ready to F. Coleman two town lots in the town of Woodbury. 6 Jun 1854. (Pp. 93-96)

Benjamin Whitt to F. Coleman a trust deed. 25 Dec 1854. (Pp. 96-97)

Robert G. Smith to James Nicholson a negro man named Edward, about 36. 13 Jun 1854. (Pp. 97-98)

J. W. Orrand to John Orrand 27 acres in the 6th District. 18 Apr 1854. (Pp. 98-99)

William Grimes to John W. Orrand 100 acres in the 6th District. 14 Jun 1854. (Pp. 99-100)

Adam Northcutt to Alexander Young 837 acres in the 5th District. 13 Jun 1854. (Pp. 100-101)

Archebald Stone and Johnathan L. Fare to M. G. Elkins 200 acres in the 1st District. 16 Jun 1854. (Pp. 101-102)

Benjamin Sapp to William Barton 70 acres in the 2nd District. 26 Jun 1854. (Pp. 102-103)

Veach Crabtree to A. B. Carnes and others one acre in the 6th District for the purpose of a meeting house. 30 Sep 1854. (Pp. 103-104)

John Melton, Executor of Ancil Melton, to Jesse Melton 40 acres in the 9th District. 29 Sep 1843. (P. 105)

James Stone to Jesse Melton 75 acres in the 7th District. 10 Dec 1846. (Pp. 106-107)

Elam McKnight to Stephen Wilson 65 acres in the 11th District.

L& Jan 1854. (Pp. 107-108)

James A. Brandon and Christopher Brandon of Arkansas to Abraham Brandon their power of attorney to settle the estate of of father Cornelius Brandon. 12 Aug 1853. (Pp. 108-109)

Hiram Brandon to Abraham Brandon his interest in the estate of Cornelius Brandon. 13 Aug 1853. (Pp. 109-110)

James Stone to William J. Stone 33 acres. 21 Feb 1850. (Pp. 110-112)

Samuel Vance to William York 265 acres in the 9th District. 24 Jun 1854. (Pp. 112-113)

Redman Bynum to Nelson Harlan 54 acres in the 12th District. 4 Dec 1852. (Pp. 113-114)

William S. Hubbard to James W. McAdow his interest in the estate of Clark Hubbard. 31 Dec 1853. (Pp. 114-115)

Robert Cox to Judith Cox his interest in 50 acres in the 11th District. 17 Sep 1853. (Pp. 115-117)

William S. Bell to Aaron Byford 85 acres in the 12th District. 31 Jul 1854. (Pp. 117-119)

Daniel Tenpenny to Alexander Higgins 50 acres in the 6th District. Bounded: Widow Thompson. 21 Aug 1854. (Pp. 119-120)

Mary Bowen petitions by her friend, Samuel Bowen, to sell land. 23 Aug 1854. (P. 121)

W. J. Stone to Isaac Gunter 35 acres in the 7th District. 31 Jul 1854. (Pp. 121-123)

C. R. Davis to Tobias Tenpenny 138½ acres in the 3rd District. 12 May 1854. (Pp. 123-124)

Mary Y. Pallett to William Sisson 175 acres in the 12th District. 31 Aug 1854. (Pp. 124-126)

James McKnight to George Peebles 50 acres on Sanders Fork. 23 Nov 1853. (Pp. 126-127)

John Williams to Thomas H. Williams 205 acres on Brawley's Fork of Carson's Fork. 5 Sep 1854. (Pp. 127-128)

Jesse B. Williams to Thomas H. Williams 200 acres in the 4th District. 5 Sep 1854. (Pp. 129-130)

Adam Elrod to his daughter, Elizabeth Mitchell, wife of James H. Mitchell 140 acres in the 5th District. 12 Aug 1854. (Pp. 130-131)

Henry A. Wiley to F. Coleman a title bond. 13 Sep 1854. (Pp. 131-132)

Washington S. Massey to B. H. Mason 248 acres in the 6th District. 21 Jul 1854. (Pp. 132-134)

William H. Travis to Daniel Tenpenny 85 acres in the 6th District. 30 Sep 1854. (Pp. 134-135)

DEED BOOK K

Henry A. Wiley to R. H. Mason a town lot in the town of Woodbury, it being the old McBroom Tavern lot. 20 Feb 1854. (Pp. 135-136)

James L. Colvert to Barton and Jarratt a mortgage. 22 Sep 1854. (Pp. 136-137)

John F. Curlee to Vinson Gaither 40½ acres in the 3rd District. 1 Apr 1854. (Pp. 138-139)

Gabriel Mears and J. P. Elkins to Thomas Elkins, Esquire, ten acres in the 8th District. 25 Apr 1854. (Pp. 139-141)

Christopher Owens to Shadrach Kelly 166 acres on Sanders Fork where the said Kelly now resides. 16 Sep 1854. (Pp. 141-142)

Daniel McGill to Burton L. McFerrin 67½ acres in the 3rd District. 8 Mar 1847. (Pp. 143-144)

Aaron Byford to Redman Bynum a tract of land in the 12th District. 26 Aug 1852. (Pp. 144-146)

William Whitmore to J. H. Whitmore a tract of land in the 5th District. 15 Mar 1852. (Pp. 146-147)

Thomas C. McLoud to Joseph Pinkerton 112 acres in the 12th District. 22 Nov 1853. (Pp. 148-149)

Johnathan Wherry to John Chappell 111 acres in the 1st District. 30 Sep 1854. (Pp. 149-150)

Mary Y. Pallett to Andrew S. Simpson four acres in the 12th District. 29 Sep 1854. (Pp. 150-151)

J. H. Alexander to J. M. Odom a tract of land in Cannon and Wilson Counties belonging to the heirs of Alexander S. Dickson, late of Wilson County. 13 Oct 1854. (Pp. 151-153)

Nace Overall of Rutherford County, Executor of R. C. Price of the same place, to E. J. Wood lot #57 in the town of Woodbury. 4 Oct 1854. (Pp. 153-154)

A. J. Inglis to John Raines 223 acres in the 11th District. 23 Sep 1854. (Pp. 155-156)

Joseph D. McKnight to P. P. Maxey seven acres. 29 Sep 1854. (Pp. 156-157)

Shadrach Kelly to A. B. McKnight 218 acres on Sanders Fork. 23 Oct 1854. (Pp. 158-159)

William Stone to Wilford Literell three acres in the 7th District. 23 Oct 1854. (Pp. 159-160)

W. C. Leech to J. W. Summer 300 acres in the 11th District. 14 Oct 1854. (Pp. 160-161)

James Wood to R. H. Mason four acres in the 6th District. 29 Sep 1854. (Pp. 161-162)

Jane Cooper to Phillip Cooper her interest in the estate of Thomas Cooper as his widow. 27 Oct 1854. (Pp. 162-163)

DEED BOOK K

Bethel Summers to William Bogle 100 acres in the 11th District. 2 Oct 1854. (Pp. 163-164)

Larkin Keeton to Joseph C. Leak 1540 acres in the 10th District. 30 Oct 1854. (Pp. 165-166)

Alexander Vinson, Robert Vinson, James A. Vinson, Berry Vinson, T. B. Brevard, Joseph Warren and wife Sophia L., Elizabeth Barkley, now Warren, formerly Vinson, Samuel Bowen and wife Ursley Ann, formerly Vinson, heirs of Richard Vinson, to T. B. Brevard their interest in 48 acres in the 6th District. Said T. B. Brevard is not one of the heirs. 1 Nov 1854. (Pp. 167-168)

Vinson heirs to Benjamin Fugett part of a 200 acre tract in the 6th District. 1 Nov 1854. (Pp. 168-170)

Nancy and Thomas McLoud to W. C. Soap 111 acres in the 12th District. 7 Sep 1854. (Pp. 170-172)

John Espey to James P. McGill 100 acres in the 12th District. 25 Oct 1854. (Pp. 172-173)

J. H. Whitmore to Jesse Bish 100 acres in the 5th District. 5 Oct 1854. (Pp. 173-174)

W. M. Mayfield to Wesley MaAdow his power of attorney to sell 100 acres in the 5th District. 25 Aug 1854. (Pp. 174-176)

Thomas Preston to W. Barrett and wife Elizabeth, formerly Preston, his interest in a tract of land owned by John Preston deceased. 3 Nov 1854. (Pp. 177-178)

A. Burger and Jacob Burger to James Ward one fourth of an acre in the 6th District. 8 Jul 1854. (Pp. 179-180)

Thomas Merritt to T. L. Todd a trust deed. 9 Nov 1854. (Pp. 180-181)

John Pendleton, Sr. to John Pendleton, Jr. 100 acres in the 8th District. 6 Nov 1854. (Pp. 181-182)

Elam McKnight to Benjamin Fugett 108 acres in the 11th District. 17 Jan 1854. (Pp. 182-183)

Elam McKnight to Stephen Wilson 33 acres in the 11th District. 20 Oct 1854. (Pp. 183-184)

John Pendleton to his son, William Pendleton 100 acres in the 5th District. 18 Oct 1854. (Pp. 184-185)

John Nokes to Henry Lance 115 acres on the east fork of Stone's River. 18 Aug 1849. (Pp. 186-187)

Tobias Tenpenny to John W. Millikin 63 acres in the 3rd District. 23 Mar 1854. (Pp. 187-188)

Mike Wilson to Wiley Davenport 25 acres in the 10th and 11th Districts. 2 Nov 1854. (Pp. 188-189)

Mike Wilson to Wesley Harriman five and a half acres in the 11th District. 2 Nov 1854. (Pp. 189-190)

John Preston died seized and possessed of 150 acres in the
6th District. Said Preston died without any will. Henry J.
Walls and wife Sarah, formerly Preston, to Thomas Preston their
interest in the estate. 4 Nov 1854. (Pp. 190-192)

L. B. Nelson to Jeremiah Scales a tract of land. 8 Aug
1854. (Pp. 192-193)

William Gross to Ealey Turner 100 acres in the 5th District.
20 Oct 1854. (Pp. 194-195)

William Elkins and wife Milly, formerly Stone, to W. B. Nokes
75 acres belonging to the estate of James Stone. 1 Aug 1854.
(Pp. 195-196)

James Petty to Mary Good 100 acres in the 4th District. 9
Nov 1854. (Pp. 196-197)

P. J. Thomas to Archebald Lewis 111 acres in the 4th District. 6 Nov 1854. (Pp. 198-199)

M. G. Elkins to James J. Prater 42 acres in the 7th District. 14 Nov 1854. (Pp. 199-200)

James H. Whiteman to John R. Ashley 49 acres in the 12th District. 12 Oct 1853. (Pp. 200-201)

Mumford Tenpenny, James A. Tenpenny, Daniel Tenpenny, Joseph
A. Brandon and wife Sarah, formerly Tenpenny, children of Richard
Tenpenny to James W. Tenpenny their interest in the estate. 11
Nov 1853. (Pp. 202-204)

Jacob Wright to John Bragg several tracts of land. 27 Dec
1842. 9 Oct 1854. (Pp. 204-204)

James S. Todd to John W. Moore 57 acres in the 12th District.
7 Oct 1853. (Pp. 205-207)

James M. Avant to Harvey L. Bush a tract of land in the
12th District. 3 May 1852. (Pp. 207-208)

Elizabeth Young, Administrator of William Young, to Thomas F.
Gaither 104 acres in the 11th District. 7 Jul 1854. (Pp. 208-
211)

Asa Todd, Administrator of Hugh Robinson; Pleasant Cothron
and wife Jane and others to John Melvin 110½ acres. 2 Apr 1853.
(Pp. 211-213)

R. H. Mason to James A. England of Perry County, Alabama
333 acres. 16 May 1853. (Pp. 213-215)

Wilford Lutrell to Isaiah Neeley 146 acres in the 7th District. 28 Oct 1854. (Pp. 215-216)

H. Lance to James Allen 43 acres in the 7th District. 4
Dec 1854. (Pp. 216-217)

Munson Hollandsworth to Ira Hollandsworth 70 acres in the
10th District. 17 Nov 1854. (Pp. 217-219)

James H. Reed to James Reed 15 acres in the 4th District.
28 Mar 1854. (Pp. 219-220)

John R. Brooks to David Travis 80 acres in the 5th District.
6 Dec 1854. (Pp. 220-221)

James M. England to John W. Orrand ten acres on Stone's
River. 15 Dec 1854. (Pp. 221-222)

William C. Miller to Joseph Hollis lot #56 in the town of
Woodbury. 19 Dec 1854. (Pp. 222-223)

R. H. Mason to James Wood eight acres in the 6th District
on Hollis' Creek. 14 Dec 1854. (Pp. 223-225)

George W. Thompson to William C. Miller lot #26 in the town
of Woodbury. 23 Dec 1853. (Pp. 225-226)

Jacob Wright to Samuel P. Travis one acre in the 1st District. 11 Apr 1854. (Pp. 226-227)

Henry Bowman and wife Mary D. to James Johnson 45 acres in
the 12th District. 27 Sep 1854. (Pp. 227-228)

Isaac M. Fuller to Samuel Vance two town lots in the town
of Woodbury, one of them being the lot that myself and family
now reside. The other being the place I have occupied as a
granary. 28 Dec 1854. (Pp. 228-230)

William Gunter to James B. Elledge two tracts of land in the
7th District, one of them being the place I now live. 4 Jan
1855. (Pp. 230-234)

Thomas P. Mitchell to Josephus Finley a trust deed. 4 Jan
1855. (Pp. 234-235)

Isaac Gunter to Isaac Marcum 33 acres in the 7th District.
5 Jan 1855. (Pp. 235-236)

James L. Kelton and wife E. E. to George W. Lawrence 62½
acres in the 1st District. 12 Jun 1854. (Pp. 237-238)

John N. Doke to A. J. Tucker 65 acres. 6 Jan 1855. (Pp.
238-239)

John N. Doke to Arthur Gaither 145 acres. 9 Jan 1855. (Pp.
240-242)

John B. Paris to Isaac C. Marcum a trust deed. 9 Jan 1855.
(Pp. 242-244)

William West to John B. Paris 240 acres on the east fork
of Stone's River. 9 Jan 1855. (Pp. 245-246)

P. T. Johnson to C. B. Summer 166 acres in the 11st District.
8 Aug 1853. (Pp. 246-247)

Aaron F. Jones and Daniel W. Jones to Alman Mullinist 18
acres in the 11th District. (Pp. 247-248)

Elam McKnight to Alman Mullinist four acres in the 11th District. 30 Dec 1854. (Pp. 248-250)

Micajah Petty to Linsy Peeler 133 acres in the 5th District.
20 Apr 1853. (Pp. 250-251)

Clark Hubbard to John W. Marshall 96½ acres in Wilson County in the 15th District. 9 Nov 1854. (Pp. 251-252)

W. W. Armstrong to John C. Leech 32 acres in the 1st District. 1 Jan 1855. ((Pp. 253-255)

Alexander Higgin to Isaac C. Marcum 60 acres in the 7th District. 24 Aug 1854. (Pp. 255-256)

Jesse Millikin to Henry Brown 90 acres in the 4th District. 11 Jan 1855. (Pp. 256-257)

Alexander McKnight and wife Mary to Briant Hare a girl slave named Elisabeth for $800. 27 Dec 1854. (Pp. 257-258)

Wiley Davenport to William C. Davenport 100 acres in the 11th District. 12 Apr 1854. (Pp. 258-259)

Micajah Petty to Alvey Guy 40 acres in the 4th District. 19 Feb 1854. (Pp. 259-260)

Jacob Byford to Ervin Cherry 15 acres in the 4th District. 6 Aug 1852. (Pp. 260-261)

William Stone to Isaiah Neely 86 acres in the 7th District. 2 Jan 1855. (Pp. 261-262)

Francis Hancock to John B. Perkins a tract of land in the 10th District. 29 Aug 1854. (Pp. 263-266)

Andrew S. Inglis to John C. Fowler and Absolom W. Fowler 50 acres in the 4th District. 5 Jan 1855. (P. 266)

John C. Fowler to Thomas Sisson 80 acres in the 5th District. 1 Jan 1855. (P. 267)

H. D. McBroom and Abel McBroom to Jane T. Blair a tract of land in the 7th District. 13 Jan 1855. (Pp. 267-268)

William West to John S. Elkins 50 acres in the 8th District. 31 Dec 1853. (Pp. 269-270)

Daniel Hight to L. D. Stewart 236 acres in the 6th District. 17 Jan 1855. (Pp. 270-271)

William C. Miller and wife Martha E., formerly Brewer, to Joseph Hollis town lot #56 in the town of Woodbury on which C. B. Davis now resides. 6 Jan 1855. (Pp. 272-273)

Joseph T. Holt to B. B. Dickins 15 acres in the 12th District. 20 Oct 1854. (Pp. 273-274)

State of Tennessee Grant #23654. 191 acres in the 1st District to John Henderson. 9 Sep 1853. (Pp. 274-275)

James R. Taylor to Henry Hoover and James H. Skelton 260 acres in the 2nd District. 9 Jan 1855. (Pp. 275-277)

William C. Leech to E. W. Owen a trust deed. 3 Feb 1855. (Pp. 277-278)

Thomas B. Brevard to A. C. Tatum 52 acres on the east fork of Stone's River. 20 Jan 1855. (Pp. 278-279)

Joseph P. Holt to Fielding Holt 130 acres on Brasley's Fork

DEED BOOK K

of Stone's River. 12 Jan 1855. (Pp. 280-281)

C. C. Good to John N. Mitchell a trust deed. 6 Feb 1855. (Pp. 281-282)

C. C. Good to R. J. Good 150 acres in the 4th District. 6 Feb 1855. (Pp. 282-284)

Joseph Ramsey to John N. Mitchell 191 acres in the 6th District. 13 Oct 1851. (Pp. 284-285)

William Preston to Jesse Patrick 100 acres in the 6th District. 15 Jan 1855. (Pp. 285-286)

Henry Lance to James H. Wood 90 acres in the 7th District. 12 Dec 1854. (Pp. 287-288)

Henry Dennis to Jesse McGee 50 acres in the 10th District. 4 Jan 1855. (Pp. 288-289)

William C. Leech to Nancy C. McAdow 60 acres in the 11th District. 3 Feb 1855. (Pp. 289-290)

Margaret Lennox and Richard Lennox to Joseph M. Stacy 50 acres on Carson's Fork of Stone's River. 30 Jul 1849. (Pp. 290-291)

Richard M. Lemay to James A. Smithson 100 acres on Barren Fork of Collins River. 3 Jan 1854. (Pp. 292-294)

John Taler to Joseph P. Holt 25 acres in the 12th District. 12 Feb 1855. (Pp. 294-295)

C. C. Good to A. F. McFerrin 50 acres in the 4th District. 2 Aug 1854. (Pp. 295-296)

A. Burger and Jacob Burger to R. H. Mason 31 acres in the 6th District. 27 Sep 1854. (Pp. 296-297)

John A. Stanley to J. W. Summer a trust deed. 3 Feb 1855. (P. 298)

Nancy Clark, widow of Joseph Clark; Joseph Clark; Zilpha Lance, formerly Clark, and husband Henry; Frances Halpaign, formerly Clark, and husband William to M. G. Elkins the life estate of the said Nancy in the estate of Joseph Clark deceased. 18 Jan 1855. (Pp. 299-300)

Alexander Finley and wife Sarah; John Epley and wife Mary; Samuel Spangler; Jesse G. Whitamore and wife Abigal; John Swanner and wife Malinda James E. Ross and wife Dicy Ann; George Epley and wife Eliza by their attorney; and Elizabeth Spangler, the heirs of Daniel Spangler to Harvy Bush 95 acres in the 5th District. Said Elizabeth Spangler is the widow. 6 Apr 1852. (Pp. 301-303)

William Young to William Barton 68 acres in the 6th District. 15 Feb 1855. (Pp. 304-305)

John Webb, trustee, to S. B. Spurlock lot #2 in the town of Woodbury. 20 Mar 1852. (Pp. 305-306)

Henry R. Perry to John Q. Weatherford lot #2 in the town of

193

Woodbury. 17 Feb 1855. (Pp. 306-307)

S. B. Spurlock to John Q. Weatherford a town lot in the town of Woodbury. 17 Feb 1855. (Pp. 307-308)

John Q. Weatherford to E. J. Wood lots #23 and 10 in the town of Woodbury. 10 Feb 1855. (Pp. 308-309)

C. C. Gunter to Joseph Moore 60 acres on the east fork of Stone's River. 16 Feb 1855. (Pp. 309-310)

William C. Leech to J. L. Fare 65 acres in the 7th District. 10 Feb 1855. (Pp. 310-311)

James A. England to Peter Tally of Rutherford County 320 acres on Stone's River. 3 Oct 1854. (Pp. 311-313)

Zachariah Thomason to B. F. Odom 43 acres in the 11th District. 13 Feb 1839. (Pp. 313-314)

Nelson Cooper to S. B. Spurlock a trust deed. 16 Jan 1855. (Pp. 314-315)

W. C. Odom to S. B. Spurlock a negro boy named Solomon, about 4. 17 Feb 1855. (Pp. 315-316)

C. B. Davis to Joseph Hollis a town lot in the town of Woodbury. Bounded: on the east by a lot formerly owned by Dr. Price. 9 Feb 1855. (Pp. 316-317)

William Wimberly to Isaac Earthman and David Travis 60 acres in the 5th District. 22 Feb 1855. (Pp. 317-318)

W. C. Leech to C. B. Summer 220 acres in the 11th District. 10 Feb 1855. (Pp. 318-319)

W. W. Earthman, J. E. Hollyburton, Levi M. Bumpass, W. M. Bumpass, M. B. Jordan, R. W. Bumpass, W. Y. Posey, Richard E. Bumpass, M. V. Bumpass, John W. Bumpass, Mary H. Hollyburton, Hardinia A. Jordan, E. J. Earthman, and Martha M. Posey, the heirs of Robert H. Bumpass to C. B. Summer 220 acres in the 11th District. 12 Feb 1855. (Pp. 319-320)

Alexander Higgins to John Higgins 41 acres in the 7th District. 25 Dec 1854. (Pp. 321-323)

Henry Dennis to F. Owen a tract of land in the 10th District. 15 Feb 1855. (Pp. 323-324)

John H. Smith to Joseph A. Dement 37 acres in the 1st District. 18 Jan 1855. (Pp. 324-325)

John P. Elkins to Gabriel Mars 12 acres in the 8th District. 21 Oct 1852. (Pp. 325-326)

Harvy Bush to John Umbarger 13 acres in the 5th District. 8 Sep 1852. (Pp. 326-327)

Hugh Craft to Samuel Pendleton 200 acres in the 5th District. 5 Aug 1851. (Pp. 327-328)

William C. Leech to Cantrel B. Odom 50 acres in the 11th District. 4 Nov 1848. (Pp. 328-329)

DEED BOOK K

Michael Wilson to Joseph Bryson 150 acres in the 11th District. 9 Jan 1855. (Pp. 329-330)

Isaac F. Smithson to Nancy Denton 200 acres in the 8th District. 5 Feb 1855. (Pp. 330-331)

John Teague and Thomas G. Wood to William Young and Mark L. Young 222 acres in the 5th District. 16 Feb 1855. (Pp. 331-332)

Jacob Wright and wife Mary of Rutherford County to William T. McKnight 203 acres on Andrews Creek. 11 Apr 1854. (Pp. 332-334)

William Hollis to William B. Ferrell and the other trustees two acres for the Methodist Episcopal Church. 15 Feb 1853. (Pp. 334-335)

Francis Spurlock to his daughter, Nancy F. Spurlock, a tract of land on Short Mountain. 5 Mar 1855. (Pp. 335-336)

Wesley Harriman to John Harriman a trust deed. 5 Mar 1855. (Pp. 336-338)

William R. Acres and John R. Sullivan to Y. L. Brevard a town lot in the town of Woodbury. 17 Feb 1855. (Pp. 338-339)

Nathaniel M. Taylor to George W. Thompson 18 acres in the 6th District. 10 Mar 1855. (Pp. 339-340)

J. L. Fare to J. B. Raines 65 acres in the 7th District. 10 Feb 1855. (Pp. 340-341)

John Muncy to Eli H. Muncy 100 acres on Barren Fork of Stone's River. 29 Dec 1854. (Pp. 341-342)

John M. Odom to Armstead G. Odom 102 acres in the 11th District. 22 Aug 1854. (Pp. 342-344)

James S. Odom to Anthony Summers four acres in the 11th District. 22 Mar 1854. (Pp. 344-345)

Thomas G. Wood to Dabney Sandridge and Caroline Sandridge a tract of land. 31 Mar 1853. (Pp. 345-349)

William Pendleton to John Pendleton 100 acres on Barren Fork of Collins River. 16 Mar 1855. (Pp. 349-350)

Samuel Pendleton to John F. Pendleton 265 acres in the 2nd District. 28 Oct 1855. (Pp. 350-351)

Josiah F. Marford, Clerk & Master, to Eley Turner, trustee, 30 acres. 15 Jan 1855. (Pp. 352-353)

William Hollis to Mumford Tenpenny two acres on Hollis' Creek. 6 Mar 1855. (P. 354)

Thomas Sullins to John Young 72 acres on the east fork of Stone's River and Clear Fork of Smith's Fork. 20 Feb 1840. (Pp. 355-356)

Alexander McKnight to John P. McKnight and Alexander G. McKnight 195½ acres in the 1st District. 28 Dec 1854. (Pp. 356-357)

DEED BOOK K

Micajah Markum to Daniel Grizzle 50 acres in the 10th District. 30 Mar 1855. (P. 358)

Micajah Markum to James Grizzle 75 acres in the 10th District. 30 Mar 1855. (Pp. 359-360)

Z. Thomason to James M. McAdow 30 acres. 14 Jul 1849. (Pp. 360-361)

G. W. McCullough is appointed power of attorney by his wife, Nancy R. McCullough to receive her share of the estate of her father, C. Curlee. 17 Apr 1855. (P. 361)

William A. Groom to James W. McAdow 26 acres in the 11th District. 13 Jan 1855. (P. 362)

Lewis Hancock to Richard H. Hancock a deed of gift of a negro boy named Joe, 7. 2 Apr 1855. (P. 363)

Thomas Sisson to Benjamin F. Creson a title bond. 17 Dec 1855. (Pp. 363-364)

J. L. Fare to James Williams and Elizabeth Hass a town lot in the town of Woodbury. 31 Mar 1855. (Pp. 364-365)

Francis Spurlock and Nancy Spurlock to Johnathan F. Blair 220 acres. 16 Apr 1855. (Pp. 365-367)

Joseph Ramsey to Thomas G. Wood lot #48 in the town of Woodbury. 25 Apr 1855. (P. 368)

Robert Bailey for love and affection to Lucinda Young, wife of Eli Young 200 acres in the 7th District. 23 Apr 1855. (Pp. 369-370)

John Farley to Thomas Elkins 50 acres in the 8th District. 4 Dec 1854. (P. 370-371)

James Reed to William Davenport 17 acres in the 11th District. 2 May 1855. (Pp. 371-372)

James W. McAdow to William A. Groom 29 acres. 13 Jan 1855. (Pp. 372-373)

W. W. McKnight to A. D. Alexander 13 acres in the 1st District. 8 Dec 1854. (Pp. 373-374)

Martha Gooding to William Gooding ten acres in the 4th District. 15 May 1855. (Pp. 374-375)

Samuel Vance to R. H. Mason a trust deed. 19 May 1855. (Pp. 375-376)

John Umbarger to Henry Brewer 95 acres in the 5th District. 9 May 1855. (Pp. 377-378)

James B. Summer to Andrew J. Bryson 125 acres in the 11th District. 7 Jul 1854. (Pp. 378-379)

Alman Rigsby to John K. Rigsby 200 acres in the 7th District. 26 Apr 1855. (Pp. 379-380)

C. B. Summers to Anthony Summers 44 acres in the 11th District. 25 Apr 1855. (Pp381-382)

DEED BOOK K

Anthony Summers to C. B. Summers 21 acres. 25 Apr 1855. (P. 382)

W. C. Leech to J. L. Fare a trust deed. 26 May 1855. (Pp. 383-384)

Dudley J. Graham and wife Elizabeth to Thomas G. Wood lot #49 in the town of Woodbury. 30 May 1855. (Pp. 384-385)

John Manus to Daniel Manus 100 acres in the 6th and 7th Districts. 4 Jun 1855. (Pp. 385-386)

David D. Hipp to James H. Mitchell five acres in the 5th District. 30 Jan 1855. (Pp. 386-387)

John Bragg to Joseph Carter 104 acres in the 1st District. 19 Dec 1854. (Pp. 387-388)

Dozier Bragg, Sr. to Joseph Carter 150 acres in the 1st District. 28 Dec 1854. (Pp. 389-390)

Roderick L. Bain to P. C. Isbell of Coffee County a trust deed. 19 May 1855. (Pp. 390-391)

Susan George and R. S. George to Daniel Tenpenny a negro boy named Millis, about 35, for $700. 4 Jun 1855. (Pp. 391-392)

Numan Hollandsworth to Peter Adams 12 acres in the 10th District. 17 Feb 1853. (Pp. 392-393)

Edwin A. Keeble to W. L. Martin 29 acres in Cannon and Warren Counties. 5 Dec 1853. (Pp. 393-394)

Jeremiah Cleveland of Bedford County to Richard Arnold 185 acres in Cannon, Bedford, and Rutherford Counties. 4 Dec 1849. (Pp. 394-395)

Mayor of Woodbury to John Webb a town lot in the town of Woodbury. 4 Jan 1854. (Pp. 395-396)

E. W. Vaughn to Samuel Vance 50 acres in the 7th District. 29 May 1855. (Pp. 396-397)

J. B. Elledge and William Gunter to Samuel Vance 75 acres in the 7th District. 29 May 1855. (Pp. 397-399)

Samuel Vance to T. J. Jetton 75 acres in the 7th District. 8 Jun 1855. (Pp. 399-400)

Thomas K. Williams to J. L. Fare a trust deed. 15 Jun 1855. (Pp. 400-402)

Jesse Gilly, Sr. to Jesse H. Gilly, Jr. 60 acres in the 12th District. 13 Jun 1855. (Pp. 402-403)

Uriah B. Bush to Francis A. Bush his power of attorney to sell his interest in a tract of land. Said Uriah B. Bush is a resident of Fulton County, Arkansas. 17 May 1853. (Pp. 403-405)

A. Stone and R. H. Mason agree to partition 248 acres in the 6th District. 23 May 1855. (Pp. 405-409)

Joseph Ramsey to Joseph Spurlock 72 acres in the 6th District. 12 Jun 1855. (P. 410)

Daniel S. Ford to Zadoc C. Bell 200 acres in the 9th District. 21 Feb 1855. (P. 411)

A. F. McFerrin to William Phillips 15 acres in the 4th District. 15 Feb 1855. (P. 412)

Alexander Higgins to the School Commissioners of the 7th District one acre on the left hand of the road going from my house to Luke Sherley's. 22 Jul 1843. (P. 413)

Newman Hollandsworth to Ira Hollandsworth 50 acres in the 10th District. 29 Jun 1855. (P. 414)

M. L. Nelson to Lewis Days 265 acres on the Barren Fork of Collins River. 6 Jul 1855. (Pp. 415-416)

Robert Simpson to Armstead Carter 186 acres in the 4th District. 16 Dec 1854. (Pp. 416-418)

John R. Sullivan and wife Ann for love and affection to Ann Fugett, wife of Townsel Fugett; James M. Brown, and Mary Brown, children of the said Ann Sullivan, the following negroes, to wit, a negro boy named David, about 2; a boy named Andy, about 4; a negro girl named Aggy, about 12. 14 Mar 1855. (Pp. 418-419)

Francis A. Bush to Anderson Lambert 225 acres in the 12th District. 13 Sep 1854. (Pp. 419-420)

S. B. Nelson and wife Sarah to M. L. Nelson a tract of land, containing 400 acres. 1 Aug 1854. (Pp. 421-422)

Richard Hancock to A. L. Hancock 128 acres in the 10th District. 13 Jul 1855. (Pp. 422-424)

A. L. Hancock and C. C. Hancock agree to partition the negroes that came to them from the estate of their mother Mary Hancock. A. L. Hancock is to receive James, Ann, Monroe, Newton, Mary, Sarah, and Alford. C. C. Hancock is to receive Nisa and child Darthula, Dilla, Silva, John, Nisan, Betsy, and Sela, an old woman . 6 Aug 1855. (Pp. 424-425)

Richard Hancock to his son, C. C. Hancock, 400 acres in the 10th District. 13 Jul 1855. (Pp. 425-427)

It is at the request of Richard Hancock that his wife, Martha, should receive at his death certain property. 13 Jul 1855. (Pp. 427-430)

C. C. Hancock bound to Martha Hancock, wife of Richard Hancock in the penal sum of $2000. 13 Jul 1855. (Pp. 430-431)

Eakin & Company to Robert S. George a quit claim deed to about 200 acres in the 6th District. 3 Jul 1855. (Pp. 431-433)

Thomas C. Word to James Higgins 36 acres in the 11th District. 23 Aug 1855. (Pp. 433-434)

M. L. Nelson to S. B. Nelson 400 acres. 24 Jun 1854. (Pp. 434-435)

Harvey L. Bush and Zachariah Bush to Francis A. Bush 60 acres in the 12th District. 12 Sep 1855. (Pp. 435-436)

DEED BOOK K

Merritt Givans to Wesley Harriman 42 acres in the 6th District. 3 Apr 1855. (Pp. 436-437)

Benjamin F. Creson and wife Sarah to Joseph A. Gooding a tract of land in the 4th District on Carson's Fork. 28 Dec 1852. 28 Dec 1852. (Pp. 437-438)

Blake Sagely to Samuel W. Gray 70 acres in the 12th District. 8 Feb 1854. (Pp. 438-439)

William Young to Joseph Spurlock 58 acres in the 6th District. 1 Aug 1855. (Pp. 439-440)

Ira Hollandsworth to James P. Gasaway 100 acres in the 16th District. 7 Jan 1855. (Pp. 440-441)

Thomas Sisson to Thomas W. Moore 12 acres in the 4th District. 2 Apr 1855. (Pp. 441-442)

Martin Cox and Caleb Cox to D. M. Freeman 138 acres in the 4th District. 19 Aug 1855. (Pp. 442-443)

John Teague to Lemuel J. Duncan a trust deed. 3 Sep 1855. (Pp. 444-445)

John C. Hays to John P. Gannon 45 acres in the 2nd District. 16 Jan 1826. (Pp. 445-446)

William B. Evans to A. B. Carnes 105 acres in the 7th District. 29 Jul 1855. (Pp. 446-447)

Richard U. Lemay to William D. Wallace 125 acres in the 5th District. 19 Dec 1854. (P. 448)

Daniel Bryson and wife Nancy to F. C. Alexander their interest in 160 acres to take effect at my mother's death. 10 Oct 1848. (Pp. 449-450)

Micajah Markum to William Vandergriff 75 acres in the 10th District. 30 Mar 1855. (Pp. 450-451)

Martin S. Hoover to John Bynum 191 acres in the 12th District. 12 Feb 1855. (Pp. 451-453)

Micajah Markum to William Vandergriff 75 acres in the 10th District. 30 Mar 1855. (Pp. 450-451)

Deputy Sheriff J. B. Raines to A. Bowen a tract of land. 2 Jun 1855. (Pp. 453-455)

Lewis Jetton, trustee of Sarah E. Weedon, enters into an agreement. 13 Sep 1855. (P. 455)

Isaac M. Gowen to George W. Thompson lots #40 and 41 in the town of Woodbury. 28 Sep 1855. (P. 456)

W. C. Odom to Warren Cummins a woman slave named Parthenia, about 20. 28 Feb 1855. (Pp. 456-457)

William R. Tally and James M. Allen to Moses Fite a girl slave named Mariah, about 5, for $500. 29 Jan 1855. (P. 457)

James M. Orrand to C. C. Odom a trust deed. 1 Oct 1855.

(Pp. 458-460)

R. L. Bain to J. W. Keel 200 acres in the 5th District. 2 Oct 1855. (Pp. 460-461)

Samuel Lester, attorney for Joseph P. Morgan, to Robert L. Manus 50 acres in the 5th District. 7 Oct 1842. (Pp. 461-462)

Henry Trott to T. J. Jetton one third of an acre in the town of Woodbury. 26 Jan 1855. (Pp. 462-463)

John A. Baird and wife Frances A. to Henry A. Wiley a trust deed. 9 Oct 1855. (Pp. 463-464)

C. T. New to William C. Miller 25½ acres in the 6th District. 9 Oct 1855. (Pp. 464-465)

Frances A. Baird and Joseph Clark to Henry A. Wiley a town lot in the town of Woodbury as a title bond. John A. Baird is now deceased. 10 Oct 1855. (Pp. 465-466)

Isaac Gooding to Catherine Jameson 53 acres in the 4th District. 25 Aug 1854. (Pp. 466-468)

William Wharton to Wiley W. Bell one acre. I am one of the partners of Bell, Wharton, & Company. 9 Oct 1855. (Pp. 468-469)

Wiley W. Bell to William R. Tally a trust deed. 11 Oct 1855. (Pp. 470-471)

Thomas Cox, guardian for John J. Marshall and (Pias) Marshall, orphans of John C. Marshall, to Isaac J. Roach of Carroll County power of attorney to sell land in Cannon County belonging to the said John C. Marshall. 28 Jul 1855. (Pp. 471-472)

Susan George and R. S. George to Ivery Simmons a title bond. 10 Oct 1855. (Pp. 473-474)

C. T. New to Moses W. McKnight the house and lot in Woodbury whereon I now live. 8 Oct 1855. (Pp. 474-475)

William Todd to A. F. McFerrin five acres in the 4th District. 21 Oct 1855. (Pp. 475-476)

David D. Hipp to Hyram Todd one or two acres in the 5th District. 21 Jun 1855. (Pp. 476-477)

Winney Peyton to R. H. Mason 75 acres purchased by my husband Harrison Peyton. 3 Oct 1855. (Pp. 477-478)

Samuel Grear to McGill & Fagan 150 acres in the 4th District. 17 Oct 1855. (Pp. 478-479)

A. D. Fugett to John F. Weedon 32 acres in the 6th District. 9 Oct 1855. (Pp. 479-480)

Aaron F. Jones to Tolbert Jones a tract of land in the 11th District formerly owned by Erasmus Jones. 24 Feb 1853. (Pp. 480-481)

John Teague to Hiram Wilson a trust deed. 17 Oct 1855. (Pp. 481-482)

William Barton to Washington S. Massey 70 acres in the 2nd District. 6 Oct 1855. (Pp. 482-483)

Nicholas Gooding to William Byford 50 acres on Stone's River in a hollow called the time kiler hollow. 30 Mar 1839. (Pp. 484-485)

William Cummins to Thomas H. Williams 500 acres on Barren Fork of Collins River. 12 Jun 1855. (Pp. 485-486)

C. B. Summer to T. R. Summer 70 acres in the 11th District. 12 Jan 1855. (Pp. 486-487)

John Moore to Fanny Moore 25 acres in the 4th District conveyed to me by the said Fanny Moore. 20 Oct 1855 as a trust deed. 20 Oct 1855. (Pp. 487-488)

Mark L. Young to T. J. and E. C. Preston 61 acres in the 2nd District. 10 Jan 1855. (Pp. 488-489)

Thomas H. Williams and Jesse B. Williams to Moses W. McKnight a trust deed. 30 Oct 1855. (Pp. 489-490)

William F. George to Susan George my house and lot in the town of Woodbury for five dollars. 25 Oct 1855. (P. 491)

A. K. Cummings to James Cummings a trust deed. 21 Oct 1855. (P. 492)

John R. Sullivan and wife Ann to Sarah E. Weedon, wife of Augustine M. Weedon and daughter of the said Ann Sullivan, a negro girl named Mary, about 2. 14 Mar 1855. (P. 493)

A. M. Weedon and wife Sarah E. to A. Burger a girl slave named Mary for $250. 1 Nov 1855. (Pp. 493-494)

H. A. Wiley to F. Coleman a town lot in the town of Woodbury, it being next to a lot formerly owned by Dr. Price. 3 Nov 1855. (Pp. 494-495)

John Farley to Mary Thomas 38 acres in the 8th District. 23 Jul 1855. (Pp. 495-496)

Isaac Young to Wiley Riggs one acre on Barren Fork of Collins River. 15 Jun 1855. (Pp. 496-497)

Isaac Brooks to Wiley Riggs 266½ acres on Barren Fork of Collins River. 10 Jan 1854. (Pp. 497-498)

Jefferson Jetton to A. Burger three fourth's of an acre in the town of Woodbury. Bounded: on the east by William West. 9 Nov 1853. (P. 498)

Elias A. Ready and wife Sarah, formerly McEwen, to Hannah M. McEwen and Margaret E. McEwen 73 acres in the 1st District. 13 Nov 1855. (Pp. 449-500)

Calvin Curlee departed this life in 1851 intestate, leaving as hiw widow, Rebecca Curlee, who still survives and as his only children, John F. Curlee, Cullen E. Curlee, David C. Curlee, Thomas G. Curlee, Peyton B. Curlee, Elizabeth Ann, wife of Joseph Youree, Nancy R. E., wife of G. W. McCullough, Ruth, wife of

Thomas Hodges. Said children to Rebecca Curlee 119 acres. 5 Nov 1853. (Pp. 500-502)

John P. Gandy and wife Sophia to Andrew J. Brandon 94 acres in the 3rd District. 27 Dec 1854. (Pp. 503-504)

(Book begins with Page 32)

James L. Kelton and wife Eliza E. to Joseph Thompson a tract of land in the 1st District. 11 Mar 1853. (Pp. 32-33)

Granville H. Johnson to Burrell P. Johnson a trust deed. 10 Nov 1855. (Pp. 33-35)

James H. Bell to Rebecca C. Bell, wife of Wiley Bell, lot #24 in the town of Woodbury. 10 Nov 1855. (Pp. 35-36)

G. W. Thompson and E. R. Thompson to M. R. Rushing a tract of land in the 6th District. 13 Nov 1855. (Pp. 36-39)

William H. Travis to Samuel D. Travis 200 acres in the 1st District. 3 Oct 1854. (Pp. 39-40)

Jesse Carter to Edward Bragg 25 acres in the 1st District. 18 Mar 1854. (Pp. 40-41)

Jesse Sisson to Ervin Cherry ten acres in the 4th District. 2 Jul 1853. (P. 42)

John Prim and wife Anna Jane to Claburn J. Gunter a tract of land that formerly was owned by Claburn Gunter, Jr. and was distributed to the Gunter heirs at his death. The land is the same place where Margaret Gunter now lives. 2 Jul 1855. (Pp. 43-44)

Joel Cherry to Amos Gaither 50 acres in the 4th District. 15 Jan 1849. (Pp. 44-45)

James M. Gunter, Sarah McDougald and husband John D. to Claborn Gunter 145 acres, it being the same land where Margaret Gunter now lives. 26 Dec 1854. (Pp. 45-47)

Jonathan G. Stone to William C. Miller 62½ acres in the 7th District. 28 Nov 1855. (Pp. 47-49)

J. J. Putman to James Higgins a negro boy named Thomas, 10, of a light copper color. 1 Nov 1855. (P. 49)

R. J. Phillips to Abel Rushing 150 acres in the 8th District. 9 Oct 1855. One half acre is reserved as a meeting house so long as the Methodists profess to worship there. 6 Dec 1855. (Pp. 50-51)

William Young and wife Uffey; Joseph Whitley and wife Elizabeth; Charley Esque and wife Mary; and Martha Gannon, heirs of Mark Gannon, to Joseph Spurlock nine and one half acres in the 6th District. 1 Aug 1855. (Pp. 51-55)

Thomas C. McLoud and wife Nancy to Azariah Gaither 21 acres in the 3rd District. 10 Aug 1853. (Pp. 55-56)

L. Holman and wife Jane C. to Samuel D. Travis 50 acres in the 1st District. 17 Dec 1855. (Pp. 56-58)

John Martin and wife Martha to Charles Hutchinson 150 acres in the 9th District. 24 Jan 1855. (Pp. 58-59)

R. S. George plot. 2 Nov 1855. (P. 60)

John B. Perkins to S. B. Sellars and W. W. Sellars 268 acres in the 10th District. 4 Jan 1856. (Pp. 61-62)

John Muncy to William C. Campbell a title bond. 31 Dec 1855. (Pp. 62-63)

A. S. McKnight to Thomas D. Summer a man slave named Henry, 23, for $1000. 31 Dec 1855. (Pp. 63-64)

George H. Keeton to William R. Bryan 50 acres in the 11th District. 2 Aug 1855. (Pp. 64-65)

William Parton to William Allen nine acres in the 8th District. 15 Nov 1855. (Pp. 65-66)

Isaac T. Hailey to John C. Mays a title bond. 29 Sep 1855. (Pp. 67-68)

John Teague to Hiram Wilson, Jr. a trust deed. 8 Jan 1856. (Pp. 69-70)

G. B. Mears to George W. Thompson 132½ acres in the 6th District. 22 Dec 1855. (Pp. 70-71)

William B. Evans to Johnathan G. Stone a tract of land in the 7th District, containing 62 acres. 7 Jan 1856. (Pp. 71-73)

James McBroom to Cooper & Finley a town lot in the town of Woodbury. 10 Jan 1856. (Pp. 73-74)

Jesse R. and Edmund W. Ferrell, by descent from their grandfather Jonathan Jones, have title to an interest in a tract of land in the 3rd District, it being the same land on which the said Jones resided and owned in his life time. Said Ferrells to C. R. Davis their interest in the land. 7 Jan 1856. (Pp. 74-75)

William B. Evans to William Elkins 70 acres in the 7th District. 23 Feb 1854. (Pp. 75-77)

Andrew Jackson Brewer to B. A. Gunter 300 acres in the 5th District. 1 Jun 1855. (Pp. 77-78)

Thomas D. Summer to Armstead Francis 153 acres in the 11th District. 7 Jan 1856. (Pp. 78-79)

John Mitchell to Lydia Williams 200 acres in the 5th District. 12 Dec 1853. (Pp. 80-81)

James J. Bogle, one of the heirs of George Bogle, to George R. Bogle his interest in a portion of land that was set apart for a dower for my mother Margaret Bogle whereon she now lives. 10 May 1855. (Pp. 81-82)

Albert T. Fagan to William McGill 100 acres in the 4th District. 10 Nov 1855. (Pp. 82-83)

McGill and Fagan to David McGill 50 acres in the 4th District. 24 Dec 1855. (Pp. 83-84)

James W. McAdow to John A. Milligan 62 acres in the 11th District. 7 Apr 1855. (Pp. 84-86)

John C. Leech to John L. Harris 32 acres in the 1st District. 7 Jan 1856. (Pp. 86-87)

Henry D. McBroom to Isaac McBroom ten acres in the 6th District. 25 Jan 1856. (Pp. 87-88)

Joel L. Melton to Samuel Young 50 acres in the 7th District. 5 May 1855. (Pp. 88-89)

Micajah Petty to William Owen 80 acres in the 4th District. 15 Mar 1854. (Pp. 90-91)

William Young to Martha Gannon 60 acres in the 6th District. 14 Sep 1855. (Pp. 91-92)

Ward Barrett, Jr. to Franklin Fann 39 acres in the 1st District. 5 Nov 1855. (P. 93)

Franklin Fann to William Reed 39 acres in the 1st District. 5 Nov 1855. (P. 94)

M. G. Elkin to James H. Wood about 400 acres in the 7th District, it being the same place whereon I now live. 4 Feb 1856. (Pp. 95-96)

J. B. Elledge to Jonathan Hendrickson a tract of land on Mountain Creek. 1 Feb 1856. (Pp. 97-99)

William Elkins to William C. Miller 70 acres in the 7th District. 4 Feb 1856. (Pp. 99-100)

Roderick L. Bain to J. L. Pendleton, trustee, a trust deed. 31 Jan 1856. (Pp. 100-102)

Samuel Phillips to Benjamin F. Woods eight acres in the 8th District. 25 Jan 1856. (Pp. 102-104)

Samuel Philips to Thomas G. Wood a trust deed. 11 Feb 1856. (Pp. 104-106)

John McClain to John W. Cunningham a tract of land in the 4th District. 17 Jul 1854. (Pp. 106-107)

John R. Sullivan to Robert S. George a tract of land in the 6th District. 11 Feb 1856. (Pp. 107-108)

Daniel F. Mitchell to John N. Mitchell 459 acres in the 4th District. 11 Feb 1856. (Pp. 109-110)

M. C. Elledge, Sheriff, to A. Boran 125 acres. 12 Feb 1856. (Pp. 111-112)

John Q. Weatherford to John Bynum a petition to sell land belonging to the heirs of Hugh Robinson. 12 Feb 1856. (Pp. 112-114)

John R. Sullivan to John F. Weedon and William C. Miller 39 acres in the 6th District. 12 Feb 1856. (Pp. 114-115)

William L. Martin to John F. Weedon his interest in 279 acres in Warren County. 12 Feb 1856. (Pp. 115-116)

Michael Wilson to William C. Jones 30 acres in the 11th District. 3 May 1855. (Pp. 116-117)

James H. Youngblood and wife Elizabeth C. to Mumford Tenpenny 50 acres on the east fork of Stone's River. 1 Nov 1853. (Pp. 117-119)

John K. Ashley to Ervin Cherry 49 acres in the 12th District. 5 Feb 1856. (Pp. 119-121)

Berry Williams to Casson Williams 110 acres in the 4th District. 13 Feb 1856. (Pp. 121-122)

Samuel Vance to William Barton a trust deed. 13 Feb 1856. (Pp. 122-124)

Marthy Lasater to her grandson, William T. Williams, a mare colt. 22 Dec 1855. (Pp. 124-125)

A. Barkley to Joseph Bryson a negro boy named Frank, about 25, for $500. 12 Feb 1856. (P. 125)

James L. Cawthon to James R. Brewer 50 acres on Barren Fork of Collins River. 14 Feb 1856. (P. 126)

M. G. Elkins to L. M. Harriman 250 acres on the east fork of Stone's River. 15 Feb 1856. (Pp. 127-128)

James Simmons to Isiah Parker 75 acres in the 4th District as a trust deed. 27 Oct 1855. (Pp. 128-130)

Henry Goodloe and J. H. Byrn enter into an agreement to change the dividing line. 15 Jan 1856. (Pp. 130-131)

Nathan Finley and Francis Cooper to Samuel Vance a town lot in the town of Woodbury. 13 Feb 1856. (Pp. 131-132)

C. B. Summer to Abraham Brandon 133 acres in the 3rd District. 18 Feb 1856. (Pp. 132-133)

John Q. Weatherford to D. M. Jarrett 75 acres in the 6th District. 25 Feb 1856. (Pp. 133-135)

D. M. Freeman to Jefferson Todd a tract of land in the 4th District. 27 Feb 1856. (Pp. 135-136)

D. M. Freeman to William Philips a tract of land in the 4th District. 27 Feb 1856. (Pp. 136-138)

Archebald Stone to G. B. Mars 15½ acres in the 6th District. 11 Mar 1851. (Pp. 138-139)

Martha Gooding to her daughter, Malinda Gooding, ten acres in the 4th District. 28 Feb 1856. (Pp. 139-140)

John Espey a deed of gift to Levina Ann Espey and Frances Elizabeth Caroline Espey 32 acres in the 12th District. 12 Jun 1847. (Pp. 140-141)

Joseph A. Gooding to William Gooding 12½ acres in the 4th District on Carson's Fork of Stone's River. 3 Mar 1856. (Pp. 141-142)

William Gooding to Joseph A. Gooding 18 acres in the 4th District. 3 Mar 1856. (Pp. 142-144)

John W. Cook to Joseph A. Gooding 22½ acres in the 4th District. 1 Mar 1856. (Pp. 144-145)

Malinda Gooding to William Gooding 22½ acres in the 4th District. 1 Mar 1856. (Pp. 145-147)

Wiley Riggs to Wesley McMahan 266½ acres in the 5th District. 5 Nov 1855. (Pp. 147-148)

John Farley to Isaac T. Blare 42 acres in the 8th District. 3 Mar 1856. (Pp. 148-150)

Jesse Millikin to Henry Brown a tract of land in the 4th District. 1 Nov 1855. (Pp. 150-151)

A. J. Philips to Thomas Winnett 40 acres in the 8th District. 12 Dec 1855. (Pp. 151-152)

Enoch Jones to Robert M. Jones 30 acres in the 9th District. 2 Feb 1856. (Pp. 152-153)

William Cummins and William Stone to B. F. Sullivan 20 acres in the 6th District. 16 Feb 1856. (Pp. 154-155)

William C. Odom to C. B. Odom a title bond. 17 Sep 1855. (Pp. 155-156)

J. L. Fare & Company to Keeble & Ready 300 acres in the 12th District. 14 Feb 1856. (Pp. 157-158)

Arthur Gaither to Catherine Bragg 145 acres in the 6th District. 12 Feb 1856. (Pp. 159-160)

Arthur Gaither to Narcissa Gaither for the consideration of her maintainance 100 acres in the 1st District. 12 Feb 1856. (Pp. 160-162)

W. B. Evans to the Trustees of the Methodist Episcopal Church a tract of land on Rock House Fork of Stone's River. 18 Sep 1855. (Pp. 162-163)

Abner Alexander to the New Hope Congregation two acres on Marshall Creek. 21 Jan 1853. (Pp. 164-165)

Benjamin Fugett to Wesley Harriman a title bond. 5 Jan 1856. (Pp. 165-166)

Henry Goodloe to Bryant Hare 158 acres in the 1st District. 17 Jan 1856. (Pp. 166-168)

William C. Leech to R. H. Mason 90 acres in the 11th District. 28 Feb 1856. (Pp. 168-169)

James McClain to John Cooper five acres in the 4th District. 21 Nov 1852. (Pp. 170-171)

John B. Parris to Isaac W. Elledge 240 acres in the 7th District. 25 Mar 1856. (Pp. 171-172)

Aden Hollandsworth to David Hutchins a tract of land in the 10th District. 7 Apr 1856. (Pp. 173-174)

State of Tennessee Grant #16652. 100 acres granted to

John Farley. 9 Jan 1830. (Pp. 174-175)

John W. Parker to Silas Parker 400 acres in the 4th District. 7 Apr 1856. (Pp. 176-177)

Newman Hollandsworth to Adam Tittle 30 acres in the 10th District. 5 Apr 1856. (Pp. 177-178)

Susanah George and William F. George to Robert L. George a town lot in the town of Woodbury, it being the house formerly occupied as a grocery house by the said William F. George. 9 Apr 1856. (Pp. 179-180)

William Cummins to Isaack Parker 115 acres in the 4th District. 21 Dec 1853. (Pp. 180-181)

William T. McBroom to A. F. McFerrin 40 acres in the 2nd District. 7 Apr 1856. (Pp. 181-183)

A. B. Carnes to John E. Mason 335 acres in the 6th District. 2 Feb 1855. (Pp. 183-184)

Henry Dennis to William Dennis a tract of land in the 10th District. 29 Dec 1854. (P. 185)

Ira Hollandsworth to Henry Dennis four acres in the 10th District. 29 Jun 1855. (Pp. 186-187)

George Turner to Isaac W. Fox 112 acres in the 7th District. 22 Apr 1856. (Pp. 187-188)

John Robinson to J. N. Patton a trust deed. 20 Mar 1856. (Pp. 189-190)

John Kinsey to Lemuel D. Evans 25 acres in the 9th District. 19 Apr 1855. (Pp. 190-192)

Ervin Cherry to Edward Alford 100 acres in the 4th District. 16 Nov 1852. (Pp. 192-193)

A. Burger to J. F. Weedon his interest as tenant in common with Edwin A. Keeble to 279 acres in Warren and Cannon Counties. 31 Mar 1855. (Pp. 193-194)

Allen R. Jones to C. H. Rollins a title bond. 12 Apr 1856. (Pp. 194-195)

Jesse B. Williams to John Mills 50 acres on Carson's Fork of Stone's River. 11 Apr 1853. (Pp. 196-197)

John Farley to Isaac T. Blair 20 acres in the 8th District. 5 May 1856. (Pp. 197-198)

William Adcock to John Mills and Nancy Mills 165 acres in the 5th District. 1 Mar 1849. (Pp. 198-199)

John Mills to Nancy Mills his interest in 165 acres in the 5th District. I and the said Nancy Mills hold the land as equal partners. 5 May 1856. (P. 200)

M. F. Todd and Malinda Coughenour enter into a marriage contract. 13 May 1856. (Pp. 201-202)

Richmond Rushing to Joseph Spurlock a tract of land. 16 May 1856. (Pp. 202-203)

Samuel Vance to Elijah Stephens a town lot in the town of Woodbury, it being the same that the Blacksmith Shop is on where H. B. Perry now works. 17 May 1856. (Pp. 203-204)

Stephen Harriman to Benjamin Fugett 50 acres in the 6th District. 5 Jan 1856. (Pp. 205-206)

John J. Bell to William Cobb about two acres in the 6th District. 26 May 1856. (Pp. 206-207)

Abram S. Hollis of Cape Girardeau, Missouri appoints Simeon Hollis his power of attorney to receive his share as one of the heirs of David Hollis. 23 Mar 1854. (Pp. 208-209)

John J. McElroy to Bartlet S. Ring 44 acres in the 12th District. 7 Mar 1856. (Pp. 209-210)

Isaac W. Elledge to Bartlet S. Ring six acres in the 12th District. 21 May 1856. (Pp. 211-212)

The estate of William Bates. Ex Parte. 9 Jun 1856. (Pp. 212-213)

Joseph C. Leake to Larkin Keaton 110 acres. 4 Jun 1856. (Pp. 213-214)

Samuel B. Barrell to M. G. Elkins 116 acres in the 7th District. 3 Jun 1856. (Pp. 214-216)

Thomas C. Word to Larkin Keaton 115 acres in the 10th District. 11 Jun 1856. (Pp. 217-218)

John W. Marshall and James W. McAdow to P. G. Leach 200 acres in the 11th District. 1 Jul 1856. (Pp. 218-219)

Fountain Owen to Nelson Owen 138 acres in the 11th District. 3 Mar 1856. (Pp. 220-221)

J. K. Gilly to John Bynum 30 acres in the 12th District. 23 Feb 1856. (Pp. 221-222)

Leroy G. Tolbert to John Bynum 48½ acres in the 12th District. 1 Mar 1856. (Pp. 223-224)

Luke Lasater to Brinkley Lasater 53 acres in the 3rd District. 1 Jul 1856. (Pp. 225-226)

Robert M. Good of Rutherford County to William H. Good 50 acres in the 23rd District of Rutherford County. 27 Feb 1855. (Pp. 226-227)

R. H. Mason to Young & McFerren 330 acres on Stone's River. 13 May 1856. (Pp. 228-230)

Sheriff to John E. Mason a town lot in the town of Woodbury. 9 Jun 1856. (Pp. 230-232)

A. C. Tatum to John Hager a negro girl named Celia Ann, about 10. 9 Jul 1856. (P. 233)

M. G. Elkins to James H. Wood 90 acres in the 7th District. 9 Jul 1856. (Pp. 234-235)

William C. Alfred and wife Sarah A., formerly Duncan, to J. L. Fare their interest, which is one eighth, in the estate of Oliver C. Duncan. 11 Jun 1856. (Pp. 235-236)

Aden Hollandsworth to Ira Hollandsworth his interest, it being three shares out of eight, in the estate of John Hollandsworth. 12 Jul 1856. (Pp. 236-237)

Jonathan Wherry to Joseph Hollis ten acres in Rutherford County on Cripple Creek. 29 Nov 1851. (Pp. 238-239)

Aden Hollandsworth to M. M. Burger 300 acres in the 10th District. 12 Jul 1856. (Pp. 239-241)

Robert M. Good to A. F. McFerrin a negro woman named Sena, about 27. 23 Jul 1856. (P. 242)

Benjamin Fugett to M. S. Fugett 208 acres in the 6th District. 29 Jul 1856. (Pp. 243-244)

M. S. Fugett to Townson Fugett 208 acres in the 6th District. 29 Jul 1856. (Pp. 244-245)

Jesse Melton to James Higgins 40 acres in the 7th District. 28 Jul 1856. (Pp. 246-247)

Alexander Higgins to James Higgins a negro girl named Lucy, about 3, for $100. 29 Jul 1856. (Pp. 247-250)

John Melton to James Higgins 35 acres in the 7th District. 6 Oct 1851. (Pp. 250-251)

A. J. Inglis to L. G. Tolbert 100 acres in the 12th District. 30 Dec 1855. (Pp. 252-253)

Squire Warren to C. C. Akers 119 acres in the 7th District. 4 Aug 1856. (Pp. 254-255)

Survey of C. B. Summers' land, containing 237 acres. 6 Aug 1856. (Pp. 256-257)

John Hayes to James J. Graham a tract of land in the 2nd District. 4 Aug 1856. (Pp. 257-258)

Townson Fugett and S. R. James to Abel Rushing 215 acres in the 6th District. 4 Aug 1856. (Pp. 259-260)

D. M. Jarratt to Elijah Neely 57 acres as a trust deed. 9 Dec 1848. (Pp. 261-262)

Thomas Hopkins of Warren County to James Todd of Rutherford County thirty   acres in Rutherford County. 16 Sep 1824.

Thomas H. Williams of Davidson County to J. L. Fare 200 acres in the 4th District. 15 Aug 1855. (Pp. 264-266)

A. C. Tatum to J. W. Orrand 52 acres in the 6th District. 4 Sep 1856. (Pp. 266-267)

Clerk & Master to J. W. Orrand 172 acres belonging to the heirs of Hugh Robinson. 4 Sep 1856. (Pp. 267-269)

E. J. Wood to John A. Wood lot #57 in the town of Woodbury.

6 Sep 1856. (Pp. 270-271)

David Epperly to J. L. Fare 200 acres in the 4th and 12th Districts. 25 Aug 1856. (Pp. 271-272)

J. L. Fare to Thompson and Barton 200 acres in the 4th and 12th Districts. 26 Aug 1856. (Pp. 262-273)

Robert K. Stephens to Alford Watson 50 acres in the 9th District. 11 Sep 1856. (Pp. 274-276)

Enos S. Weatherspoon to Joseph Bogle 30 acres in the 11th District. 22 Nov 1847. (Pp. 276-277).

Joseph Bogle to Joseph and R. J. E. McKnight 135 acres. 15 Sep 1856. (Pp. 277-278)

Joseph Ramsey to Susan Harper, Administratrix of Thomas Nokes, 15 acres in the 6th District. 15 Sep 1856. (Pp. 279-280)

R. H. Mason to A. M. Fisher a title bond. 19 Sep 1856. (Pp. 280-281)

William Cobb to J. J. Bell a quit claim to one third of the steam mill at Woodbury. 15 Sep 1856. (Pp. 281-282)

Wiley W. Bell and John J. Bell to William R. Talley a trust deed. 15 Sep 1856. (Pp. 282-285)

David McGill to Albert T. Fagan four acres in the 4th District. 24 Dec 1855. (Pp. 286-287)

Samuel Bryson. Procession of land. 23 Sep 1856. (Pp. 287-288)

Jasper M. Stone and wife Mary to Thomas J. Thompson their interest, it being one sixth, in 85 acres on which Sarah Thompson resides. Said Sarah Thompson holds a life interest. 4 Sep 1856. (Pp. 288-290)

Ivy Bush to Jonathan G. Davis 160 acres in the 5th District. 7 May 1853. (Pp. 290-291)

William Whitmon to Ivy Bush 160 acres in the 5th District. 5 Nov 1849. (Pp. 291-292)

Isaac Neely, Sheriff, to Charles Espey 149 acres. 1 Sep 1856. (Pp. 293-294)

Robert A. Smith to Henry Hoover 130 acres as a trust deed. 27 Sep 1856. (Pp. 295-297)

Thomas Adamson to John W. Matthews 35 acres in the 10th District. 20 Sep 1856. (Pp. 297-298)

Delilah Bosley to Jeremiah Scales, trustee for his wife, Rachel G. Scales, 500 acres known as the Clement place and the place that Henry Maney formerly lived. 6 Oct 1856. (Pp. 299-300)

John W. Summers and William C. Leech to R. H. Mason a tract of land in the 11th District. 28 Feb 1856. (Pp. 301-302)

Anthony Summers to R. H. Mason 27 acres in the 11th District. 6 Oct 1856. (Pp. 303-304)

R. H. Mason to J. F. Weedon a tract of land in the 11th District, containing 420 acres. 6 Oct 1856. (Pp. 304-306)

Isaiah Neely to Joseph Ramsey a town lot in the town of Woodbury, it being the lot whereon the Widow Perry lives. 25 Sep 1856. (Pp. 307-308)

Rebecca Curlee to T. G. Curlee 115 acres in the 8th District. 2 Sep 1856. (Pp. 308-309)

Adam Elrod to his daughter, Eliza B. Ferrell, wife of William B. Ferrell 190 acres in the 5th District. 10 Sep 1856. (Pp. 310-311)

Anthony Summers to James S. Odom 30 acres in the 11th District. 25 Apr 1855. (Pp. 311-312)

John Hager to A. C. Tatum 203 acres in the 2nd District. 15 Sep 1856. (Pp. 313-314)

Tobias Tenpenny, one of the heirs or Richard Tenpenny, to James W. Tenpenny and Richard Tenpenny, Jr. his interest in the estate. 30 Jan 1854. (Pp. 315-316)

B. T. McFerrin to Samuel Nesbit 98 acres in the 3rd District. 4 Oct 1856. (Pp. 317-318)

A. F. Todd to William Thompson 15 acres in the 5th District. 15 Dec 1855. (Pp. 318-319)

Micajah Petty to James Cook 110 acres in the 4th District. 11 Sep 1856. (Pp. 319-320)

Archebald Stone to Abel Rushing a negro boy named Bob, about 27, for $200. 14 Oct 1856. (Pp. 321-323)

William Cummings to Catharine Finley ten acres in the 5th District. 9 Mar 1855. (Pp. 323-324)

Isaac Neely, Sheriff, to William Ready some personal property belonging to James Ready. 14 Oct 1856. (Pp. 325-327)

Thomas Hale to William L. Dodd a tract of land in the 11th District. 1 Jul 1854. (Pp. 327-328)

Abel Rushing to John Rushing 200 acres as a trust deed. 23 Oct 1856. (Pp. 328-330)

Washington Kennedy to William L. Covington 87 acres in the 6th District. 16 Oct 1856. (Pp. 330-332)

R. J. Bond to William R. Bogle 130 acres in the 11th District. 4 Oct 1856. (Pp. 332-333)

W. T. McBroom to A. P. Mullinax 50 acres in Harricane Creek in the 11th District. 15 Sep 1856. (Pp. 333-334)

Nathaniel M. Taylor to William L. Covington 30 acres in the 6th District. 17 Oct 1856. (Pp. 335-336)

Andrew N. Johnson to John Higgins 80 acres in the 6th District. 19 Sep 1856. (Pp. 337-338)

Elijah Neely to his three sons, to wit, Robert Walkup Neely, Nathan Lyon Neely, and James Blakely Neely, and also his daughter, Polly Jane Neely, 135 acres, it being the place upon which myself and family now live. Bounded: Elizabeth Neely, the widow of Nathan Neely, and their children. 5 Nov 1856. (Pp. 339340)

Asa Smith to Franklin Coleman lot #4 in the town of Woodbury. 7 Nov 1856. (Pp. 341-342)

Abel McBroom to Franklin Coleman a town lot in the town of Woodbury. Bounded: west of the Christian Church. 7 Nov 1856. (Pp. 342-343)

Joseph Ramsey to Barton and Thompson a negro boy named Stephen, 19, for $1250. 14 Oct 1856. (P. 344)

William T. McBroom to Eli H. Muncy 60 acres in the 2nd District. 10 Nov 1856. (Pp. 345-346)

William Cummins to John Hipp 100 acres in the 5th District. 10 Oct 1856. (Pp. 346-348)

Adam Elrod to T. J. Preston a tract of land in the 2nd District. Bounded: Mary Preston and John F. Preston. 30 Sep 1856. (Pp. 348-349)

A. D. Stephens and R. L. Stephens to Mary Tassey, wife of Alexander Tassey 151½ acres in the 1st and 2nd Districts. 13 Oct 1856. (Pp. 349-351)

James Todd to Walter Wilson a tract of land in the 4th District. 19 Nov 1856. (Pp. 351-352)

David D. Hipp to James P. Pendleton 175 acres in the 5th District. 29 Nov 1856. (Pp. 353-354)

Archebald Stone to Gabriel Hume 54 acres. 8 Dec 1856. (Pp. 354-356)

Thomas G. Wood, Clerk & Master, to Archebald Stone 125¼ acres in the 6th District, it being land belonging to George St. John's heirs, to wit, John St. John, Berry St. John, Arthur St. John, Martin St. John, William St. John, and Thomas St. John, and other children. 18 Apr 1855. (Pp. 357-359)

Daniel F. Weedon and wife Maria L. to George W. Thompson a town lot in the town of Woodbury. 5 May 1856. (Pp. 359-360)

Gabriel Mears and James Mears to S. J. Odom 37 acres in the 8th District. 18 Nov 1856. (Pp. 361-362)

H. A. Wiley to Jesse Barnes one half acre in the town of Woodbury. 16 Nov 1856. (Pp. 362-363)

Alex Tassey and wife Mary to W. S. Massie a tract of land in the 2nd District. 15 Nov 1856. (Pp. 363-364)

William A. Barkley to John N. Doak his one sixth interest in a tract of land in the 2nd District. 1 Aug 1854. (P. 365)

William Soape to David Sommers as the trustee for the children of James Allman 50 acres in the 12th District. 22 Nov 1856. (Pp. 366-367)

Samuel B. Barrell to John Muncy 135½ acres on the Barren Fork of Collins River. 1 Dec 1855. (Pp. 367-368)

Archebald Stone to James K. Eason a negro boy named Henry, about 16, of yellow complexion for $400. 10 Nov 1847. (P. 369)

G. N. Northcut to Micajah Massie 35 acres in the 9th District. 29 Nov 1856. (P. 370)

James B. Summers to John F. Davenport seven and one half acres in the 11th District. 1 Dec 1856. (Pp. 371-372)

John Pendleton to Israel Long 450 acres in the 8th District. 10 Jan 1856. (Pp. 372-375)

William G. Melton to Jesse Lawrence 38 acres in the 7th District. 17 Dec 1856. (Pp. 275-376)

Jesse Lawrence to William G. Melton 50 acres in the 7th District. 17 Dec 1856. (Pp. 376-378)

James T. Breshears to Joseph Bogle 145 acres in the 7th District. 20 Dec 1856. (Pp. 378-380)

William Bogle to William B. Wilson 100 acres in the 11th District. 4 Sep 1856. (Pp. 380-381)

Allen R. Jones to Christopher Rollins 100 acres in the 10th District. 6 Jan 1857. (Pp. 381-382)

Ann Lansden to William C. Donnell 130 acres in the 11th District. Bounded: Nancy McAdow. 4 Oct 1856. (Pp. 382-383)

Henry Hoover to Robert A. Smith a quit claim to 130 acres in the 2nd District. 27 Sep 1856. (Pp. 383-384)

John L. Work to R. H. Mason a negro boy named Ellis, about 25, for $1400. Said Work is a resident of Rutherford County. 5 Jan 1856. (Pp. 384-385)

John Muncy to William Columbus Campbell 170 acres on the 5th District. 26 Dec 1856. (Pp. 385-386)

A. F. McFerrin to James Todd 75 acres in the 4th District. 24 Oct 1856. (Pp. 386-387)

Survey of the land of Michael Jones in the 11th District. 9 Dec 1856. (P. 388)

Survey of the land of H. C. Summers in the 11th District. 15 Jan 1857. (Pp. 389-390)

William Hunt to Stephen Harriman a negro woman named Amanda, about 17, and her infant child who is about three months. 22 Sep 1856. (P. 390)

B. B. Cooper to James Higgins 40 acres in the 11th District. 20 Jan 1856. (Pp. 391-392)

214

Col. John Stump, Henry Stump, and Robert Lanier of Davidson County to Samuel K. Laughlin in consideration of certain professional services their interest in 293 acres in Warren County. 15 Mar 1838. (Pp. 392-394)

Survey of the lands of Joseph Bryson. 21 Jan 1857. (Pp. 395-397)

T. H. Smith to S. B. Spurlock two boy slaves named Alford and Brady for $1200. 28 Jan 1857. (P. 398)

J. L. Fare to M. W. McKnight and D. L. Fare the School House property in the town of Woodbury containing one half acre. 19 Jan 1857. (Pp. 398-399)

Joseph Simpson to Andrew S. Simpson 18 acres in the 12th District. 19 Oct 1835. (Pp. 399-400)

John Harriman to Stephen Harriman a trust deed. 27 Jan 1857. (Pp. 401-402)

Joshua Barton to his son, William Barton, 300 acres on the east fork of Stone's River. 29 Jan 1857. (Pp. 402-404)

Charles F. Jones to William B. Jones a trust deed. 26 Jan 1857. (Pp. 404-406)

William B. McLaughlin and Levina Tolbert enter into a marriage contract. Said McLaughlin is a resident of Coffee County and said Tolbert is a resident of Bedford County. 2 Oct 1856. (Pp. 406-408)

Jane McLaughlin, Mary Ann McLaughlin, William McLaughlin, Daniel W. Mitchel and wife Elenar, heirs of Dawson McLaughlin, have title to 125 acres in the 2nd District. Said parties to James Vassar their interest in the said land. 14 Aug 1856. (Pp. 408-409)

Aden Hollandsworth to Ira Hollandsworth a tract of land in the 10th District. 28 Feb 1857. (Pp. 409-411)

James Stone to Jesse Lawrence 16 acres. 31 Aug 1852. (Pp. 411-412)

Elizabeth Farley to J. F. Blair all my life estate that was assigned to me out of the land of my husband John Farley. 22 Nov 1856. (Pp. 412-413)

W. R. Talley to R. H. Mason one acre in the 6th District. 3 Feb 1857. (Pp. 413-415)

Joseph Bryson, Sr. to Joseph Bryson, Jr. 65 acres in the 11th District. 9 Feb 1857. (Pp. 415-416)

Jesse J. Farley to J. F. Blair his interest in the estate of John Farley. 5 Dec 1856. (Pp. 416-417)

Jeremiah Scales to Joseph Walker of Rutherford County 402 acres in the 4th District. 9 Feb 1857. (Pp. 417-419)

Alexander McKnight to Bryant Hare ten acres in the 1st District. 20 Jan 1857. (Pp. 419-420)

Henry Goodloe to Bryant Hare two acres in the 1st District. 10 Feb 1857. (Pp. 420-421)

John W. Ware to C. H. Gasaway two acres in the 9th District. 28 May 1856. (Pp. 421-422)

William Cummings to Anuel Rains 250 acres in the 5th District. 21 Dec 1853. (Pp. 422-423)

William T. Dodd to Hiram N. Dodd 23 acres in the 10th District. 31 Dec 1856. (Pp. 423-424)

Nancy Mitchel and husband Stephen to Martin L. Prater 20½ acres in the 6th District. 5 Jun 1856. (Pp. 424-426)

Bryant Hare to Henry Goodloe the following slaves, to wit, Charles, Henry, George, Henry, Jim, Delpha, Fanny, Crecy, Nancy, Ruben, Ann, Edmond, Isham, America, Crecy being the same as set forth in a deed made by Bennet Rucker to Henry Goodoe as trustee for his wife Mirian and her children except Isham, America, Crecy which are children of said Ann. 17 Dec 1856. (P. 426)

Fountain Owen to William Dodd three acres in the 10th District. 1 Aug 1856. (P. 427)

William McGill to James McFerrin 18¼ acres in the 4th District. 25 Mar 1856. (Pp. 428-429)

Alexander McKnight to Henry Goodloe ten acres. 20 Jan 1857. (Pp. 429-430)

William and Thomas Sisson with Polly and Sally Sisson, the heirs of James Sisson, to Jesse Sisson, one of the heirs of said Sisson, 100 acres. 25 Mar 1845. (Pp. 430-431)

William R. Hill to David Epperly and W. S. Cawthon 68 acres in the 12th District. 2 Feb 1857. (Pp. 431-432)

George Grizzle to Claborne Gunter four and a half acres in the 9th District. 12 Feb 1857. (P. 433)

Thomas Sisson to Benjamin F. Creson 53 acres in the 4th District. 11 Feb 1856. (Pp. 434-435)

William R. Whitamore to William R. Hill 68 acres in the 12th District. 23 May 1854. (Pp. 435-436)

D. M. Jarratt to William Gilly a tract of land on the east fork of Stone's River. 9 Feb 1857. (Pp. 436-437)

M. R. Rushing to William L. Covington one acre in the 6th District. 9 Feb 1857. (Pp. 437-438)

Charles Marcum to Johnathan L. Blair 100 acres in the 9th District. 4 Feb 1857. (P. 439)

Wesley Harriman to Benjamin Fugett 50 acres in the 6th District. 24 Dec 1856. (P. 440)

Edward Bragg to Jesse Carter 100 acres. 10 Feb 1854. (Pp. 441-442)

DEED BOOK L

John Webb to Young & McFerrin a town lot in the town of Woodbury. Bounded: on the south by High Street. 10 Feb 1857. (Pp. 442-443)

Jesse Carter to William B. Hays 100 acres in the 1st District. 21 Aug 1856. (Pp. 443-444)

Jonathan L. Blair to Charles Marcum 51 acres in the 9th District. 4 Feb 1857. (Pp. 444-445)

J. B. Martin and R. J. Wood to William W. May 200 acres in the 5th District. 6 Nov 1854. (Pp. 445-447)

Jacob M. Keykendoll to William W. May 100 acres in the 5th District. 5 Dec 1855. (Pp. 447-448)

William W. May to Jacob M. Keykendoll 200 acres in the 5th District. 16 Feb 1857. (Pp. 448-450)

William L. Covington to M. R. Rushing one acre in the 6th District. 9 Feb 1857. (Pp. 450-451)

Jane Allen to A. F. McFerrin and Burton L. McFerrin 60 acres in the 8th District. 9 Jan 1856. (Pp. 451-452)

Larkin D. Stewart to Washington S. Massey a part of the tract of land that the said Stewart lives on in the 2nd District. 17 Feb 1851. (Pp. 452-453)

T. C. Ward to H. C. Summer 284 acres in the 11th District. 12 Feb 1857. (Pp. 453-454)

R. U. Lemay to James Kerly several tracts of land in the 6th District. 26 Dec 1853. (Pp. 454-456)

State of Tennessee Grant #18545. 129 acres to Samuel Phillips. 23 Jul 1845. (Pp. 456-457)

William B. Evans to William H. Wilcher a tract of land in the 6th District. 18 Sep 1855. (P. 458)

John F. Weedon to William C. Miller 95 acres in the 6th District. 6 Oct 1856. (Pp. 459-460)

Isaac W. Elledge to Bartlet S. Ring 240 acres in the 12th District. 20 Feb 1857. (Pp. 460-462)

Silas Parker to Isaac Kirklin 100 acres in the 4th District. 21 Feb 1857. (Pp. 463-464)

John Pendleton to John Bragg 100 acres in the 5th District. 10 Feb 1857. (Pp. 464-465)

Joseph C. Leak to James Sloan 2043 acres on Canal and Sycamore Creeks of the clear fork of Smith's Fork. 19 Feb 1857. (Pp. 465-466)

A. F. Jones to Samuel Jones 40 acres. 15 Sep 1856. (P. 467)

William Cummings to William Spry 100 acres in the 5th District. 20 Sep 1855. (P. 468)

William Barton to William Cox a tract of land in the 11th

District. 21 Dec 1854. (P. 469)

Isaac Kirklin to A. J. Burkett and Jeremiah Bush 50 acres in the 12th District. 18 Feb 1857. (P. 470)

George Ashford to William Wilsher 88 acres in the 6th District. 4 Mar 1857. (Pp. 470-472)

Daniel Thomas and wife Mary, formerly Farley, to J. T. Blair their interest in the estate of John Farley. 28 Feb 1857. (Pp. 472-473)

J. W. Orrand to William Davenport 35 acres in the 11th District. 28 Feb 1857. (Pp. 473-474)

R. H. Mason to Warren Cummings 20 acres in the 6th District. 6 Mar 1857. (Pp. 475-476)

William T. Tolbert to S. T. Tolbert his one ninth part of two tracts of land. 15 Dec 1855. (Pp. 476-478)

Lydia Williams to Wesley McMahan five acres in the 5th District. 21 Feb 1857. (Pp. 479-481)

Lydia Williams for love and affection to Mary Ann Nunnally and her two children, Ellis and Lydia, 200 acres in the 5th District. 5 Mar 1857. (Pp. 481-483)

R. L. McKnight for love and affection to Sarah E. Byrn four slaves, to wit, Mary, Ruben, Rosiloh, and Sarah. 12 Mar 1857. (Pp. 483-484)

R. L. McKnight for love and affection to Jamima H. McLin 195 acres. 25 Mar 1857. (Pp. 484-485)

Elijah Anderson to Hardin Taylor 25 acres on Carson's Fork of Stone's River. 19 Dec 1856. (Pp. 485-486)

John Martin to R. B. Martin 252 acres in the 5th District. 23 Oct 1852. (Pp. 487-488)

Benjamin Fugett to Thomas Keele a negro woman named (Mariah), about 21, for $900. 28 Nov 1856. (P. 488)

Survey of the land of Joseph Carter. 30 Mar 1857. (Pp. 489-490)

J. M. Burger to G. M. Burger a house and lot in the town of Woodbury, it being the house that W. F. George formerly occupied as a grocery house. 21 Feb 1857. (P. 491)

Alford Watson to E. E. Blair 30 acres in the 9th District. 16 Mar 1857. (Pp. 492-493)

George W. Woods to Nathan L. Woods 75 acres in the 8th District. 4 Apr 1856. (P. 494)

Alexander McKnight to Moses McKnight 36 acres in the 1st District. 6 Apr 1857. (Pp. 495-496)

Alexander McKnight, Executor of Moses McKnight, to S. H. McKnight 21 acres in the 1st District. 11 Jan 1851. (Pp. 496-497)

DEED BOOK L

T. F. Mancy to his son, Philip Mancy, 50 acres in the 1st District. 3 Apr 1857. (Pp. 497-499)

John Mitchel and wife Elizabeth to Margaret Ferrell, wife of John Ferrell 150 acres in the 5th District. 9 Mar 1857. (Pp. 499-500)

M. P. Parton to H. E. Ford a tract of land in the 8th District. 24 Mar 1857. (Pp. 500-501)

John B. Wood to J. C. Alexander 150 acres in the 9th District. 4 Apr 1857. (Pp. 501-503)

M. G. Elkins to Benjamin Sapp a contract to build a sawmill. 6 Apr 1857. (Pp. 503-504)

W. W. McKnight to L. F. Porterfield 15 acres in the 1st District. 11 Apr 1857. (Pp. 504-505)

S. H. McKnight to L. F. Porterfield 21 acres in the 1st District. 11 Apr 1857. (Pp. 505-506)

Zadock Duncan to Ervin Cherry 213 acres in the 5th District. 28 Jul 1855. (Pp. 506-507)

Benjamin Williams to Lewis Jetton 82½ acres in the 2nd District. 21 Apr 1857. (Pp. 507-509)

Elizabeth Barrett and Robert R. Mars enter into a marriage contract. 25 Apr 1857. (P. 509)

Lewis Jetton to William A. McBroom and the other trustees two acres for a meeting house to be called New Hope. Said church is to be located in the 1st District on the waters of Locke's Creek. 1 Oct 1856. (P. 510)

Joseph Clark, attorney for Francis Halpaign of Marian County, Arkansas, to M. G. Elkins his interest a tract of land descended to me as one of the heirs of Joseph Clark deceased. Also, my interest in the dower of Nancy Clark. 17 Sep 1855. (Pp. 511-512)

Archebald Stone to Franklin Coleman a title bond. 28 Apr 1857. (Pp. 513-514)

Benjamin Wallace to James Warren a title bond. 27 Apr 1857. (P. 514)

Washington S. Massie, Administrator of Adam Elrod, to H. A. Wiley a negro girl named Mary, about 17, for $1400. 9 Feb 1857. (Pp. 515-516)

Jeremiah Scales and wife Rachel G. to James G. Ligon a trust deed. 11 May 1857. (Pp. 516-518)

J. J. Farley to J. T. Blair his interest in the estate of John Farley. 4 May 1857. (Pp. 518-519)

J. R. Ferrell and E. W. Ferrell to R. C. Jones 100 acres in the 3rd District. 18 Feb 1851. (Pp. 519-520)

William C. Jones to William Wilson 30 acres in the 11th District. 30 May 1857. (Pp. 521-522)

Sarah and A. F. Todd, Benjamin Wilson, Hiram Wilson, Hollis Wilson, Granville and Mary Todd, A. J. Wilson, R. M. and Elizabeth J. Hall, heirs of H. Wilson, to John Wilson 56 acres in the 4th District. 30 May 1857. (Pp. 522-523)

H. Wilson heirs to Walter Wilson 25½ acres in the 4th District. 30 May 1857. (Pp. 523-525)

H. Wilson heirs to Elizabeth Jane Hall 45¼ acres in the 4th District. 30 May 1857. (Pp. 525-529)

The heirs of Hiram Wilson to Granville Todd 25½ acres in the 4th District. 30 May 1857. (Pp. 529-530)

Francis A. Bush to Zachariah Bush a tract of land in the 12th District. 10 Dec 1855. (Pp. 530-531)

Harvey L. Bush to Zachariah Bush 100 acres in the 12th District. 2 Jun 1857. (Pp. 532-534)

John B. Armstrong to William Barton 245 acres in the 1st District. 18 Apr 1857. (Pp. 534-536)

Joseph Bryson to John D. Harris 13 acres in the 11th District. 20 Mar 1857. (Pp. 536-537)

William West to Benjamin Lawrence 102 acres as a trust deed. 11 Jun 1857. (Pp. 537-538)

Henry Brown to Walker Todd 80 acres in the 4th District. 11 Jun 1857. (Pp. 538-540)

Edward Gaither to Thomas Campbell 29 acres in the 2nd District. 7 May 1856. (Pp. 540-541)

William West to A. F. Todd 75 acres in the 8th District. 10 Jun 1857. (Pp. 541-542)

James Sullivan and Andrew Sullivan, by descent from their father William Sullivan, have title to a tract of land in the 6th District. Said Andrew Sullivan to the said James Sullivan his interest. 3 Jul 1857. (Pp. 542-543)

John Finley to Isaac Finley certain tracts of land on the dry fork of the east fork of Stone's River. 26 Sep 1841. (Pp. 544-545)

Josephus Finley, George Finley, Absolom Finley, Andrew S. Simpson and wife Elander, Elvisa Finley, J. J. Owen and wife Alethy, Thomas Finley, William C. Cathey and wife (Nancy), heirs of Isaac Finley, to George and Absolom Finley their interest in a tract of land in the 2nd District. 5 Jan 1857. (Pp. 544-545)

William Phillips to Newson Phillips 60 acres in the 4th District. 9 Jan 1857. (Pp. 545-546)

James Rogers to Wilburn Rogers his interest in the land of his father, John B. Rogers. 4 Jul 1857. (Pp. 546-547)

Thomas Elkins to Isaiah Neely three acres in the 8th District. 23 Jun 1857. (Pp. 547-549)

William Wilson to Michael Wilson 30 acres in the 11th District. 17 Aug 1857. (Pp. 549-550)

Robert S. George to A. F. McFerrin a tract of land on the Turnpike Road. 13 Aug 1857. (Pp. 551-552)

Eli H. Mancy to William C. Campbell 100 acres in the 5th District. 16 Feb 1857. (Pp. 552-553)

Aden Hollandsworth to Benedict Jetton 150 acres in the 10th District. 19 Aug 1857. (Pp. 553-555)

Peter (Adom) to C. H. Rawlings 37 acres in the 10th District. 19 Aug 1857. (Pp. 555-556)

Caleb Cox to Mary Finley his interest in a tract of land in the 2nd District. 23 Jan 1854. (Pp. 556-557)

John F. Curlee to A. F. McFerrin 50 acres in the 3rd District. 9 Jan 1854. Pp. 558-559)

Andrew J. Brandon to Daniel Tenpenny 94 acres in the 3rd District. 31 Jul 1856. (Pp. 559-560)

Edward Alford to Hiram Wilson 100 acres in the 4th District. 15 Dec 1856. (Pp. 561-562)

Joseph Carter to James J. Bynum 89 acres in the 12th District. 8 Sep 1857. (Pp. 562-563)

Joseph Carter to H. B. Bush 70 acres in the 12th District. 8 Sep 1857. (Pp. 563-564)

John Teague and wife Sarah E. to John Pendleton 50 acres in the 4th District. 1 Sep 1857. (Pp. 564-565)

Spencer Gilly to George N. Northcut 161 acres on Mountain Creek in the 9th District. 27 Oct 1856. (Pp. 566-567)

William Todd to A. F. McFerrin 35 acres in the 4th District. 9 Jan 1857. (Pp. 567-568)

A. F. McFerrin to N. D. Chiswell 100 acres in the 4th District. 16 Nov 1855. (Pp. 569-570)

Jeptha R. Halcum to Thomas P. Mason 100 acres in the 9th District. 5 Dec 1846. (Pp. 570-571)

S. J. Odom to George Finley 37 acres in the 8th District. 15 Jan 1857. (Pp. 571-572)

N. D. Chiswell to Ruben Elam 100 acres in Warren County. 17 Mar 1857. (Pp. 572-573)

Mathew S. Bogle to Benjamin A. Hancock 100 acres in the 11th District. 28 Aug 1852. (Pp. 574-575)

Lenzey Peeler, Sarah Peeler, Cato Ann King, and George King to Hardin Taylor 33 acres in the 5th District. 23 Nov 1854. (Pp. 575-576)

Abel McBroom to Young & McFerrin 121 acres in the 6th District. 18 Sep 1857. (Pp. 577-578)

William T. Alexander to John A. George, Administrator of Charles P. Alexander, his share of the estate of the said Charles P. Alexander. 1 Mar 1854. (P. 578)

Emeline McMahon and William McMahon to John A. George their share of the estate of Charles P. Alexander. 24 Sep 1857. (P. 578)

M. S. Alexander to John A. George his share of the estate of Charles P. Alexander. 19 Sep 1857. (P. 579)

J. L. Fare to John A. George, Guardian for the heirs of Charles P. Alexander, five dollars in full of his fee. 13 Feb 1852. (P. 579)

John R. Ashley to William D. B. Duncan 50 acres in the 12th District. 3 Oct 1857. (Pp. 579-580)

Henry L. Duggan to William McKnight 29 acres in the 11th District. 6 Oct 1857. (P. 581)

T. J. Jetton to W. B. Nokes a title bond. 6 Oct 1856. (Pp. 582-583)

Elam McKnight to William S. McKnight 125 acres in the 11th District. 7 Aug 1857. (Pp. 583-584)

Charles (Bevin) to Joshua Vassar 50 acres in the 2nd District. 11 Oct 1842. (Pp. 584-585)

F. C. Alexander to Henry S. Duggan 160 acres in the 11th District. 7 Apr 1856. (Pp. 585-586)

Daniel Tenpenny to Samuel P. Gannon 95 acres in the 3rd District. 5 Oct 1857. (Pp. 586-587)

John Pedon to Thomas Campbell a tract of land on Locke's Creek. 7 Jan 1847. (Pp. 587-588)

William Thompson to Thomas L. Todd 15 acres in the 8th District. 17 Sep 1857. (Pp. 588-589)

A. G. Petty to James Cook one acre in the 4th District. 29 Dec 1856. (P. 589)

John St. John to Nicholas Harris a title bond. 3 Nov 1832. (P. 590)

Aden Hollandsworth to Peter Adams four and one half acres in the 10th District. 19 Aug 1857. (Pp. 590-591)

Jacob M. Kuykendoll to W. C. Tynes a tract of land on Barren Fork of Collins River. 13 Apr 1857. (Pp. 591-592)

David Patton, Administrator of David M. Patton, to Andrew L. Simpson 80 acres in the 12th District. 25 Feb 1857. (Pp. 593-594)

James Perry to A. N. Fisher a trust deed. 6 Oct 1857. (Pp. 594-595)

William A. McKnight to Benjamin Fugett 154½ acres in the 10th District. 8 Oct 1857. (Pp. 595-597)

Lewis Hancock to Richard A. Hancock 475 acres in the 10th District. 10 Oct 1857. (Pp. 597-600)

Lewis Hancock to Benjamin F. Hancock a negro boy named Jack, about 9, for love and affection. 10 Oct 1857. (P. 600)

Benjamin Davis of Rutherford County to Joshua Vassar of the same place 30 acres in Rutherford County. 13 May 1824. (Pp. 601-602)

Martin Cox to Caleb Cox a tract of land in the 4th District. 13 Oct 1857. (Pp. 602-604)

Calvin D. Curlee to A. F. McFerrin 150 acres in the 3rd District. 25 Aug 1856. (Pp. 604-605)

William D. B. Duncan to Ervin Cherry 213½ acres in the 5th District. 3 Nov 1856. (Pp. 605-606)

A. F. McFerrin to E. C. Preston 60 acres in the 3rd District. 15 Oct 1857. (P. 607)

Benjamin Webber to Benjamin F. Creson a certain portion of the home tract of land to be used for the benefit of my wife, Rebecca, and my daughter. 15 Oct 1857. (Pp. 608-609)

Thomas Barrett and wife Margaret to Henry A. Haas his power of attorney to receive their share of the estate of John Haas, father of the said Margaret Barrett. 15 Oct 1857. (Pp. 609-610)

Fielding Holt to Richard Holt 100 acres in the 12th District. 14 Feb 1857. (Pp. 610-612)

William West to A. F. Todd 60 acres in the 8th District. 10 Jan 1855. (Pp. 612-613)

David Hutchins to Joshua Jetton 30 acres in the 10th District. 12 Oct 1857. (Pp. 613-614)

Thomas Hopkins to Benjamin Davis 30 acres in Rutherford County in the 2nd District. 16 Sep 1824. (Pp. 614-615)

Aden Hollandsworth to Benedict Jetton 25 acres in the 10th District. 12 Oct 1857. (Pp. 616-617)

Caleb Cox to G. W. Lawrence 142 acres in the 4th District. 13 Oct 1857. (Pp. 617-618)

James Jamison to David Byford 16 acres in the 4th District. 30 May 1857. (P. 619)

James Jsmison to Robert Jamison 103 acres in the 4th District. 30 May 1857. (Pp. 619-621)

David D. Hipp to George B. Hipp 200 acres in the 5th District. 10 Oct 1857. (Pp. 621-622)

Josiah Cramians to Benjamin Davis 20 acres in Rutherford County on the north branch of the Horse Spring Fork of the East Fork of Stone's River. 19 Mar 1823. (Pp. 623-624)

James J. Trott to Fisher & Jetton his interest in 50 acres

in the 5th District. 7 Oct 1857. (Pp. 624-625)

William West to John H. Wharton and Abel Rushing lot #26 in the town of Woodbury. 18 Nov 1857. (Pp. 626-627)

Benjamin Webber states that his wife, Rebecca, has heretofore filed her bill in Chancery Court for a divorce and alimony. Said parties enter into an agreement in which the said Rebecca received 378½ acres on Brawley's Fork. 14 Feb 1857. (Pp. 627-629)

John F. Weedon to James H. Byrn 162½ acres in the 11th District. 29 May 1857. (Pp. 629-630)

Clement R. Davis, Commissioners to sell the land of Cornelius Brandon deceased, to Joseph A. Brandon 219 acres in the 3rd District. 6 Dec 1856. (Pp. 630-632)

William Barton to W. T. McBroom a tract of land on Canal and Harrican Creeks. 20 May 1856. (Pp. 632-633)

William T. McBroom to C. W. Thompson 800 acres on Canal and Harrican Creek. 13 Feb 1857. (Pp. 633-634)

James Clift to his daughter N. J. Ellen Clift, a certain rosewood piano. 28 Sep 1857. (Pp. 634-635)

John E. Mason to B. L. McFerrin lot #46 in the town of Woodbury. 8 Dec 1857. (Pp. 635-636)

Joseph Hollis to John F. and R. J. St. John lot #56 in the town of Woodbury. 14 Dec 1857. (Pp. 636-637)

Abbott, Charles R. 13,58
Abel, Thomas G. 55,59,84,
  116
Ables, Thomas G. 54
Abston, Elizabeth 104
Acres, C. C. 148
Acres, William R. 98,195
Adams, Abner 42,83,118
Adams, Abraham 13
Adams, Candace 167
Adams, Drufina 116
Adams, Henry 46
Adams, Isham, 11,12,31,33,
  65
Adams, James 116
Adams, James M. 167
Adams, M. 154
Adams, Peter 34,51,85,114,
  126,130,133,197,222
Adams, Polly 31
Adams, Samuel B. 167
Adams, Susannah 65
Adams, T. W. 154
Adams, Thomas 46
Adams, William W. 94,100,
  181
Adams, Willie 65
Adamson, Joseph 16
Adamson, Thomas 211
Adamson, Thomas A. 85
Adamson, William 96
Adamson, Wills 6,22,26
Adcock, Isaac 79
Adcock, Jacob 105,121,
  124,140
Adcock, Mark 35
Adcock, William 208
Adom, Peter 221
Akers, C. C. 170,210
Akers, Campbell 87
Akers, Campbell C. 119
Akers, Elizabeth 137,176
Akers, Meredith 86,117,
  137,176
Akers, William P. 160
Akers, William R. 117,126,
  136
Alexander, A. 52
Alexander, A. C. 175,185
Alexander, A. D. 91,127,
  147,151,175,196
Alexander, A. M. 64,76,77,
  78,84,109
Alexander, Abner 78,96,97,

207
Alexander, Abner C. 45
Alexander, Abraham D. 151
Alexander, Acalus 4
Alexander, Acheles 59,69
Alexander, Achelus 94
Alexander, Achilles 34
Alexander, Akelus 80
Alexander, Andrew M. 48,49,71
Alexander, B. B. 177
Alexander, Benjamin F. 17
Alexander, Calvin H. 55
Alexander, Charles 69,172
Alexander, Charles P. 13,18,19,29,
  55,57,75,86,125,135,172,222
Alexander, Ezekiel 35
Alexander, F. C. 177,179,185,199,
  222
Alexander, J. C. 219
Alexander, J. H. 184,188
Alexander, James H. 3,8,9
Alexander, John D. 53
Alexander, John H. 184
Alexander, M. C. 135
Alexander, M. S. 222
Alexander, Mark 88
Alexander, Martha 151
Alexander, Mary 97
Alexander, Mary A. 125
Alexander, Mary J. 171
Alexander, Oswin 121
Alexander, William T. 222
Alford, Edward 208,221
Alfred, Sarah A. 210
Alfred, William C. 210
Allen, B. F. 146
Allen, Benjamin 40
Allen, Benjamin F. 173
Allen, David 2
Allen, Hugh 28
Allen, James 17,44,190
Allen, James M. 199
Allen, Jane 217
Allen, John 2,6
Allen, Levi D. 154
Allen, Rufus R. 154
Allen, Thomas 23
Allen, U. D. 159
Allen, Widow 2
Allen, William 204
Allman, James 214
Alman, Stephen 5
Alman, William 5,8
Alman, William L. 27

Alman, William T. 26
Almond, William T. 26
Anders, Ephraim 74
Anderson, Carroll 145
Anderson, Elijah 218
Anderson, John 63
Anderson, Joseph M. 106
Anderson, Mary 145
Anderson, William 41
Anderson, Wills 2
Andrews, Elaner 152,172
Andrews, Eleanor 109
Andrews, Ephraim 64,66,
    71,77,79,112,152,185
Andrews, Jane 109,152,172
Andrews, John 22,64,66
Andrews, John M. 115
Andrews, Perses 64
Andrews, Samuel H. 64,66
Anglin, David W. 4,16
Anthony, Martha 155
Arey, Daniel J. 166
Arey, Mary A. 166
Argo, Mary 147
Argo, Thomas 147
Argo, Thomas P. 147
Armstrong, E. M. 62
Armstrong, Elijah 32,145
Armstrong, J. R. 163
Armstrong, John B. 163,
    171,220
Armstrong, Knott 23
Armstrong, Knox 83
Armstrong, M. W. 186
Armstrong, Margaret 145
Armstrong, Thomas T. 17
Armstrong, W. W. 192
Arnold, America 138
Arnold, Richard 131,197
Asher, Lexington 105
Ashford, B. C. 169
Ashford, Bazel 128
Ashford, George 120,121,
    126,142,162,218
Ashley, John K. 206
Ashley, John R. 190,222
Assary, James L. 15
Athey, Elijah 127
Avant, James M. 71,190
Avent, James M. 166
Bailey, Eli 14,122,131
Bailey, John N. 43,113,
    127
Bailey, Joseph 52,62,125
Bailey, Robert 29,38,48,

50,117,129,165,196
Bailey, Vincent 126,155
Bain, R. L. 200
Bain, Roderick L. 197,205
Baird, Frances A. 96,200
Baird, John A. 96,200
Baird, Lemuel M. 71
Baker, Elizabeth 8
Baker, Jonathan 153
Bankhead, John 172
Banks, John M. 113,114,117,138
Banks, Lot 130
Banks, Stephen 130
Banning, Thomas 164
Barclay, James 160
Baren, Abraham 138,139
Barkley, A. 206
Barkley, Elizabeth 151,154,189
Barkley, Henry C. 67
Barkley, James 10,15,19
Barkley, John 25,67
Barkley, John, Jr. 25
Barkley, Mary 67
Barkley, Nancy A. 67
Barkley, Robert A. 67
Barkley, Sarah 67
Barkley, William A. 67,213
Barnes, Jesse 213
Barnes, Thomas 83
Barnett, A. 42
Barnett, Ally 155
Barnett, Anderson 23,42
Barratt, Martha 184
Barrell, Samuel B. 209,214
Barret, Ward, Sr. 67
Barrett, Eli 127
Barrett, Elizabeth 189,219
Barrett, George C. 83,102,144
Barrett, Harmon 6,32,38,49,50
Barrett, Hayman 5
Barrett, John 126,127,146,163,171
Barrett, Margaret 223
Barrett, Polly 5
Barrett, Thomas 6,109,137,183,223-
Barrett, W. 189
Barrett, Ward 22,161,166
Barrett, Ward, Jr. 205
Barry, John 106,145
Bartley, John 22
Barton, Dale 21
Barton, Hale 21
Barton, Jane 75,185
Barton, John 114
Barton, Joshua 17,21,22,23,37,40,
    65,95,129,142,160,179,185,215

Barton, Robert 172
Barton, Sarah 182,186
Barton, Thomas 185
Barton, William 40,75,112,
  116,125,128,138,144,151,
  160,169,179,182,185,186,
  193,201,206,215,217,220,
  224
Barton, William, Jr. 41,75
Basham, John 56
Basham, Johnathan 177
Basham, Jonathan 81
Bashaw, John 41
Bass, Ezekiel 80
Bass, John M. 2
Bastian, Andrew 148
Bastian, John 148
Bateman, Johnathan 14
Bates, Benjamin 120
Bates, S. 99
Bates, William 6,7,30,32,
  33,36,37,41,50,54,55,58,
  59,62,67,75,87,98,99,102,
  106,112,116,120,147,209
Baughman, Jacob 97,127
Baughman, Nancy 97,127
Beaird, Frances M. 150
Beaird, Francis A. 153
Beaird, John A. 150,153
Bean, Elizabeth 20
Bean, Richard H. 20
Benson, Joseph 106
Benson, Peggy N. 106
Benson, Solomon 106
Beaty, Allen 49,54
Beaty, Eleazar 74,80
Beaty, Elizabeth 19,56
Beaty, Isaac 19,20
Beaty, James 19
Beaty, William D. 78
Beech, A. C. 130
Beetly, James G. 106
Bell, Abraham L. 65,73
Bell, Eli 112,120
Bell, Elisha 45,54
Bell, J. J. 211
Bell, James 45,57,96
Bell, James H. 203
Bell, John H. 129,144,150
Bell, John J. 209,211
Bell, Lewis 29
Bell, Martha 65,73,96
Bell, Rebecca C. 203
Bell, Samuel 15,29
Bell, Sarah 112

Bell, Susanah 30,45,65,73
Bell, W. S. 150
Bell, Wiley 203
Bell, Wiley W. 200,211
Bell, William 45
Bell, William S. 129,187
Bell, Zadoc C. 198
Bennett, Benjamin 20,21
Bennett, Collin 22
Bennett, Elizabeth 21
Bennett, G. W. 22
Bennett, Henry 22
Bennett, James 22
Bennett, John M. 6,20,21,22
Bennett, Nancy 21,22
Bennett, Rebecca 21
Bennett, Richard 21
Bennett, Taylor 20
Bennett, Thad 21
Bennett, William 21,22
Berger, Abraham 37,38
Berger, Jacob 33
Berry, John 62
Bethel, Cantrell 9,17
Bethel, Tilman 16,23
Bevin, Charles 222
Bichel, John 72
Bickel, Michael 122
Bickle, John 86,139
Bickle, Michael 2,86
Bilbro, B. H. 186
Billingsley, Elizabeth 114
Billingsley, Joshua 114
Bish, Jesse 189
Bishop, George 14
Blair, E. C. 147
Blair, E. E. 218
Blair, Elkin C. 156
Blair, Ira L. 70,103
Blair, Irey 68
Blair, Isaac 147
Blair, Isaac T. 114,140,142,156,
  208
Blair, J. F. 215
Blair, J. T. 175,218,219
Blair, James 147,156,178
Blair, Jane T. 192
Blair, John 53
Blair, Johnathan F. 196
Blair, Johnathan L. 216
Blair, Jonathan F. 217
Blair, Sarah 186
Blair, William 93,121,122,124,147,
  157
Blanton, John 131

Blare, Isaac T. 207
Blew, Ruben 42
Blount, G. R. 36
Bogle, A. J. 150,153
Bogle, Andrew 13,99,152,
155
Bogle, Andrew J. 56,88,
173,179,182
Bogle, Emily 179
Bogle, George 14,34,35,
71,72,74,76,113,114,
145,150,204
Bogle, George R. 204
Bogle, Isabel 21
Bogle, James 72
Bogle, James J. 204
Bogle, John 173,182
Bogle, Joseph 59,68,105,
136,165,167,211,214
Bogle, Joseph H. 31,37,
104,119,128,176,179
Bogle, Joseph, Sr. 167
Bogle, Margaret 204
Bogle, Mathew S. 221
Bogle, Matthew 113,176,
179
Bogle, Robert 152
Bogle, Samuel 21
Bogle, Sarah 68,80
Bogle, Thomas 21
Bogle, William 71,129,
133,189,214
Bogle, William R. 71,
105,167,171,212
Boles, Samuel B. 62
Bond, R. J. 124,136,212
Bond, Richard J. 64,81,
171
Bond, William 124
Boran, A. 205
Bosley, Delilah 60,179,
211
Bosley, John 60
Bostic, H. P. 103
Bostic, Hardin P. 93
Bowen, A. 199
Bowen, Absolom 127
Bowen, Deadamia 180
Bowen, James T. 73
Bowen, John 110
Bowen, John S. 50
Bowen, Mary 187
Bowen, Moses 55
Bowen, Samuel 151,154,
180,187

Bowen, Thomas 40,129
Bowen, Usly 151
Bowen, Usly A. 154
Bowen, William 180
Bowen, William C. 79
Bowen, William G. 180
Bowers, Hezekiah 10
Bowling, Henry C. 181
Bowling, John 149,151
Bowling, Matthew W. 181
Bowman, Benjamin 126
Bowman, Daniel 84,126
Bowman, Henry 91
Bowman, James S. 84
Bowman, James T. 60,73,78,80,85,
88
Bowman, Mary D. 191
Bowman, Michael 175
Boyd, Elizabeth 104
Boyd, Isbel 104
Boyd, P. W. 104
Boyd, Robert 74,115
Boyd, Robert L. 104
Boyd, William 77,104
Boyd, William T. 104
Bradford, James Y. 24,37
Bradford, Thomas 17,19,23
Brady, Harriet R. 13
Brady, William 13
Bragg, Catherine 207
Bragg, Dosher 29
Bragg, Dozier 73,77,133,147,166
Bragg, Dozier, Jr. 173
Bragg, Dozier, Sr. 171,197
Bragg, Edward 29,52,62,73,159,
172,203,216
Bragg, Elizabeth M. 168
Bragg, John 73,77,78,104,190,197,
217
Bragg, Nancy J. 173
Bragg, Sally L. 173
Bragg, Thomas 109,124
Bragg, W. M. 133
Bragg, William M. 136,173,179
Bralley, Prior 122
Brandon, Abraham 75,187,206
Brandon, Andrew J. 202,221
Brandon, Armstrong 111
Brandon, Calvin 182
Brandon, Christopher 187
Brandon, Cornelius 75,111,170,
175,176,177,182,187,224
Brandon, Hiram 75,187
Brandon, James A. 187
Brandon, John 146

228

Brandon, John E. 170
Brandon, Joseph A. 16,20,
  79,111,146,190,224
Brandon, Mary 175,177,182
Brandon, R. W. 121
Brandon, Robert W. 115,116,
  120,121,128
Brandon, Sarah 190
Brashears, Elizabeth 106
Brashears, James L. 106
Brashears, Melvay 52
Brashears, Saldon 17
Braswell, Sampson 21
Bratten, William 107
Bratten, William G. 119,172
Bratton, Henry A. 107
Bratton, William 172
Bratton, William G. 176
Brent, Elizabeth 75
Brent, Solomon 75
Brents, Johnson 31
Brents, Solomon 31
Breshears, James T. 214
Brevard, T. B. 102,142,166,
  169,189
Brevard, Thomas 62
Brevard, Thomas B. 98,105,
  115,132,147,159,192
Brevard, Y. L. 195
Brevard, Zebulon 131
Brevard, Zebulon L. 180
Brewer, Andrew J. 204
Brewer, B. 119
Brewer, Benjamin 63,79,102,
  125
Brewer, Henry 196
Brewer, J. 119
Brewer, J. B. 116
Brewer, Jackson 160
Brewer, James R. 206
Brewer, Jesse 79,89,102,125
Brewer, John 39,164
Brewer, Martha 141,143,161
Brewer, Martha E. 192
Brewer, Robert 160
Briant, John 161
Briant, Joshua W. 16
Briant, Solomon 16,25
Brien, B. 134
Brien, J. 134
Brien, John S. 131
Brien, Manson M. 78,137
Brien, Narcissy B. 6
Brien, Pascal W. 6
Brients, Elizabeth 32

Brients, Solomon 32
Brients, Thomas 32
Briggs, H. W. 77
Britton, James 90
Britton, Washington 33
Brooks, Isaac 201
Brooks, Isaac, Jr. 106
Brooks, Joab 112
Brooks, Joel 138
Brooks, John R. 175,191
Broomfield, Elizabeth 75
Brown, D. Q. 4
Brown, Elizabeth 4,53,73,86,95,
  99
Brown, Henry 192,207,220
Brown, James 20,21
Brown, James F. 23
Brown, James M. 2,3,8,9,10,32,40,
  42,48,56,57,58,61,79,198
Brown, John 2,6,7,10,17,24,26,27,
  30,33,36,40,41,42,44,46,47,48,
  58,61,167
Brown, Joseph F. 47,59,60,63
Brown, Joshua 21
Brown, M. D. 73
Brown, Martin D. 153
Brown, Mary 198
Brown, Nancy 116,117
Brown, Richard 142
Brown, Sarah 167
Brown, William 20
Brown, Wyatt A. 86
Brownfield, Betsy 5
Brownfield, William 38,44
Brownston, Daniel 9
Brownston, Isaac 9
Bruce, Jane 6
Bruce, Marcus D. 6
Brunston, Daniel M. 20
Brunston, Isaac 20
Bryan, Andrew J. 171
Bryan, William R. 204
Bryant, Alexander 136,142
Bryant, John W. 110,122,144
Bryant, Samuel C. 32
Bryford, Aaron 41,74
Bryson, Andrew J. 196
Bryson, Daniel 199
Bryson, Fanny 30
Bryson, Frances 96,132
Bryson, Francis 35,56,139
Bryson, George 34
Bryson, Hiram 46
Bryson, John 58,67,83,97
Bryson, Joseph 24,73,78,81,88,96,

Bryson, Joseph 118,140,
  150,160,182,195,206,
  215,220
Bryson, Joseph, Jr. 136,
  153,215
Bryson, Joseph, Sr. 82,
  124,135,215
Bryson, Lacky 56
Bryson, Locky 139
Bryson, Nancy 199
Bryson, Robert 83,152
Bryson, Samuel 14,45,56,
  76,97,139,211
Bryson, Samuel L. 78
Bryson, William 26,27,30,
  54,59,84,96,139,140
Bryson, William B. 74
Bullard, Elisha 3,8
Bullard, Henry 3,8
Bumpass, John W. 194
Bumpass, Levi M. 194
Bumpass, M. V. 194
Bumpass, R. W. 194
Bumpass, Richard E. 194
Bumpass, Robert H. 194
Bumpass, W. M. 194
Bundervant, John 88
Burge, Amy 54
Burge, Brevard 54
Burge, Henry 54
Burge, William 54
Burge, Wright 54
Burger, A. 141,143,154,
  164,167,172,173,185,
  187,193,201,208
Burger, Abraham 40,63,
  132,135,180
Burger, G. M. 218
Burger, J. M. 218
Burger, Jacob 53,75,117,
  139,164,167,189,193
Burger, James M. 67
Burger, James W. 60
Burger, M. M. 210
Burger, S. N. 173
Burger, Samuel E. 17,95,
  106
Burger, Samuel N. 143,164
Burk, Samuel 69,174
Burke, Samuel 12,84
Burket, Henry 174,178,184
Burkett, A. J. 218
Burkett, John 177
Burnett, Anderson 99
Burnett, Samuel 54

Burton, H. M. 118,164
Burton, Hardy M. 71,77
Burton, William 88
Bush, Amandy M. 182
Bush, Francis A. 197,198,220
Bush, H. B. 221
Bush, Harvey 113,193,194
Bush, Harvy L. 182,190,198,220
Bush, Ivy 77,112,151,211
Bush, Ieremaih 218
Bush, Uriah B. 111,178,197
Bush, Willis W. 182
Bush, Zachariah 35,46,52,53,74,77,
  94,113,198,220
Butcher, Martha 86
Butcher, Richard 8,56,60,86,173
Byford, Aaron 24,71,85,94,112,134,
  148,187,188
Byford, Aron 55,104
Byford, David 223
Byford, Elizabeth 23
Byford, Hardy 24,26
Byford, Henry 23,24
Byford, Jacob 156,167,192
Byford, Jane 113
Byford, William 40,141,201
Bynum, George 34
Bynum, James J. 221
Bynum, John 63,145,147,205,209
Bynum, John, Sr. 34
Bynum, Polly 95
Bynum, Redman 133,187,188
Bynum, William 95,119,145,147
Bynum, Pumphrey 13
Bynuns, Pumphrey 2
Byrn, J. H. 206
Byrn, James H. 224
Byrn, Sarah E. 218
Byrn, W. B. 84
Byrn, William B. 115
Byrns, James H. 100
Byrns, James W. 126
Byrs, W. B. 81
Caffey, Medford 45
Caffy, Medford 33,86
Cain, Martha A. 97
Cain, W. L. 97
Caldwell, David 91,97
Calvert, Elizabeth 161
Calvert, Harriet 161
Calvert, William J. 161
Calvert, William J., Jr. 161
Cameron, Washington 15
Campbell, Albert G. 41
Campbell, Eldridge 23,25

Campbell, Eldridge H. 122
Campbell, Henderson 122
Campbell, Judge C. 13,32
Campbell, P. W. 6
Campbell, Robert A. 44,60, 75
Campbell, Sally S. 31
Campbell, Thomas 220,222
Campbell, William 97,169, 173
Campbell, William C. 204, 214,221
Cann, Joseph H. 56
Cannady, John C. 13,37,38
Cannon, Agnes T. 56
Cannon, Araminta 184
Cannon, James 154
Cannon, Letsy 59
Cannon, Martin 184
Cannon, Raford 154
Cannon, Robert T. 92
Cannon, Samuel 154
Cannon, Willis 59
Cantrell, G. W. 21
Cantrell, Stephen 4,5,92
Cantrell, Watson 9,91
Capps, Q. A. 129
Capshaw, William 99
Carder, David 61
Carens, A. B. 175
Carnahan, Burton L. 166
Carnahan, Elizabeth 97, 127
Carnahan, Hiram 97,127
Carnahan, James 96,127
Carnahan, Jane 97,127
Carnahan, John 127
Carnahan, Mary 127
Carnahan, Nancy 127
Carnahan, Newton C. 87, 89,96,138,164
Carnahan, Sarah 105,166
Carnes, A. B. 173,186,199, 208
Carnes, Alexander B. 155
Carson, Elizabeth 154
Carson, Isabella 155
Carson, James 155
Carson, James M. 155
Carson, Joseph 155
Carson, Margaret M. 155
Carson, Mary E. 155
Carson, Robert 3,80,81,82, 111,154,155,156,167,177
Carson, Robert, Sr. 154

Carson, Samuel 154,155,156,159, 167,177,178
Carson, William 124,154
Carter, Armstead 118,149,198
Carter, Armstrong 49,63,84,85
Carter, Cullin 27
Carter, Jesse 83,147,152,166, 203,216,217
Carter, Joseph 118,149,158,197, 218,221
Caruthers, Mary 114,118
Caruthers, Maxwell 25,114,118
Carver, David 16
Cathy, Nancy 220
Cathy, William 101,110
Cathy, William C. 220
Caughanour, David 15,165
Caughnor, David 24
Cavat, Thomas 8
Cavatt, Thomas 10
Cavett, Thomas 12,33,34,37,45
Cawthon, Harvey S. 156
Cawthon, Hugh R. 131
Cawthon, James L. 133,179,206
Cawthon, Jane 145
Cawthon, Pleasant 128,133,145, 156
Cawthon, W. S. 216
Cawthorn, James 115
Cawthron, James 121,126
Chahill, Edmund M. 29
Chambers, Maxwell 65,73
Champion, Catherine F. 58
Champion, John B. 58
Chaney, John 37
Chaney, John L. 37,41
Chappell, John 117,188
Cheatham, Elizabeth 60
Cheatham, Jack 150,153
Cheatham, L. P. 60
Cheatham, L. R. 67
Cheatham, Leonard P. 60
Cheatham, Permelia 153
Cherry, Daniel 18
Cherry, Ervin 146,151,153,155,167, 192,203,206,208,219,223
Cherry, James 31,57
Cherry, Joel 3,12,16,28,46,82,114, 119,146,150,203
Chery, Erin 109
Childers, John 54
Childress, John 47
Childress, Stephen 83
Childrup, John 40
Chiswell, N. D. 221

231

Clark, Andrew 176
Clark, Archabald A. 176
Clark, Frances 193
Clark, James 14
Clark, Jane 176
Clark, John 57,177
Clark, John W. 176,177
Clark, Joseph 3,17,24,34,
  83,193,200,219
Clark, Margaret 177
Clark, Mary 176
Clark, Mary A. 176
Clark, Nancy 181,193,219
Clark, Robert 176
Clark, Robert A. 176
Clark, Robert N. 177
Clark, William 176,177
Clark, William S. 101
Clark, Zilpha 193
Clarke, Joseph 57
Clement, Hezekiah 49,107
Clements, Hezekiah 111
Cleveland, Jeremiah 197
Clift, Ellen 224
Clift, James 224
Clift, N. J. 224
Clifton, Henry H. 36
Cloyd, David 102
Clymer, Thomas 10
Coalman, Franklin 69,72
Cobb, William 209,211
Cochran, Jane 2
Cochran, W. F. 2
Coffee, Joshua M. 55,74
Coffee, Medford 87
Coggin, Daniel 20,21
Cogwell, Fanny 49
Cogwell, Frederick 49
Cogwell, Richard 49,67
Coinghour, David 60
Coit, James 31
Coleman, F. 89,186,187,
  201
Coleman, Frances 69
Coleman, Franklin 34,93,
  114,128,132,139,165,167,
  213,219
Collins, William 46,148,
  171
Colvert, J. L. 141
Colvert, James L. 180,188
Colvert, Johannah 180
Colwell, David 136
Conley, George W. 40,50
Conn, Richard J. 50

Connelly, Caroline 126
Connelly, James 126
Cook, James 129,142,167,168,212,
  222
Cook, John W. 129,142,207
Cooper, A. 178
Cooper, Abraham 34,68,71,73,118,
  158,161,178
Cooper, B. B. 74,172,181,214
Cooper, Benjamin B. 30,55,73,94
Cooper, Benny 182
Cooper, Frances 19,28,34
Cooper, Francis 76,88,164,206
Cooper, Jane 182,184,188
Cooper, John 3,9,80,102,207
Cooper, John G. 184
Cooper, Nelson 194
Cooper, Phillip 182,188
Cooper, Rebecca 172
Cooper, Sarah 147,181
Cooper, Silas 23
Cooper, Thomas 34,44,93,182,184,
  188
Cooper, Visa 102
Cooper, William 13
Cothran, Jane 190
Cothran, Pleasant 40,190
Couch, William H. 130
Couch, Willis F. 115,133
Coughamour, David 72,115
Coughenour, David 76
Coughenour, Malinda 76,208
Coughinour, David 62,65
Covington, William 61,146
Covington, William L. 42,50,81,
  109,212,216,217
Cowen, Isaac M. 128
Cowen, Nelson 72
Cowen, William D. 115,155
Cox, Caleb 83,98,126,139,153,154,
  199,221,223
Cox, Isaac W. 208
Cox, James 69,159
Cox, Judith 69,159,187
Cox, Judy 57
Cox, Martin 52,54,56,72,83,139,
  143,199,223
Cox, Peter 72,110,138,178
Cox, Robert 187
Cox, Thomas 200
Cox, William 217
Cox, William H. 133
Crabtree, Veach 144,161,170,173
Craft, Hugh 54,156,173,194
Craft, John 54,146

232

Craft, Katharine 146
Craft, Levi 146
Craft, William 3,16,54
Craighead, John B. 60
Craighead, Levenia 60
Cramians, Josiah 223
Crane, Josiah M. 165
Crane, Mary A. 125
Crane, William 105,125,
 160
Creason, Abram 132
Creason, James 132
Creson, Abraham 112
Creson, Benjamin 107
Creson, Benjamin F. 196,
 197,216,223
Creson, James C. 178
Creson, Joshua 167
Creson, Lewis 178,182
Creson, Sarah 107,199
Crips, Peter 14
Crockett, George 22,37
Crook, James 22
Crook, Martin D. 139,141
Cropper, Abraham 56
Cross, John 109
Crowder, David 17,19
Cummings, A. K. 201
Cummings, Benjamin 18,95,
 98,179
Cummings, Benjamin, Jr. 18
Cummings, Jackson G. 94
Cummings, James 179,201
Cummings, John 98,119,143
Cummings, Moses 18,39,50,
 98
Cummings, Sinclair 50
Cummings, W. W. 109
Cummings, Warren 78,82,102
Cummings, William 12,23,50,
 62,91,94,103,130,181,212,
 216,217
Cummins, David 59
Cummins, James 145
Cummins, John 147
Cummins, M. C. 132
Cummins, Moses 37,163
Cummins, Moses H. 131
Cummins, P. D. 87
Cummins, W. S. 3
Cummins, Warren 138,142,
 159,162,175,199,218
Cummins, William 42,59,144,
 153,155,170,201,207,208,
 213

Cunningham, John W. 205
Cunningham, William 6
Curlee, C. 196
Curlee, C. E. 180
Curlee, Calvin 98,100,124,201
Curlee, Calvin D. 223
Curlee, Cullen 85,165
Curlee, Cullen E. 201
Curlee, David C. 201
Curlee, Elizabeth A. 201
Curlee, John F. 127,173,188,201,
 221
Curlee, Nancy R. 201
Curlee, Peyton B. 201
Curlee, Rebecca 201,202,212
Curlee, Ruth 201
Curlee, T. G. 212
Curlee, Thomas G. 201
Curler, Cullin 49
Curles, Calvin 58
Curtis, Elizabeth 15,24,28
Dale, William 19
Daley, William 77
Daniel, John 58,71,102
Daniel, Mitchell 25,100,109,117,
 119,134,142,150
Daniel, Peter 80,102
Daniel, Thurston 45,74,134
Daniels, John 10
Daniels, Mitchell 12
Daniels, Pompey 32
Dasher, Daniel 4
Dasher, Henry 56,58
Dasher, John H. 143
Dasher, Rebecca 56
Dasher, Richard P. 4
Davenport, Abraham 73
Davenport, Absolom 63,86,165
Davenport, Auley 22
Davenport, Edmund 22,124
Davenport, Elizabeth 112
Davenport, George 42,165
Davenport, Hardy 112
Davenport, Henry 112
Davenport, John B. 161,162
Davenport, John F. 214
Davenport, Joseph 112
Davenport, Reuben 144
Davenport, Warren 165
Davenport, Wiley 46,78,153,162,
 164,189,192
Davenport, Wilie 69
Davenport, William 112,196,218
Davenport, William C. 192
Davenport, Willie 63

Davis, A. P. 178
Davis, Anderson S. 41
Davis, Benjamin 223
Davis, C. B. 118,132,135,
170,192,194
Davis, C. C. 73
Davis, C. R. 36,39,82,83,
107,116,187,204
Davis, C. Reed 27,35,38,
42
Davis, Caleb B. 126
Davis, Clement R. 46,49,
149,159,166,168,171,
178,224
Davis, David 47
Davis, Hannah M. 14
Davis, John 9,126,172
Davis, Jonathan G. 211
Dawson, William J. 63
Days, Lewis 198
Deloach, Boykin 96,138
Deloach, James 96
Deloach, John 138
Deloach, Sarah 73,96
Dement, Joseph 109
Dement, Joseph A. 125,
152,172,194
Denby, Samuel 53,75,79,
133,171,178
Denby, William 171,177,
178
Dennis, Henry 16,87,
118,127,162,171,173,
193,194,208
Dennis, Margaret 20,33,
100,108
Dennis, Mathew 151
Dennis, William 208
Denton, Elizabeth 20
Denton, Hugh L. 20
Denton, Isaac C. 20
Denton, John M. 62
Denton, Mary 20
Denton, Nancy 195
Denton, Telford 20
Denton, William 20
Desha, Robert 20
Destiny, Salina 99
Devenport, Wiley 23
Dickens, Agnes 137
Dickens, B. B. 92,95,
113,134,149
Dickins, B. B. 38,55,
68,71,74,89,192
Dickins, Baxter B. 14,

17,63,65,71,82,112,160
Dickins, Baxter B., Sr. 74
Dickins, Thomas 184
Dickinson, Agnes 137
Dickson, Alexander S. 184,188
Dickson, Araminta 184
Dickson, Elizabeth 184
Dickson, Emily 184
Dickson, Ezekiel 184
Dickson, J. H. 184
Dickson, James 154
Dickson, John M. 184
Dickson, Joseph K. 184
Dickson, Joseph R. 131
Dickson, Levi W. 184
Dickson, Rebecca 184
Dill, Joseph 141
Dill, Parson 19
Dillard, James 2,9
Dinby, Samuel 33
Doak, John N. 167,171,175,213
Dobbs, Elijah 141,169
Dodd, Hiram 36
Dodd, Hiram N. 69,216
Dodd, Richard 14
Dodd, Walker 108
Dodd, William 99, 216
Dodd, William L. 212
Dodd, William T. 216
Dodge, Everett K. 52
Doke, John N. 144,191
Donnell, William C. 115,133,176,
214
Dosier, Henry 4
Douglass, B. 180
Douglass, H. 180
Douglass, H. L. 173
Douglass, Jesse L. 143
Douglass, Jesse T. 160
Douls, Joseph 42
Dowell, Peter 81
Dozier, Abey 165
Dozier, Henry 152
Dozier, Jonathan 152
Dozier, Rebecca 139
Dramon, Jesse 73
Dubois, Andrew 136
Dubois, Andrew C. 134
Dubois, Elias H. 136
Duggan, Aaron 76
Duggan, Aron 74
Duggan, Henry L. 222
Duggan, Henry S. 74,76,222
Duke, Gideon 54
Duke, Mordacai J. 78,81

Duke, Samuel 85
Duncan, Clary 79
Duncan, H. D. 35
Duncan, Josiah 2,6,22,26
Duncan, Lemuel 103,161
Duncan, Lemuel J. 126,199
Duncan, Oliver C. 109,135, 210
Duncan, S. H. 26,41
Duncan, Sarah A. 210
Duncan, Thomas W. 2,9,14
Duncan, William 78,79
Duncan, William D. 222, 223
Duncan, Zadoc 219
Dunkin, Lemuel 22
Dunn, John A. 8,19
Durham, Cyril 61
Early, Caleb 41,50
Earthman, E. J. 194
Earthman, Isaac 163,194
Earthman, Margaret 162
Earthman, W. W. 194
Eason, James K. 37,44,66, 68,78,79,81,115,148,162, 167,214
Eddings, Evan 124,141,144
Eddings, John 26,27,36
Eddings, John, Sr. 11
Eddings, R. G. 164
Eddings, Richard 11,28,30, 36
Eddings, Richard D. 118
Edge, Edward W. 9
Edmondson, Samuel 97,99
Edmondson, Thomas 97
Edmonson, Samuel 75,82,87, 105
Edwards, Alfred 127
Edwards, Archabal 6
Edwards, Archebald 11,12, 113
Edwards, F. A. 107
Edwards, Fasha 64
Edwards, Martha 98
Edwards, Mary 51
Edwards, Matthew 10,26, 27,36,64
Edwards, Patience 51
Edwards, Upha 127
Eeels, Thomas S. 105
Elam, Henry 35,94
Elam, James H. 83
Elam, John 35
Elam, Mary 89

Elam, Reuben 82,153,221
Elam, Samuel 48
Eledge, Joseph L. 27
Eledge, Joseph, Sr. 27
Eledge, William F. 27
Elem, Reuben 45
Elem, Ruben 48
Elkins, D. L. 176
Elkins, Dillard 105
Elkins, Dillard L. 175
Elkins, Elizabeth J. 72
Elkins, Gabriel 9
Elkins, J. P. 188
Elkins, John D. 67,85,145
Elkins, John O. 106
Elkins, John P. 194
Elkins, John S. 192
Elkins, M. G. 94,129,157,181,186, 190,193,205,206,209,219
Elkins, Milly 190
Elkins, Moses 24
Elkins, Murfrey G. 89
Elkins, Paralee 159
Elkins, Peggy A. 72
Elkins, Polly 92
Elkins, Shadrack 138
Elkins, Susan 138
Elkins, Thomas 9,38,58,66,82,86, 91,92,105,124,162,175,176,188, 196,220
Elkins, William 13,47,96,121,124, 190,204,205
Elledge, Isaac H. 125
Elledge, Isaac W. 56,78,81,84,85, 98,132,207,209,217
Elledge, J. B. 197,205
Elledge, James B. 132,160,163,191
Elledge, Joseph 92,125
Elledge, Joseph L. 54,125
Elledge, Joseph S. 49
Elledge, M. C. 205
Elledge, Malissa J. 181
Elledge, W. C. 186
Elledge, William 91
Elledge, William F. 43,125
Elliott, George 1
Elrod, Adam 1,7,36,57,79,94,95, 143,145,158,159,187,212,213,219
Elrod, Jeremiah 16
Elum, Henry 40
Elum, John 40,47
England, James A. 185,190,194
England, James M. 191
England, Jane 127
England, John M. 97

England, M. A. 127
England, Mary 97,127
England, Sterling 97
England, T. E. 127
English, Andrew 132,133
Enos, Henry 50,134
Epley, Eliza 193
Epley, George 193
Epley, John 107,175,193
Epley, Mary 193
Epperly, David 211,216
Esary, James 77,85,96,98
Esary, James L. 85,87,102
Esley, Charles 53
Esley, George 57
Esley, Mary 56,57
Eson, James K. 149
Espey, Alexander 53,77
Espey, Charles 2,57,211
Espey, Frances E. 206
Espey, George 57,86
Espey, John 85,86,122,189,
   206
Espey, Levina A. 206
Espy, Charles 184
Espy, George 21
Espy, John 21
Espy, John L. 172
Espy, Robert 21
Esque, Charley 203
Esque, Mary 203
Essary, James 22,27,33,37,
   44,161
Essary, James L. 15,24,28,
   141,144,156,157
Estes, John 29,61,76,81
Estill, Wallis 63
Estill, Wallis, Jr. 63
Evans, C. C. 39
Evans, Charles C. 39,108
Evans, James 18
Evans, John H. 108,155
Evans, Joseph 14,47
Evans, Lemuel D. 208
Evans, Onedimus 21
Evans, Samuel C. 61,170
Evans, Sarah 14
Evans, W. B. 207
Evans, William 58
Evans, William B. 16,38,
   170,199,204,217
Evans, William E. 42,47,68
Ewell, Dabney 35,40,52,133
Ewing, James 44,54,76
Ewing, Randall 54

Ewing, William B. 54,81,158
Fagan, Albert 84,120
Fagan, Albert T. 36,37,127,168,
   204,211
Fagan, R. A. 163
Fagan, Robert 40,53
Fagan, Robert A. 84,95
Fagan, Robert L. 3,24,28,38
Fagan, Robertson L. 121,122
Fagan, Robison L. 110
Fagan, Sintha 122
Fagg, Godfrey M. 45
Faire, William H. 64
Falkenberry, William 25
Fann, Franklin 154,161,205
Fann, Grundy 117,142,170,179
Fann, John 111
Fare, D. L. 215
Fare, J. L. 126,135,138,176,194,
   195,196,197,207,210,211,215,222
Fare, J. S. 134
Fare, Johnathan L. 186
Farler, John 139,207
Farler, Patton 139
Farley, Elizabeth 215
Farley, J. J. 219
Farley, Jesse J. 215
Farley, John 128,196,201,208,215,
   218
Farley, Mary 218
Farris, Joel 39,95
Farris, Jonathan 53
Faulkenberry, Daniel 114
Faulkenberry, David 28,114
Faulkenberry, Hugh P. 114
Faulkenberry, Jacob 38,42,47,59,
   63
Faulkenberry, William 42,114
Fearn, Sally 20
Fearn, Thomas 20
Felps, Kelin 43
Felton, Thomas, Jr. 23
Felton, Thomas, Sr. 23
Ferguson, James 91,105,120
Ferguson, Mary 91,105,120
Ferrell, E. W. 219
Ferrell, Edmund W. 204
Ferrell, Eliza B. 212
Ferrell, Elizabeth W. 108
Ferrell, Enoch 59
Ferrell, Enock 80
Ferrell, J. R. 219
Ferrell, James 7,19,20,40
Ferrell, Jesse R. 204
Ferrell, John 99,145,219

Ferrell, Ligston 119
Ferrell, Margaret 219
Ferrell, Robert S. 116
Ferrell, William 119,122,
  157,162,178
Ferrell, William B. 195,212
Ferris, J. 33
Ferris, Josiah 27,41,114
Finger, John 56
Finley, Absolom 220
Finley, Alexander 20,57,118,
  184,193
Finley, Catharine 212
Finley, Daniel 75,160,161,
  169,174
Finley, Edmund 41,66,71,162
Finley, Elvisa 220
Finley, George 220,221
Finley, Isaac 59,60,220
Finley, John 43,59,71,76,
  127,129,159,162,171,220
Finley, Josephus 191,220
Finley, Lathan 37
Finley, Mary 221
Finley, Nathan 23,26,27,55,
  86,143,162,206
Finley, Nathaniel 66
Finley, Sarah 193
Finley, Thomas 220
Fisher, A. M. 211
Fisher, A. N. 222
Fisher, Abner 78
Fisher, John 18,36,37,44,
  61,69,73,79,87,94,109,
  127,128,145,157,160
Fite, Daniel 185
Fite, David 2
Fite, Elizabeth 6
Fite, Henry 11,17
Fite, Jacob 19
Fite, John 16
Fite, John, Sr. 11
Fite, Leonard 6
Fite, Moses 2,11
Floyd, William 19
Fogg, Godfrey M. 63
Ford, Abram W. 9
Ford, Daniel S. 128,198
Ford, George T. 12,25,27,
  36,38,40,53,90,98,106,
  134,138,145
Ford, H. E. 219
Ford, Henry, Jr. 109
Ford, Henry M. 109
Ford, Jordan H. 9

Ford, Mary 120
Ford, Matthew B. 88
Ford, Thomas 178
Forester, Robert E. 155
Fork, Henry 16
Foster, Charles G. 96
Foster, Horace 55
Foster, James F. 159,163
Foster, Lewis T. 81
Foster, Richard 45
Foster, William N. 105,144
Fouston, Josiah 114
Fowler, Absolom W. 192
Fowler, Aleathy 39
Fowler, Benjamin 75
Fowler, John C. 180,192
Fowler, Joseph 3
Fowler, Milton 18,34
Fowler, R. 109,120,122,124,140,
  146
Fowler, Regin 136,146,149
Fowler, Rezin 39,86,152,153,154,
  156,174,181
Fowler, Rizen 32,100,102,106
Fowler, Thomas 39,41
Francis, Armstead 74,79,108,113,
  172,204
Francis, Armsted 35,53
Francis, E. 74
Francis, Elizabeth H. 113
Francis, Epaphaditus 35,74
Francis, Epaproditus 121
Francis, M. 121
Francis, Melcesdic 67
Francis, Melchisidic 108,113,114
Francis, Micajah 75
Francis, Milas F. 64
Frazer, John 27,104
Frazer, Sally 27
Frazier, Elizabeth 27
Frazier, Robert F. 27
Freas, Jacob W. 166,179
Free, Benjamin 58
Freeman, D. M. 199,206
Freeman, Willis M. 103
Freeman, Willy M. 95
Freeze, Benjamin 174
Freeze, Elizabeth 174
Freeze, John 174
Freeze, Sarah 174
Freeze, Sarah E. 174
Freeze, Solomon 156,174
Frias, Jacob M. 166
Frias, Jacob W. 179
Frith, Henry 2

Frogden, Nathan F. 94,96
Fuget, Benjamin 102
Fugett, A. D. 117,125,
    126,141,144,200
Fugett, Alfred D. 115
Fugett, Ann 198
Fugett, B. M. 149,166
Fugett, Benjamin 100,102,
    109,126,134,142,151,
    152,159,166,180,183,
    189,207,209,210,216,
    218,222
Fugett, M. S. 210
Fugett, Townsel 198
Fugett, Townson 210
Fulk, John D. 56
Fuller, Isaac M. 191
Fuller, Isaac N. 169,170
Fuller, J. N. 160,169
Fuston, Jesse G. 87
Fuston, Josiah 126,148
Gaither, Amos 122,124,203
Gaither, Arthur 163,191,
    207
Gaither, Asariah 37
Gaither, Azariah 122,132,
    179,203
Gaither, Razel 138
Gaither, Bazzel 132
Gaither, Bozel 122
Gaither, Bozzell 126
Gaither, Brice 122
Gaither, Edmund 179
Gaither, Edward 176,220
Gaither, Elizabeth 122
Gaither, Narcissa 207
Gaither, Thomas F. 190
Gaither, Vincent 53,61,
    188
Gandy, John P. 97,173,202
Gandy, Sophia 202
Gannon, Alfred 53
Gannon, Bechum 70
Gannon, Brachus 40
Gannon, Elizabeth 184
Gannon, George 4,38,103,
    106,125,168,181,185
Gannon, John 184
Gannon, John P. 199
Gannon, Mark 39,112,135,
    203
Gannon, Martha 1,203,205
Gannon, Mary 1,39
Gannon, Patsey 1,39,52,
    135

Gannon, Polly 39
Gannon, Samuel P. 222
Gannon, Widow 1
Garner, Francis 27
Garrison, Samuel 19
Garrison, Samuel J. 50
Gasaway, C. H. 216
Gasaway, James P. 199
Gather, Edward 163
Gatten, Edward 92
Gatter, Amos 95
Gatton, Harmon 169
Gatton, Hiram 150
George, J. A. 135
George, James 54
George, James A. 56,58,60
George, James O. 39,40,43,66,68,
    69,70,83,101,107
George, John A. 39,40,43,49,56,
    69,75,102,105,110,125,172,174,
    222
George, Leonard 28
George, R. S. 146,197,200,203
George, Robert 4,56
George, Robert S. 198,205,221
George, Susan 197,200,201
George, Susanah 208
George, W. F. 218
George, William F. 43,67,139,150,
    153,171,201,208
Gibson, Richard 107
Gilley, Caleb H. 80
Gilley, Caleb M. 91
Gilley, Gideon 81
Gilley, Isaac 81
Gilley, Jesse 88,115
Gilley, Jesse H. 87,97,113
Gilley, Jesse, Sr. 110
Gilley, Peterson 68,70
Gilley, Spencer 81
Gilliam Jesse 19,24,179
Gilliam, John 11
Gillim, Jesse 88
Gillim, William 56
Gilly, J. H. 151
Gilly, J. K. 209
Gilly, Jesse 133
Gilly, Jesse, Jr. 197
Gilly, Jesse, Sr. 185,197
Gilly, John 185
Gilly, Peterson 9
Gilly, Sarah 63
Gilly, Simeon 133
Gilly, Simpson 63
Gilly, Spencer 221

Gilly, William 39,216
Gipson, James 9
Gipson, Jesse 26
Givan, George L. 18
Givan, William J. 18
Givans, Merritt 199
Givens, Merritt 138,162,
  182
Givens, William 162
Givens, William A. 162
Givins, Mary 138
Givins, Merit 33,39,48
Givins, Solomon J. 38,48
Givins, William 25,71
Givins, William A. 71,142
Glascock, Moses H. 46,139
Glasscock, Jesse 151
Glover, Thomas 11,19
Godwin, Allen 114,115,176
Godwin, Benjamin A. 175
Godwin, Isabella 177
Godwin, Rebecca 175,176
Godwin, William 176,177
Goggin, E. T. 18
Goggin, Edmund T. 23
Goggin, Nancy 23
Goggin, Polly 26
Goggin, William 26
Good, C. C. 175,193
Good, Christopher 12
Good, Christopher C. 115
Good, Elizabeth 12
Good, George B. 115
Good, Henry 44
Good, James B. 63
Good, Lucinda 149
Good, Mary 190
Good, R. J. 193
Good, Robert J. 115
Good, Robert M. 63,209,
  210
Good, Sarah 149,160
Good, Sarah J. 156
Good, William H. 209
Goodin, James 102
Goodin, Nicholas 102
Gooding, Abraham 66,109,
  170
Gooding, Isaac 200
Gooding, James 73,76,102
Gooding, Joseph 73,102,
  206
Gooding, Joseph A. 135,
  199,207
Gooding, Malinda 149,206,

207
Gooding, Martha 3,73,83,102,128,
  147,149,196,206
Gooding, Nicholas 17,20,40,201
Gooding, William 54,73,83,128,
  196,206,207
Goodloe, A. M. 156
Goodloe, Henry 107,108,206,216
Goodloe, S. J. 133
Goodloe, Samuel J. 133,134,135
Goodlow, Alfred M. 180
Goodlow, Henry 148,180,207
Goodner, James 18
Goodner, John 9
Goodright, Isaac 168
Gordin, Levina 133
Gordin, Robert 133
Gordon, George D. 33
Gordon, Jesse 88
Gordon, John 157
Gordon, Levina 145
Gordon, Louisa 170
Gordon, Robert 111,145,151,161
Gossett, German 18
Gossett, John 14
Gotcher, William M. 163,179
Gowan, Alfred P. 89
Gowan, Alfred T. 82
Gowan, William D. 30
Gowen, Alfred P. 56
Gowen, Isaac M. 121,144,199
Gowen, J. M. 149,157,166
Gowen, William D. 132,158
Graham, Dudley 133
Graham, Dudley J. 133,134,144,
  160,197
Graham, Elizabeth 144,160,197
Graham, James J. 210
Graham, John 6
Graham, Joseph 21
Graves, John 6,15
Gray, James 66
Gray, Samuel 64
Gray, Samuel W. 199
Grear, Samuel 131,132,136,200
Green, Curry 139
Greenstaff, Dillard 107
Greer, James 29
Greir, Jane 145
Griffith, Jonathan 16
Grimes, Britton 104
Grimes, George 106
Grimes, William 38,104,186
Grimmitt, William H. 113
Grissam, John 180

239

Grissom, Nancy 138
Grissom, Pryor 118
Grissom, Samuel 74
Grizzle, Daniel 172,196
Grizzle, George 31,54,63,
136,216
Grizzle, Isaac 168,176
Grizzle, James 196
Grizzle, William 185
Groom, William 172
Groom, William A. 196
Groose, William 103
Gunter, Augustin S. 47
Gunter, B. A. 204
Günter, C. C. 121,181,194
Gunter, Claborn 203
Gunter, Claborn C. 157
Gunter, Claborn J. 203
Gunter, Claborn, Jr. 203
Gunter, Claborne 216
Gunter, Clabourn 29,46,
47,87
Gunter, Claiborne C. 57
Gunter, Isaac 63,147,173,
177,187,191
Gunter, James M. 203
Gunter, John 25
Gunter, Margaret 203
Gunter, Samuel 43,46,105,
121,122
Gunter, William 54,80,93,
145,147,158,163,165,
191,197
Guy, Alvey 192
Guy, Willis 150,151,156
Haas, Betsy 5
Haas, Elizabeth 26
Haas, Henry A. 223
Haas, John 223
Haas, Joseph H. 8,28
Haas, Phillip 11
Hagan, Ellen R. 185
Hager, John 209,212
Hailey, Isaac I. 182
Hailey, Isaac T. 204
Halcom, Jeptha 71
Halcum, Jeptha R. 221
Hale, Benjamin 98,142,153
Hale, Benjain, Sr. 99
Hale, John 142
Hale, Joseph 74
Hale, Oliver, Jr. 35
Hale, Thomas 153,212
Haley, B. B. 111

Haley, James 144
Haley, John W. 58,75
Haley, Joshua 171
Haliton, James 154
Hall, B. M. 174
Hall, Benjamin 92
Hall, Elizabeth 220
Hall, Elizabeth J. 220
Hall, H. B. 144
Hall, James 118
Hall, John W. 81
Hall, Joseph 105
Hall, R. M. 178,220
Hall, Reuben 152
Hall, William J. 159
Halpaign, Frances 193,219
Halpaign, William 193
Halpain, Elizabeth 27
Halpain, John 25,27
Halpain, Joseph 27
Halpain, Margaret 27
Halpain, William 27
Hamilton, Francis G. 64
Hamilton, James 185
Hamilton, James W. 128
Hamilton, Jane E. 64
Hammond, Larkin W. 111,136
Hammons, Charles A. 155
Hammons, Ezekiel 86
Hancock, Alfred L. 72,99,156,166
Hancock, Alfred S. 58
Hancock, B. J. 173,178
Hancock, Benjamin A. 221
Hancock, Benjamin F. 223
Hancock, Bluford J. 178
Hancock, C. C. 108,153,198
Hancock, Charles 138
Hancock, Charles J. 105,153
Hancock, Christopher C. 122
Hancock, Eliza 147
Hancock, Frances 169,173
Hancock, Francis 192
Hancock, L. R. 173
Hancock, Lewis 46,92,100,131,153,
167,169,196,223
Hancock, Lewis R. 153
Hancock, Martha 198
Hancock, N. L. 147
Hancock, Richard 14,19,46,57,79,
97,122,127,131,174,198
Hancock, Richard A. 223
Hancock, Richard H. 196
Haney, John 59,65
Haney, William 23,36

Haney, Willis W. 36,53
Hankins, James 147
Hare, Briant 192,207
Hare, Bryant 215,216
Hare, John P. 59,63,93,
  97,148,153
Harlan, Nelson 187
Harper, Joseph 30,37,45
Harper, Susan 211
Harpoole, Daniel 25
Harrell, Reuben 1560
Harriman, John 215
Harriman, L. M. 206
Harriman, Stephen 209,
  214,215
Harriman, Wesley 126,189,
  195,199,207,216
Harris, John D. 220
Harris, John L. 182,205
Harris, Nicholas 222
Harris, Philip 109
Harrison, John 172,195
Hart, Henry 14,21,45
Hart, Solomon 35
Hathaway, Abram 128
Hathaway, Ana 2
Hawkins, James 100
Hawkins, John 173
Hawkins, Joseph 173
Hawkins, Reuben 169,173
Hawthorn, John M. 84
Hayes, Benjamin 34,39,59,
  115
Hayes, Henry 12,151,155
Haynes, Charles E. 159
Haynes, Everett 124,157
Haynes, Ivery J. 72
Haynes, John 210
Haynes, Juie 54
Hays, Benjamin 59,62,70,
  79,85,86
Hays, David 104
Hays, Ezekiel 50,52,62,
  67
Hays, Henry 23,64,65,112,
  122
Hays, Hugh 23
Hays, John 23,97,102,131,
  151,185
Hays, John C. 163,171,179
Hays, Nancy 23
Hays, Nathaniel 147
Hays, Peter 23
Hays, Samuel 165
Hays, Stith 121,175,178

Hays, William 23
Hays, William B. 217
Henderson, Agnes M. 119
Henderson, Agnes W. 94,104,157
Henderson, Barnett 20
Henderson, Baulding 104
Henderson, J. T. 119
Henderson, James 119
Henderson, James T. 104,109,112,
  116,120,127,131,135,139,142,
  145,157
Henderson, John 100,192
Henderson, Logan 56
Henderson, Lucinda 20
Henderson, Pleasant 104,145
Henderson, Robert C. 104
Henderson, William 2
Henderson, William G. 28
Henderson, William Y. 1,28,34,49
Hendricks, Joseph 59
Hendrickson, James 10
Hendrickson, Jonathan 139,205
Hendrickson, Josias 9
Henson, James 8
Herald, Reuben 172
Herman, John 93
Herndon, G. L. 136,141
Herrell, Whitmale 131
Hewit, Ann 176
Hewit, John 176
Hickerson, William P. 106
Hickman, Edwin 10
Hickman, John P. 10
Hickman, Thomas 21
Hicks, Archebald 61,84,132
Hicks, Lewis 11
Higgins, Alexander 63,65,113,145,
  150,186,187,192,194,198,210
Higgins, Elijah 29,66,85,98,145,
  151
Higgins, James 35,36,62,89,145,
  148,198,203,210,214
Higgins, John 21,29,32,45,46,62,
  71,76,85,145,150,166,194,213
Higgins, Mary 45,62,85
Higgins, Mary A. 99
Higgins, Nancy A. 98
Higgins, Robert 151
Higgins, Wesley 145
Higgins, Westley 45
Higgins, William 34,35,62,69,145,
  148,159
Hight, Daniel 192
Hill, John M. 54
Hill, William R. 216

Hipp, David D. 39,95,138, 139,158,197,200,213,223
Hipp, George B. 223
Hipp, John 213
Hodges, Ruth 202
Hodges, Thomas 202
Hofer, Adam 118
Hogg, James 60
Hogwood, Alexander W. 61
Hogwood, David 139
Hollandsworth, Aden 150, 151,152,169,179,207,210, 215,221,222,223
Hollandsworth, Elizabeth 165, 167
Hollandsworth, Ira 121,125, 149,150,157,162,165,166, 167,168,170,171,173,190, 198,199,208,210,215
Hollandsworth, John 125,49, 150,153,167,168,169,210
Hollandsworth, John D. 179
Hollandsworth, John, Sr. 125
Hollandsworth, Joseph 179
Hollandsworth, Josiah 169
Hollandsworth, Munson 190
Hollandsworth, Namen 148
Hollandsworth, Namon 150
Hollandsworth, Newman 160, 198,208
Hollandsworth, Numan 197
Hollingsworth, John 50,111, 114,119
Hollis, Abram S. 209
Hollis, David 57,112,114,209
Hollis, David, Sr. 96
Hollis, Esther 57,73
Hollis, James 80,166
Hollis, James B. 42,127,134
Hollis, Jesse 36,39,53,79, 143,154
Hollis, John 3,23,26,28,57, 73,112,117,118,171
Hollis, Joseph 57,132,191, 192,194,210,224
Hollis, Lewis 124,141
Hollis, Mary A. 166
Hollis, Micajah 3
Hollis, Patsy 96
Hollis, Simeon 131,209
Hollis, William 35,38,60, 154,195
Hollis, William C. 96
Hollis, William, Sr. 53
Hollyburton, J. E. 194

Hollyburton, Mary H. 194
Holman, Jane C. 203
Holman, L. 203
Holman, Lazarus 29
Holt, Alvis 26
Holt, Fielden 75
Holt, Fielding 15,38,146,162,192, 223
Holt, Fielding, Sr. 168
Holt, Herrod 28
Holt, James D. 15,38
Holt, Joseph 129
Holt, Joseph P. 137,160,192,193
Holt, Joseph T. 192
Holt, Lilly 26
Holt, Richard 104,129,146,160,223
Holt, Thomas 113,150
Holt, William 146,162,168
Hoodenpyle, Phillip 30
Hooker, William M. 104,124
Hooper, Edward E. 12
Hoover, Daniel 13
Hoover, Henry 192,211,214
Hoover, Jacob 173,180
Hoover, Martha S. 13,116,130,163
Hoover, Thomas H. 139,159
Hopkins, Allen 86
Hopkins, George W. 94
Hopkins, John P. 83,85,87,94,95, 98
Hopkins, Joseph W. 94,144
Hopkins, Thomas 2,3,9,16,23,41,53, 89,91,210,223
Hopkins, Thomas H. 54,65,70,75,85, 94
Hopper, Moses 84
Hopper, Robert 92
Horn, Joseph 124,177
Howard, Frank 80
Howard, Frankey 54
Howard, William 54,55
Howerston, Henry 118
Howerston, Philip 118
Hubbard, Clark 141,162,184,187,191
Hubbard, William S. 187
Hume, Ann L. 169
Hume, David 169
Hume, Gabriel 8,25,31,36,43,44,55, 109,111,125,130,149,156,158,162, 168,169,213
Hume, Martha 162
Hume, Sarah A. 162
Hume, William C. 169
Hunt, Emily 184
Hunt, William 214

Hunter, Peter 170,171,175, 179
Huntsucker, Peter 62
Hurt, R. M. 184
Hutchins, Benjamin 157
Hutchins, David 207,223
Hutchinson, Charles 203
Hutt, Isaac 88
Ibby, James 98
Ibby, William R. 98
Inglis, A. J. 107,151,170, 179,188,210
Inglis, Alexander 139
Inglis, Andrew S. 139,192
Inglish, Alexander 46,77,89
Isbell, P. C. 197
Iverson, Uriah 66
Jackson, Burton 96
Jackson, Elizabeth 156
Jackson, Henderson 61
Jackson, William P. 111,144, 152
Jacobs, Alford 156
Jacobs, Cullen E. 129,136
Jacobs, Elizabeth 65,72
Jacobs, John A. 62,72
Jacobs, William 156,164
James, Buchanan 50
James, Buckhannon 44
James, Daniel 10
James, Isbel 98
James, James L. 50
James, James S. 104
James, John 147
James, S. R. 210
James, Samuel R. 162
James, Thomas 10
James, William 14,44
James, William R. 98
Jameson, Catherine 200
Jameston, James 157
Jamison, James 223
Jamison, Nancy E. 65,73
Jamison, Robert 223
Jamison, Samuel 107
Jamison, William 65,73
Jaragin, Allen 10
Jarnagin, Jesse 11
Jarnegan, Jesse 54
Jarnigan, Jesse 37
Jarratt, C. H. 121
Jarratt, C. R. 119
Jarratt, Catharine 112
Jarratt, Claburn R. 112
Jarratt, D. M. 99,182,210,

216
Jarratt, David M. 46,51,80,91,93, 98,104,111,121,122,130,133,144, 162
Jarratt, H. R. 32,36,37,39,42,45, 46,55,78,81,82,83,86,88,117
Jarratt, Higdon R. 61,63,81
Jarratt, P. M. 181
Jarrell, John 8
Jarrett, D. M. 76,206
Jarrett, David M. 69
Jarrett, H. R. 17,76
Jenkins, Charles 2
Jenkins, Mary 2
Jennings, E. C. 166
Jennings, Jacob 18
Jernigan, Jesse 81
Jernigan, Jessey 110
Jernigan, Nathan 151
Jetton, Benedict 221,223
Jetton, Jefferson 201
Jetton, John B. 45,85,116
Jetton, Joshua 223
Jetton, Lewis 21,30,88,125,144, 149,150,151,168,179,199,219
Jetton, Louis 43
Jetton, T. J. 197,200,222
Johnson, Allen 13
Johnson, Andrew N. 170,213
Johnson, Bryan 103
Johnson, Burrell P. 203
Johnson, Cave 78
Johnson, Granville H. 203
Johnson, James 191
Johnson, Jesse 12,14,58,61
Johnson, John 11
Johnson, P. T. 191
Johnson, Richard P. 57
Johnson, T. T. 121
Johnson, William C. 29
Jones, A. F. 217
Jones, Aaron 159
Jones, Aaron F. 151,154,166,172, 181,191,200
Jones, Allen 142,146,155
Jones, Allen R. 152,160,214
Jones, Alsa 26
Jones, Annett 153
Jones, Betsy 5
Jones, Charles F. 215
Jones, D. W. 154
Jones, Daniel 184
Jones, Daniel W. 191
Jones, David 107,116,146
Jones, E. H. 67

Jones, E. H. 67
Jones, E. R. 152
Jones, Edmund 6
Jones, Elevean 110
Jones, Elihu 146
Jones, Enoch 107,207
Jones, Ephraim A. 115
Jones, Erasmus 57,64,115,
  159,200
Jones, Erasmus, Jr. 81
Jones, Erasmus, Sr. 81
Jones, Frederic 9
Jones, J. J. 57,158,160
Jones, John 5,38,44
Jones, John D. 14
Jones, Jonathan 3,82,116,
  204
Jones, Joseph 5,44
Jones, Joseph W. 154
Jones, Leven 91
Jones, Levenia 26
Jones, Levin 41,112,131,
  139
Jones, Mahaley A. 166
Jones, Maney R. 171
Jones, Mary 71,105
Jones, Michael 54,81,214
Jones, Michel 71,76
Jones, Nancy R. 171
Jones, R. C. 219
Jones, Rannel 71
Jones, Ransom 136
Jones, Richard 63
Jones, Richard C. 146
Jones, Robert M. 128,207
Jones, Samuel 217
Jones, T. G. 137
Jones, Thomas E. 153
Jones, Thomas G. 155
Jones, Tolbert 200
Jones, William B. 215
Jones, William C. 205,219
Jones, William R. 171
Jones, Wilson Y. 168
Jordan, Hardenia 194
Jordan, Joshua 141
Jordan, M. B. 194
Jourdan, Stephen 135
Justice, John B. 138
Justis, William 106
Kearsey, Henry 54
Keaton, George H. 124
Keaton, Isaac 61
Keaton, Isaac A. 127
Keaton, Isham 9

Keaton, Larkin 85,134,209
Keeble, Edward A. 180
Keeble, Edwin A. 13,197,208
Keel, J. W. 200
Keel, Thomas 102
Keele, John C. 77
Keele, John G. 64
Keele, Thomas 218
Kees, Erasmus 94,134
Kees, Erasmus S. 94,96
Keeton, George H. 204
Keeton, Isaac 178
Keeton, Issac A. 167
Keeton, Larkin 189
Keith, J. S. 121,139,146
Keith, James 158
Keith, James J. 158,159
Keith, James S. 59,159
Keith, John S. 158,159
Kellough, James 67
Kellough, John 102
Kelly, Saderick 70
Kelly, Shadrach 165,188
Kelly, William 166
Kelton, E. E. 191
Kelton, Eliza 181
Kelton, Eliza E. 203
Kelton, James L. 112,115,191,203
Kelton, John L. 181
Kemp, Cinthia 9
Kennedy, Drucilla 67
Kennedy, James H. 67
Kennedy, Martha A. 162
Kennedy, Washington 1,12,135,169,
  212
Kennedy, William B. 67
Kerkendall, Jacob M. 98,104
Kerkendall, Norris 108
Kerley, James 217
Kersey, Henry 56,64
Keykendoll, Jacob M. 122,217
Kies, Erasmus S. 72
Kimbro, Rolly P. 155
King, Cato A. 221
King, George 5,221
King, James C. 33
King, John 77,208
King, Robert 57
King, Sally 5,160
King, William 74,166,171
Kirk, William 52
Kirkland, Isaac 178
Kirklin, Isaac 217,218
Kirsey, Henry 42
Kirsey, John 116

Kneeland, Ira C. 30
Knight, Ralph 83
Knott, Benjamin 23
Knott, George W. 23
Knott, Joseph 23,30,127
Knox, John W. 136
Knox, Joseph 36,62,68,127,
   136
Knox, Joseph, Jr. 50,51
Knox, Joseph, Sr. 50,68,
   127
Knox, William A. 36,37,53,
   84,120,127
Kurby, Henry 31
Kuykendoll, Jacob M. 222
Labby, Elizabeth 112
Labby, Pleasant 112
Lack, Elizabeth 53
Lack, Robert 58
Lack, William 53
Lain, Jacob A. 42
Lain, Noah W. 112
Lamberson, Leonard 2,6,121
Lamberson, Mary D. 6
Lambert, Anderson 198
Lambert, Edmund 62,63,72
Lambert, Edward 144
Lambert, James 107,111,143
Lambert, Jane 35
Lamberth, Edmund 84
Lamberth, James 73
Lamberth, Jane 84
Lance, Claton 111
Lance, Gabriel 18,48,52,88,
   131
Lance, H. 190
Lance, Henry 57,121,185,
   189,193
Lance, James H. 18,88
Lance, Matilda 111
Lance, Samuel 34,69,87,88
Lance, Thomas 69
Lance, Zilpha 57,193
Landers, James 135
Landsden, Hugh B. 115,133
Lane, David 43,45
Lane, Jacob A. 43
Lanier, Robert 215
Lansden, Ann 214
Lansden, Robert W. 39,71,
   104,132,177
Lanson, Hugh B. 81
Lasater, Brinkley 79,98,
   102,209

Lasater, Johnathan 94
Lasater, Luke 166,171,180,209
Lasater, Marthy 206
Lasiter, Hardy 18,37
Lasiter, Luke 18,28,37,44
Lassiter, Brinkley 6
Laswell, Samuel 8,73,82,95
Laughlin, S. H. 62
Laughlin, Samuel H. 28,78,147
Laughlin, Samuel K. 215
Lawing, Samuel 10
Lawrence, Alexander 43
Lawrence, Benjamin 220
Lawrence, G. W. 223
Lawrence, George 168
Lawrence, George W. 191
Lawrence, Jesse 47,48,67,134,147,
   148,149,155,170,174,214,215
Lawrence, John 9
Lawrence, John H. 80,91
Leach, P. G. 209
Leach, Thomas 56
Leach, W. C. 165
Leach, William C. 76,172
Leak, J. C. 180
Leak, Joseph C. 180,189,217
Leake, Joseph C. 209
Leash, Abner S. 56
Ledbetter, Hugh 99,125,126,129
Lee, Robin 65
Lee, William 58
Leech, Abner S. 110,135
Leech, D. G. 154
Leech, John C. 192,205
Leech, P. G. 136
Leech, Thomas 110,143
Leech, Thomas K. 110,125,141,175
Leech, W. C. 188,194,197
Leech, William C. 110,135,139,141,
   142,145,149,154,155,165,174,175,
   176,177,178,182,192,193,194,207,
   211
Leek, Thomas 24,125
Lefever, Zachariah 24
Leigh, Washington 24,136,171
Leigh, William 169,170
Leiper, A. J. 147
Leiper, John 124
Leiper, S. H. 147
Lemay, Lewis 16,22,23
Lemay, R. U. 217
Lemay, Richard 8,69,115
Lemay, Richard A. 12,22,23,25
Lemay, Richard H. 91

Lemay, Richard M. 37,134,
  136,193
Lemay, Richard U. 185,199
Lemay, Richard W. 111,143
Lemmons, John 163
Lennox, Margaret 193
Lennox, Richard 193
Lenox, Margaret 15
Lester, Samuel 200
Lewis, Archebald 26,60,190
Lewis, Delilah 27
Lewis, Russell 27
Libbey, Joseph 41
Libby, Elizabeth 127
Libby, Pleasant 127
Ligon, James G. 219
Linder, Nathaniel 9
Literell, Wilford 135,188
Little, Hiram Y. 135
Littrel, Wilford 111
Locke, Robert 13
Long, Israel 214
Lowe, John T. 9
Lowe, Thomas 105,145,146
Lowe, Walter 9
Lowell, William 47
Loyd, James 145
Lusk, Byrd 115
Lutrell, Wilford 190
Lynn, Daniel D. 174
Lynn, Jackson 81
Lynn, Martha 174
Lyon, Elizabeth 11
McAdow, Ann 76
McAdow, Eliza 76
McAdow, Elizabeth 161
McAdow, J. W. 76
McAdow, James 29,66,76
McAdow, James B. 147,149
McAdow, James, Jr. 29
McAdow, James M. 196
McAdow, James, Sr. 29
McAdow, James W. 29,72,
  76,172,187,196,204,209
McAdow, John A. 130,147,
  149
McAdow, Madison 76
McAdow, Marshall 76
McAdow, Martha 143
McAdow, N. 76
McAdow, Nancy 214
McAdow, Nancy C. 143,193
McAdow, Nubern S. 76
McAdow, Wesley 189
McAdow, William 74,104,

117,130,149
McAdow, William P. 150
McAdow, William S. 130,131,141,
  142
McBroom, Abel 1,3,4,7,32,57,69,
  75,79,87,127,130,143,179,186,
  192,213
McBroom, Abel, Jr. 179,182,186
McBroom, Alexander 79,110,112,
  137,138,183
McBroom, B. L. 113
McBroom, B. T. 182,184
McBroom, Benjamin F. 75,169,179
McBroom, Benjamin T. 64,69,70,75,
  87,179,182,186
McBroom, H. D. 4,5,64,67,81,99,
  113,134,141,192
McBroom, Henry D. 1,3,4,5,32,57,
  75,130,161,179,182,185,186,205
McBroom, Isaac 76,205
McBroom, James 204
McBroom, Jesse 32,141
McBroom, John D. 26,29,32,179,182,
  186
McBroom, John P. 186
McBroom, Robert 156
McBroom, Robert C. 174
McBroom, Sarah 179,182,185,186
McBroom, Sary 75
McBroom, W. T. 182,212,224
McBroom, William 186
McBroom, William A. 219
McBroom, William F. 179
McBroom, William J. 182
McBroom, William T. 87,141,154,
  184,185,208,213,224
McCabe, William H. 178
McCahill, Edmond 130,143,147
McCaslin, Hannah 144,145
McCasline, Hannah 133
McClain, James 73,207
McClain, John 36,52,65,72,85,87,
  94,95,114,121,122,124,126,132,
  154,156,205
McClain, Susannah 73
McClane, John 100,108
McClarin, John 16
McCleroy, John J. 105
McConnegal, Barbary 66
McCormack, William 8
McCrary, John 95,106
McCrary, Sary M. 106
McCullough, G. W. 196,201
McCullough, James 128
McCullough, Nancy R. 196,201

McCullough, William G. 124
McDaniel, Samuel 75
McDonald, James 29
McDougal, John P. 93
McDougle, Archebald 36
McDowell, Luke 19
McElroy, James 85
McElroy, James J. 36
McElroy, John J. 10,50,61,
  64,209
McEwen, Hannah M. 201
McEwen, Josiah 78
McEwen, Josiah, Jr. 68
McEwen, Josiah, Sr. 79,80
McEwen, Margaret E. 201
McEwen, Sarah 126,201
McFaddin, Candow S. 160
McFerrin, A. F. 15,32,42,
  43,49,50,56,94,97,103,
  105,107,120,121,129,131,
  132,135,136,141,174,175,
  193,198,200,208,210,214,
  217,221,223
McFerrin, Alexander F. 157
McFerrin, B. F. 94,107
McFerrin, B. L. 2,3,4,15,
  32,40,42,48,49,50,63,
  68,74,91,94,103,105,
  110,121,129,131,136,
  141,224
McFerrin, B. T. 72,212
McFerrin, Benton 110
McFerrin, Benton L. 83
McFerrin, Burton L. 188
McFerrin, James 216
McFerrin, William 127
McGee, James C. 19
McGee, Jesse 146,157,170,
  173,193
McGee, Joseph C. 44,45
McGee, Levina A. 159
McGill, Daniel 188
McGill, David 31,68,95,
  100,107,147,166,204,211
McGill, James 95,107,117,
  128,129
McGill, James P. 189
McGill, Nancy 95
McGill, William 129,147,
  166,204,216
McGlocklin, Dawson 52,127,
  167
McGlocklin, William 62
McIver, John 120,124,125,
  137,162

McJarret, David 73
McKee, James 76
McKee, William 116,142
McKnight, A. B. 188
McKnight, A. M. 98,108
McKnight, A. Miller 148
McKnight, A. S. 144,145,162,167,
  171,201
McKnight, Abagail 98
McKnight, Abner S. 138
McKnight, Albert 37
McKnight, Albert M. 138
McKnight, Alexander 3,13,23,29,53,
  77,78,96,98,148,149,162,168,180,
  181,192,195,215,216,218
McKnight, Alexander G. 195
McKnight, Andrew 81,181
McKnight, Andrew M. 83,98,138,148,
  149
McKnight, Daniel 181
McKnight, David 59,63,74,104,157
McKnight, Drewry 17
McKnight, Elam 138,141,178,186,189,
  191,222
McKnight, Elizabeth 80,174
McKnight, Elizabeth R. 185
McKnight, Enos 76,86
McKnight, George D. 181
McKnight, H. M. 98
McKnight, James 20,41,187
McKnight, James D. 81,83
McKnight, James M. 83
McKnight, James T. 63,104,115,157,
  162,181
McKnight, John M. 17,23,24,59,63,
  81,98,181
McKnight, John P. 149,195
McKnight, Joseph 181,211
McKnight, Joseph D. 158,188
McKnight, Lucy E. 162
McKnight, M. W. 215
McKnight, Mary 192
McKnight, Moses 12,49,91,107,125,
  168,181,218
McKnight, Moses W. 200,201
McKnight, R. J. 211
McKnight, R. L. 218
McKnight, Richard 100
McKnight, Richard L. 29,58,63,80,
  99
McKnight, S. H. 121,181,184
McKnight, S. R. 218
McKnight, S. T. 168
McKnight, Samuel F. 13
McKnight, Samuel H. 125,181

McKnight, Sarah J. 181
McKnight, T. C. 88
McKnight, W. W. 107,181,
   196,219
McKnight, W. Wilberford 168
McKnight, William 80,105,
   150,222
McKnight, William A. 222
McKnight, William S. 222
McKnight, William T. 195
McKnight, William W. 80,93,
   108,121,141,147,174,185
McKnight, Williford 149
McLaughlin, Dawson 215
McLaughlin, Jane 215
McLaughlin, Mary A. 215
McLaughlin, William 215
McLaughlin, William B. 215
McLin, James S. 67
McLin, Jamima H. 218
McLin, L. C. 40
McLin, William E. 12,58,
   67,93,96
McLoud, Nancy 189,203
McLoud, Thomas 189
McLoud, Thomas C. 188,203
McMahan, Jonathan 160
McMahan, Rebecca 160
McMahan, Wesley 207,218
McMahon, Emeline 222
McMahon, William 222
McMin, John 76
McNairy, John 119
McNary, Robert 59
Magness, Berry P. 84
Malone, Lewis 159,164
Manaham, James 53,56,84,92
Manakin, James 77
Mancy, Eli H. 221
Mancy, Philip 219
Mancy, T. F. 219
Manes, Daniel 23
Maney, Henry 120,124,177,
   179,211
Maney, Joel 134
Maney, L. M. 177
Manning, Henry 105
Manus, Daniel 129,197
Manus, Daniel F. 116
Manus, John 185,197
Manus, Robert L. 200
Marah, Joseph 145
Marah, Sarah 145
Marchbanks, James 72
Marchbanks, Johnathan 98,

104
Marchbanks, Jonathan 86
Marcum, Charles 216,217
Marcum, Isaac 191
Marcum, Isaac C. 191,192
Marcum, Micajah 91,96,147,177,196
Marcum, Samuel 177
Marcum, William 61,91
Marford, Josiah F. 195
Markham, Micager 103
Markum, Isaac 174
Markum, John L. 158
Markum, Micajah 196,199
Marlin, Amzi W. 180
Mars, G. B. 109,206
Mars, Gabriel 194
Mars, Robert R. 219
Marshall, Eliza J. 102
Marshall, John C. 200
Marshall, John J. 200
Marshall, John W. 172,191,209
Marshall, Pias 200
Marshall, Robert 29,39,47,91,129,
   149,177
Marshall, Samuel B. 45
Martin, A. W. 91
Martin, Alexander 66
Martin, Ann W. 91
Martin, C. J. 125
Martin, J. B. 217
Martin, J. C. 52,129,159
Martin, J. T. 185
Martin, James 88
Martin, James C. 86
Martin, John 56,60,61,97,101,203,
   218
Martin, John C. 48,63,65,66,71,77,
   85,104,112,120,127,133,158,170,
   180,185
Martin, John, Jr. 84,88
Martin, John, Sr. 78
Martin, Joseph G. 148
Martin, Louis G. 25
Martin, Martha 203
Martin, Micajah 88
Martin, Patsey 60
Martin, R. B. 218
Martin, Robert 88
Martin, Sophia B. 112,159,185
Martin, Tarver 19
Martin, W. L. 197
Martin, William C. 88
Martin, William L. 205
Martin, Winney 71
Martin, Zavener 9

Mason, B. H. 187
Mason, John E. 208,209,224
Mason, Joseoh 65
Mason, R. H. 116,139,142,
  146,157,158,162,163,168,
  171,173,174,179,180,185,
  186,188,190,191,193,196,
  197,200,207,209,211,212,
  214,215,218
Mason, Reynea H. 142
Mason, Thomas P. 221
Massey, Micajah 178
Massey, W. S. 166
Massey, Washington S. 147,
  149,156,187,200,217,219
Massie, Micajah 214
Massie, W. S. 213
Mathis, Sampson 87
Matthews, Drury 3
Matthews, John W. 152,211
Matthews, Matthew 47
Maxcy, Phillip C. 181
Maxey, Nancy 165
Maxey, P. P. 188
Maxey, Phillip 48
Maxey, T. F. 45
Maxey, Walter 165
May, William W. 217
Mayfield, W. M. 189
Mays, Benjamin 94
Mays, John C. 204
Meadleton, John B. 6
Meadleton, William 15
Mears, Elijah 48,62,76
Mears, G. B. 120,166,204
Mears, Gabriel 188,213
Mears, George W. 14,26,27,
  30
Mears, Goldberg 76
Mears, Goldsborough 46
Mears, Goldsbury 30
Mears, James 62,73,213
Mears, John M. 48
Mears, William 29,41,46
Mears, William F. 127
Medford, Henry 13,68
Medley, James 104
Medlin, James 99,102,116,
  117
Melton, Aneil 52,82,92,
  124,131,186
Melton, George C. 131
Melton, James 13,17,125,
  131
Melton, Jesse 92,186,210

Melton, Joel 120
Melton, Joel D. 82
Melton, Joel L. 205
Melton, John 58,82,114,119,121,
  124,131,186,210
Melton, John D. 124
Melton, John, Jr. 17
Melton, John, Sr. 17
Melton, John W. 158
Melton, Joseoh 122
Melton, Mary 124
Melton, Polly 125
Melton, Squire 121
Melton, William 114,122
Melton, William G. 214
Melton, William S. 86,96,113,147,
  170
Melvin, John 190
Melvin, William E. 59
Merit, Thomas 11,34
Merritt, Thomas 47,189
Mers, William F. 110
Metcalf, Marcus A. 47,73,76,77
Middleton, William 35,40
Middleton, William H. 35
Miles, Allen 111,135
Miles, Delila 135
Miles, James 5
Miles, John 161,174,184
Miles, Robert S. 184
Miligan, Jesse 17
Miller, C. M. 123
Miller, James 52
Miller, Martha E. 192
Miller, William C. 97,128,144,191,
  192,200,203,205,217
Milligan, Albert G. 170
Milligan, Alexander 137,171
Milligan, Elizabeth 100,145
Milligan, James 71,74,96,145
Milligan, Joel 161,181,182
Milligan, John 137
Milligan, John A. 204
Milligan, Nancy A. 100
Milligan, William 35
Milligan, William W. 11,45
Millikan, Sarah 122
Millikin, Albert G. 88,93,108,121,
  122,129,132,136,137,143,170,177
Millikin, Austin S. 107
Millikin, Jesse 88,120,175,177,192,
  207
Millikin, John W. 108,129,143,152,
  189
Millikin, M. G. 170

Mills, John 208
Mills, Nancy 208
Milton, Ancil 4
Milton, John 5,17,27,65,66
Milton, William C. 158
Mitchel, Daniel W. 164,215
Mitchel, Dorothy 164
Mitchel, Elenar 215
Mitchel, Elizabeth 219
Mitchel, John 129,156,219
Mitchel, John N. 143
Mitchel, nancy 216
Mitchel, Stephen 164,216
Mitchel, Stephen A. 146
Mitchell, Daniel F. 205
Mitchell, David 77
Mitchell, Elizabeth 187
Mitchell, Isaac L. 169
Mitchell, James 4,15,19,
  24,33,45,88,92
Mitchell, James H. 187,197
Mitchell, James M. 44
Mitchell, John 204
Mitchell, John A. 162
Mitchell, John N. 47,173,
  193,205
Mitchell, Robert 44,62,77,
  83
Mitchell, Stephen 62
Mitchell, Stephen A. 81,92,
  107,145,174
Mitchell, Thomas P. 191
Moffet, Henry 128
Moffitt, Henry 117,139
Montgomery, Andrew 154
Montgomery, Archebald 163
Montgomery, Eleanor 154
Montgomery, John 108
Montgomery, Susan 163
Moody, Lydia 4
Moore, Abenon 76
Moore, Abner 62
Moore, Adam J. 34
Moore, Alexander 161
Moore, Alexander S. 122,181
Moore, Drufina 116
Moore, E. Jane 26
Moore, Eletha L. 105
Moore, Elizabeth 5,30,138
Moore, Elizabeth J. 10,26,
  30
Moore, Fanny 201
Moore, Jacob 59,65,68,69
Moore, James T. 119
Moore, Jesse 67

Moore, Jesse G. 7,10,26,30,42,61
Moore, John 7,165,201
Moore, John L. 25,26,71
Moore, John W. 190
Moore, Joseph 29,148,149,194
Moore, L. B. 15,58,76,148,154,168,
  181
Moore, Lemuel G. 116
Moore, Little B. 75
Moore, Pamelia 96
Moore, Pendleton 23
Moore, Samuel 5,7,30,60,65,83,87,
  102,108,151,152
Moore, Samuel R. 151
Moore, Stephen 99
Moore, Templeton 96
Moore, Thomas W. 171,199
Moore, Warren 152
Moore, William 10,26,27,30,32,79,
  138
Moore, William N. 105
Morford, Josiah F. 82
Morgan, Alexander 106,107,141,163,
  171
Morgan, Allen 55,166
Morgan, Catherine 141
Morgan, James D. 30
Morgan, John 13,32,78
Morgan, Joseph 40
Morgan, Joseph D. 2,21,41
Morgan, Joseph P. 200
Morin, Louis A. 68
Moris, Hiram 174
Morris, Henry 108
Morris, Hiram 64,155
Morris, William 99,129
Morrison, Andrew 37
Morton, A. W. 152,172
Morton, J. J. 152,172
Morton, Jesse B. 152
Morton, William J. 152
Moses, Hiram 174
Mosier, Richard P. 11
Moss, Gabriel 103
Moss, William 103
Mottley, Samuel 158
Mullinax, A. P. 212
Mullinax, Abner 105
Mullinax, Alman 78,169
Mullinist, Alman 191
Mullins, Daniel C. 56,61,64,66,101
Mullins, Dozier 85,86,99,116
Mullins, Ezekiel 34,84,131
Mullins, J. 61
Mullins, John 54,86,87,104,115,114

Mullins, John A. 84
Mullins, John W. 100,109,
  117,118,125,126,128,169
Mullins, Joseph 63,64,83,
  86
Mullins, Jubelee 63
Mullins, Mr. 117
Mullins, Nancy 162
Mullins, Widow 169
Muncy, Eli H. 195,213
Muncy, John 195,204,214
Murphy, Stephen 15
Murray, William H. 45
Murry, John 164
Murry, William H. 88
Myers, George W. 100
Nance, C. W. 93,180
Napier, R. C. 60
Nash, Benjamin 180
Nash, William 114
Neeley, Elijah 18,27,99,
  153,174,181
Neeley, Isaiah 12,40,95,
  98,220
Neeley, Joshua 13,90
Neeley, Nathan 11,15,26,
  27,30,38,40,43,48,49,91
Neely, Elijah 152,155,159,
  161,210,213
Neely, Eliza 56
Neely, Elizabeth 213
Neely, Isaac 211,212
Neely, Isaiah 109,192,212
Neely, James B. 213
Neely, Nathan 5,72,102,104,
  213
Neely, Nathan L. 213
Neely, Peggy 106
Neely, Polly J. 213
Neely, Robert W. 213
Neely, Sarah 159
Nelson, Charles L. 125,152,
  162,164,170,180
Nelson, James R. 180
Nelson, John 87,121,126
Nelson, L. B. 178,190
Nelson, M. L. 198
Nelson, M. S. 170
Nelson, S. B. 198
Nelson, Samuel B. 159
Nelson, Sarah 198
Nesbit, Alexander 126,176
Nesbit, Ephraim 96,108
Nesbit, Samuel 212
Nesbitt, Alexander 117

New, C. T. 146,200
New, Charles T. 49
Newby, Hezekiah B. 21
Newby, Nancy 21
Newby, Nathan 52
Nichol, William 115
Nichols, Delinda 4
Nichols, Elizabeth J. 136
Nichols, Joseph 136
Nichols, Joshua 136
Nichols, Mary E. 136
Nichols, Thomas P. 4
Nichols, William 62,66,71,145,170,
  182
Nicholson, Clementine 136
Nicholson, James 186
Nivins, Joseph 17,46
Nokes, John 121,157,189
Nokes, Salvina 99
Nokes, Sophrona 80
Nokes, Thomas 58,68,69,82,84,85,
  86,105,122,211
Nokes, Thomas, Jr. 13
Nokes, W. B. 190,222
Nokes, William 105,108,109,156
Nokes, William B. 66,85,99,170,
  181
Nokes, William C. 84
Norris, Almira 110
Norris, Elizabeth 110
Norris, Isaac 110
Norris, Martha 125,134
Norris, Nathan J. 41,110,134
Norris, Nathan L. 125
Norris, Thomas 110
North, Seth J. 45
Northcut, Adrian 75
Northcut, G. N. 214
Northcut, George N. 221
Northcut, Woodson 60,80
Northcutt, Adam 186
Northcutt, Frances 14
Northcutt, Woodson 16,44,45
Norton, William 33
Nunnally, Ellis 218
Nunnally, Lydia 218
Nunnally, Mary A. 218
Oaks, Hezekiah 34
Odom, A. J. 178
Odom, Armstead G. 113,179,195
Odom, B. F. 72,120,137,177,194
Odom, Benjamin F. 148
Odom, C. B. 207
Odom, C. C. 199
Odom, Cantrel B. 194

Odom, Eliza 179
Odom, Eliza J. 113
Odom, J. M. 178,184,188
Odom, James 66,116,117,
  120
Odom, James L. 162
Odom, James S. 52,68,73,
  75,195,212
Odom, James T. 117
Odom, John M. 120,195
Odom, Lucy 68
Odom, Mary 75,148
Odom, R. W. 68,73,117
Odom, S. J. 93,137,213,
  221
Odom, Samuel C. 76,98,
117,174,184
Odom, Sarah S. 172
Odom, Shadrack J. 116,
  172,177
Odom, W. C. 194,199
Odom, William C. 28,29,
  78,89,93,117,207
Odum, James 21
Odum, James S. 20
Ogles, John 94
Oliver, Augustine 59
Oliver, Augustine S. 12
Oliver, Augustus 53
Oliver, Daniel M. 89,101
Oliver, Ibby N. 101
Oliver, J. N. 89
Oliver, Jane H. 89,101,
  132
Oliver, Thomas 6
Orr, Alexander 21,22,43,
  48,129,130,154,180
Orr, E. A. 43,48,102,113,
  129,131,154
Orr, Eleazar 48,100
Orr, Eleazar A. 84,130,
  143
Orr, J. D. 54
Orr, James D. 43,71,74
Orr, Leanar 109
Orr, Robert 14
Orran, John 155,159
Orrand, J. W. 108,186,
  210,218
Orrand, James M. 199
Orrand, John 138,186
Orrand, John W. 186,191
Orrand, T. J. 138
Overall, Jacob 18
Overall, Nace 188

Owen, Alethy 220
Owen, Christopher 59,76,136
Owen, E. W. 192
Owen, Elbert 72,103
Owen, Elizabeth 167
Owen, F. 194
Owen, Fountain 72,79,83,85,99,
  108,118,119,177,209,216
Owen, J. J. 220
Owen, Lemuel 167
Owen, Moses 86
Owen, Nelson 72,74,98,103,172,209
Owen, Permelia 76
Owen, Rebecca E. 83
Owen, William 205
Owens, Christopher 188
Owens, Fountain 19
Owens, Moses 69
Pace, William 53,56,59,60
Pafford, Randall 28
Pallet, Abram 10
Pallet, Abram C. 10
Pallett, Abraham C. 137
Pallett, Abram 137,176
Pallett, Abram C. 137
Pallett, G. W. 137
Pallett, James Y. 137
Pallett, Jane 137
Pallett, Mary Y. 137,170,176,187,
  188
Pallett, Robert 27
Pallett, Thomas A. 137
Palmer, Rachel 14
Panken, L. D. 77
Pankey, Ewell 77
Paris, J. B. 164
Paris, Jane 125
Paris, John B. 125,137,191
Paris, Johnathan 42
Paris, Jonathan 107
Paris, Solomon C. 42,58
Parish, William C. 121
Park, Isaack 208
Parker, Cornelius 117,142
Parker, Isaiah 109,129,170,206
Parker, John 119,153
Parker, John W. 137,208
Parker, Levi 87,125
Parker, Samuel 168
Parker, Sarah 125
Parker, Silas 208,217
Parker, Thomas 9,114
Parkhurst, Daniel 12,14,34,45
Parks, Frankey 94
Parris, Jane 92

Parris, John B. 91,92,207
Parris, Jonathan 92
Parrish, William C. 141
Parsons, Ludlam M. 59
Partin, William 52
Parton, Aaron V. 134
Parton, M. P. 219
Parton, William 6,12,33,
 134,165,204
Paterson, John 81
Patrick, James 44
Patrick, Jemima 109
Patrick, Jesse 109,193
Patrick, William 116,120
Patrick, William C. 117,
 120
Patten, Mary 86
Patterson, Elizabeth 21
Patterson, Joab 21
Patterson, John 47,116,
 159
Patterson, Nancy 21
Patterson, Robert 117
Patterson, William 21
Patton, David 51,68,74,
 79,89,93,131,132,222
Patton, David M. 222
Patton, J. N. 208
Patton, Jane 156
Patton, John 132
Patton, John F. 131
Patton, Matthew 38
Patton, Nancy 132
Patton, Robert 156
Patton, Robert J. 170
Patton, Thomas J. 83
Patton, William 43
Pearce, Beverly 19
Pearson, Daniel 84
Pearson, John W. 15
Peay, T. T. 163
Pebles, George 91
Peden, Eliza 70
Pedon, John 109,111,117,
 222
Pedon, Minford 173
Pedon, Nancy J. 173
Peebles, George 37,41,
 100,187
Peeler, King 161
Peeler, King S. 180
Peeler, Linzy 160,191,
 221
Peeler, Sarah 221
Pelar, Linzy 156

Pelham, Alexander 154
Pelham, Isham 100,165
Pelham, Levi 100,165
Pelham, William 154
Pendergrass, Henry 8
Pendleton, Ann E. 147
Pendleton, Benjamin 1,2,13,17,19,
 36,47,48,56,57,58,59,67,93,99,
 117,121,130,132
Pendleton, Edmond 59,66,106
Pendleton, Eliza 117
Pendleton, Eliza A. 130,149
Pendleton, J. L. 205
Pendleton, James 83,118
Pendleton, James P. 213
Pendleton, John 6,17,30,32,38,47,
 83,87,118,145,146,153,165,167,
 168,178,189,195,214,217,221
Pendleton, John F. 195
Pendleton, John, Jr. 189
Pendleton, John, Sr. 189
Pendleton, Joseph W. 111
Pendleton, Samuel 146,173,194,195
Pendleton, William 189,195
Penn, A. C. 24,33,114
Penn, Abram C. 82
Perkins, John B. 181,192,204
Perry, Ann M. 185
Perry, Edmond 185
Perry, H. R. 162
Perry, Henry 99
Perry, Henry R. 10,111,115,156,159,
 162,164,167,168,185,193
Perry, Jackson 185
Perry, James 222
Perry, James D. 158
Perry, James P. 92
Perry, Jessa L. 6
Perry, Jesse L. 10
Perry, John 43
Perry, John W. 185
Perry, Malissa 185
Perry, Martha 185
Perry, Moses 185
Perry, Powell 185
Perry, Widow 212
Persons, Samuel D. 105
Petiff, William A. 87
Pettis, George 84
Petty, A. G. 222
Petty, Alexander 15,17,20,24
Petty, Ambrose 15,22,29,34,46,81
Petty, Irvin 182,184
Petty, James 94,132,136,143,155,
 165,182,190

Petty, John 16,34,53,60,
77,84,85,86,89,92,94,
95,100,115,122,157,163,
168
Petty, Micajah 5,26,34,
67,87,109,134,138,141,
144,151,181,191,192,
205,212
Petty, William J. 182
Peyton, Harrison 170,200
Peyton, W. H. 155
Peyton, William H. 65,95,
108
Peyton, Winney 102,200
Philips, A. J. 70,207
Philips, B. H. 107
Philips, Benjamin H. 25,
136
Philips, Peter 107
Philips, Samuel 205
Philips, William 145,206
Phillips, Andrew 95
Phillips, Benjamin H. 19
Phillips, Elizabeth 151
Phillips, James 8
Phillips, Newson 220
Phillips, R. J. 203
Phillips, Samuel 50,217
Phillips, William 20,21,
33,198,220
Pickett, Andrew 21
Pierce, Jesse 159
Pike, William 33
Pillow, Levi 49
Pinkerton, Joseph 1,5,
18,22,30,92,114,139,
157,166,179,188
Pinkston, Mathew 55
Pistole, James 6
Pistole, Pleasant 6
Pittard, Elijah 62,69
Pitts, Sarah 173
Poff, Mary A. 103
Pogue, Samuel 9
Polly, James 103
Pope, Mark A. 41
Porter, Hugh 36,132
Porterfield, John 55
Porterfield, John H. 53
Porterfield, L. F. 110,
219
Posey, Martha M. 194
Posey, W. Y. 194
Powell, Henry 118,172,184
Powell, Thomas 179

Powell, William 172
Prater, James J. 157,190
Prater, James M. 157
Prater, Martin L. 216
Pratt, William A. 22
Preston, E. C. 178,201,223
Preston, Eli 66,126
Preston, Elijah C. 150
Preston, Elizabeth 189
Preston, John 80,189,190
Preston, John F. 134,135,147,150,
213
Preston, Mary 126,213
Preston, Sarah 190
Preston, T. J. 178,201,213
Preston, Thomas 189,190
Preston, Thomas J. 150
Preston, William 29,35,66,80,88,
93,126,134,135,142,143,150,151,
156,191
Preston, William T. 160
Price, Dr. 170,194,201
Price, James 52,68
Price, Jane 167
Price, Lydia 167
Price, May 167
Price, R. C. 188
Price, Reter 167
Price, Richard 106,111
Price, Richard C. 49,63,93,117,
128,129,138,141
Price, Robert C. 15
Price, Sarah 167
Price, William 111,167,168
Prim, Anna J. 103
Prim, John 203
Prim, William W. 133
Pumphrey, Lewis 37,44
Putman, J. J. 103
Rackley, Wiley 120
Raines, J. B. 195,199
Raines, James 49
Raines, John 188
Rains, Aniel 60
Rains, Annual 77,84,86,87,92,100,
115,124,136,216
Rains, Anuel 21,67
Rains, Isaac 96,143
Rains, Larkin 86,96
Ramsey, James 26
Ramsey, Joseph 7,10,13,17,26,27,30,
31,32,42,46,47,50,51,56,58,64,72,
75,76,82,86,87,93,97,98,99,100,
106,115,118,124,125,129,130,134,
135,149,174,193,196,197,211,212,

Ramsey, Joseph 213
Randles, Churchwell B. 88
Ransdell, Churchwell B. 12
Ransom, John C. 74,89
Ratcliff, Aaron 27
Rawlings, C. H. 221
Rawson, Hiram 8
Rayburn, Johnson 32
Rea, William 27,136
Ready, Charles 5,147,161,
   186
Ready, Elias A. 201
Ready, James 117,212
Ready, Lucretia 115
Ready, Sarah 201
Ready, William 212
Redin, John 67
Redman, Solomon 9
Reed, David B. 170
Reed, Elezar 69
Reed, Frederick 89
Reed, George W. 174
Reed, Hale 23
Reed, Hugh 2,3,8,16,17,18,
   39,85,93
Reed, James 34,190,196
Reed, James H. 174,190
Reed, John 4
Reed, John H. 3
Reed, Lemuel A. 53,55
Reed, William 205
Reeves, Elizabeth 99
Reeves, George W. 99
Reeves, Polly 161
Reeves, Sally 161
Reglasbooks, John 69
Reynolds, Benjamin F. 43
Reynolds, Clinton B. 16
Reynolds, Elisha 13,86
Reynolds, John 9,15
Rich, Obadiah 16
Richardson, Barnard 22
Richardson, Brice M. 23,45
Richardson, Elizabeth 70,
   91
Richardson, Elizabeth P. 85
Richardson, H. W. 103,106
Richardson, Samuel 28,51,
   70,85,91
Richardson, Thomas 185
Richardson, Thomas W. 91,
   116
Richmond, Thomas 44
Riggs, Wiley 201,207
Rigsby, Alman 118,196

Rigsby, Almon 18
Rigsby, John 39
Rigsby, John H. 163
Rigsby, John K. 126,196
Rigsby, Paul 12
Rigsby, Thomas 57
Rigsby, William T. 126,163
Ring, Bartlet S. 209,217
Ring, John 56,84
Ring, William 88,97
Ring, William, Sr. 112
Roach, Isaac J. 200
Roberts, C. L. 105
Roberts, Calvin 105
Roberts, Calvin W. 114
Roberts, Cyrus L. 23,50,61,85
Roberts, Cyrus R. 26
Roberts, Granville 37,105
Roberts, Grenville 166
Roberts, J. M. 166
Roberts, James 73,105
Roberts, James M. 37,55,92,135,
   146,166
Roberts, Martha 105,166
Roberts, S. G. 166
Roberts, Sarah 105
Robertson, F. D. 60
Robertson, Felix 60
Robertson, Hugh 69
Robertson, James 60
Robertson, James R. 60
Robertson, Jesse B. 35
Robertson, John M. 60
Robertson, William B. 60
Robinson, Edward 2,11
Robinson, Elizabeth 106
Robinson, Euphama 145
Robinson, Hannah 145
Robinson, Hugh 28,51,53,59,60,77,
   86,89,114,116,124,145,150,152,
   190,205,210
Robinson, Jane 145
Robinson, Jessa B. 4,114
Robinson, Jesse 60
Robinson, Jesse B. 124,128,133,145
Robinson, Jesse H. 144
Robinson, Jessey B. 107,113
Robinson, John 128,131,208
Robinson, Levina 145
Robinson, Peggy 11
Robinson, Richard W. 160
Robinson, Silas A. 30,44,106,110,
   131,133,150
Robinson, Wiley H. 124
Robinson, Willis H. 74

Robison, Hugh 77,120
Robison, L. M. 92
Robison, Silas A. 93,145
Robison, Wilie H. 77
Robison, Willie H. 95
Rodgers, Catherine 141
Rodgers, Daniel M. 141
Rodgers, Elizabeth 109
Rodgers, Henry D. 141
Rodgers, James H. 141
Rodgers, John 8,77,107,
  141
Rodgers, John B. 89,109
Rogers, George 137
Rogers, James 220
Rogers, John 15,46,53,
  65,94,106
Rogers, John B. 107,117
Rogers, R. H. 119,131
Rogers, Wilburn 220
Rogers, William 106,107
Rollins, C. H. 208
Rollins, Christopher 214
Rolston, David N. 181
Rolston, William 50
Rose, Elijah B. 40
Rose, Elisha B. 132,177
Rose, G. W. 8,13,103
Rose, J. G. 29,39
Rose, John G. 100
Rose, Leroy 103
Ross, David 73,102
Ross, Dicy A. 193
Ross, G. B. 3
Ross, James E. 193
Rossen, Highram 28
Roughton, James H. 138
Roughton, T. H. 138
Roughton, Thomas H. 92,
  115,157
Rucker, Benjamin 177
Rucker, Bennett 99,107,
  108
Rucker, Elizabeth 177
Rucker, Gideon 48,50,66,112,
  120
Rucker, James H. 112
Rucker, Jane 112
Rucker, Joice 86
Rucker, S. W. 120
Rucker, Samuel 112
Rucker, Samuel W. 170
Rucker, T. S. 119,120
Rucker, Thomas S. 112
Rugle, Jasper 7

Rushing, Abel 181,203,210,212,
  224
Rushing, John 212
Rushing, M. R. 203,216,217
Rushing, Richmond 208
Russell, Mary 73
Russell, Samuel J. 73
Russell, Samuel P. 26
Rusworm, John J. 76
Ryan, B. R. 97
Sadler, Euphama 145
Sadler, Euphania 133
Sadler, Fanny C. 152
Sadler, George W. 90,133,145,152
Sadler, Phany 90
Sadler, Thomas 35,36,37,43,46
Saffel, Amos 14
Saffel, Milus 91
Saffle, Milas 50
Sageley, Blake 11,14,30,32,79,106,
  199
Sagely, Blake 83,92,182
Sanders, Elihu 93
Sanders, Marshall 157
Sanders, Mary C. 71
Sandridge, Caroline 129,195
Sandridge, Dabney 129,180,195
Sandridge, Damer 111
Sandridge, Eliza 150,153
Sandridge, Hallah 111
Sandridge, Huldy 129
Sandridge, Louisa 150,153
Sandridge, Louiza 111
Sandridge, Mela 111
Sandridge, Permelia 150
Sandridge, Richard 111
Sanes, Noah W. 148
Sanford, E. R. 148
Sanford, Elijah R. 158
Sanford, Elizabeth 180
Sanford, Elizabeth R. 134,151,158
Sanford, Thomas B. 122,142,148,
  151,157,158
Sapp, Benjamin 5,18,47,83,100,
  105,111,125,134,136,137,145,
  146,149,154,155,166,181,186,219
Sapp, G. B. 2
Sapp, Granberry 18,22
Sapp, Green B. 35
Sapp, Jessa 2
Saul, Henry 13,30
Sauls, Abraham 50
Sauls, Henry 49,50
Sauls, James K. 98
Sauls, John K. 24,78,93,127,151,170

Sauls, Rhoda 127
Sauls, William 91
Saunders, James 124
Scales, Jeremiah 190,211,
  215,219
Scales, Rachel G. 211,219
Scott, David 25
Scott, James 8,12
Scott, Thomas S. 40
Scovil, Ashley 42
Scovil, Nelson 42
Scurlock, William 128
Seal, Edward C. 98
Seawell, Jesse Q. 63,65,
  67,70,78
Sellars, S. B. 204
Sellars, W. W. 204
Sewell, Jesse 57
Sewell, Jesse Q. 97
Shackleford, Daniel 11
Shackleford, Harrison 161
Shackleford, Mary 161
Shaw, John L. 33,42,71,75
Shaw, Robert L. 16
Shelby, Moses 27,112
Sheppard, Mary 110,120
Sheppard, Peyton 120
Sherley, Luke 45,53,82,198
Sherlock, Joseph 115
Sherrill, George 111
Sherrill, George W. 89
Silliman, Thomas 179
Silvertooth, G. W. 154
Silvertooth, Jacob 154
Simmons, Ivery 200
Simmons, James 4,206
Simpson, Andrew L. 222
Simpson, Andrew S. 188,
  215,220
Simpson, Elander 220
Simpson, Jane 167
Simpson, John 144
Simpson, Joseph 25,38,49,
  117,120,139,157,166,215
Simpson, Nancy 33
Simpson, Peter 8,9,38,117,
  166,167,178
Simpson, Robert 143,180,
  198
Simpson, Valentine 31,37,
  40,46,66,100
Simpson, William 33
Sisson, Ann 110,113
Sisson, Anna 161
Sisson, Henry 103,107

Sisson, James 4,8,15,16,24,75,
  107,110,111,114,115,128,147,
  161,169,173,175,216
Sisson, Jesse 128,133,134,145,161,
  169,174,203,216
Sisson, Jesse, Jr. 160
Sisson, Jesse, Sr. 115
Sisson, Polly 174,216
Sisson, Sally 174,216
Sisson, Thomas 103,107,111,134,161,
  174,175,191,196,199,216
Sisson, Widow 161,175
Sisson, William 96,107,153,161,170,
  174,175,187,216
Sisson, Wilson 83
Skelton, James H. 192
Sloan, James 217
Smart, Thomas C. 168
Smartt, Sarah 147
Smartt, Thomas C. 147
Smith, Anna 173
Smith, Arthur 5
Smith, Asa 64,71,85,125,137,156,213
Smith, Clementine 186
Smith, David 29
Smith, Guy 67
Smith, Harrison 63,106
Smith, Hector 142
Smith, Helton 50
Smith, James 49,57,79,86,173
Smith, John 112
Smith, John C. 111
Smith, John H. 17,95,152,165,194
Smith, John J. 115
Smith, John N. 173
Smith, John Y. 117
Smith, Jonathan 77,87,126
Smith, Joseph 73
Smith, Joseph H. 28,43,47
Smith, Lewis L. 160
Smith, Lucy 152
Smith, Nicholas 104,113
Smith, O. B. 186
Smith, Penelope 104
Smith, Penelope J. 113
Smith, R. A. 129,134,135,139,150,
  155,158,170,172,175
Smith, r. H. 165
Smith, Robert A. 49,116,144,155,
  211,214
Smith, Robert G. 186
Smith, Standford 163
Smith, Stanfield 95,104,168
Smith, Stanford 12,60,63,72,79,110,
  134,169,171,172,179,185

Smith, Stanton 172
Smith, Swinfield 81,174
Smith, T. H. 215
Smith, Thomas H. 152,165
Smith, Turner B. 70,104,
106,144,163,174
Smith, William 21,44,78,
96,112,161
Smith, Williamson 87
Smithson, Albert 41
Smithson, Hiram 91
Smithson, Isaac F. 195
Smithson, James 101,182
Smithson, James A. 193
Smithson, John C. 171
Smoot, alexander N. 161,
179
Smoot, Neely 155
Smoot, William 164
Sneed, W. H. 48
Snipes, Britton W. 112,
134
Soap, Elizabeth 18,68,
69,93
Soap, Isaac 88
Soap, James 18
Soap, W. C. 189
Soap, William 103
Soap, William C. 107,143,
170
Soape, Jemima 39
Soape, Joseph 19
Soape, William 214
Sommers, David 214
Spandler, Daniel 118,181,
193
Spangler, Elizabeth 193
Spangler, Jacob 27,98
Spangler, Samuel 27,103,
181,193
Spears, Samuel 64,131
Spence, Brent 2
Spicer, B. B. 140,159,160
Spicer, Brovel 146
Spicer, Catharine A. 10
Spicer, David O. 6,10,22
Spicer, Hardy 32
Spicer, Lucy W. 10,22
Spicer, Robert G. 10,13,
22
Spicer, Solomon 127
Spry, Frances 134
Spry, William 217
Spurlock, Drury 68
Spurlock, Frances 67

Spurlock, Francis 27,31,33,166,
177,195,196
Spurlock, James 33
Spurlock, James A. 177
Spurlock, John A. 27
Spurlock, Joseph 38,42,67,157,158,
180,197,199,203,208
Spurlock, Josiah 127
Spurlock, Nancy 196
Spurlock, Nancy F. 195
Spurlock, S. B. 128,164,193,194,
215
St. John, Ann 52
St. John, Arthur 213
St. John, Berry 213
St. John, Catharine 22,31
St. John, F. G. 55,116
St. John, Frederick A. 96
St. John, Frederick G. 45
St. John, French G. 52
St. John, George 14,22,31,213
St. John, George, Sr. 96
St. John, Hamon 99
St. John, Harmon 101
St. John, John 15,34,50,213,222
St. John, John F. 224
St. John, Martin 213
St. John, R. J. 224
St. John, Thomas 22,32,34,46,55,80,
213
St. John, William 213
Stacy, Joseph M. 193
Stacy, William 30,94,117,119,173
Stair, Lewis 129
Standley, John 28
Standley, John A. 66
Stanford, James 23
Stanley, John A. 71,193
Stare, Lewis 97
Starnes, Frederick P. 157
Starr, Lewis 133
Steel, Edward G. 178
Steel, James A. 36
Stephens, A. D. 213
Stephens, Anderson P. 185
Stephens, B. C. 8
Stephens, Benjamin C. 1,33
Stephens, Benjamin G. 43
Stephens, Elijah 7,8,12,49,62,91,
98,209
Stephens, Frederick P. 116
Stephens, Job 56,71
Stephens, Job B. 12
Stephens, Jobe 5,58,157
Stephens, R. L. 213

258

Stephens, Richard L. 185
Stephens, Robert 5,12
Stephens, Robert H. 58
Stephens, Robert K. 31,56,
  59,61,103,169,185,211
Stephens, Sampson 31,42,
  45,58,71,100,103,134,
  163,168,169
Stevens, Elijah 180
Stewart, David M. 37
Stewart, James W. 29,61
Stewart, L. D. 192
Stewart, Larkin D. 217
Stewart, Martin 28,65
Stewart, Robert M. 79
Stewart, William 147
Still, John M. 65
Stokes, Edmund P. 20
Stokes, William B. 15,49
Stone, A. 97,108,149,
  176,197
Stone, A. R. 55,77,97
Stone, Allen R. 19,25,29,
  33,41,77
Stone, Archable 71
Stone, Archebald 35,37,
  38,43,52,53,63,65,78,
  93,122,123,130,131,139,
  145,158,169,181,186,
  206,212,213,214,219
Stone, Archibald 5,12
Stone, Benjamin A. 98
Stone, James 36,61,72,95,
  108,138,158,173,186,
  187,190,215
Stone, James H. 37,125
Stone, Jasper M. 211
Stone, John B. 13,34,38,
  45,47,48,126
Stone, John W. 108,127
Stone, Johnathan G. 204
Stone, Jonathan G. 203
Stone, Lawrence 69
Stone, Luaner 88
Stone, Mary 211
Stone, Milly 190
Stone, P. F. 33
Stone, Parker F.22,24,25,
  29,46,77,118,184
Stone, Sarah 52
Stone, Susan 125
Stone, W. J. 187
Stone, William 23,25,40,
  42,46,67,109,113,147,163,
  174,188,192,207

Stone, William J. 187
Stone, William, Sr. 120
Stoneman, John H. 29
Stover, James 35
Stover, James W. 35
Stroud, Anna 165
Stroud, Anny 168
Stroud, John H. 52,156,160
Stroud, John W. 28,36,89,95,101,
  107,115,132,138,149
Stroud, M. A. 156
Stroud, Marchel 15
Stroud, Marshall 16,53
Stroud, Mary 160
Stroud, Oran 17,34,54
Stroud, Oran B. 34
Stroud, Walter 93,106,139,149
Stroud, William 39,52,87,89,91,96,
  105,108,138,165
Stroud, William D. 107,132,135,
  139,142,143,156,165,168
Stroud, William, Jr. 95,108
Stroud, William, Sr. 95,132
Stroughonbourgh A. 48
Stuart, Daniel M. 60,63
Stump, Frederick 89
Stump, Henry 215
Stump, John 76,215
Sullins, James 155
Sullins, James, Jr. 150
Sullins, Jesse 23,64
Sullins, Jesse, Sr. 86
Sullins, Thomas 195
Sullins, William 29,155
Sullivan, Andrew 220
Sullivan, Ann 198,201
Sullivan, B. F. 207
Sullivan, Cadijah 39
Sullivan, Caleb 32,44
Sullivan, Calvin 30
Sullivan, Caswell 39
Sullivan, Hanna 82
Sullivan, Harry 82
Sullivan, James 52,82,138,151,220
Sullivan, Jane 138
Sullivan, John E. 8
Sullivan, John R. 13,30,75,100,
  121,122,126,129,133,136,139,157,
  198,201,205
Sullivan, Martha 105,166
Sullivan, Minty 61
Sullivan, T. G. 109,142,145,173
Sullivan, Thomas G. 170,173,185
Sullivan, William 15,58,61,82,220
Sullivan, William L. 10,60

Summar, Lucinda 172
Summar, W. C. 172
Summars, B. H. 182
Summer, Baldy H. 147,185, 186
Summer, C. B. 175,182,191, 194,201,205
Summer, Elizabeth 136
Summer, Emmey 113
Summer, H. C. 217
Summer, J. W. 188,193
Summer, James B. 196
Summer, John W. 86,113,151, 165,177,182
Summer, Joseph D. 84
Summer, Mary 147,185
Summer, Matthew 113
Summer, T. R. 201
Summer, Thomas D. 113,127, 204
Summers, Anthony 52,62,76, 195,196,197,212
Summers, Bethel 189
Summers, C. B. 177,196,197, 210
Summers, H. C. 214
Summers, Henry C. 55
Summers, James B. 45,82, 171,214
Summers, John W. 36,41,42, 74,79,142,144,165,167,211
Summers, Robert J. 23,35,89
Summers, Thomas D. 47,91,108
Summers,Alexander H. 79,174
Sutton, Edmond 174
Sutton, Margaret T. 174
Sutton, Mary 45,174,181
Sutton, Roxanna P. 174
Swanner, Henry 181
Swanner, J. W. 146
Swanner, Jacob 146
Swanner, John 193
Swanner, Malinda 193
Sweeton, Amos 77
Tackett, David 9
Taler, John 193
Talley, W. R. 215
Talley, William R. 211
Tally, P. C. 117
Tally, Peter 194
Tally, William R. 199,200
Tassey, A. 174
Tassey, Alex 213
Tassey, Alexander 65,185,213
Tassey, Mary 174,185,213

Tassey, Meshac 49
Tassey, Nancy 49
Tassy, Dosamur 104
Tatum, A. C. 192,209,210,212
Taylor, Charles 182
Taylor, E. R. 119
Taylor, Edmund 7,56,64,65,99,102, 108,109,119,143
Taylor, Elizabeth 31,114,118,160
Taylor, Elizabeth R. 119,120,121, 122
Taylor, Hardin 218,221
Taylor, James 1,3,4,5,16,18,19,33, 35,39,46,55,67,75,100,102,103, 104,108,109,110,113,119,120,122, 135,141,177
Taylor, James A. 127
Taylor, James R. 114,118,119,192
Taylor, John L. 132,141
Taylor, Katherine 58
Taylor, Mary 109
Taylor, Mollie 182
Taylor, N. M. 135
Taylor, Nathan M. 124,141,142
Taylor, Nathaniel M. 103,109,110, 135,143,146,195,212
Teague, John 116,168,174,195,199, 200,204,221
Teague, Sarah E. 168,174,221
Teal, Robert 185
Teasley, Henderson 156
Teasley, Jane 156
Teasley, Mary 156
Teasley, William 156
Tedder, Rhoda 127
Tedder, Thomas 127
Telford, N. C. 160
Teneson, James B. 164
Tenneson, Edmund 6
Tennison, Hiram 70,74,79
Tennison, Margaret 73
Tennison, Martin 73
Tenpenny, Daniel 67,70,96,98,112, 124,175,177,187,190,197,221,222
Tenpenny, David 25
Tenpenny, James 100,108
Tenpenny, James A. 190
Tenpenny, James W. 126,128,152,190, 212
Tenpenny, Joseph 79
Tenpenny, Mumford 40,147,190,195, 206
Tenpenny, Richard 40,42,45,115, 190,212
Tenpenny, Richard, Jr. 212

Tenpenny, Sarah 190
Tenpenny, Tobias 79,170,
  187,189,212
Terry, H. R. 168
Thomas, Abner 75
Thomas, Allen 65,92,112
Thomas, Anderson J. 32
Thomas, Blackman C. 17
Thomas, Daniel 218
Thomas, Henry 61,86
Thomas, Iverson J. 55,61,
  132,136
Thomas, J. H. 172
Thomas, Jacob 27
Thomas, Jacob A. 142
Thomas, James 35,56
Thomas, John G. 82
Thomas, Mary 201,218
Thomas, P. J. 112,190
Thomas, Peter J. 28,134,
  157
Thomas, Ridley 185
Thomas, Samuel N. 86
Thomason, Daniel 20
Thomason, Mary 20
Thomason, Pleasant A. 14
Thomason, Z. 153,196
Thomason, Zachariah 46,61,
  83,85,94,96,194
Thompson, Anson 91,100,120
Thompson, Ason 105
Thompson, C. W. 224
Thompson, Caroline 100
Thompson, E. R. 203
Thompson, G. W. 203
Thompson, George W. 126,
  149,185,191,195,199,204,
  213
Thompson, James A. 100
Thompson, James P. 31
Thompson, Jason 30,119
Thompson, John M. 119
Thompson, Johnson 88
Thompson, Joseph 203
Thompson, Mary 91,105,120
Thompson, Meredith 65
Thompson, Polly 100
Thompson, Sarah 100,211
Thompson, Susanah 30
Thompson, Thomas 25,35,40,
  87,105,120
Thompson, Thomas J. 100,211
Thompson, Widow 187
Thompson, William 17,28,100,
  212,222

Thompson, Zachariah 31,92
Thrower, Henry 51
Thurston, George W. 75,80
Tilford, N. C. 149
Tittle, Adam 92,99,145,208
Tittle, Anthony 31,80
Tittle, George 118
Tittle, Hiram 92,99,118
Tittle, Hiram Y. 145
Tittle, Hyram Z. 66
Tittle, John 145
Tittle, Mary 145
Tittle, Millie J. 145
Tittle, Missouri M. 145
Tittle, Nancy 31
Tittle, Robert 34,46,80
Tittle, Samuel 16,34,46,66,80,85,
  92,98,99,145
Tittle, Susan 85,98
Tittle, Susannah 80,99
Todd, A. F. 99,212,220,223
Todd, Asa 77,152,167,190
Todd, Daniel 167
Todd, Elizabeth 132,177
Todd, Granville 220
Todd, Hiram 89,120,163
Todd, Hyram 200
Todd, J. S. 163
Todd, James 103,177,210,213,214
Todd, James, Jr. 49,132
Todd, James P. 48
Todd, James S. 178,190
Todd, Jefferson 113,206
Todd, Jesse 20,28,47,52
Todd, John A. 57
Todd, M. F. 109,208
Todd, Mary 220
Todd, Micajah F. 48
Todd, Milton 110
Todd, Nancy A. 50
Todd, Pinkney 117,119,167
Todd, Ransom 167
Todd, Sarah 220
Todd, T. L. 189
Todd, Thomas J. 57
Todd, Thomas L. 5,50,222
Todd, Thomas S. 26
Todd, W. T. 163
Todd, Walker 220
Todd, William 26,44,63,125,139,
  168,178,200,221
Todd, William, Jr. 110
Tolbert, James J. 184
Tolbert, James R. 112,138
Tolbert, L. G. 210

261

Tolbert, Leroy G. 209
Tolbert, Levina 215
Tolbert, S. G. 168
Tolbert, S. T. 184,218
Tolbert, William T. 218
Toliver, Augustus 79
Toliver, John 55
Tomlinson, William H. 35
Trammel, Thomas 21
Travers, Milas F. 65
Travis, Amos 176
Travis, Anderson 72
Travis, Barton W. 65
Travis, Daniel 65,71
Travis, Daniel G. 176
Travis, Davil 136,162,
  165,182,191,194
Travis, Eleanor 72
Travis, Jane 91
Travis, John 72
Travis, John A. 36
Travis, Milas F. 48,64,
  65,66,67
Travis, Miles F. 152
Travis, Milus F. 25
Travis, Samuel C. 104
Travis, Samuel D. 203
Travis, Samuel P. 191
Travis, Solomon 21,24,67,
  84,99
Travis, William 136,182
Travis, William A. 71,97,
  122
Travis, William H. 69,104,
  158,159,187,203
Trewitt, Elijah 11
Trewitt, Nancy 11
Trewitt, Tabitha 11
Trewitt, William 11
Trewitt, Wingate 11
Tribble, Peter 173
Trigg, Abraham 135
Trigg, Alexander 135
Trigg, Amandy M. 182
Trigg, William J. 182
Trimble, Joseph 57,75,86,
  111,112
Trott, Henry 103,104,111,
  115,117,118,122,167,172,
  175,200
Trott, Henry, Jr. 1,3,7,11,
  12,13,18,26,30,31,32,37,
  38,39,49,52,62,69,98,104
Trott, J. J. 50,166

Trott, James J. 18,20,38,52,58,
  74,128,144,223
Tubb, John 130
Tucker, A. J. 191
Tucker, John 6,30
Tucker, Pleasant W. 28
Tumby, Temple 67
Turner, Esley 190
Turner, Frances 103,118
Turner, Francis 27,42,63,148,163
Turner, George 176,208
Turner, Thomas L. 13,34,38,41,50
Turner, Wilson 88
Turney, Bowman 31
Turney, Frances 31
Turney, George 31
Turney, Isaac 31
Turney, John C. 31
Turney, Joseph 16,20
Turney, Lemuel 7,11,13,31,58
Turney, Pleasant 31
Turney, Polly 11
Turnley, Alyette 47
Tuttle, John 76
Tynes, W. C. 222
Umbarger, John 181,194,194
Underhill, Samuel 53,59,65,79,89
Vance, Eliza 142
Vance, Elizabeth 97
Vance, John 87,97
Vance, Joseph 68,80
Vance, Samuel 14,87,92,93,94,96,
  97,102,110,111,125,127,128,163,
  169,171,174,175,176,182,187,191,
  196,197,206,209
Vance, Sarah 125
Vance, Thomas 14,32,69,104
Vandergriff, William 199
Vannatta, Samuel 10
Vannay, Hannah P. 141
Vantrease, John 10,19
Vassar, James 167,215
Vassar, Joshua 107,165,222,223
Vasser, Rutty 82
Vaughn, E. W. 197
Vaughan, Edmund W. 90
Vaughan, John S. 19
Vincent, Richard 15,48,53
Vinson, Alexander 151,154,189
Vinson, Ann 151
Vinson, Berry 102,189
Vinson, Elizabeth 154,189
Vinson, James A. 128,151,154,189
Vinson, Mary 154

Vinson, Richard 5,16,42,
  43,48,72,80,91,102,
  128,151,154,189
Vinson, Robert 1,6,8,14,
  18,33,37,43,93,151,154,
  165,169,189
Vinson, Ursley 189
Wade, Noble 185
Wade, P. M. 25
Wade, G. W. 152,172
Wade, John T. 75
Walker, Abraham L. 62
Walker, Alfred 62
Walker, Burrel 110
Walker, Burwell 54
Walker, Burwell J. 79
Walker, Charles B. 79,80
Walker, George 36,40,46,
  85,97,102
Walker, James H. 97
Walker, John P. 53,79,93
Walker, Joseph 215
Walkup, Elijah N. 186
Walkup, Robert 36
Wall, J. Y. 91
Wall, John W. 95
Wallace, Benjamin 176,
  180,219
Wallace, Campbell 87
Wallace, Henry 18
Wallace, R. H. 6
Wallace, Richard H. 87
Wallace, William D. 199
Walls, Edmond 81,83,88,
  126,133
Walls, H. M. 80
Walls, Henry J. 190
Walls, Henry M. 88
Walls, Martha 126
Walls, Sarah 190
Wammack, Thomas 126,130
Ward, James 189
Ward, John 125,131,143,
  146,168,169,171
Ward, John B. 105
Ward, T. C. 217
Ward, Thomas C. 160
Ward, William 161
Ware, John W. 159,216
Warley, Edith 53
Warren, Alexander 175
Warren, Arthur 3,6,20,25,
  52,55,94,120,168
Warren, Arthur, Jr. 138
Warren, David 20

Warren, David T. 38,60,86
Warren, Elizabeth 189
Warren, Henry 6,7,8,18,20,22,25,
  50,59,65,79,83,93,138
Warren, Henry, Sr. 20
Warren, James 219
Warren, John 138
Warren, Joseph 19,43,48,49,58,
  151,154,189
Warren, Nancy A. 175
Warren, Sophia 151,154
Warren, Sophia L. 189
Warren, Squire 210
Warren, Zachariah 86,91,103,173
Washington, Thomas 45,63
Watson, Alford 211,218
Watson, James N. 68
Watson, Lance 68
Watson, Laner 67
Watson, Larner 6
Watson, Leanner 28
Watson, Mereda 14
Watts, James 80
Watts, Milton E. 125
Watts, William E. 59
Weaden, Daniel F. 77
Weatherford, J. D. 118
Weatherford, John Q. 93,108,163,
  174,193,194,205,206
Weatherspoon, Enos S. 211
Weatherspoon, Winphrey 11
Webb, J. W. 87
Webb, John 18,37,44,115,162,167,
  168,193,197,217
Webb, John, Jr. 105
Webber, Benjamin 49,55,65,68,82,
  84,96,113,118,143,155,167,223,
  224
Webber, Benjamin F. 144,167,178
Webber, Benjamin, Sr. 144,150
Webber, Francis M. 82
Webber, George W. 82
Webber, John 147,178
Webber, John A. 118,143,150,155,
  171,182
Webber, Philip 147
Webber, Rebecca 223,224
Webber, Richard 20,84,96,105
Weber, John 77,113
Weber, Philip 77
Webster, Johnathan 1
Weed, Otis H. 73
Weeden, A. M. 81,84,97,102,105,
  115,116,119,121,141,180,201
Weeden, Augustine M. 117,201

Weeden, D. F. 120
Weeden, Daniel 77,104
Weeden, Daniel F. 73,85,
  86,112,119
Weeden, J. F. 119,212
Weeden, John F. 119,136,
  158,217
Weeden, Maria L. 112,148
Weeden, Mary 119
Weeden, Mary J. 108
Weeden, Paulina J. 81
Weedon, A. M. 128,129,
  133,135,142,150,153,
  155,156,165
Weedon, Ann 161
Weedon, Augustine M. 129,
  149,161
Weedon, D. F. 122
Weedon, Daniel F. 129,138,
  148,161,213
Weedon, Elizabeth 161,165
Weedon, George W. 161,165
Weedon, J. F. 208
Weedon, John F. 122,155,
  161,165,200,205,224
Weedon, Lewis 153
Weedon, Maria L. 138,213
Weedon, Martha 161
Weedon, Mary J. 122
Weedon, Sarah E. 148,150,
  153,199,201
Weedon, William 161
Welch, John 3
Wendel, Thomas 59
Wendell, David 12,20
West, Charles H. 178
West, James 34
West, M. S. 6
West, Malinda 178
West, Michael 50
West, Thomas 6,18
West, William 13,14,17,28,
  33,48,49,50,61,67,68,70,
  82,86,100,102,128,145,
  149,152,163,171,175,184,
  191,192,201,220,223,224
Wetmore, Elen 147
Wetmore, W. J. 147
Weymouth, Benjamin 65,66,
  89
Weymouth, Benjamin F. 43
Whaley, Elijah 26
Whaley, Henrietta 22
Whaley, Margaret 26

Whaley, Seth 26
Whaley, Thomas 2,22,26
Wharey, Johnathan 95
Wharry, Jonathan 43
Wharton, Ann 161
Wharton, Ann M. 121,161
Wharton, John H. 224
Wharton, William 27,59,69,158,
  161,165,182,200
Wheelin, John 93
Wherry, Betsy 63
Wherry, Cynthia A. 52
Wherry, Elizabeth 52,53,63
Wherry, Jackson 52,63
Wherry, Jackson L. 52,53
Wherry, Johnathan 30,188
Wherry, Jonathan 34,63,134,163,
  168,210
Wherry, Levesta 52
Wherry, Levetta B. 53
Wherry, Mira 52
Wherry, Mira P. 53
Wherry, Oliver H. 52,53
Whitamore, Abigal 193
Whitamore, Jesse G. 193
Whitamore, William 88,111
Whitamore, William R. 216
White, William 88
Whitely, Betsy 135
Whitely, Elizabeth 38,39,52
Whitely, Joseph 38,39,52,135
Whiteman, James H. 190
Whitemare, William 55
Whitemore, James 89
Whitemore, William 87,89,157
Whiterly, Daniel B. 77
Whiteside, Jenkins 27
Whitfield, Alford 30,105,176
Whitfield, Alfred 143
Whitfield, Allen 44
Whitfield, Ansel 44
Whitfield, Arthur A. 44
Whitfield, Benjamin 131
Whitfield, Eli 30
Whitfield, Elizabeth 131
Whitfield, George 106
Whitfield, Green W. 114
Whitfield, John 42
Whitfield, Mathew 131,151
Whitfield, Roda 105
Whitfield, Thomas 49,106
Whitfield, Thomas G. 164
Whitfield, Thomas Y. 114
Whitfield, Willis 30,44,114,143,

Whitfield, Willis 164,176
Whitfield, Willis, Jr. 106
Whitfield, Willis, Sr. 106
Whitfield, Wright 114
Whithorne, W. J. 79
Whitley, Elizabeth 203
Whitley, Joseph 203
Whitley, Sullivan 89
Whitlock, John 173
Whitlock, Sally S. 173
Whitlock, Sterling 10
Whitman, William 211
Whitmore, J. H. 188,189
Whitmore, James 69
Whitmore, William 188
Whitsitt, John A. 168
Whitt, Benjamin 186
Whittemore, James H. 133
Whybrenl, Thomas 80
Whylvent, Thomas 31
Wilcher, William 91
Wilcher, William H. 217
Wiley, Frances A. 2,32
Wiley, H. A. 201,213,219
Wiley, Henry 2,8,32,76,
  175
Wiley, Henry A. 187,188,
  200
Wiley, Mary 96
Willard, Beverly 98
Willard, Beverly, Sr. 98
Willard, Elijah 98
Willard, James D. 98
Willard, John 28,34
Willard, Joseph 41,43
Willard, William 28,66,98,
  154
Williams, Benjamin 219
Williams, Berry 206
Williams, Betsy 172
Williams, Casson 206
Williams, Elizabeth C. 176
Williams, Gabriel 12,75
Williams, James 20,39,85,
  95,122
Williams, James M. 176
Williams, Jesse B. 68,169,
  172,187,201,208
Williams, John 53,64,68,
  74,94,95,130,157,187
Williams, Lemuel T. 176
Williams, Lydia 204,218
Williams, McKisack 12
Williams, Melchideck 36,68,
  75

Williams, Nancy M. 176
Williams, Nathan 41,47,59
Williams, Parmenas 16
Williams, Rhoda L. 176
Williams, Rhody L. 176
Williams, Robert B. 61
Williams, Sampson 11
Williams, Tempa 176
Williams, Thomas 18,156,169
Williams, Thomas H. 137,187,201,
  210
Williams, Thomas J. 68,69,83,122,
  156
Williams, Thomas K. 72,197
Williams, Tilda P. 176
Williams, William 15,60,74,82,111
Williams, William J. 66
Williams, William T. 206
Williard, John 98
Williard, Joseph 77
Williard, William 98
Willis, Mary 131
Willis, Temperance 88
Willis, Wila 34
Willis, William 110,131
Willis, Willie 88
Wilsher, C. M. 142
Wilsher, William 83,142,218
Wilson, A. J. 220
Wilson, Allen 100,126,137,138
Wilson, Benjamin 180,220
Wilson, H. 220
Wilson, Hiram 94,179,200,220,221
Wilson, Hiram, Jr. 204
Wilson, Hiram, Sr. 95
Wilson, Hollis 220
Wilson, James 32
Wilson, James A. 19
Wilson, John 220
Wilson, Michael 99,172,195,205,221
Wilson, Mike 189
Wilson, Stephen 27,152,172,186,189
Wilson, Stephen 178
Wilson, Thomas 21
Wilson, Walter 213,220
Wilson, William 64,219,221
Wilson, William B. 214
Wimberly, Hardy 163,165
Wimberly, Hardy, Sr. 165
Wimberly, Isaac 165
Wimberly, Johnathan 38
Wimberly, Jonathan 21,165
Wimberly, Susan 165
Wimberly, William 172,194
Wimbly, Hardy 91

Wing, Halsey R. 157
Winnett, Thomas 207
Winters, James E. 154
Winters, Margret 154
Witherspoon, Alexander 82
Witherspoon, Ebenezar A. 76
Witherspoon, Elihu 35,82
Witherspoon, Eliza 17,76
Witherspoon, Enos 19,82
Witherspoon, Enos S. 82
Witherspoon, Enos T. 17
Witherspoon, James C. 76
Witherspoon, John H. 109
Witherspoon, John K. 102
Witherspoon, Lewis F. 82
Witherspoon, Tirza 82
Witherspoon, William E. 102,
   109
Witherspoon, Winphrey 23
Witt, John 16,20,28,56,103,
   153
Womack, Thomas 51,114,133
Wood, A. J. 128
Wood, Andrew J. 36,40,52,
   55
Wood, B. F. 55
Wood, Benjamin F. 52,57
Wood, E. J. 172,188,194,210
Wood, Elizabeth 159,161
Wood, G. W. 23
Wood, George D. 23
Wood, George W. 24
Wood, James 5,12,16,43,47,
   49,52,56,64,65,69,74,78,
   100,135,156,188,191
Wood, James H. 193,205,209
Wood, John 24,44,52,56,65,
   69,74,78
Wood, John A. 210
Wood, John B. 219
Wood, John H. 16,19,25,33,
   40,42,52,54,57,61,69,78,
   79,80,93.95,111,121,128,
   129,149,174,175,180
Wood, John J. 164,181
Wood, John, Sr. 5,19
Wood, John W. 93
Wood, Joseph 12
Wood, Nathan 23,24
Wood, R. J. 152
Wood, Roxanna P. 174
Wood, T. G. 66,145
Wood, Thomas 12,22
Wood, Thomas C. 78
Wood, Thomas G. 36,40,44,46,

50,69,78,80,82,93,110,118,148,
153,156,157,159,163,168,174,195,
196,197,205,213
Wood, Thomas J. 69,94,151
Wood, William 12,18,20,52,58,133,
134,159,161
Woodall, Thomas 20
Woodall, William C. 134,135
Woodberry, Levie 1
Woodruff, R. W. 151
Woodruff, Robert W. 131
Woodruff, Temperance 131
Woods, Benjamin F. 205
Woods, George W. 218
Woods, J. J. 143
Woods, John 124
Woods, Nathan 22
Woods, Nathan L. 218
Wooldridge, John 21
Word, James C. 97,144
Word, Sarah 24
Word, T. C. 74
Word, Thomas 24,41
Word, Thomas C. 30,44,57,78,81,
   89,102,110,118,146,184,209
Word, Thomas G. 150,198
Word, William 39,41
Work, John L. 214
Work, Margaret 14
Wrather, Elizabeth 138,144
Wrather, F. D. 126,129,130,133,
   134,135,136,138,139,144,158
Wrather, Farman D. 130
Wright, Jacob 30,31,32,41,44,77,
   78,83,84,92,129,149,160,190,191,
   195
Wright, John 2,13,32
Wright, Mary 195
Wright, Susan J. 158
Wright, William B. 158
Yeargan, James 11
Yeargin, John 13
Yoakum, H. 37
Yoakum, Henderson 10,80,84,89,93,
   114
York, William 187
Yount, Alexander 11,130,173,186
Young, Andrew H. 72
Young, David 2
Young, Eli 81,196
Young, George W. 135
Young, Henry 11,24,148,151
Young, Isaac 48,89,132,135,201
Young, Isaac B. 122,129,132,176
Young, Isaac R. 177

Young, James 72
Young, Jane 111
Young, John 16,23,63,64,
83,100,113,125,150,169,
171,172,195
Young, John H. 132,147
Young, John S. 87,124
Young, Joseph 15,35,91,
176
Young, Lucinda 196
Young, M. L. 178
Young, Mark 141
Young, Mark L. 159,160,
178,195,200
Young, Mary 89
Young, Nancy 137
Young, Samuel 62,92,205
Young, Samuel C. 137,176
Young, Thomas D. 38
Young, Thomas R. 41
Young, Ufa 135
Young, Uffey 203
Young, Uffy 39,52
Young, W. M. 1
Young, William 11,20,34,39,
52,58,62,80,111,132,135,
139,148,151,162,180,190,
193,195,199,203,205
Youngblood, Arthur 12,48,
156
Youngblood, Cyreny 120
Youngblood, Elizabeth 156
Youngblood, Elizabeth C. 206
Youngblood, Henry 156
Youngblood, James C. 105,120
Youngblood, James H. 163,206
Youngblood, Joseph 100,105,
110
Youngblood, Josiah S. 12,
25,31,36,51,156
Youree, Andrew H. 75
Youree, Elizabeth A. 201
Youree, Joseph 201
Yourie, Ephraim 136
Yourie, Mary 136
Yourie, Thomas N. 136

Academy, Brawley's Fork 112
Bailey's Meeting House 165
Bank of Tennessee 79,85
Baptist Church, Brawley's
  Fork 112,114
Baptist Church, Eleventh
  District 81
Baptist Church, Hopewell 88
Baptist Church, Maxwell 88
Baptist Church, Sanders Fork 91
Baptist Church, Separate 88
Blacksmith Shop 209
Bradyville Academy 89
Christian Church, Woodbury
  213
Cumberland Presbyterian Church,
  Eleventh District 81
Cumberland Presbyterian Church,
  Sanders Fork 88
Cumberland Presbyterian Church,
  Thyatira 89,93
Fake's Brick Moulder 5
Female Academy 128
Hopewell Meeting House 110
Liberty Meeting House 175
Liberty School House 161,175
Long Island Bank 80
McBroom Tavern 188
Methodist Episcopal Church 195,
  203
Methodist Episcopal Church,
  Bailey's 165
Methodist Episcopal Church,
  Eleventh District 81
Methodist Episcopal Church,
  Fifth District 139
Methodist Episcopal Church Camp-
  ground, Ninth District 133
Methodist Episcopal Church,
  Prospect 106
Methodist Episcopal Church,
  Rock House Fork 207
Methodist Episcopal Church,
  Woodbury 97
Murfreesborough & Liberty Turn-
  pike Company 152
New Hope Congregation 207
Presbyterian Church, Sanders
  Fork 88
Rocky Point Meeting House 110
School, Sanders Fork 88
School, Seventeenth District 39
School, Seventh District 198

School, Tenth District 131
Town Spring 4
Willis' Meeting House 110,131

www.ingramcontent.com/pod-product-compliance
Lightning Source LLC
Chambersburg PA
CBHW021856020426
42334CB00013B/359